Recovering Political Philosophy

Series editors
Timothy W. Burns
Baylor University
Waco, TX, USA

Thomas L. Pangle
University of Texas at Austin
Austin, TX, USA

Postmodernism's challenge to the possibility of a rational foundation for and guidance of our political lives has provoked a searching re-examination of the works of past political philosophers. The re-examination seeks to recover the ancient or classical grounding for civic reason and to clarify the strengths and weaknesses of modern philosophic rationalism. This series responds to this ferment by making available outstanding new scholarship in the history of political philosophy, scholarship that is inspired by the rediscovery of the diverse rhetorical strategies employed by political philosophers. The series features interpretive studies attentive to historical context and language, and to the ways in which censorship and didactic concern impelled prudent thinkers, in widely diverse cultural conditions, to employ manifold strategies of writing, strategies that allowed them to aim at different audiences with various degrees of openness to unconventional thinking. Recovering Political Philosophy emphasizes the close reading of ancient, medieval, early modern and late modern works that illuminate the human condition by attempting to answer its deepest, enduring questions, and that have (in the modern periods) laid the foundations for contemporary political, social, and economic life. The editors encourage manuscripts from both established and emerging scholars who focus on the careful study of texts, either through analysis of a single work or through thematic study of a problem or question in a number of works.

More information about this series at
http://www.palgrave.com/gp/series/14517

Gustave de Beaumont
Alexis de Tocqueville

On the Penitentiary System in the United States and its Application to France

The Complete Text

Translated by Emily Katherine Ferkaluk

Gustave de Beaumont
Beaumont-sur-Dême
Sarthe, France

Alexis de Tocqueville
Metz, Moselle, France

Recovering Political Philosophy
ISBN 978-3-030-09993-0   ISBN 978-3-319-70799-0   (eBook)
https://doi.org/10.1007/978-3-319-70799-0

© Emily Katherine Ferkaluk, under exclusive license to Springer International Publishing AG, part of Springer Nature 2018
Softcover re-print of the Hardcover 1st edition 2018
Translated from *Du Système pénitentiaire aux États-Unis et de son application en France, suivi d'un appendice sur les colonies pénales et de notes statistiques* by Gustave de Beaumont and Alexis de Tocqueville (H. Fournier, Paris, 1833).
This work is subject to copyright. All rights are solely and exclusively licensed by the Publisher, whether the whole or part of the material is concerned, specifically the rights of translation, reprinting, reuse of illustrations, recitation, broadcasting, reproduction on microfilms or in any other physical way, and transmission or information storage and retrieval, electronic adaptation, computer software, or by similar or dissimilar methodology now known or hereafter developed.
The use of general descriptive names, registered names, trademarks, service marks, etc. in this publication does not imply, even in the absence of a specific statement, that such names are exempt from the relevant protective laws and regulations and therefore free for general use.
The publisher, the authors, and the editors are safe to assume that the advice and information in this book are believed to be true and accurate at the date of publication. Neither the publisher nor the authors or the editors give a warranty, express or implied, with respect to the material contained herein or for any errors or omissions that may have been made. The publisher remains neutral with regard to jurisdictional claims in published maps and institutional affiliations.

Cover credit: Stefano Bianchetti / Alamy Stock Photo

Printed on acid-free paper

This Palgrave Macmillan imprint is published by the registered company Springer International Publishing AG part of Springer Nature.
The registered company address is: Gewerbestrasse 11, 6330 Cham, Switzerland

To David.

Series Editors' Preface

Palgrave's *Recovering Political Philosophy* series was founded with an eye to postmodernism's challenge to the possibility of a rational foundation for and guidance of our political lives. This invigorating challenge has provoked a searching re-examination of classic texts, not only of political philosophers, but of poets, artists, theologians, scientists, and other thinkers who may not be regarded conventionally as political theorists. The series publishes studies that endeavor to take up this re-examination and thereby help to recover the classical grounding for civic reason, as well as studies that clarify the strengths and the weaknesses of modern philosophic rationalism. The interpretative studies in the series are particularly attentive to historical context and language, and to the ways in which both censorial persecution and didactic concerns have impelled prudent thinkers, in widely diverse cultural conditions, to employ manifold strategies of writing—strategies that allowed them to aim at different audiences with various degrees of openness to unconventional thinking. The series offers close readings of ancient, medieval, early modern and late modern works that illuminate the human condition by attempting to answer its deepest, enduring questions, and that have (in the modern periods) laid the foundations for contemporary political, social, and economic life.

No translation of Gustave de Beaumont's and Alexis de Tocqueville's *On the Penitentiary System in the United States and its Application to France* has been easily available in English for some time, and the unreliability and incompleteness of the only English version, that of America's first political scientist, Francis Leiber (originally published in 1833), makes pressing the need for an accurate, complete translation. Emily Katherine

Ferkaluk's translation meets this need wonderfully. It takes full advantage of the first published edition of Tocqueville's *Du Système Pénitentiaire aux États-Unis, et de son application en France; suivis d'un appendice sur les Colonies Pénales et de notes statistiques* (H. Fournier Jeune, 1833) to produce a complete, scrupulously literal, yet readable English translation. Ferkaluk has devoted herself to this task because, in the first place, she sees (and gives us solid reason to see) that Tocqueville's interest in penology was no mere pretext for visiting America, as he sometimes pretended, but was quite sincere: It emerged from his professional and familial political experiences, and continued manifesting itself in the public debates over penal reform in which he continued to engage throughout the 1840s. In the second place, Ferkaluk realizes that Tocqueville's observations concerning prison reform are of abiding interest, both to students of Tocqueville and to those with an interest in humanely and civically approaching the questions of crime and emprisonment, as moral and civic phenomena that compel citizens to address the minds and hearts of criminals. In this neglected work we see Tocqueville engaging in the kind of reflection and policy-making at which he excelled as a statesman, and which he recommended (and exemplified) for citizens of the emerging modern democracies.

Timothy W. Burns
Thomas L. Pangle

Acknowledgements

A book is a product of a great many people's wisdom, encouragement, support, advice, and hard work. For this book, I am especially grateful to Richard Dougherty, whose discussions of Tocqueville as a political thinker first inspired this project and whose critical review of early drafts were indispensable to its success. I am also grateful to Tiffany Miller, Gerard Wegemer, Joshua Parens, and the anonymous reviewers at Palgrave Macmillan for their helpful and thoughtful comments on various drafts of the project. I am enormously grateful to Stephen Maddux, whose sophisticated instinct in the French language allowed for careful emendation of the translation; to Mae Dewhurst, who provided much needed proofreading of the translation and many helpful suggestions for revision; and to Zane Merkle, who assisted in creating the index. I am thankful to the staff at the Yale Beinecke Rare Book and Manuscript Library, who spent many days assisting me with research in the Yale Tocqueville Manuscripts; I am also thankful to the Johns Hopkins Sheridan Library for their help with the Francis Lieber papers. Many thanks go to Mark Caleb Smith, whose faithful encouragement and advice guided me at different stages of writing and editing. I am also grateful to Michelle Chen, whose enthusiasm for the project and editorial skills were invaluable in carrying this manuscript to publication. Many thanks go to Timothy Burns, John Stegner, and the rest of the editorial team at Palgrave, who supported and refined the project. I am thankful also for Bruce and Nan Ransom, and to the Braniff Graduate School at the University of Dallas, who each generously funded the project at different times. Finally, I am grateful to my mother and father for their encouragement and inspiration; to Hanna, whose intellectual friendship and massive support I cherish; and to David, whose love, faith, and reassurance grounded me during writing and editing. I take full responsibility for any remaining errors in the introduction or translation of this work. *Soli Deo Gloria*

Contents

Translator's Introduction — xv

List of Documentary Evidence — xxxi

Preface — xxxix

Part I — 1

Chapter 1: History of the Penitentiary System — 3

Chapter 2 — 25

Chapter 3: Reform — 57

Chapter 4: Financial Part — 83

Part II — 93

Chapter 1 — 95

Chapter 2 — 99

xii CONTENTS

Part III: On Houses of Refuge   121

Chapter 1   123

Chapter 2   141

Part IV: Appendices   147

Appendix: On Penal Colonies   149

Appendix: Alphabetical Notes   171

Appendix No. 4: Agricultural Colonies   197

Appendix No. 5: On Public Education   201

Appendix No. 6: Pauperism in America   207

Appendix No. 7: Imprisonment for Debts in the United States   213

Appendix No. 8: Imprisonment of Witnesses   215

Appendix No. 9: Temperance Societies   217

Appendix No. 10: Inquiry into the Philadelphia Penitentiary   219

Appendix No. 11: Conversation with Mr. Elam Lynds   233

Appendix No. 12: Excerpts   239

Appendix No. 13: Regulations of the Connecticut Prison   247

Appendix No. 13 Bis.: Regulations from Mr. Welles
for the Boston House of Refuge   257

Appendix No. 14: Letter from Mr. Barrett, Chaplain
of the Wethersfield Penitentiary   265

Appendix No. 15: Conversation with the Director
of the Philadelphia House of Refuge   269

Appendix No. 16: Statistical Notes   271

Appendix No. 17: Statistical Observations and Comparisons   287

Appendix No. 18: Some Points of Comparison Between
France and America   311

Appendix No. 19: Financial Part   321

Index   335

Translator's Introduction

The translation within this book is the product of an effort to discover the purpose, meaning, and relevance of Alexis de Tocqueville's first and little-studied work, *On the Penitentiary System in the United States and its Application to France*. As is well known, Tocqueville and Gustave de Beaumont toured United States penitentiaries from April 1831 to February 1832 as representatives of the French government. During their travels, the French commissioners gathered official documents and conducted research on the finances, administration, and regulations of at least fourteen American prisons and penitentiaries.[1] *On the Penitentiary System* is the product of their official investigation on behalf of the French government, designed to elucidate whether one of two primary American penitentiary systems (Philadelphia or Auburn) could be implemented to successfully reform French prisons. The work was published in France and America in 1833; in August of that same year, the work was awarded the Monthyon prize by the *Académie des Sciences Morales et Politiques*. While much scholarly attention has been given to the more famous written works resulting from the American journey (Tocqueville's *Democracy in America* and Beaumont's *Marie, or Slavery in the United States*), little scholarship has been undertaken to grasp the relative contribution *On the Penitentiary System* makes to understanding Tocqueville's political thought as a whole.[2] There has, perhaps, been a dearth of scholarship on Tocqueville's first published work in part because we have not yet had a complete English translation of the work. This book remedies that problem by making an English translation of the work available in its entirety.

Many scholars also suggest that Tocqueville's study of penitentiaries was not a genuine policy endeavor, and thus remains an unimportant area of research. George Wilson Pierson argues that Tocqueville's journey to America was conducted in large part for political purposes: to advance his own stagnating political career in the French government and to avoid political unrest surrounding the rise of the July Monarchy in the summer of 1830 (1938, pp. 27–28, 31). Eduardo Nolla also argues that the trip to America was initially a means to preserve Tocqueville's political career, rather than an end in itself (de Tocqueville 2010). Hugh Brogan agrees that "For Tocqueville, whether at this date or years later, prison reform was never to be more than a secondary concern, a means to an end" (2006, p. 143–5). Michelle Perrot similarly states that the idea to study penitentiaries was, in some part, only a pretext for Tocqueville's greater desire to study democracy (1984, p. 7). Thorsten Sellin says that Tocqueville's and Beaumont's interest in prisons "was peripheral" (1964, p. xv). These notions are partially affirmed by Tocqueville's private words to his friend Charles Stoffels, when he wrote from America that his study of penitentiaries was "a very honorable pretext that makes us seem particularly to merit the interest of the government, whatever it may be, and that assures us its good will upon our return."[3] Tocqueville thus acknowledges that the trip was planned in part to aide both Tocqueville's and Beaumont's political careers.

Despite general consensus in scholarship that Tocqueville's interest in American penitentiaries was merely pragmatic, there are several reasons to believe that Tocqueville's interest in penology, broadly speaking, was sincere.[4] Not only did Tocqueville's father experience the vicious conditions of the French prison system under the Reign of Terror (1793), but Tocqueville himself observed numerous prisons in France during his work as a *juge auditeur* and later *juge suppléant* (Pierson 1938, p. 18, 31). In particular, Tocqueville visited the house of detention at Poissy in September 1830, from which he wrote a report on the poor conditions of French prisons. The study in penitentiary systems was, at least in part, a project stemming from Tocqueville's professional and familial political experiences.

Moreover, Tocqueville and Beaumont continued to work in French penal reform after the initial publication of *On the Penitentiary System*. The pair published two subsequent editions of the report in response to French political debates in 1840 and 1843–44 over penal reform. In 1840, a committee of the Chamber of Deputies in the Constituent Assembly was appointed to report on a prison reform bill submitted by de Rémusat, Minister of the Interior (Sellin 1964, p. xxxvi). Tocqueville was the *rapporteur*, and Beaumont a member, of the committee. The Government eventually withdrew the bill for revision.[5] A revised project appeared in 1843, introduced by the new Minister of the Interior, Count Duchâtel. Tocqueville was again the *rapporteur*; a debate took place over seventeen days in 1844 regarding the project. During debates on the bill, Tocqueville argued forcefully in support of the Pennsylvania system over the Auburn system. Although the Chamber adopted a modified version of the bill, its enactment was interrupted first by the February Revolution in 1848, and again with the conclusion of the Second Republic by Louis Napoléon Bonaparte's *coup d'état* in December, 1851 (Sellin 1964, p. xxxviii). According to Sellin, Tocqueville's and Beaumont's "hopes for a basic reform of the prison system were not to be fulfilled during their lifetimes. The construction of cellular prisons was ordered stopped in 1853 and in some prisons the cellblocks already built were ordered razed. The following year, the transportation of convicts to penal colonies was introduced" (1964, p. xxxix). Despite their ultimate failure to establish penitentiaries in France, Tocqueville's and Beaumont's work in penal reform for over two decades lends weight to the understanding that their interest in penitentiaries was not simply a pretext for their journey to America. Consequently, *On the Penitentiary System* plays a greater role in understanding Tocqueville as a political thinker and statesman that has yet to be seen.

Why Study Penitentiaries?

The historical context of nineteenth century France explains the immediate purpose behind Tocqueville's and Beaumont's study of American penitentiary systems. When Tocqueville and Beaumont left for America, there was no doubt that France needed to reform its criminal justice system. At the time, imprisonment was just beginning a transition from being used to hold suspects or witnesses prior to trial or the execution of sentences, rather than as a punishment for convicted crimes. Prisons in the seventeenth and eighteenth centuries contained criminal men awaiting their actual punishment, women or children sentenced to hard labor, wayward children abandoned by their parents, vagrants, and the insane. Tocqueville and Beaumont emphasize in both their *Mémoire* (the formal request for permission from the French government to travel to America as official representatives) and *On the Penitentiary System* the problem of the amount of growing recidivism among criminals in France, a fact directly linked to the condition of French prisons. By overcrowding prisons and mixing the guilty with the innocent, the French criminal justice system was acting as a laboratory or school for crime. Additionally, reducing recidivism required an emphasis on rehabilitation that French prisons lacked. Tocqueville and Beaumont thus responded to a political and social need in France to reform the criminal justice system.[6]

This need was recognized within the intellectual and political climate of French and American humanitarianism that characterizes the historical context for Tocqueville's and Beaumont's study of prison reform.[7] Seymour Drescher notes that French humanitarianism grew out of the enlightenment, "led by highly educated aristocratic and bourgeois intellectuals" who "gradually formulated a broad program designed to systematize and secularize a national program of public welfare in matters of education, health, old age, criminality, and especially indigence and charity" (1968, pp. 93–95).[8] These intellectuals are referred to as "publicists" within the text of *On the Penitentiary System*. According to *Le Trésor de la Langue Française informatisé*, "*publiciste*" has two meanings: first, a publicist is a person who writes on public law or is an expert on public law.[9] Second, a publicist is more generally a journalist. Thus, a publicist is a blend of academic intellectual and popular journalist; or in the case of penal reform, a mix of philosopher and philanthropist. As a practical example, Francis Lieber, the German intellectual who first translated *On the Penitentiary System* into English in America, called himself a "publicist" (Freidel 1947, p. 173). Tocqueville and Beaumont directly react to the political ideas and philanthropical work of these publicists in *On the Penitentiary System*, arguing that such persons have let their penal imaginations run away from their control.

More particularly, in writing *On the Penitentiary System*, Tocqueville and Beaumont responded to growing public interest in penal reform during their time. In 1790, Honoré Gabriel Riqueti, compte de Mirabeau crafted a report calling for the establishment of **maisons d'amélioration** in each department, with separate cells for each prisoner and a system of forced labor. Mirabeau's penal report to the Constituent Assembly was followed in 1791 by a report from Louis-Michel le Peletier, marquis de Saint-Fargeau, representing the Committees on the Constitution and on Criminal Legislation. Le Peletier presented a penal code that included the abolishment of the death penalty in most cases, along with the establishment of *maisons de peine* (prisons for those receiving punishment), the *cachot* (a dungeon, often used to lock up prisoners who violated prison rules), the *gêne* (which was to combine solitary confinement with labor), and the *prison* (prisons for the arrested). The proposed penal code was adopted in part, authorizing the institution of four forms of imprisonment (chains in *maisons de force, réclusion*, the *gêne*, and *détention*). However, le Peletier's reform was never enacted due to the Reign of Terror beginning in September 1793.

Alternatively, in their *Memoir* Tocqueville and Beaumont identify de Montalivet's prison reform work in 1810 as the beginning of French political concerns over establishing penitentiaries during their era (Beaumont and Tocqueville 1984). Perrot describes the multiple studies of penitentiaries preceding Tocqueville's and Beaumont's, conducted in England by John Howard and Jeremy Bentham and filtering into France via the scholarship of Duke Decazes, Villermé, Marquet-Vasselot, Ginouvier, Taillandier, and Charles Lucas (1984, p. 8–9). Additionally, within the text of *On the Penitentiary System*, Tocqueville and Beaumont often refer to the work of Rochefoucauld-Liancourt, who first travelled from France to study American penitentiaries and published his findings in *Des prisons de Philadelphie par un Européen* (1796). By 1819, the Royal Prison Society was established as a government advisory board; members also acted as inspectors of the Paris prisons (Drescher 1968, p. 126). In sum, Tocqueville and Beaumont were neither the first nor the last to conduct a study of the American penitentiary system.[10]

Although the report's overall tone is one of pragmatic policy making, Tocqueville's and Beaumont's *Mémoire* reveals a more fundamental motive behind their study of American penitentiaries. Beaumont and Tocqueville defend the need to study penitentiaries in response to a great "evil" that threatens French society with "ruin and destruction," namely the issue of increasing crime in proportion to the civilizational progress of society (Tocqueville 1984, p. 49). The problem is a contradiction in terms, since increasing civilization ought to hypothetically decrease crime. Instead, civilizational progress seems to have created a new set of social problems: the authors identify vagabondage, laziness, and theft as the highest increasing offenses in France.[11] There is thus an apparent paradox between criminality and civilization. In its study of the penitentiary's claim to be able to reform human nature, *On the Penitentiary System* broadly answers two questions that arise from the paradox: why the parallel relationship between increasing civilization and increasing crime exists, and what to do to resolve the social problems stemming from the relationship. In answering these questions, Tocqueville and Beaumont intend to test the extravagant promise of progress and publicists to rid society of problems such as poverty or crime, and instead offer a moderate civic solution to the problem of recidivism.

Practically, *On the Penitentiary System* acts as an educative tool for the French public. The work counteracts the influence of publicists over the French public and gives tools to the public to empower itself to take on the responsibility of penal reform. *On the Penitentiary System* teaches citizens how to think in terms of a new, moderate political science: theory must be tempered by experience, especially experience that teaches us the universal nature of human beings. Theory must also be tempered by self-knowledge, the type which shows us our political limits in terms of unique national resources and character. Throughout the text, Tocqueville and Beaumont evaluate different penal institutions in terms of the American experience and French socio-political circumstance; by looking to individual national experiences, they intend to give the French public necessary self-knowledge of their own capacity and potential limits to resolving the problem of increasing crime.

Politically, this rhetorical purpose for *On the Penitentiary System* assumes that the public is capable of rightly caring for issues such as crime or poverty through civic institutions, rather than through a centralized government. At first, Tocqueville's and Beaumont's report seems directed solely at those with influence over the public—publicists or legislators whose ideas establish the goals of political and social institutions and who therefore need a healthy understanding of human nature and a good amount of experience to ensure they do not abuse their own penal imaginations. However, this is not the audience to which Tocqueville and Beaumont give their report. Rather, *On the Penitentiary System* ultimately seeks to empower the general public to take control of directing their own penal imagination, rather than be subject to the imaginative whims of publicists and philosophers. At the basis of the arguments in *On the Penitentiary System* stands Tocqueville's and Beaumont's assumption that the public imagination is at least partially responsible for political policies that are either beneficial or harmful to both the individual and the nation. *On the Penitentiary System* is written for a democratic citizenry and is intended to inspire noble political action in local communities.

Why Translate *On the Penitentiary System*?

Notably, although there were two revisions of the first French edition of *On the Penitentiary System* published during the authors' lifetimes, there has been only one semi-complete English translation. Upon returning to France, Tocqueville and Beaumont asked their newly-made acquaintance in America, Francis Lieber, to translate their report and publish it in America. The three were introduced in Boston towards the conclusion of Tocqueville's and Beaumont's journey, and would meet again in Paris in 1844 (Pierson 1938, pp. 377, 439; Perry 1882, p. 91).[12] Lieber's singular translation of *On the Penitentiary System* may be called a revision in its own right, since he undertook a major editorial role when translating the text on behalf of his friends. In particular, Lieber added his own "Preface and Introduction of the Translator" and a lengthy appendix on the Pennsylvania penitentiary system. Additionally, Lieber explicitly replaced some of the original appendices with his own rather than translating them; in other appendices, Lieber wrote more than double the original excerpt or cut out significant portions. Lieber also added lengthy footnotes throughout the main text directly engaging and often contradicting Tocqueville and Beaumont in both opinion and fact. The result of Lieber's efforts is a text that stands on its own and in contrast to the original report drafted and published by the two Frenchmen.

Significantly, Tocqueville wrote to Beaumont in November 1833 that he was "not completely satisfied" with Lieber's translation.[13] Tocqueville complained of the weighty notes "in which, in his [Lieber's] capacity as a foreigner, he feels himself obliged to contradict the smallest truths that we utter about America" (Pierson 1938, p. 708). Tocqueville deduces from Lieber's revision of *On the Penitentiary System* both an extreme fear of centralization and "an incorrigible conceit" that is peculiarly American. Taking Tocqueville's criticisms of the translation to heart, we have brought the first complete, literal translation to English readers.

It is our hope that the new translation of *On the Penitentiary System* clears the pathway for further studies of Tocqueville's political work in French penal reform and penal thought. Additionally, more work can be done to systematically compare the ideas in *On the Penitentiary System* with those of Tocqueville's major works, *Democracy in America* and *The Old Regime and The Revolution*. This future work is part of an ongoing project to understand Tocqueville's political thought as a philosophy that asks questions of and appeals to universal truths, as well as undergirds the prudent decision making of the legislator. Tocqueville was not simply a politician, nor was he thoroughly a philosopher. Tocqueville's political thought instead demonstrates a blend of understanding policy alternatives to particular problems in light of potentially absolute answers to universal questions. Moreover, while Tocqueville's larger works present his deeper insights into political philosophy, such as an understanding of the ideas that explain modern human activity, the ideas are sometimes obtusely presented in his major work's length and organization. *On the Penitentiary System* presents scholars of Tocqueville the unique opportunity to read a concise work that demonstrates Tocqueville's philosophical method applied to a particular political problem facing his nation during a specific time. Future comparisons of the case study on penitentiaries to the themes of Tocqueville's larger works will therefore help us to see his philosophical ideas more clearly.

Not only does *On the Penitentiary System* have the potential to give us a deeper understanding of Tocqueville as both politician and philosopher, but Tocqueville's lessons in *On the Penitentiary System* are also fruitful for recognizing the theoretical questions that undergird our current movement for penal reform. *On the Penitentiary System* was written at the cusp of a fundamental change in how the study of penology (a discipline not yet systematized) approached crime. While there was a shift from emphasizing public torture or other corporal punishments as primary penal methods, there was also a new concern to reform the inward state of the human being in order to allow the prisoner to re-enter society and be empowered to lead an honest life. The means to achieve such a goal were to lock the prisoner away from society; corporal punishment was largely replaced with incarceration.

In our modern era, we are questioning not only the efficacy of incarceration as the primary penal method for enforcing criminal justice, but also its status as a "moral" institution.[14] The initial goals established at the beginning of the penitentiary movement in America have gone unrealized. Rather than reducing recidivism and the number of criminals in general, penitentiaries have instead resulted, in our time, in the problem of mass incarceration. Sara Benson concisely expresses the scholarly consensus on the reason for the rise of prisons since the 1970's: "drug war politics accelerated prison construction into the 1990s, as conservative law and order politics joined with racial liberalism to build a prison nation" (2015, p. 384). Whether one agrees or disagrees with those reasons for the increase in prison sentencing, it is generally (and bipartisanly) acknowledged that mass incarceration does little to deter or reduce crime rates, while also being expensive for the state (Reddy 2015; *Prison and Crime* 2014). Additionally, our modern incarceration system instills within prisoners anti-democratic social behavior; many former convicts cannot vote, act on juries, or participate in other crucial citizen political activities (Weaver and Lerman 2010; Reddy 2015, p. 8). In contemporary American society, mass incarceration thus represents a deeply problematic form of punishment in need of reform (Redburn et. al 2014).

Tocqueville's policy recommendations in *On the Penitentiary System* are especially important for guiding both the method and content of contemporary prison reform. We learn from Tocqueville how to moderate our expectations of what government should (and can) accomplish in relation to the individual, how to avoid foreign political complications rooted in poor domestic policy, and how to strengthen civic associations so as to avoid the growth of government. The work also enables us to see more clearly the strengths and weaknesses of relying on incarceration as the primary means of punishment. Today, we are asking questions about whether new forms of public policy, such as probationary or restorative justice programs, faith-based recidivism programs, community corrections alternatives, or electronic monitoring, would be better suited than incarceration to achieving re-integration of the prisoner into society and reducing recidivism.[15] Discerning which programs can be both sustainable and successful in terms of morally reforming the individual necessitates returning to the questions Tocqueville and Beaumont asked when evaluating the status of penitentiaries in the nineteenth century.

Most importantly, the qualitative study of *On the Penitentiary System* shows us the theoretic groundwork that needs to occur before evaluating modern penal policies. We need to see that punishment is not only a formative social institution, but is also in a crucial way dependent on the formative influence of society. Tocqueville and Beaumont argue that the penitentiary has a restorative effect on offenders when individual community members are intimately involved in the penitentiary's discipline. *On the Penitentiary System* thereby provides the groundwork for how to conserve the notion that crime is both a moral and social problem. This dual problem that prisons face, in seeking to transform the minds and hearts of offenders, can be solved in part by recognizing our civic responsibilities to care for such persons within a democracy.

Note on the Translation

As mentioned above, Tocqueville and Beaumont published three French editions of *Système Pénitentiaire* during their lifetime. The first French edition was published by H. Fournier Jeune in Paris, 1833. The second edition was published by Charles Gosselin in 1836 as Tocqueville's and Beaumont's response to French criticism of their report; most notably, the edition includes an expanded introduction (Pierson 1938, p. 710).[16] The title of the second edition was revised to include: *Seconde édition, entire mentre fondue et augmentée d'une introduction*. A third edition of *Système Pénitentiaire* was published in 1845 under the revised title *Système pénitentiaire aux États-Unis et de son application en France; suivi d'un Appendice sur les colonies pénales et de notes statistiques (3e édition augmentée du Rapport de M. de Tocqueville sur le projet de réforme des prisons et du texte de la loi adoptée par la Chambre des Députés)*. The third edition includes a summary of reform enacted in France from 1837–1845, written by Tocqueville, as well as his report to the Chamber in 1845.

The most recent publication of the French text can be found in J.P. Mayer's definitive edition of Tocqueville's *Oeuvres Complètes, Écrits sur le système pénitentiaire en France et a l'étranger, Tome IV*. Volume 4 is printed in two parts. This definitive edition combines different components of the second and third editions of *Du Système Pénitentiaire* into a singular, annotated French text. The edition also includes the original *Mémoire* submitted to the French Government by Beaumont and Tocqueville, published documents from Tocqueville's participation in the French parliamentary debates surrounding prison reform from 1843–44, previously unpublished notes on prisons and penal colonies of France and Switzerland, as well as letters written by Tocqueville regarding penitentiary reform.

Three versions of the first edition of *On the Pénitentiaire System* have been published in the English language. W.B.S. Taylor partially translated and published the work in England in 1833. Also in 1833, Francis Lieber translated the first edition and published the work in Philadelphia, PA. Lieber's interleaved manuscript, including handwritten notes and revisions to his original publication of the translation, can be found at the Johns Hopkins University Sheridan Special Collections Library. However, Lieber never published a second edition including those revisions. Thorsten Sellin published a revised edition of Lieber's translation in 1964, omitting Lieber's footnotes and many of the appendices.[17]

The following translation was made from the first published edition of *Du Système Pénitentiaire aux États-Unis, et de son application en France; suivi d'un appendice sur les Colonies Pénales et de notes statistiques*, written by Gustave de Beaumont and Alexis de Tocqueville and published by H. Fournier Jeune in Paris, 1833. The first published edition was chosen for translation for three reasons. First, the complete fair copy of the original manuscript no longer exists. Portions of the original manuscript, along with drafts of notes, appendices, and statistics, can be found at the Yale University Beinecke Rare Book & Manuscript Library. The translator has utilized original source material as much as possible, while still recognizing the need to provide a complete English text. Copies of the first published edition of *On the Penitentiary System* can be found at the Huntington Library Rare Books Collection and at the Bibliothèque nationale de France.

Second, the first French edition is the text Francis Lieber would most likely have received for translation and simultaneous publication in America with the French publication. Lieber begins his "Translator's Preface and Introduction" by saying, "MM. de Beaumont and de Tocqueville had the kindness to send me, a few months ago, their work on the Penitentiary System in the United States, before it had issued from the press in Paris, requesting me, at the same time, to translate it, if possible, for the American public" (Beaumont and Tocqueville 1833, p. v). Notably, Lieber also ends the preface by remarking that "the translator received information from Paris on the day when this introduction went to press, that a second edition of the original was preparing," thereby indicating that the first edition was the text he translated. This translation will thus potentially be useful to any scholar wishing to contrast French and American penal reform in the nineteenth century, because it allows for a comparison of Lieber's changes to the original French text he used.

Third, the first edition reflects the authors' original reflections on both penitentiaries and on American society and politics. The later editions of the text reflect Tocqueville's and Beaumont's reactions to French political developments in penal reform, as well as their matured consideration of the problems connected to establishing penitentiaries. On the other hand, the first edition presents the reader with a prefatory lens through which to better understand Tocqueville's most recognized work, *Democracy in America*.

Without compromising on the readability of the English translation, we have attempted to render the words as literally to the original French text as possible. Hence, significant words have been given a consistent translation throughout the text and an explanation for translation choice occurs in endnotes at the place the word first appears. Words that are particularly important to the penal discussion in *On the Penitentiary System* are as follows: *corruption; dompter; morale; pécule; régime* (as compared to *discipline, système, administration*); the potential distinction between *condamnés, prisionnier, détenus; surveillance;* the differences between *châtiment, peine, délit.* We also note an explanation and definition, where appropriate, of peculiar French penal terms such as *départemens, conseils généraux,* and *les condamnés correctionnellement.* Paragraph breaks are retained from the original; grammar and spelling have been updated to adhere to the rules of modern English. Beaumont's and Tocqueville's original footnotes are numbered in the translation and hold the same position that they originally occupied in the French text; editorial notes, including commentary on the French text and some of Lieber's significant variations, are preceded by a [*]. Additionally, Tocqueville's and Beaumont's alphabetical notes retain their original places within the text and refer to the appendix "Alphabetical Notes" at the end of the document. Finally, it is worth noting that what follows this introduction is the first complete English translation of the first French edition written by Tocqueville and Beaumont, omitting only four pages of drawings of various penitentiaries originally appended to the French publication and the original Table of Contents.

Emily Katherine Ferkaluk
Boston, 2018

NOTES

1. Those institutions are as follows: The Sing-Sing prison in Ossining, NY; the Auburn Penitentiary in NY; Eastern State Penitentiary on Cherry Hill Street, Philadelphia, PA; Walnut Street prison, Philadelphia, PA; prison in Pittsburgh, PA; prison in Wethersfield, CT; prison in Boston, MA; prison in Baltimore, MD; prisons in Kentucky, Tennessee, Ohio, Louisiana, Maine, and Vermont.
2. Several scholars have commented briefly on the importance of *On the Penitentiary System* as a potentially prefatory work to *Democracy in America.* See: Brogan 2006, p. 234; Dunn 1985, p. 401; Drolet 2003, p. 129. There are only two mentions of penitentiary systems in *Democracy.* The first occurs in I.1.2 as an example of how to distinguish "what is of Puritan origin or of English origin" in the American democracy (Tocqueville 2000, p. 44). The second mention occurs in the chapter I.2.7, "How the Omnipotence of the Majority in America Increases the Legislative and

Administrative Instability that is Natural to Democracies" (Tocqueville 2000, p. 238).
3. Letter of 11 October 1831 to Charles Stoffels. Yale Tocqueville Manuscripts. General Collection, Beinecke Rare Book and Manuscript Library, Yale University. A.VII.
4. I am not the first to make such an assertion; Avramenko and Gingerich give a detailed argument that "though prison reform served as a pretext for Tocqueville's journey to America, his interest in penology was genuine" (2014, p. 62).
5. For Tocqueville's speech, see Tocqueville 1968, pp. 70–90. Pierson provides a more detailed description of the political opposition which led to Tocqueville's and Beaumont's struggle to pass actual prison reform (pp. 711–713).
6. Tocqueville's work in penal reform is intimately related to his political interest in the governance of the French Algerian colonies. The intersection of both political efforts suggests a common philosophical or principled ground from which Tocqueville acted as a statesman.
7. For a general review of the American intellectual and political climate of the time, see Barnes 1921, pp. 35–60.
8. See also Sellin's history of French prison reform prior to Tocqueville's and Beaumont's journey, p. xix–xxxix. Sellin carefully situates the work of Rochefoucauld, Lucas, and Livingston in the French reform movement.
9. Sellin argues that the groundwork for "reform of the law of crime and punishment" in France was laid by Montesquieu in his *Persian Letters,* Rousseau's *Social Contract,* Voltaire and the Encyclopedists, and the Marquis of Beccaria's work *On Crimes and Punishment* (1964, p. xx). In 1788 a translation of John Howard's *State of Prisons,* written to establish penitentiaries in England, appeared in France. In 1819 Decazes established the Royal Society of Prisons in France, whose members included La Fayette, La Rochefoucauld-Liancourt, de Broglie, and Guizot (1964, p. xxxii). Finally, in 1827 Charles Lucas petitioned the Chambers to introduce the penitentiary System in France (Sellin 1964, p. xxxv).
10. After Tocqueville's and Beaumont's trip, two more observations of the American penitentiary system were conducted on behalf of England (William Crawford) and Russia (Julius) in 1835. In 1836, the French sent Frédéric-Auguste Demetz and Guillaume-Abel Blouet to study the Cherry-Hill penitentiary again.
11. These crimes result in part from industry fluctuations that cannot keep up with job demands. Hence, part of the problem of crime is the need to find new markets to give "unoccupied arms [...] the chance to work" (Tocqueville 1984, p. 51). Tocqueville and Beaumont will examine in detail the proper relationship between the economy of the penitentiary and commercial markets within the local community.

12. Lieber and Tocqueville maintained a sporadic correspondence following the translation; for translations of some of their letters, see: Perry 1882, pp. 140, 191–3; Tocqueville 2009, pp. 60–62, 65, 67–82, 84, 87, 99, 132, 145, 154, 161, 183, 231, 260.
13. Tocqueville to Beaumont, 1 Nov. 1833, Paris. Yale Tocqueville Manuscripts. General Collection, Beinecke Rare Book and Manuscript Library, Yale University. C.1.a.2.
14. Based on the following reports, incarceration is both expensive for the nation and does not significantly contribute to lowering crime rates: Roeder et. al 2015; "FBI Releases Crime Statistics" 2015; Harcourt 2011. Bernard Harcourt connects the birth of the penitentiary system in the eighteenth century with modern mass incarceration on the basis of the "illusion" that the free market can run successfully on a natural order.
15. Enn gives evidence that it was the general public, rather than lawmakers, who emphasized the need for greater expansion of incarceration in response to crime (2014, pp. 857–872). Enn's argument agrees with Tocqueville's and Beaumont's emphasis on social mores as the responsible agents for punitive measures.
16. The criticism came primarily from the Inspector General of the Maisons de Détention, Mr. de La Ville de Mirmont, in his publication *Observations sur les maisons centrales de détention, à l'occaision de l'ouvrage de MM. de Beaumont et de Tocqueville*, 1833. Mirmont argued that the Pennsylvania system "was impossibly expensive and impractical," while the Auburn system was "no better than the dormitories of the *maisons centrales*."
17. Lieber's first edition was re-published in 1868 without any revisions. Two additional reprints of Lieber's translation were published by Augustus Kelley (1970) and Archon Books Paperbacks (1979). An abridged edition of Lieber's translation was also published by Patterson Smith (1981).

References

Avramenko, Richard and Robert Gingerich. 2014. "Democratic Dystopia: Tocqueville and the American Penitentiary System." *Polity* 46 (1): 56–80.

Barnes, Harry Elmer. 1921. "The Historical Origin of the Prison System in America." *Journal of the American Institute of Criminal Law and Criminology* 12 (1): 35–60.

Beaumont, Gustave de and Alexis de Tocqueville. 1984. "Note sur le Système Pénitentiaire et la Mission Confiée Par M. Le Ministre de l'Intérieur a MM. Gustave de Beaumont et Alexis de Tocqueville." In *Écrits sur le système pénitentiaire en France et à l'étranger, Tome IV, Vol. 1*, edited by Michelle Perrot, 50–80. Paris: Gallimard.

———. 1833. *On the Penitentiary System in the United States and Its Application in France, with an Appendix on Penal Colonies and also Statistical Notes.* Translated by Francis Lieber. Philadelphia: Carey, Lea & Blanchard.
Benson, Sara. 2015. "A Political Science of Punishment: Francis Lieber and the Discipline of American Prisons." *New Political Science* 37 (3): 382–400.
Brogan, Hugh. 2006. *Alexis de Tocqueville: A Life.* New Haven: Yale University Press.
Drescher, Seymour. 1968. *Dilemmas of Democracy: Tocqueville and Modernization.* Pittsburgh: University of Pittsburgh Press.
Drolet, Michael. 2003. *Tocqueville, Democracy, and Social Reform.* New York: Palgrave Macmillan.
Dunn, Thomas. 1985. "Friendly Persuasion: Quakers, Liberal Toleration, and the Birth of the Prison." *Political Theory* 13: 387–407.
Enn, Peter K. 2014. "The Public's Increasing Punitiveness and Its Influence on Mass Incarceration in the United States." *American Journal of Political Science* 58 (4): 857–872.
"FBI Releases 2014 Crime Statistics." *Uniform Crime Report, Crime in the United States, 2014.* https://www.fbi.gov/about-us/cjis/ucr/crime-in-the-u.s/2014/crime-in-the-u.s.-2014/resource-pages/fbi-releases-2014-crime-statistics.pdf. Accessed April 21, 2016.
Freidel, Frank. 1947. *Francis Lieber: Nineteenth-Century Liberal.* Baton Rouge: Louisiana State University Press.
Harcourt, Bernard. 2011. *The Illusion of Free Markets.* Cambridge, MA: Harvard University Press.
Perrot, Michelle. 1984. "Tocqueville Méconnu." In *Œuvres Complètes: Écrits sur le système pénitentiaire en France et à l'étranger, Tome IV, Vol. 1,* 7–44. Edited by Michelle Perrot. Paris: Gallimard.
Perry, Thomas Sergeant. 1882. *The Life and Letters of Francis Lieber.* Boston: James R. Good and Company.
Pierson, George Wilson. 1938. *Tocqueville in America.* Baltimore: Johns Hopkins University Press.
Prison and Crime: A Complex Link. Pew Center on the States, Sept. 2014. http://www.pewtrusts.org/~/media/assets/2014/09/pspp_crime_webgraphic.pdf?la=en. Accessed September 6, 2017.
Redburn, Stephen, Jeremy Travis, Bruce Western, eds. 2014. *The Growth of Incarceration in the United States: Exploring Causes and Consequences.* Washington, D.C.: The National Academies Press.
Reddy, Vikrant. 2015. *A New Agenda for Criminal Justice.* Edited by Yuval Levin and Ramesh Ponnuru. The Conservative Reform Network.
Roeder, Oliver, Lauren-Brooke Eisen, Julia Bowling. 2015. "What Caused the Crime Decline?" *Brennan Center for Justice at NYU School of Law.* http://www.brennancenter.org/sites/default/files/analysis/What_Caused_The_Crime_Decline.pdf. Accessed April 21, 2015.

Sellin, Thorsten. 1964. "Introduction." In *On the Penitentiary System in the United States and Its Application to France*, edited by Thorsten Sellin, xv–xl. Carbondale: Southern Illinois University Press.

Tocqueville, Alexis de. 1968. "On Prison Reform." In *Tocqueville and Beaumont on Social Reform*. Edited and translated by Seymour Drescher, 50–80. New York: Harper Torchbooks.

———. 1984. *Œuvres Complètes: Écrits sur le système pénitentiaire en France et à l'étranger, Tome IV, Vol. 1*. Edited by Michelle Perrot. Paris: Gallimard.

———. 2000. *Democracy in America*. Translated and edited by Harvey Mansfield and Delba Winthrop. Chicago, IL: University of Chicago Press.

———. 2009. *Tocqueville on America After 1840: Letters and Other Writings*. Edited and translated by Aurelian Craiutu and Jeremy Jennings. Cambridge: Cambridge University Press.

———. 2010. *Democracy in America: Historical-Critical Edition of De la Démocratie en Amérique, Vol.1*. Edited by Eduardo Nolla. Translated by James T. Schleifer. Indianapolis: Liberty Fund.

Weaver, Vesla M. and Amy E. Lerman. 2010. "Political Consequences of the Carceral State." *The American Political Science Review* 104 (4): 817–833.

List of Documentary Evidence[1]

The authors have, on their return from America, placed in the hands of the Minister of Commerce and Public Works six volumes in-folio, containing documents fully described below:

First Volume

Massachusetts

1. Report for the year 1820 on the Charlestown prison near Boston.
2. Report for the year 1821.
3. Report for the year 1822.
4. Report for the year 1823.
5. Report for the year 1824.
6. Report for the year 1825.
7. Report for the year 1826.
8. Report for the year 1827.
9. Report for the year 1828.
10. Report from the inspectors of the new penitentiary for the year 1829.
11. Report for 1830.
12. Laws of the State of Massachusetts, concerning the penitentiary and rules of the prison.[2]
13. Some statistical documents on the prison, and a handwritten note from the superintendent who gave them to us.
14. Regulations of the former prison (1823).

xxxi

Connecticut

15. Report from the Commission charged to inspect the old Newgate prison (1825).
16. Report from the Commission charged to inspect the old Newgate prison for 1826.
17. Report from the Commission charged to construct a new prison (1827).
18. Report from the inspectors of the Wethersfield prison (1828).
19. Report from the inspectors of the Wethersfield prison (1829).
20. Report from the inspectors of the Wethersfield prison (1830).
21. Report from the inspectors of the Wethersfield prison (1831).
22. Laws of Connecticut relating to the penitentiary system (1827).
23. Statistical table of crimes and misdemeanors from 1790 to 1831.
24. Letter addressed to us by Mr. Barrett, chaplain of Wethersfield, on the penitentiary system (7 October 1831).
25. Copy of a contract between the superintendent of Wethersfield and a contractor.
26. Handwritten note delivered to us by Mr. Barrett on Wethersfield discipline (October 1831).

Second Volume

New York- Old Newgate Prison

1. Original document delivered to us by the Secretary of State (Mr. Flagg), containing a report on Newgate from 31 December 1817; another from 31 December 1818; and a third from 20 January 1819.
2. Report from the assessor of the State of New York on Newgate (2 March 1819).
3. Report from the inspectors of the Newgate prison, from 21 January 1820.
4. Report from the inspectors of the Newgate prison, of 1824 and 1827 for 1823 and 1826.
5. Statistical tables presenting the number and nature of crimes in the State of New York, copied by us from the registers of the Newgate prison.

6. Statistical tables presenting the number of prisoners, of those pardoned, escaped, and those who died, and the figure of expenses of the old Newgate prison from 1797 to 1819.

Singsing Penitentiary

7. Report from the inspectors to the legislature (1825).
8. Report from the inspectors to the legislature from 1827 for 1826.
9. Report from the inspectors to the legislature from 1828 for 1827.
10. Report from the inspectors to the legislature from 1829 for 1828.
11. Report from the inspectors to the legislature from 6 January 1830.
12. Report from the inspectors to the legislature from 5 January 1831.
13. Report from the inspectors to the legislature from 12 January 1832.
14. Report from Mr. Hopkins on Mr. Elam Lynds (19 March 1831).
15. Handwritten note on the discipline of Singsing. (Handed to us by Mr. Tiltse, the superintendent of that prison).
16. Plan of Singsing and note from Mr. Cartwright, containing an estimate and quote[3] of the expenditures of this prison.

Auburn Penitentiary

17. Handwritten report of the commissioners charged to inspect Auburn (16 March 1818).
18. Report from the inspectors of the Auburn prison from 1st February 1819.
19. Report from the inspectors of the Auburn prison for the year 1820.
20. Report from the inspectors of the Auburn prison from 1st January 1824 for 1823.
21. Report from the inspectors of the Auburn prison from 26 January 1825 for 1824.
22. Report from the inspectors of the Auburn prison from 2 February 1826 for 1825.
23. Report from the inspectors of the Auburn prison from 8 January 1827 for 1826.
24. Report from the inspectors of the Auburn prison from 5 January 1828 for 1827.
25. Report from the inspectors of the Auburn prison from 1st January 1829 for 1828.

Third Volume

Continuation of Auburn

1. Report from the inspectors of Auburn prison from 18 January 1830 for 1829.
2. Report from the inspectors of Auburn prison from 24 January 1831 for 1830.
3. Report from the inspectors of Auburn prison from 30 January 1832 for 1831.
4. Summary on the construction and discipline of Auburn, by Gershom Powers (1826).
5. Report from Gershom Powers on the Auburn Prison (1828).
6. Letter from Gershom Powers in response to Edward Livingston (1829).
7. Report from Messrs. Hopkins and Tibbits on the Auburn prison (13 January 1827).
8. Gershom Powers' remarks on disciplinary punishments (1828).
9. Inquiry on Auburn's discipline and the prison's system.
10. Handwritten note delivered to us by the accounting agent (Clark) of Auburn, relating to the order and the discipline of this prison.
11. Conversation that we had with Mr. Smith, chaplain of the Auburn prison.

Fourth Volume

Maryland—Former prison and new Baltimore penitentiary

1. Legislative documents concerning the Maryland penitentiary (1819).
2. Rules of the new penitentiary (22 December 1828).
3. Report from the directors of the penitentiary (23 December 1828).
4. Report from the directors of the penitentiary (21 December 1829).
5. Report from the directors of the penitentiary from 20 December 1830.
6. Observations of Mr. Niles on the penitentiary (22 December 1829).
7. Letter from Mr. Mac-Evoy on the same subject (4 December 1831).
8. List of executions in Maryland from 1786 to date.

Pennsylvania —Prisons of Walnut Street, Pittsburgh, and the Cherry-Hill Penitentiary

9. Report to the legislature on the penitentiary system (27 January 1821).
10. Summary account[4] from Roberts Vaux on the penitentiary system of Pennsylvania (1826).
11. Letter from Roberts Vaux to William Roscoe on the same subject (1827).
12. Letter from Edward Livingston to Roberts Vaux on the same subject.
13. Observations on the same subject by Dr. Bache (1829).
14. Description of the new penitentiary (1829).
15. Constitution of the Prison Society of Philadelphia.
16. First and Second Reports on the New Penitentiary (1831).
17. Acts of the legislature containing new penal laws, combined with the new penitentiary system. Rules for the prison.
18. Letter from Dr. Bache on the new penitentiary system, contained in an edition of the journal *Of Law*.
19. Three issues of *Hazard's Register*, containing some statistical documents on the penitentiary system of Pennsylvania.
20. Samuel Wood's letter on the penitentiary system (1831).
21. Report from the commissioners who drafted the Penal Code of Pennsylvania (24 December 1827).
22. *On the Penitentiary System of Pennsylvania*, by Mease (1828).

Fifth Volume

General Documents on the Penitentiary System, or indirectly connected thereto

1. Six Reports from the Boston Prison Society from 1826 to 1832.
2. Report of Mr. Gray regarding the creation of labor workshops for released convicts.
3. Report serving as an introduction to the code of prison discipline, by Edward Livingston. 1827.
4. On the abolition of the death penalty, by the same.
5. Reflections on the penitentiary system, by Mr. Carey of Philadelphia. 1831.

6. Essay on the penal code of Pennsylvania, by Tyson.
7. Report of 1831 on the Temperance Society of New York.
8. Report of 1831 on the Temperance Society of Pennsylvania.
9. Medical statistics of Philadelphia, by Emerson. 1831.
10. Report on the primary schools of Pennsylvania. 1831.
11. Laws relating to Pennsylvania schools.
12. Three statistical tables on the state of health in Baltimore.
13. Report on the funds intended for Connecticut schools.
14. Letter addressed to us by Mr. Elam Lynds on the penitentiary system (10 October 1831).
15. Opinion of Mr. Elam Lynds on the penitentiary system (handwritten note personally handed to us on 8 July 1831).
16. Statistical table on the number of crimes in Ohio.
17. Another table on the number of crimes in Ohio since 1815.
18. Letter from the honorable Mr. MacLean, judge of the United States Supreme Court, on the penitentiary system.
19. Statistical tables on condemnations pronounced in the city of New York by the Courts of Oyer and Terminer from 1785 to 1795.
20. Statistical tables of condemnations pronounced by the Supreme Court.
21. Statistical tables of condemnations pronounced by the Supreme Court from the year 1800 to 1810; and from 1820 to 1830.
22. General table of condemnations pronounced in the State of New York during the year 1830 for crimes, criminal offences, and minor offences (except for judgements made by police officers).
23. Handwritten note from Mr. Welles, judge (at Wethersfield), containing his opinion on the penitentiary system, the estimated cost of a prison for 500 prisoners, and the estimation of maintenance expenses.
24. Copy of a letter addressed to Mr. Hozack of New York by William Roscoe.

Sixth Volume

House of Refuge (New-York)

1. Opening speech for the New York House of Refuge, 1826.
2. Report from 1827 on the House of Refuge.

3. Report from 1828 on the House of Refuge.
4. Report from 1829 on the House of Refuge.
5. Report from 1830 on the House of Refuge.
6. Report from 1831 on the House of Refuge.
7. Report from 1832 on the House of Refuge.
8. Rules of the New York House of Refuge, and appeal to the inhabitants of New York by the Prison Commission, to obtain charity relief.

Philadelphia and Boston

9. Appeal from the directors of the Philadelphia House of Refuge[5] to obtain funds (1826).
10. Speech given by Mr. J. Sergeant for the opening of the Philadelphia House of Refuge.
11. New appeal from the directors of the House of Refuge to their fellow-citizens (1828).
12. 1st Report on the Philadelphia House of Refuge (1829).
13. 2nd Report on the Philadelphia House of Refuge (1830).
14. 3rd Report on the Philadelphia House of Refuge (1831).
15. Rules of the Boston House of Refuge (1830).
16. Report from the commission entrusted with the establishment of a house of refuge in Baltimore.
17. Model of an apprenticeship contract for juvenile delinquents of Philadelphia.
18. Investigation into the New York House of Refuge.
19. Various documents, seven in number, on the New York House of Refuge.

All these compose one hundred twenty-seven articles that, classified as stated above into 6 volumes in-folio, were placed by the Minister of Commerce and Public-Works into the archives of the bureau.

The master of requests, Secretary-General of the Bureau[6] of Commerce and Public-Works, acknowledges receipt from Messrs. de Beaumont and de Tocqueville of the volumes named above, that were deposited in the library section of the archives of the bureau:

The master of requests, Secretary-General
Signed: Edmond Blanc

Notes

1. *The "List of Documentary Evidence" marks the beginning of Tocqueville's and Beaumont's work *On the Penitentiary System*; the authors listed the research documents they supplied with their official report to the French government, and often refer to such documents throughout their work. Lieber notes, and the translator agrees: "We give this list, because it will be agreeable to those interested in the work, and in prisons in general, to know from what sources the authors derived their information, besides personal inspection" (Beaumont and Tocqueville 1833, p. xxxix).
2. *Note that a distinction exists in the French between "penitentiary" and "prison" as designated by their respective words. In the following text, "le pénitencier" will always be translated "penitentiary," while "la prison" will be translated "prison" to mark the difference.
3. *The French has: "devis et estimation," a phrase which probably means list of things to be done (*devis*) + the costs (*estimation*).
4. *The *Trésor de la Langue Française informatisé* defines "notice" as: "brief text intended to summarily present a particular subject."
5. *Usually translated "shelter" today; I have chosen to keep "Houses of Refuge," since Lieber also refers to the institutions by that name in his preface and appendix.
6. *Lieber notes: "There is no word in English for the French *ministere* [...] or for the German *ministerium*, because, in fact, the thing itself does not exist in England or the United States; it belongs essentially to *bureaucracy* (Beaumont and Tocqueville 1833, p. xliv).

References

Beaumont, Gustave de and Alexis de Tocqueville. 1833. *On the Penitentiary System in the United States and Its Application in France, with an Appendix on Penal Colonies and also Statistical Notes*. Translated by Francis Lieber. Philadelphia: Carey, Lea & Blanchard.

"Trésor de la Langue Française informatisé." *Center National de Ressources Textuelles et Lexicales*. http://atilf.atilf.fr/. Accessed September 9, 2017.

Preface

Society,[1] in our time, experiences a restiveness that appears to us to have two causes:

The one, wholly psychological;[2] there is within intelligences[3] an activity that does not know where to spend itself, in minds an energy that lacks sustenance, and that devours society, for want of other prey.

The other, wholly material; it is the physical distress of the working population that lacks labor and bread, and whose corruption,[4] beginning in distress, ends in prison.

The first evil is due to the intellectual wealth of the population; the second, to the penury[5] of the poor classes.[6]

How to close the first of these wounds? Its remedy seems to depend more upon circumstances than upon human beings. Regarding the second, more than one effort has already been made to heal it;[7] but it is not yet known whether success was [ever] possible.[8]

Such is the insufficiency of human institutions, that we see[9] disastrous consequences result from establishments which in theory promise only happy results.[10]

In England, it was assumed that one was drying up the source of crime and poverty by giving work and money to all the unfortunate; and one sees the number of the poor and criminals grow each day in that country.

There is not a single philanthropic institution, the abuse of which is not all but customary.

The best directed charity[11] gives rise to new forms of poverty: and any help offered to an abandoned child causes others to be abandoned. The more one looks at this depressing spectacle of public beneficence fighting human sufferings without success, the more one recognizes that there exist ills against which it is noble to struggle, but that our old societies seem powerless to heal.[12]

Yet the wound exists, visible to all eyes. There are in France two million paupers and forty thousand liberated convicts going out of the *bagnes*[13] or some of the other prisons.[14]

Frightened by such a menacing evil, public opinion seeks the remedy for it from a government that does not cure it, perhaps because it judges it incurable.

Yet if it is true that this social vice cannot be eradicated, it appears equally certain that there exist some circumstances helping to aggravate it, and some institutions whose influence renders it less disastrous.

Various voices are raised at this moment to indicate to the government the path it should follow.

Some ask for the establishment of agricultural colonies in the still uncultivated parts of French soil, on which the arms of convicts and the poor might be useful.

This system, which obtains great success in Belgium and Holland, is worthy of the fixed attention of politicians.[15]

There are others who, struck especially with the danger presented to society by liberated convicts, whose corruption has increased in prison, think that a great part of the evil would be remedied, if, during the imprisonment of criminals, they were subjected to a penitentiary system that, instead of further depraving them, rendered them better.[16]

Persuaded that the moral reform of the criminal is impossible, and that his presence in society is always an imminent danger, a few writers, one of whom has just received a prize from the French Academy, would like all malefactors to be deported outside of France.[17]

In the middle of this clash of diverse opinions, some of which are not irreconcilable with each other, it appeared to us that it might be useful to introduce into the discussion some authentic documents on one of the important points in dispute.

Such has been the origin of the voyage we have undertaken under the auspices of the French government.

Commissioned to conduct an investigation in the United States on the theoretical and practical principles of the penitentiary system, we have accomplished this mission; the government has received our report;[18] now it is to the country that we must give an account of our labors.

If our research is judged useful, we will owe it to the generous hospitality that we received in the United States. Everywhere in that country establishments of all kinds were opened to us and all information was furnished with an eagerness by which we have been deeply touched.

The importance of our inquiry was understood in America; and public functionaries of the highest order, as well as men given over to the private life, vied with each other in facilitating its accomplishment.

We have had no way of showing our gratitude for such benevolence. But if this book should ever, by public report, reach America, we are happy to think that the inhabitants of the United States will find here a feeble expression of our profound gratitude.

Notes

1. *Importantly, Beaumont and Tocqueville chose "society" as the first word of the text.
2. *The French word used is "morale," which can be understood in three main ways. First, "morale" designates the mind, psyche, or other things of a spiritual nature, i.e. the opposite of what is physical or outwardly visible, and can therefore be translated in English as "psychological." Second, "morale" references the mores, customs, or habits of a society at a certain time. Third, "morale" refers to a morality system or morals; i.e., notions of good and bad. Thus, "morale" will be translated throughout as either "moral" or "psychological," depending on its context.
3. *Whereas Lieber translates the entire second sentence as dealing with the "mind," two distinct French words are used. Although the semantic fields somewhat overlap, "l'esprit" means an "incorporeal substance" or supernatural power which operates on and within the soul, and is often used to signify the use of imagination, conception, or judgment as intellectual faculties (*Dictionnaire*, 1:679). On the other hand, "intelligence" is broader: "intellectual faculty, capacity of hearing, of conceiving, of comprehending; or, spirit…" (*Dictionnaire*, 1:46). "Esprit" is consistently translated "mind" in the text; "intelligence" as "intelligence."
4. *The French word "la corruption" designates not only moral deterioration but also the corrosion of metals or other material objects. Thus, the use may be considered as in between the moral and material meanings of the word. The word will be consistently translated as "corruption" throughout the text.

5. *"La misère" often means "extreme poverty."
6. *Tocqueville and Beaumont draw a distinction between "working population" and "poor classes" that Lieber leaves out.
7. *Lieber has, instead of "cure it," "free mankind from it." It is an interesting change considering Lieber's use of medical analogy in his own translator's preface.
8. *Note that "était" is strangely in the imperfect indicative.
9. *Beaumont and Tocqueville use several words indicating sight in their preface: "voit," "regarder."
10. *Later, the use of "funeste" (translated consistently as "disastrous") will take on a more complicated meaning when used with "sanity," since "funeste" can mean "fatal" at times.
11. *"L'aumône" clarifies that the charity is financial aid.
12. *Again, Lieber does not translate "guérir" as "to heal," choosing an alternative verb.
13. *"Les bagnes" were historically a type of French prison connected to compulsory labor typically in ship-yards (notably, the arsenals at Rochefort, Brest, and Toulon). The *bagnes* were used for long-term convicts sentenced to hard labor. At the time of Tocqueville's and Beaumont's report, there were four different types of penal institutions in France, all of which were established by the national government: the *bagnes*; *maison d'arrête*, which temporarily held those charged with offences and those sentenced to more than a year in prison who were waiting to be transferred to a *maison centrale*; *maison de justice*, similar to the *maison d'arrête* but only existing in the assize court towns; *maisons de correction*, which held those sentenced to less than a year; *maisons centrales*, "for all sentenced to imprisonment for more than a year, or to hard labor, or to those condemned to *travaux forces* for offences committed in prison" (Chisholm 1910, p.793).
14. See *Des Colonies Agricoles*, by Mr. Huerne de Pommeuse; Statistical Tables at the end of the volume.
15. See the work cited in the previous note.
16. *"Rendît" is in the imperfect subjunctive, thus indicating a past action that did not achieve completion.
17. Mr. Ernest de Blosseville, author of *Histoire des Colonies pénales dans l'Australie*. Paris, 1831. The system of deportation, to which public opinion in France seems rather generally favorable, appears to us to be surrounded by dangers and obstacles. See the Appendix on Penal Colonies.
18. This report has been handed to the Minister of Commerce and Public Works. Count d'Argount has received it with an interest for which the authors must here express their gratitude.

References

Blosseville, Ernest de. 1831. *Histoire des Colonies Pénales de l'Angleterre dans l'Australie*. Paris: Adrien le Clere.

Chisholm, Hugh. 1910. *Encyclopedia Britannica: A Dictionary of Arts, Sciences, Literature, and General Information*, Vol. 10, 11th ed. New York: Encyclopedia Britannica Company.

Dictionnaire de l'Académie française, 6th Edition, Vol. 1 and 2 (1832–5). http://artfl-project.uchicago.edu/node/17. Accessed September 9, 2017.

Pommeuse, Huerne de. 1832. *Des Colonies Agricoles et de leurs Avantages*. Paris: Imprimerie de Madame Huzard.

Part I

Chapter 1: History of the Penitentiary System

Birth of the penitentiary system in 1786. — Influence of the Quakers. — Walnut Street Prison in Philadelphia: its defects and advantages. — The Duke of La Rochefoucauld-Liancourt. — Discipline[1] of Walnut Street adopted by several States; its fatal[2] effects. —Origin of Auburn. — Pittsburg. — Cherry-Hill. — Disastrous experiment of complete solitary imprisonment; it is followed by the Auburn system, founded on isolation and silence; success of this system in several States of the Union. — Wethersfield: creation of Singsing, by Mr. Elam Lynds. —Establishment of houses of refuge in the State of New York. —Pennsylvania abandons the system of complete solitude without labor: new discipline of imprisonment combined with new penal laws. —Which States have not yet made any reform in their prisons; in what way this reform is incomplete in the States where it has occurred— Inhumanity[3] of some criminal laws in certain States. —Summary.

Although the penitentiary system in the United States is a new institution, its origin goes back to times that are already far from us. The first thought of reform in the American prisons belonged to a religious sect in

---

* *Historique*, used in the title, differs slightly from *histoire*: *Histoire* is the narrative of actions, events, and circumstances; whereas, *historique* is the "simple recitation of facts in their order and circumstances." See *Dictionnaire* 1: 892–3.

Pennsylvania. The Quakers, whose principles abhor all bloodshed, had always protested against the inhumane laws that the colonies kept from their mother country. In 1786 their voice managed to be heard, and from this period the death penalty, mutilation, and the whip were successively abolished in almost all cases by the Pennsylvania legislature;[4] henceforth, convicts had a less cruel fate to undergo. The punishment of imprisonment was substituted for corporal punishments, and the law authorized the courts to inflict solitary imprisonment in a cell, day and night, upon all those guilty of capital crimes. It was then that the Walnut Street prison was established in Philadelphia. The convicted prisoners were classified there according to the nature of their crimes, and special cells were constructed to contain those whom the courts of justice had sentenced to complete isolation: these cells also served to subdue individuals who did not submit to prison discipline. The solitary prisoners did not work.[5]

This innovation was good, but incomplete.

The impossibility of submitting criminals to a useful classification has since been recognized; and solitary imprisonment without labor has been condemned by experiment. However, it is fair to say that the trial of this theory was not long enough to be decisive; the authority accorded to all Pennsylvania judges by the laws of 5 April 1790 and 22 March 1794, to send to the Walnut prison convicted prisoners who previously would have been detained in local county jails, did not take long to produce in this prison such overcrowding that the difficulties of classification increased, at the same time the number of cells became insufficient.[6]

To tell the truth, a penitentiary system did not yet exist in the United States.

If someone asks why this name was given to the discipline of imprisonment that had been established, we will answer that then, as today, in America the abolition of the death penalty was not distinguished from the penitentiary system. People said: *instead of killing the guilty, our laws put them in prison; thus, we have a penitentiary system.*

The conclusion did not quite follow. It is very certain that the death penalty applied to most crimes is irreconcilable with a discipline of imprisonment; but once this punishment has been abolished, the penitentiary system does not yet exist; it is still necessary that the criminal whose life has been spared be placed in a prison whose discipline renders him better. For if this discipline, instead of reforming, only further degrades him, it would not be a *penitentiary system*, but only a *bad system of imprisonment*.

For a long time, France shared in the error of the Americans in this regard. In 1794 the Duke of La Rochefoucauld-Liancourt published an interesting article on the Philadelphia prison; he declared that this city had an excellent prison system, and everyone repeated it.[7]

However, the Walnut Street prison could produce none of the effects that are expected from this system. It had two principal defects: it corrupted the convicts who worked together by the contagion[8] of mutual communications. It corrupted by idleness the individuals plunged into isolation.

The true merit of its founders was to abolish the sanguinary laws of Pennsylvania, and, by introducing a new system of detention there, of drawing public attention to this point...

Unfortunately, no distinction was made from the beginning between what was worthy of praise in this innovation and what deserved blame.

The punishment of isolation, applied to the criminal in order to conduct him to reform by reflection, rests upon a philosophical and true idea. But the authors of this theory had not surrounded it with that which could make it practicable and salutary. Yet their mistake was not immediately perceived; and the success of the Walnut-Street prison, highly praised in the United States still more than in Europe, gave credence in opinion to its defects as well as its advantages.

The first State that showed itself eager to imitate Pennsylvania was New York, which, in 1797, adopted a new prison system with new penal laws.

Solitary imprisonment without labor was allowed here as in Philadelphia; but just as at Walnut-Street, it was reserved for those who were especially sentenced to undergo it by the courts of justice, and for those disobedient to the regulations of the prison. Thus, solitary imprisonment was not the ordinary discipline of the establishment; it was the exclusive lot of serious criminals who, before the reform of penal laws, would have been sentenced to death. Moreover, those guilty of lesser crimes were crammed pell-mell into the prison; unlike the prisoners in the cells, they were made to work during the day; and the only disciplinary punishment that their guard had a right to inflict on them, in the case of infraction to the regulations, was solitary imprisonment with bread and water.

The Walnut Street prison was imitated by others: Maryland, Massachusetts, Maine, New-Jersey, Virginia, et cetera, adopted successively the principle of solitary imprisonment applied only to a certain class of criminals (*a*) in each of these States; the reform of criminal laws preceded that of the prisons.

Nowhere did this system of imprisonment have the success that was expected of it. In general, it was ruinous to the public treasury; it never effected the reform of prisoners;[9] every year the legislature of each State voted allocations of considerable funds to sustain the penitentiaries, and the perpetual return of the same individuals into the prisons proved the inefficacy of the discipline to which they were subjected.[10]

Such results seemed to demonstrate the defect of the whole system; however, instead of accusing the theory itself, its execution was attacked. It was thought that all the evil resulted from the insufficient number of cells and the crowding of prisoners in the prison, and that the system, such as it was established, would be fruitful in happy consequences if a few new constructions were added to the already existing prisons. Therefore, new expenses and new efforts were made.

Such was the origin of the Auburn prison (1816).

This prison, which has since become so celebrated, was first established on an essentially defective plan; it confined itself to some classifications, and each of its cells was intended to receive two convicts:[11] it was of all combinations the most unfortunate; it would be better to mix fifty criminals together in the same living quarters than to put two together. This disadvantage was soon felt, and in 1819 the legislature of the State of New York decreed the erection of a new building at Auburn (the North Wing) to augment the number of solitary cells; altogether, it must be remarked that no idea as yet existed of the system that has since prevailed. It was not thought to submit the totality of the convicts to the cellular system; its application was only to be made to a greater number; —at the same time, the same theories brought the same attempts to Philadelphia, where the small success of the Walnut prison would have convinced the inhabitants of Pennsylvania of its powerlessness for good, if the latter, following the example of the inhabitants of New York, had not found, in some faults of execution, a reason to vindicate the principle.[12]

In 1817, the legislature of Pennsylvania decreed the erection of the penitentiary at Pittsburgh, for the western counties, and in 1821 that of the Cherry-Hill penitentiary, for the city of Philadelphia and the eastern counties.[13]

The principles that were to be followed for the construction of these two establishments were not, however, in total conformity to those that had presided over the erection of Walnut; in this latter prison, classifications had formed the predominant system, of which solitary imprisonment was only an accessory: in the new prisons, classifications were abandoned, and a solitary cell was to be prepared to receive each convict. The criminal was not to leave his cell day or night, and all work was forbidden him in his solitude. Thus, complete solitary imprisonment that, at Walnut, was only an accident, came to be the foundation of the system of Pittsburgh and Cherry-Hill.

The experiment that was undertaken promised[14] to be decisive: no expense was spared to give to the new establishments a construction worthy of their purpose, and the buildings that were built resembled palaces more than prisons.

However, even before the laws that had ordained their erection were executed, the Auburn prison had been tried out in the State of New York. Heated debates took place, on this occasion, within the legislature; and the public was impatient to know the result of the new experiments that had just been made.

The northern wing having been almost finished in 1821, eighty criminals were placed there, an individual cell given to each of them (*b*). This trial, from which such a fortunate outcome was promised, was fatal to most of the prisoners: in order to reform them, they had been subjected to complete isolation; but this complete solitude, when nothing distracts nor interrupts it, is beyond the strength of man;[15] it consumes[16] the criminal without respite and without pity; it does not reform, it kills.

The unfortunates on whom this experiment was performed fell into a state of depression so manifest that their guards were struck with it: their lives seemed in danger, if they remained longer in the prison, undergoing the same discipline;[17] five of them, during a single year, had already succumbed to it (*c*); their psychological state was no less alarming: one of them had become insane; another, in a fit of despair, had taken advantage of a moment when the jailer brought him something to rush out of his cell, running the almost certain risk of a mortal fall.

Confident of similar results, the system was definitively judged. The Governor of the State of New York pardoned twenty-six of those in solitary detainment; those to whom this favor was not accorded went out during the day and were allowed to work in the common workshops. Ever since this time (1823), the system of isolation without restriction ceased to be practiced at Auburn entirely: —they soon acquired proof that this discipline, deadly to the sanity of the criminals, was powerless to effectuate their reform. Of the twenty-six convicts whom the Governor pardoned, fourteen returned shortly into the prison following new convictions.[18]

This experiment, so deadly to those who were chosen to undergo it, was of a nature to jeopardize the fate of the penitentiary system.[19] After the disastrous effects of isolation, it was to be feared that the whole principle would be rejected: it would have been a natural reaction. They were wiser: the idea persisted that the solitude which causes criminals to reflect, and separates them from each other, exercises a beneficial influence; they sought only a way to avoid the disadvantages of isolation while retaining its advantages. It was believed that this end could be reached by leaving the convicts in their cells during the night and making them work during the day, in common workshops, in an environment of complete silence.

Messrs. Allen, Hopkins, and Tibbits, who, in 1824, were charged by the legislature of New York with inspecting the Auburn prison, found this new rule[20] established there. They greatly praised it in their report, and the legislature sanctioned the new system with its formal approbation.

Here an obscurity presents itself that has not been in our power to dissipate. We see the famous Auburn system suddenly being born and emerging from the ingenious combination of two elements that seem, at first glance, incompatible: isolation and congregation. But what we cannot perceive clearly is the creator of this system, of which nevertheless someone must have had the first thought...

Is the State of New York indebted to Governor Clinton for this [creation], whose name, in the United States, is connected to all useful and beneficial enterprises?

Does the honor belong to Mr. Cray, one of the directors of Auburn, to whom Judge Powers, who was himself at the head of that establishment, seems to attribute the merit?

Finally, can Mr. Elam Lynds, who has certainly contributed much to putting this new system into practice, also claim the glory of its invention?[21]

We shall not attempt to answer these questions, interesting to the persons whom we have just named, and to the country that saw them born, but of little importance to us.

Besides, does not experience teach us that there are some innovations of which the honor does not belong to one person, because they are due to simultaneous efforts and to the progress of time?[22]

The establishment of Auburn, since its beginning, obtained extraordinary success; and it did not take long to excite the highest degree of public attention. A remarkable revolution took place in minds; the direction of a prison formerly confided to obscure jailers was now aspired to by men occupying a high social position in the world: and Mr. Elam Lynds, a former Captain of the United States Army, and Judge Powers, a magistrate of a rare merit, derived honor in [public] opinion and in their own eyes by filling the offices of directors of Auburn.

However, the adoption of a cellular system applied to all convicts of the State of New York rendered the Auburn prison insufficient, which, after the successive augmentations it had received, contained only five hundred fifty cells;[23] the necessity of a new prison was therefore felt. It was then that the plan for Singsing was resolved upon by the legislature (1825). This plan was executed in a manner that deserves to be reported.

Mr. Elam Lynds, who had just proved himself at Auburn, of which he was the superintendent, left this establishment, took with him a hundred prisoners accustomed to obeying him, led them to the site where the projected prison was to be built, and there, encamped on the banks of the Hudson, without any shelter to receive him, without walls to shut in his dangerous companions, he set them to work, making each one a mason or carpenter, having no other force to keep them in obedience but the firmness of his character and the energy of his will.

For several years the convicts, whose number was gradually increased, worked thus to build their own prison; and today the Singsing penitentiary contains one thousand cells, all constructed by criminals who have been contained there.[24] At the same time (1825), an establishment of another nature was born in the City of New York, but one that does not occupy a lesser place among the innovations whose history we are retracing. We mean the house of refuge founded for juvenile delinquents.[25]

There exists no establishment that is better in accord with experience. It is well known that most of the persons on whom the criminal justice system inflicts its rigors have been unfortunate before they became guilty. Misfortune is particularly dangerous for those whom it befalls at a still-tender age; and it is very rare that the orphan without inheritance and without friends, or a child abandoned by its parents, avoids the traps that are wide open to their inexperience, and does not pass within a short time from poverty to crime. Affected by the fate of young delinquents, several charitable persons from the City of New York conceived the plan of a house of refuge, intended to serve as an asylum and to procure for them the education and means of existence that fortune had refused them: the first subscription produced 30,000 dollars (159,000 f.); thus an eminently useful establishment was raised by the sole power of a charitable association, and an establishment that is better, perhaps, than the penitentiary prisons, since the latter punish crime, while the house of refuge tends to prevent it.

The experiment performed at Auburn in the State of New York, the fatal effects of isolation without work, did not prevent Pennsylvania from continuing its trial; and in the course of the year 1827 the Pittsburgh penitentiary began to receive prisoners. Each convict was locked away day and night in a cell, where he was not allowed to work. This solitude, which in theory was to be complete, was not so in fact. The construction of the penitentiary is so faulty, that it is very easy to hear from one cell what is happening in another; in this manner each convict found a daily distraction in communication with his neighbor, that is, the occasion for an inevitable corruption;[26] and as these criminals did not work, it could be said that their sole occupation was mutual corruption. This prison was thus worse than even that of Walnut; for, owing to their relations among themselves, the prisoners of Pittsburgh were reformed as little as those of Walnut-Street; and while the latter compensated society through their work, the others passed their whole time in an idleness harmful to themselves and burdensome to the public treasury (*d*).

The poor outcome of this establishment proved nothing against the system that had given it birth, because its defects of construction rendered its execution impossible; however, the proponents of the theories on which it had been founded began to cool. This impression became even more vivid in Pennsylvania, when the disasters caused by solitude without work in the Auburn prison were learned, as well as the fortunate outcome of the new rule founded on isolation by night with common work during the day.[27]

Warned by such striking results, Pennsylvania seemed afraid that she had started off in a bad direction; she felt the need to submit the question of solitary imprisonment without work to a new examination, [already] implemented at Pittsburgh, and intended for the Cherry Hill penitentiary, whose construction was already well advanced.

The legislature of this State therefore appointed a committee to examine which was the better system of imprisonment. Messrs. Charles Shaler, Edward King, and T.L. Wharton, commissioners charged with this mission, have, in a very remarkable report, exhibited the diverse systems then in force (20 December 1827), and they conclude their discussion by recommending the new Auburn discipline, which they proclaim superior.[28]

The authority of this inquiry had a powerful [effect] on [public] opinion;[29] however, it aroused serious opposition on the part of some: Roberts Vaux in Pennsylvania, Edward Livingston in Louisiana, continued to support the doctrine[30] of complete isolation of criminals.

The latter, whose writings are imbued with so elevated a philosophy, had prepared for Louisiana, his native country, a criminal code and a code of reform for the prisons.[31] His profound theories, little understood by those for whom they were intended, had more success in Pennsylvania, for which they were not made. In this superior work, Mr. Livingston accepted, for most cases, the principle of labor for the prisoners; he also showed himself less the defender of Pittsburg than the adversary of Auburn; he recognized the good rule of this latter prison, but he rose up strongly against the corporal punishments used to maintain it. Mr. Livingston and those who supported the same doctrines had to combat a powerful fact: the uncertainty of their theories not yet tested, and the proven success of the system they attacked. Auburn's prosperity continued to grow; everywhere the marvelous effects of its rule were vaunted, and they were retraced each year with great energy in a work justly celebrated in America, and that has mightily contributed to direct public opinion in the United States on the penitentiary system to the point where it has arrived; we mean the annual public reports by the Boston Society of Prisons. These reports, which are the work of Mr. Louis Dwight, give a distinct preference to the Auburn system (*e*).

All the States of the Union were attentive witnesses to the controversy between the two contrary systems.

In this fortunate country, which has neither neighbors to disturb it from without, nor interior dissensions which distract it from within, nothing more is necessary, in order to excite public attention in the highest degree, than the trial of some principle of social economy. As the existence of society is not put in jeopardy, the question is not how to live, but how to improve.

Pennsylvania was perhaps more than any other State interested in these restless debates: as the rival of New York, it had to show itself zealous to retain in every respect the rank its advanced civilization gives it among the most enlightened States of the American Union.

It adopted a system that suited at once the austerity of its mores and its philanthropic tendencies; it rejected isolation without labor, whose fatal effects experience had brought attention to everywhere, and it preserved the complete separation of prisoners, a severe punishment that, to be inflicted, does not need the support of corporal punishments.

The Cherry-Hill penitentiary, founded on these principles, is then nothing other than the combination of Pittsburg and Auburn. It has retained from Pittsburg isolation by night and day, and introduced the labor of Auburn into the solitary cell (*f*).

This revolution in the discipline of Pennsylvania prisons was immediately followed by a general reform of criminal laws. All punishments were made milder; the rigors of solitary imprisonment allowed an abridgement of their duration; the death penalty was abolished in all cases except in that of premeditated murder (*g*).

While the States of New York and Pennsylvania made serious reforms in their laws, each adopting a different system of imprisonment, the other States of the Union did not remain impassive and inactive in the presence of the great spectacle offered them.

Since the year 1825 the plan of a new prison on the Auburn model had been adopted by the legislature of Connecticut; and the Wethersfield penitentiary had succeeded the old prison of Newgate.

Despite the weight that Pennsylvania had just put in the balance in favor of complete isolation with labor, the Auburn system, that is to say common labor during the day with isolation during the night, continued to obtain preference; Massachusetts, Maryland, Tennessee, Kentucky, Maine, and Vermont have adopted the Auburn plan by turns and have taken it as a model for the new prisons that they have constructed (*h*).

Several States did not limit themselves to establishing prisons for sentenced criminals, but they have also, in imitation of New York, founded houses of refuge for juvenile delinquents that are like an appendix to the penitentiary system. These establishments were organized at Boston in 1826 and at Philadelphia in 1828. There is every indication that Baltimore will also soon have its own house of refuge.

Besides, it is easy to predict that the impulse for reform given by New York and Philadelphia will not stop in the States we named above.

Thanks to the happy rivalry that exists among all the States of the Union, and to the advertising that binds together all parts of the immense body, each State follows the reforms that are made among the others and shows itself impatient to imitate them.[32]

It would be wrong today to judge all the States of the Union by the picture that we have presented of the innovations accepted by some of them.

Accustomed as we are to seeing our central government attract all to itself and to imprint a uniform direction on all parts of administration in the diverse provinces, we sometimes imagine that it is the same in other countries; and comparing the centralization of Washington with that of Paris, the individual States of the Union to our departments,[33] we are tempted to think that innovations made in one necessarily take place in others.[34] However, nothing of the sort happens in the United States.

These States, bound together by their common federal tie, are, in respect to everything that concerns their common interests, subjected to a single authority.[35] But outside these general interests they preserve their personal independence, and each of them is sovereign master to govern itself as it pleases. We have spoken of nine States that have adopted a new prison system: there are fifteen that have still made no change.[36]

In these latter, the former system reigns in all its force: crowding with prisoners, mingling of crimes, ages, and sometimes sexes, mixture of the indicted and convicted, of criminals and debtors, of the guilty and witnesses;[37] considerable mortality, frequent escapes, absence of all discipline, no silence that might lead the criminal to reflection; no labor that accustoms them to honestly earn their living; insalubrity of the place, which destroys health; cynicism of the conversations which corrupt; idleness that depraves; the assemblage, in a word, of all defects[38] and all immoralities: such is the spectacle offered by the prisons that have not yet entered into the way of reform (*i*).

Alongside one State whose penitentiaries could serve as a model, one finds another whose prisons offer the example of everything that ought to be avoided. Thus, the State of New York is without contradiction one of the most advanced in the path of reform, and New Jersey, which is separated from it only by a river, has retained all the defects of the former system.

Ohio, which possesses a penal Code remarkable for the mildness and humanity of its provisions, has barbarous prisons. We groaned profoundly when, visiting the prison at Cincinnati, we found half the prisoners chained with irons and the rest plunged into an infected dungeon; and we cannot describe the painful impression that we experienced when, examining the prison of New Orleans, we saw men confounded pell-mell with pigs in the middle of every kind of filth and refuse.[39] In locking up criminals, nobody thinks of making them better, but only of breaking their malice; they are chained like ferocious beasts; instead of being corrected, they are brutalized.[40]

If it is true that the penitentiary system is entirely unknown in the region that we just reviewed, it is equally certain that this system is incomplete even in the States where it is in force.[41] Thus in New York, in Philadelphia, in Boston, there are new prisons for convicts whose punishment exceeds one or two years imprisonment; but establishments of a similar nature do not exist to receive individuals whose punishment is less, or those awaiting trial who have been arrested as suspects.[42] In respect to the latter nothing has been changed; disorder, confusion, mixture of ages and morals, all defects of the old discipline meet here for them: we have seen in the house of arrest in New York (Birdwell) more than fifty indicted persons[43] together in the same room.[44] These prisoners are those for whom well-regulated prisons ought to have been built first. It is easy to conceive in fact that the indicted who has not been declared guilty, and the convict who has committed only a light offence, ought to be surrounded by much greater protection than the guilty who are more advanced in crime and whose culpability has been recognized.

The accused are sometimes innocent and always presumed such. How could we suffer them to find in prison a corruption that they did not bring with them?

If they are guilty, why place them first in a house of arrest appropriate for corrupting them further, only to reform them afterwards in the penitentiary prison, where they will be sent after their condemnation (*j*)?

Clearly there is a gap in a prison system that presents similar anomalies.

These shocking contradictions proceed mainly from the overall defect in aggregating various parts of administration in the United States.

The larger prisons (State prisons), corresponding to our central prisons, belong to the State that directs them; then come the county jails, which the county manages; and finally, the city prisons, which are governed by the city itself.

The individual administrations in the States being almost as independent of each other as the States are among themselves, it results that they hardly ever act uniformly and simultaneously. While one makes a useful reform in the ambit of its authority, another remains inactive and attached to routine traditions.

We shall see below how this independence of localities, which harms the totality of all their actions, has nevertheless a beneficial influence in impressing on each of them a prompter and more energetic progress in the direction it freely follows.

For that matter, we will not point out any longer what is defective in the prison system of the United States: if France chooses one day to imitate the American penitentiaries, the most important thing for her will be to know those that can serve as models. The new establishments will thus be the only object of our examination.

We have seen from what precedes that few States have completely changed their system of imprisonment; the number of those that have modified their penal laws is even more limited. Several of them still possess part of the inhumane laws that they received from England.

We will not speak of the southern States, where slavery is in force; every place where one half of society is cruelly oppressed by the other one must expect to find in the law of the oppressor a weapon always ready to strike nature that revolts or humanity that complains. The death penalty and blows; here is the whole penal Code for slaves.[45] But if we throw a glance at the States themselves that no longer have slaves, and whose civilization is most advanced, we will see this civilization is allied, in some, with penal laws full of mildness, and mingles, in others, with all the rigors of a Draconian code.

Let us compare with the laws of Pennsylvania only those of New England, which is perhaps the most enlightened region of the American Union. In Massachusetts, there are ten different crimes punished by death, among others rape and burglary.[46] Maine, Rhode-Island, and Connecticut count the same number of capital crimes.[47] Among these laws, some contain the most infamous tortures, such as the pillory; others, revolting cruelties, such as branding and mutilation.[48] There are also some that order fines whose tax is the equivalent of a confiscation.[49] While one finds these remainders of inhumanity in States that possess an old civilization, there are others that, born yesterday, have banished from their laws all cruel punishments that are not justified by the interest of society. Thus, Ohio, which is certainly not as enlightened as New England, possesses a penal Code much more humane than those of Massachusetts and Connecticut.

Next door to a State where the reform of penal laws seems to have arrived at its summit, we find another whose criminal laws are imprinted[50] with all the brutalities of the former system. It is thus that the States of

Delaware and New Jersey, so behind in the path of innovations, border on Pennsylvania, who, in this respect, marches at the head of all the others.[51]

We would forget the purpose of our report if we spent any more time on this point. We were obliged to present a survey of the penal legislation of the United States because it exercises a necessary influence on the very question that occupies us.

It is easy to see, in fact, to what extent the punishments that degrade the guilty person are incompatible with the purpose of the penitentiary system that proposes to reform him. How can we hope to reform the morality of a man who carries on his body indelible signs of his infamy, either because the mutilation of his limbs incessantly reminds him of his crime, or because the mark imprinted on his forehead perpetuates its memory?[52]

Should we not address pious prayers to God that the last traces of a vanishing inhumanity should disappear from all the United States, and notably from those that have adopted a penitentiary system with which they are irreconcilable, and whose existence renders them more shocking?[53]

However, let us not blame this nation for advancing slowly on the path of innovations. Must not such changes be the work of time and of public opinion?[54] — There are in the United States a certain number of philosophical minds who, full of theories and systems, are impatient to put them into practice; and if they had power themselves to make the law of the country, they would efface by a stroke of the pen all the old customs, for which they would substitute the creations of their genius and the decrees of their wisdom. Rightly or wrongly, the people do not move as fast as they; they [the people] consent to changes, but they want them progressive and partial (*k*). Perhaps this prudent and reserved reform, effected by an entire people, whose entire habits are practical, will be better than the hasty trials that would result from the enthusiasm of ardent minds and the seduction of theories.[55]

Whatever may be the obstacles yet to be overcome, we do not hesitate to declare, in the United States the cause of reform and progress appears assured to us.

Slavery, that shame of a free people, sees each day some territories over which it extended its empire escape its yoke; and the men themselves who possess the most slaves, have found in their souls[56] the inner conviction that slavery will not have a long duration.

Each day sees the softening of some one of the sufferings that injure humanity; and in the most civilized States of the North, where these punishments are still written in the laws, their application has become so rare, that they are as though fallen into disuse.

The movement of amelioration has begun. The States that have not yet done anything are conscious of their wrong; they envy the fate of those that have preceded them in the race and are impatient to imitate them.

Finally, it is a fact worth remarking that the modification of penal laws and that of prison discipline are two associated reforms that, in the United States, are never separated.

Our special task is not for us to expound on the first; the second alone will fix our attention.

The various States in which we have seen a penitentiary system in force pursue the same goal: the improvement of prison discipline. But they employ, to achieve this goal, different means. It is these diverse means that have been the object of our investigation.

Notes

1. *Lieber most often translates "régime" as "discipline" (Beaumont and Tocqueville 1833, p. 1). There are many possible English translations of "régime:" system, discipline, discipline, regulation, etc. In the French, "régime" can also mean "order," "diet," or "all legal or regulatory provisions or practices governing an institution, establishment, or a particular activity." Tocqueville and Beaumont use "régime" in this latter sense to argue that the penitentiary has a specific organization that enforces a particular rule of life upon inmates. Although the English sense of "regime" has acquired negative or totalitarian connotations in modern times, in the tradition of political thought the word signifies a peculiar system of government, mode of organization, or administration, coming from the Old French and Latin "disciplinen." "Regime" in the classical sense (*politeia* in Ancient Greek) signified a form that the political order takes, embodying a specific way of life in a society directed towards a particular goal. Notably, "régime" also differs from "système," which means in a political sense: "collection of organizational methods, practices, and procedures designed to ensure a defined function." Thus, in order to both account for the peculiar meaning of "régime"as well as to distinguish "régime" from "système" (also used in the text), it is translated consistently as "discipline" unless referring to "diet;" the phrase "régime d'emprisonnement" is translated "system of imprisonment." The French "discipline" is translated as either "rule" or

"discipline." See *Dictionnaire* 2:599, 805; "Trésor de la Langue Française informatise" (Hereafter: TLFi) "système" and "régime."

2. *In using the word "funeste," Tocqueville and Beaumont suggest that complete solitude can have fatal effects, i.e. consequences leading invariably to death. "Funeste" can also imply what relates to unhappiness, ruin, or desolation; i.e. "negative," "disastrous," or "regrettable." I keep the more dramatic interpretation here because the authors seem to indicate that death, rather than simply depression or other negative psychological effects, are the ultimate effects of this penal discipline. There is a connection between our psyches and our physical bodies.
3. *The French word is "barbarie," which could also be translated "barbaric" in contemporary usage.
4. Today, the death penalty is pronounced by the Code of Pennsylvania only in the case of assassination, poisoning and arson.
5. These cells were and still are thirty in number in the Walnut Street prison.
6. See Letter from Samuel Wood to Thomas Keltera. Philadelphia, 1831. See summaries of the original and successive efforts to improve the rule of the prison at Philadelphia, and to reform the criminal Code of Pennsylvania, by Roberts Vaux.
7. See *Des Prisons de Philadelphie, par un Européen* (La Roçhefoucauld-Liancourt), in the IV year of the republic. Paris.
8. *While Lieber translates "la contagion" as "contamination," I have chosen to keep the medical undertones as implied in the French.
9. See Statistics, financial part. See Report to the Legislature, by the Comptroller of the State of New York. 2 March 1819. See the Fifth Report of the Boston Prison Society, pages 412, 423, and 454. See also Report on the Connecticut Prison and on that of Massachusetts.
10. See our Statistical Observations on the Various States of the Union, No. 17, Comparative Table of Re-committals. "It is a sad truth that most of the convicts do not reform during their detention, but, on the contrary, are hardened in their wickedness, and are, after their liberation, more vicious and more consumed with crime than they were before" (Report of 20 January 1819, to the New York Legislature).
11. The Auburn prison, that is to say the South Wing, built in 1816, 1817 and 1818, contained sixty-one cells, and twenty-eight chambers each of which afforded room for eight to twelve convicts.
12. *Stephen Maddux pointed out that the phrase "absoudre le principe" has a vague and peculiar meaning in its French usage. The idea is that, rather than discarding the principle itself as defective, Pennsylvanians sought out a way to blame the execution of the principle.
13. Cherry-Hill is the new penitentiary of Philadelphia, implemented only in 1829.

CHAPTER 1: HISTORY OF THE PENITENTIARY SYSTEM   19

14. *Or, "bid fare."
15. *Here I have taken Lieber's translation; the more literal rendering is: "above human forces." "Des forces de l'homme" is a poetical plural, meaning "the resources that an individual human being has."
16. *Lieber has "destroys," but it is noteworthy that Tocqueville and Beaumont use the same word to describe the condition of prisoners when corrupted or when subjected to complete solitude without labor: consume. The word describes physical withering and/or moral dejection of a person (TLFi).
17. *Lieber does not translate "soumis au même régime," perhaps to detract from the implication that absolute solitude as a penal measure is dangerous to the health of prisoners.
18. See Report of Gershom Powers, 1828, and handwritten note of Elam Lynds.
19. *Instead of "fate," Lieber translates as "success" (Beaumont and Tocqueville 1833, p. 6).
20. *"Discipline," according to TLFi, has two primary meanings: in the first place, "discipline" can mean "instruction, moral direction." In the second place, discipline can mean "imposed rule." It is in the latter sense that we translate the word.
21. [Public] opinion in the United States generally attributes to Mr. Elam Lynds the creation of the system finally adopted in the Auburn prison. This opinion is also that of Messrs. Hopkins and Tibbits, charged, in 1826, with inspecting the Auburn prison. See p. 23; and of Mr. Livingston, see his *Introduction to a system of penal laws*, p. 13, edition of 1817, Philadelphia. We have found this opinion contested only in a letter addressed by Mr. Powers to Mr. Livingston, in 1829. See this letter p. 5 and following.
22. *Note the interesting combination of causes: human effort and historical progress.
23. In 1813, Auburn still had only three hundred eighty cells. On 12 April 1824, the legislature ordered the construction of an additional one hundred seventy cells. *Lieber corrects the authors here, noting that only an additional sixty-two cells were built, rather than one hundred seventy (7).
24. The manner in which Mr. Elam Lynds has built Singsing would no doubt be found incredible, were it not a recent fact and well known in the United States; in order to understand it, it is necessary to know all the resources that an energetic man can find in the new rule of American prisons; if one desires to form an idea of the character of Mr. Elam Lynds, and of his opinions on the penitentiary system, they have only to read the Conversation that we had with him, and that we believe we have transcribed in its entirety. See [Appendix] no. 11.
25. *At the time of the writing, France had one equivalent institution to American houses of refuge: the Abbe Ausoux in Paris, established in 1827.

26. *Stephen Maddux pointed out that the combination of "opportunity" and "inevitable" suggests the meaning that once the occasion exists, even if occurring randomly or by chance, the corruption is inevitable.
27. It was not only in the Auburn prison that solitary imprisonment without work exercised the most disastrous influence on the psychological and physical health of the prisoners. The experiments made in the prisons of Maryland, Maine, Virginia, and New Jersey were no more successful; one mentions, in this latter prison, the names of ten individuals killed by solitary imprisonment. See the Fifth Report of the Boston Society, p. 422. In Virginia, when the governor ceased to pardon the convicts, there was no example of any of them surviving the onset of a sickness. (See Report of the editors of the Penal Code of Pennsylvania, p. 30).
28. This report is one of the most important legislative documents in existence on the American prisons. It has been, in Europe, the subject of a special study by certain publicists.
29. *Lieber translates "l'opinion" as "public opinion," which seems implied. However, Tocqueville and Beaumont are careful to insert the modifier "public" elsewhere in the text.
30. *The TLFi provides a better understanding of "doctrine" as "the ensemble of principles or statements, systematized or not, translating a certain conception of the universe, of human existence, of society..." in order to guide human conduct or formulate models of thought. It is interesting that Tocqueville and Beaumont choose to use the word "doctrine," since up to this point they have characterized complete isolation as a theory or principle. "Doctrine" perhaps reflects how Vaux and Livingston view complete isolation: not as a theory that ought to be tested, but as a guiding rule that must be defended. The use of the word "doctrine" is also interesting considering the religious beginnings of penitentiary systems.
31. *Lieber contests this assertion as "a great mistake" since Livingston received his education in New York and his writings "are of a decided Anglo-American character" (Beaumont and Tocqueville 1833, p. 10).
32. *Here, Tocqueville and Beaumont seem to refer to the political importance of newspapers in the young American democracy, a theme Tocqueville later expands in *Democracy in America* I.2.3 and II.2.6 (Tocqueville 2000, pp. 172–180, 493–496). Another word for translating "advertising" would be "publicity."
33. *The departments in France were originally created to function administratively between the "regions" and the "commune" as political divisions of the country; they thus represent both an institutional and territorial organization within the nation
34. Mr. Charles Lucas, who has published a very respected work on the penitentiary system, has fallen into error on this point. "Two systems," he

writes, "are presented, the one exclusive to the Old World, and the other to the New. The first is the system of deportation followed by Great Britain and Russia, the second is the penitentiary system established in *all the States of the Union.*" "...The penitentiary discipline," he says a little further, "that Caleb Lownes gave in 1791 to Pennsylvania, where it has spread *almost simultaneously in all the States of the Union...*" See *Du système pénal et du système répressif en général* by Mr. Charles Lucas. Introduction, p. 58, 59 and 60.
35. That of Congress.
36. In Ohio, in New-Hampshire and some other States, a system of imprisonment has been established; but it is a bad prison discipline, and not a penitentiary system.
37. See [Appendices] Notes on Imprisonment for Debts and On the Imprisonment of Witnesses, No. 7 and 8.
38. *The French word is "les vices."
39. The place which locks up convicted criminals, in New Orleans, cannot be called a prison: it is an awful cesspool, in which they are crowded, and which is appropriate only for those filthy animals found here together with the prisoners: it must be observed all those who are prisoners here are not slaves: it is the prison for free men. It appears, however, that the necessity of a reform in the discipline of prisons is felt in Louisiana; the governor of this State told us that he would incessantly ask the legislature for an allocation of funds for this object. It seems equally certain that the system of imprisonment in Ohio is about to be entirely changed.
40. In general, for their prisons as for all the rest, the southern States are far behind those of the North. In some of them the reform of the prison discipline is not asked for by public opinion; quite recently the penitentiary system was abolished in Georgia, having been established a year before.
41. If the law of 30 March 1831 is executed in Pennsylvania, this State will soon have the most complete system of imprisonment which has existed in the United States. This law orders the erection of a prison on the plan of solitary imprisonment, intended to receive indicted persons, debtors, witnesses, and those sentenced to a short prison sentence: — See *Acts of the General Assembly Relating to the Eastern Penitentiary and to the New Prisons of the City and County of Philadelphia,* p. 21.
42. The prison of Blackwell-Island at New York, all newly built, is the only one which has been made to receive prisoners convicted of small offences.
43. *Note that "condamnes" is translated two ways in the text, depending on the context in which it is found: 1. Convicted or Sentenced, 2. Convict(s). There is a total of 8 words to designate the persons sentenced to imprisonment in the text: *condamnes, malfaiteur/malfrat* (both translated

"malefactor"), *criminal* (translated "criminal"), *détenu/forçat/prisonnier* (all translated "prisoner"), *délinquant* (translated "delinquent").
44. In this prison, where there are only the indicted, no regard is paid to the different crimes with which they are charged, to the youth of the one, to the old corruption of others. All these individuals have not a bed, nor a chair, nor a board, nor a couch, on which to lay their head. They do not have a yard where they can breathe clean air. — A few steps away there is a perfectly ordered prison, which contains convicted criminals. The best and most vicious prisons are found in the United States.
45. There are no prisons to shut up slaves: imprisonment is too expensive! Death, whipping, exile cost nothing! In order to exile them, they are sold, which yields profit. See Statistical Notes on the State of Maryland.
46. We comprise in this number the crimes against the federal government, that of high treason against the United States, piracy, theft of the government's mail.
47. The laws of the latter State also pronounce in seven particular cases the punishment of life imprisonment.
48. A law of Connecticut orders that the mother hiding the death of her natural child will be exposed to the galleries for one hour with a rope noosed around her neck.
   — Another law of Massachusetts orders one fine against fornication; it adds that if the convict does not pay this fine within twenty-four hours he receives six lashes of the whip. The one guilty of blasphemy is, according to the laws of the same country, sentenced to the pillory and the whip. Those in Rhode-Island who commit the crime of forgery are sentenced to the pillory. During his exhibition a piece of each ear is cut off and he is branded with the letter C (*counterfeiting*). After all this, he submits to imprisonment not exceeding six years.
49. For example, one law of the State of Delaware orders a fine of 10,000 dollars (54,000 fr.) for a single crime.
50. *The choice of word describing the effect of law on the penal system mirrors the effect of punishment on the criminal's body in the act of branding.
51. The laws of the State of Delaware pronounce the death penalty against six different crimes (not including capital crimes provided by the federal law of the United States).
   —Here is how they punish forgery: the guilty is sentenced to a fine, to the pillory, to three months of isolation in a cell; at the expiration of his punishment the convict must wear on his back, for at least two years and not more than five years, the letter F (forgery) imprinted on his cloak in scarlet color; this letter must be six inches long and two inches wide.

Poisoning is punished as follows:

The guilty can be sentenced to a fine of 10,000 dollars, to one hour of the pillory, and to be publicly whipped; he must receive sixty properly applied lashes, the law says (well laid on); then he submits to four years of imprisonment, after which he is sold as a slave for a time not exceeding fourteen years.

Here is one other serious punishment pronounced for a very slight offence: twenty-one lashes are the punishment for those who pretend to be a sorcerer or magician. In New Jersey, any individual convicted in recurrence for murder, rape, arson, theft, forgery, and sodomy, is punished by death...

52. In the United States, the brand is placed ordinarily on the forehead... In the month of June, 1829 the recommitted convict was marked in Boston at the moment of exiting prison, by tattooing them on the arm; on them was written these words: Massachusetts State prison (Central prison of Massachusetts). This custom was repealed 12 June 1829.
53. We do not contest against society the necessity of punishing by death those of its members who have violated its laws. We believe even that the conservation of this punishment is in certain cases still indispensable to maintain social order. But we believe equally that any time the death penalty is given in the law without an absolute necessity, it is only a useless cruelty and an obstacle to the penitentiary system, which has as its object to reform those whose life society saves.
54. *Compare to above, where Tocqueville and Beaumont attribute progress to human effort and the progress of time.
55. Among the philosophers in the United States who call for the abolition of the death penalty, Mr. Edward Livingston must be distinguished. He does not dispute with society its right to take away the life of those of its members that it is interested in subtracting from within; he maintains only that the terrible punishment, which can strike without remedy an accused innocent, does not produce in general the effects that are intended, and that it can be effectively replaced by less rigorous punishments that cause society less vivid impressions, but more durable. Placed on this terrain, the question is not resolved, but it is reduced to its true terms. See *Remarks on the Expediency of Abolishing the Punishment of Death*. By Edward Livingston. Philadelphia, 1831.
56. *The first use of the word for "soul."

References

1831. *Acts of the General Assembly Relating to the Eastern Penitentiary and to the New Prisons of the City and County of Philadelphia*. Philadelphia: J. W. Allen.

Beaumont, Gustave de and Alexis de Tocqueville. 1833. *On the Penitentiary System in the United States and Its Application in France, with an Appendix on Penal Colonies and also Statistical Notes.* Translated by Francis Lieber. Philadelphia: Carey, Lea & Blanchard.

Dictionnaire de l'Académie française, 6th Edition, Vol. 1 and 2 (1832–5). http://artfl-project.uchicago.edu/node/17. Accessed September 9, 2017.

1830. *Fifth Annual Report of the Board of Managers of the Prison Discipline Society.* Boston: Perkins and Marvin.

La Rochefoucauld-Liancourt. 1819. *Des Prisons de Philadelphie, par un Européen.* Paris: Madame Huzard.

Livingston, Edward. 1831. *Remarks on the Expediency of Abolishing the Punishment of Death.* Philadelphia: Jesper Harding.

Lucas, Charles. 1827. *Du système pénal et du système répressif en général, de la peine de mort en particulier.* Paris: Charles-Béchet.

Powers, Gershom. 1828. *Report of Gershom Powers, Agent and Keeper of the State Prison at Auburn, Made to the Legislature, January 7, 1828.* Albany: Croswell and Van Benthuysen.

Tocqueville, Alexis de. 2000. *Democracy in America.* Translated and edited by Harvey Mansfield and Delba Winthrop. Chicago, IL: University of Chicago Press.

"Trésor de la Langue Française informatisé." *Center National de Ressources Textuelles et Lexicales.* http://atilf.atilf.fr/lexicographie/. Accessed September 9, 2017.

Vaux, Roberts. 1826. *Notices of the Original and Successive Attempts to Improve the Discipline of the Prison at Philadelphia and to Reform the Criminal Code of Pennsylvania.* Philadelphia: Kimber and Sharpless.

Chapter 2

Discussion. — Object of the Penitentiary System. — First section: what are the fundamental principles of this system? — Two distinct systems: Auburn and Philadelphia. — Examination of these two systems. — How are they similar; how do they differ.

The penitentiary system, in its proper sense, applies only to individuals convicted and subject to the punishment of imprisonment for the expiation of their crime.

In a less restricted sense, it can be extended to every arrested person, whether their arrest precedes or follows the sentence; that is, whether these persons are arrested as accused of a crime or as convicted for having committed it; in this broader sense, the penitentiary system includes prisons of any kind, central houses, houses of arrest and refuge, etc.

It is also in this latter sense that we will understand it.

We have already said that in the United States, the prisons corresponding to our houses of arrest, that is, cells intended for provisionally arrested defendants and those individuals sentenced to a short term of imprisonment, have undergone no reform. Consequently, we will not speak of them: we can present in this regard only a theory; and it is to practical observations above all that we give our attention.

We will therefore immediately direct our attention to penitentiaries as such, which in the United States contain convicts who, according to our laws, would be sent to the central houses of correction, houses of detention, and to the *bagnes*.[1]

The punishment of imprisonment, in the different States where it is pronounced, is not varied like in our laws. In the French system, one distinguishes between simple imprisonment, seclusion, and forced labor; each of these punishments has characteristics that belong to it; imprisonment in the United States has a uniform character; it differs only in its duration.

It is divided into two principal classes: 1. Imprisonment from one month to one or two years, applied to police infractions and misdemeanors; 2. Imprisonment from two to twenty years, or for life, which serves to repress the more serious crimes.

It is for the convicts who are found in the second class that a penitentiary system exists in the United States:[2]

In what does this system consist and what are its fundamental principles?
How is it put into action?
By what disciplinary means is it maintained?
What results have been obtained in respect to reformation of the inmates?
What have been its effects from a financial account?
What lessons can we adopt from this system for the improvement of our prisons?

Such are the principal questions on which we will present the summary of our observations and research.

After having accomplished this task, we will conclude our report by examining houses of refuge for juvenile delinquents; these establishments are rather schools than prisons, but they do not form a less essential part of the penitentiary system, since the discipline to which these young prisoners are subjected has as its object to punish those who have been declared guilty, and it proposes the reformation of all!

First Section

Of what does the penitentiary system consist, and what are its fundamental principles?

In the United States, there are two perfectly distinct systems: the system of Auburn and that of Philadelphia.

Singsing in the State of New York, Wethersfield in Connecticut, Boston in Massachusetts, Baltimore in Maryland, are founded on the Auburn model.[3]

On the other side, Pennsylvania is found completely alone.

These two systems, contrary to each other on important points, have, however, a common basis without which no penitentiary system is possible; this basis is the *isolation* of prisoners (*l*).

Anyone who has studied the interior of prisons and the mores[4] of prisoners has acquired the conviction that the communication of these men with each other makes their moral reformation impossible, and even becomes for them the inevitable cause of a hideous corruption. This observation, which is justified by daily experience, is becoming an almost popular truth in the United States; and the publicists who agree the least on the mode of execution of the penitentiary system agree on this point, that no good system can exist without the separation of criminals.[5]

It was believed for a long time that to remedy the evil that arises from the communication of prisoners with each other it sufficed to establish a certain number of classifications in the prison. But after having tried this way, its ineffectualness has been recognized. There are similar punishments and crimes called by the same name, but there are no two moral persons who are alike; and every time convicts are mixed together, there necessarily exists a disastrous influence of one on the others, because, in the association of the cruel,[6] it is not the least guilty who acts on the criminal, but the most depraved who has an effect on the one who is the least.

It is therefore necessary, given the impossibility of classifying prisoners, to come to the separation of all (*m*).

This separation, which prevents the cruel person from being harmful to others, is favorable to himself.

Thrown into solitude, he reflects. Placed alone in the presence of his crime, he learns to hate it: and if his soul is not yet desensitized to evil, it is in isolation that remorse will come to assail him.

Solitude is a severe punishment, but such a punishment is merited by the guilty. "A prison intended to punish," says Mr. Livingston, "would soon cease being an object of fear, if the convicts who fill it could entertain there at their pleasure the social relations in which they were indulging before having become prisoners."[7]

However, whatever the crime of the guilty, no one has the right to take life from him, when society wants only to deprive him of his liberty. Such would be, however, the result of complete isolation, if no distraction came to soften the rigor.

This is the reason why labor is introduced into the prison. Far from being an aggravation of punishment, it is a true benefit for the prisoner.

But even when the criminal does not find an alleviation of his sufferings, he should nevertheless be forced to engage in it. It is idleness that led him to crime; in working, he will learn how to live honestly.

From another point of view, the labor of the criminal is still necessary: his imprisonment, expensive for society when he is idle, becomes less onerous when he works.

The prisons of Auburn, Singsing, Wethersfield, Boston, and Philadelphia rest therefore on these two united principles: isolation and labor. These principles, to be beneficial, ought not to be separated: the one is ineffective without the other.

In the former Auburn prison, they tried isolation without labor, and the prisoners who did not become insane, or who did not die of despair, re-entered society only to commit new crimes.

At Baltimore in this moment they are trying the system of labor without isolation, and this trial does not appear favorable.

While allowing half the principle of solitude, they reject the other half; the penitentiary of this city contains a number of cells equal to that of the prisoners who are locked up during the night; but during the day they permit them to communicate together. Assuredly, separation at night is the most important; however, it is not sufficient. The relationships that criminals have with each other is necessarily corrupting; and these relationships must be avoided if one wishes to preserve the prisoners from any mutual contagion (*n*).

Thoroughly convinced of these truths, the founders of the new penitentiary of Philadelphia wanted each prisoner to be locked in an individual cell day and night.

They thought that the complete and material separation of criminals can alone secure them from a mutual defilement, and they have adopted the principle of isolation in all its rigor. According to this system, the convict once thrown into his cell remains confined there until the expiration of his punishment: he is separated from the whole world; and the penitentiary full of malefactors like himself, but isolated from one another, does not even present to him a society in the prison: if it is true that, in establishments of this nature, all evil comes from the relations that prisoners have amongst themselves, we are forced to acknowledge that nowhere is vice more surely evaded than at Philadelphia, where the prisoners are in the material impossibility of communicating together. It is incontestable that this perfect isolation shelters the prisoner from all disastrous contagion.[8]

As solitude is in no other prison more complete than in Philadelphia, nowhere also is the necessity of labor more absolute. At the same time, it would be inaccurate to say that labor is imposed in the Philadelphia penitentiary; it can be said more correctly that the honor of labor is granted. When we visited that penitentiary, we spoke consecutively with every prisoner (*o*). There is not one who has not spoken to us of laboring with a kind of gratitude, and who has not expressed to us the idea that without the help of constant occupation, life would be insufferable to him.[9]

During the long hours of solitude, without this distraction what would become of the man left to himself, prey to the remorse of his soul and to the terrors of his imagination? Labor fills the solitary cell with an interest; it fatigues the body and rests the soul.

It is highly remarkable that these men, most of whom have been led to crime by laziness and idleness,[10] are reduced, by the torments of isolation, to find in labor their unique consolation: in detesting idleness, they accustom themselves to hate the primary cause of their misfortune; and labor, in comforting them, makes them love the only means they will have of honestly earning their living one day.

The founders of Auburn also acknowledge the necessity of separating the prisoners, to prevent any communication between them, and to subject them to the obligation of labor; but in order to arrive at the same goal, they follow a different path.

In this prison, like in those that are founded on its model, the prisoners are locked up in their solitary cells only during the night. During the day, they work together in common workshops, and since they are subjected to the law of a rigorous silence, though united, they are still isolated by that fact. Labor in union and in silence is therefore the characteristic that distinguishes the Auburn system from that of Philadelphia...

Because of the silence to which the prisoners are sentenced, this congregation offers, it is said, no disadvantage, and presents many advantages.

They are united, but no psychological link exists between them. They see without knowing each other. They are in society, without communicating together; there is between them neither aversion nor sympathy. The criminal who plans an escape project or an attack on the life of his guards does not know in which of his companions he can find assistance.

Their congregation is wholly material, or, to put it better, their bodies are together and their souls [are] isolated; and it is not the solitude of the body that is important, it is that of the intelligences. At Pittsburgh the prisoners, although materially separated, are not alone, since psychological communications exist among them. At Auburn they are really isolated, though no wall separates them.

Their meeting in the workshops is therefore not dangerous: it has further, it is said, a merit all its own, that of accustoming the prisoners to obedience.

What is the principal object of punishment in relation to him who is subjected to it? It is to give him sociable habits, and first to teach him to obey. The Auburn prison has on this point, its partisans say, a manifest advantage over that of Philadelphia.

Perpetual imprisonment in a cell is an irresistible fact which curbs the prisoner without fighting, and thus strips his submission of every kind of morality; locked up in this narrow space, he does not have, properly speaking, to observe discipline. When he is silent, he keeps a forced silence; if he works, it is to escape the boredom that overwhelms him: in a word, he obeys much less the established rule than the physical impossibility of acting otherwise.

At Auburn, on the contrary, labor, instead of being a consolation for the prisoners, is, in their eyes, a painful task of which they would be fortunate to rid themselves. In observing silence, they are incessantly tempted by it to break the law. They are subjected to the discipline, and yet they may not be [disciplined]. They have some merit in obeying, because their obedience is not a necessity. It is thus that the Auburn discipline gives to prisoners the habits of sociability that are not found in the Philadelphia prison (*p*).

We see that silence is the principal basis of the Auburn system; it is what establishes among all the prisoners that psychological separation that deprives them of any dangerous communications, and leaves them only the social relations that are inoffensive to them.

But here is presented another serious objection against this system; partisans of the Philadelphia prison say that to pretend to reduce a great number of collected malefactors to complete silence is a veritable chimera; and that this impossibility ruins from top to bottom the system whose sole foundation is silence.[11]

We think that there is great exaggeration in this reproach. Certainly, we cannot admit the existence of a discipline pushed to such a degree of perfection that it guarantees the rigorous observation of silence amidst a great number of united individuals, whose interest and passions excite to communicate together. We can say, however, that if in the prisons of Auburn, Singsing, Boston, and Wethersfield, silence is not always strictly observed, the cases of infraction are so rare that they are scarcely dangerous.

Admitted, as we have been, into the interior of these various establishments, and going there at every hour of the day without being accompanied by anyone, visiting in turn the cells, workshops, chapel, and the yards, we have never been able to surprise a prisoner uttering a single word; and yet we have sometimes spent entire weeks in observing the same prison.

At Auburn, there exists a layout of the site that singularly facilitates the discovery of any contravention to the rule. Each of the workshops, where the prisoners work, is surrounded by a gallery from which one can see them without being seen by them. We have often, from the benefit of this gallery, spied on the conduct of the prisoners, whom we have not found in fault a single time. There is, moreover, a fact that proves better than any other to what extent silence is maintained by this discipline; it is what takes place at Singsing. The prisoners of this prison are occupied with extracting stone in quarries located outside the walls of the penitentiary; so that 900 criminals, watched by only 30 guards, work in liberty in the middle of an open countryside without any chain fettering either their feet or their hands. Clearly, the lives of the guards would belong to the prisoners if material force was sufficient for the latter; but they lack psychological force. And why are these 900 united malefactors weaker than the 30 individuals who command them? Because the guards communicate freely among themselves, coordinate their efforts and have every power of association;[12] while the convicts, separated from each other by silence, have, despite their numerical force, all the weakness of isolation. Let us suppose for an instant that the prisoners have the least facility of communication; immediately the order is reversed: the meeting of their intellects, carried out by speech, has taught them the secret of their strength; and their first infraction to the law of silence destroys the whole rule.

The admirable order that reigns at Singsing, and which silence alone can maintain, proves then that silence is observed there (q).

We have shown the general principles on which the Auburn and Philadelphia systems are based: now, how are these principles put into action? How and by whom are the penitentiary establishments administered? What is the interior order and the discipline of each day? This is what we will explain in the following section.

SECOND SECTION: ADMINISTRATION

Administration. — Superintendent. — Clerk. — Inspectors. — Who appoints them. — Their privileges. — Their salary. — Importance of their choice. — Influence of public opinion. — Daily discipline of the prison. — Rising; going to sleep; labor, meals. — Nourishment. — Cafeteria. — Point on reward for good conduct. — Point on unproductive labor. — Difficulty of labor in the solitary cells of Philadelphia. — Enterprise: how it differs from the system established in France. — Absence of any *pécule*, except at Baltimore.[13]

The administration of the prison is everywhere entrusted to a superintendent[14] whose authority is more or less extensive. At his side is found a clerk or accountant, responsible for the financial part of the establishment.

Above the superintendent, three inspectors have the high direction and moral surveillance of the prison,[15] and finally below him a more or less considerable number of inferior guards are his agents.

At Auburn, Singsing, Philadelphia and Wethersfield, the superintendent is appointed by the inspectors; at Boston, he is appointed by the governors;[16] in Connecticut, the inspectors are appointed by the legislature; in Massachusetts, by the Governor of the State, and in Pennsylvania, by the Supreme Court. Everywhere the power that appoints the superintendent revokes it at its discretion.

We see that the choice of persons who direct the penitentiary establishments belongs to significant authorities.

Regarding jailors [or, inferior guards], their nomination in the prisons of Singsing, Wethersfield, Boston and Philadelphia belongs to the superintendent himself; at Auburn, they are chosen by the inspectors.

The superintendents of prisons are all, with the exception of those of Philadelphia, required to give sufficient guaranty of their good management.[17] The functions of the inspectors are gratuitous at Philadelphia and Wethersfield; they are only slightly compensated in the other prisons. The sum that they receive in Massachusetts hardly amounts to their travel expenses.[18] They are always chosen from the inhabitants of the locality.[19] The men most distinguished by their social position aspire to pursue this employment; it is thus that at Philadelphia, among the number of inspectors of the penitentiary, one notes Mr. Richards, mayor of the city, and at Boston, Mr. Gray, senator of the State of Massachusetts.

Although the inspectors are not the immediate agents of administration, they are however the masters of it. They make the regulations that the superintendent is responsible for executing, and they constantly survey this execution; they can even modify it at their discretion, according to the demands of circumstances; in no case do they take part in the acts of administering; the superintendent alone administrates because he alone is responsible. They have everywhere the same legal authority; however, they do not exercise it in the same manner in each of the prisons that concern us. Thus, at Singsing the surveillance of the inspectors appeared superficial to us, while at Auburn and Wethersfield their intervention in the affairs of the prison is much more felt.

In sum, we can say that the functions of inspectors are more extended in the law than in reality; while the superintendent, whose written authority is not very great, is found however [to be] the soul of the administration.

The most important position to fill in the prison is therefore without doubt that of the superintendent. It is in general entrusted, in the penitentiaries of the United States, to honorable men appropriate by their skill to functions of this nature. Thus, the Auburn prison has had by turn for directors Mr. Elam Lynds, former Army Captain, and Mr. Gershom Powers, Judge of the State of New York. At Wethersfield, Mr. Pillsbury; at Singsing, Mr. Robert Wiltse; at Boston Mr. Austin, former Navy Captain; all are men distinguished by their knowledge and their capacity. To a great probity and a deep sense of their duties they add much experience and that perfect knowledge of men [that is] so necessary in their position. Among the superintendents of the American penitentiaries we have above all to note Mr. Samuel Wood, director of the new Philadelphia prison, a man of superior mind, who, influenced by his religious sentiments, abandoned a lucrative career in order to devote himself to the success of a useful establishment.

The inferior agents, the under-wardens, are not as distinguished either by their social position or by their talent. They are, however, in general intelligent and honest. Responsible for the surveillance of labor in the workshops, they almost always have a special and technical knowledge of the professions exercised by the inmates (*r*).

The salary of the various employees, without being exorbitant, is nevertheless considerable enough to provide to some an honorable existence, and to others all the necessities of life.[20]

Moreover, it is not by the amount of sums paid to them that the merit of prison employees should be judged.

In Virginia, the superintendent of the Richmond prison annually receives 2000 dollars (10,600 fr.). Yet he is director of one of the worst prisons of the United States; while the superintendent of Wethersfield, which is one of the good ones, if not the best, receives for his whole salary only 1200 dollars (6,360 fr.).[21] We can make the same observation in comparing the good prisons to each other: thus, in Connecticut, the sum total paid for the salary of the various employees of Wethersfield amounts to only 3713 dollars 33 c. (19,680 fr. 64 c.), for one hundred seventy-four prisoners; while in Boston, the same expenditure for two hundred seventy-six prisoners amounts to 13,171 dollars 55 c. (69,809 fr. 21 c). Thus, at Boston, where the number of prisoners is not double those that are at Wethersfield, the expenses of the employees costs three and a half times more than in this latter prison.[22]

In exposing the organization of the new establishments, we have been struck with the importance that is attached to the choice of individuals who direct them. As soon as the penitentiary system appears in the United States one sees the staff change in nature. One found only vulgar men to be jailers of a prison; the most distinguished men offer themselves to manage a penitentiary, where there is a moral direction to impress.

We have seen how the superintendents, however elevated their character and position was, were subject to the control of a superior authority, the inspectors of the prison. But there is still above them, and above the inspectors themselves, an authority stronger than any other, not written in the laws, but all-powerful in a free country; it is that of public opinion; the innovations that are made in this matter having excited general attention, [public opinion] is directed entirely on this point and it exercises its vast influence without obstacles.[23]

There are countries where public establishments are so much considered by the government as its personal thing that it prohibits entrance to them to simply whoever pleases, just as a proprietor defends that of his house according to his good pleasure. They are a kind of administrative sanctuary into which no profane person can enter. These establishments in North America are thought of as belonging to all. Thus, the prisons are open to any who wishes to enter them, and each can get knowledge of the interior order that presides there. There is no exception to this liberty except in the Philadelphia penitentiary. There one can still, if one wishes, visit the buildings and the interior of the establishment. It is only forbidden to see the inmates, because the visits of the public would be contrary to the theory of complete solitude that forms the foundation of the system.

Instead of avoiding the inspection of the public, the superintendents and inspectors of prisons solicit the investigation and attention of anyone.[24] Each year, the inspectors give an account of the financial situation and the moral state of the prison either to the legislature or to the governor; they indicate existing abuses and improvements to be made. Their reports, printed by order of the legislatures, are immediately handed over to public report and controversy; the newspapers, whose number there is immense,[25] faithfully reproduce them. In this way, there is not an inhabitant of the United States who does not know how the prisons of his country are governed, and who is not able, whether by his opinions, or by his fortune, to contribute to their improvement. General interest being thus excited, individual societies are formed in each town for the progress of prison discipline: every public establishment is carefully examined; every abuse is discovered and pointed out. If it is necessary to construct new prisons, individuals add their funds to those of the State to meet the costs. This general attention, source of a perpetual vigilance, causes an extraordinary zeal and extreme circumspection on the part of prison employees that they would not have if they were placed in the shadows. This surveillance of public opinion that is the cause of their discomfort also provides compensation for them, for it is what makes their functions elevated and honorable, base and obscure as they were.

We have just seen the elements that compose the prison. Let us now examine how it acts in the sphere of its organization. At the arrival of the convict in the prison, a doctor verifies the state of his health. They make him take a bath; they cut his hair and give him a new outfit according to the uniform of the prison. At Philadelphia, he is led to his solitary cell from which he never leaves; it is there that he works, eats, and rests; and the construction of this cell is so complete that there is never necessity for him to leave it.[26]

At Auburn, at Wethersfield, and in other prisons of the same nature, he is first plunged into the same isolation, but it is only for a few days, after which they make him leave his cell to occupy him in the workshops.[27] At daybreak the prisoners are awakened to the sound of a bell signaling the time to rise; the jailors open the doors. The prisoners form a line under the supervision of their respective guards, and go first into the hall where they stop to wash their hands and their faces, and from there go into the workshops where they are immediately put to work. The labor is not interrupted until dinnertime. There is not a single moment allocated to recreation.[28]

At Auburn, when the hour of breakfast and dinner arrives work is suspended and every inmate meets in a large dining hall. At Singsing and in every other penitentiary they retire into their cells, and each eats separately there. This last rule appears to us preferable to that of Auburn. It is not without drawbacks and even danger to assemble such a large number of criminals in the same place, whose congregation makes the maintenance of discipline much more difficult.

In the evening, at the setting of the sun, work stops and every convict leaves the workshops to return to their cells. The rising, going to sleep, eating, leaving the cells, entering the workshops, everything during the day takes place in the most profound silence, and nothing is heard in the prison save the sound of those who march and the movement of the laborers who work. But when the day is finished and the prisoners are returned to their solitary cells, the silence that is in the confines of these vast walls, where so many criminals are confined, is a silence of death. At night, we often walked these ringing and silent[29] galleries where the clarity of a lamp shines incessantly: it was as though we walked through catacombs; there were a thousand living beings there and yet there was solitude.

The order of a day is that of the whole year. Thus, all the hours of the convict follow one another with an overwhelming uniformity, from the time he enters the prison until the expiration of his punishment. Labor fills the whole day. The whole night is given entirely to rest. Since the labor is arduous and rough, long hours of rest are necessary; they do not disturb the inmate between bedtime and sunrise. Before having slept, as well as after, he still has time to contemplate his solitude, his crime, and his misery.

Without doubt, not every penitentiary has a similar discipline; but every inmate of a prison is treated the same way. There is even more equality in the prison than in society.

Everyone wears the same clothes and eats the same bread. Everyone labors: there exists in this respect a distinction only in the results of those who have a natural aptitude to one profession more than another. In no case can work be interrupted. They have recognized the disadvantage of determining a task, after the accomplishment of which the prisoner would be free to do nothing. It is crucial for the inmate as well as for the prison order that he labor without stopping; for him, because idleness is disastrous to him; for the prison, because according to the observation of Judge Powers fifty individuals who work are more easily watched than ten convicts who do nothing.[30]

Their food is healthy, abundant, but coarse;[31] it must sustain their strength and not provide for them any sensations that are simply agreeable.

No-one can follow a different diet from that of the prison. Every fermented beverage is forbidden there; they only drink water.[32] The convict who possesses wealth nevertheless lives like the poorest of all: and we do not see in the new American prisons those cafeterias that are encountered in ours and that sell to the prisoners anything that can satisfy their gluttony. The abuse of wine is unknown there because the use of it is prohibited.

This discipline is simultaneously moral and just. It is not necessary that the site where society has placed criminals to repent present scenes of pleasure and debauchery. It is wrong to leave the rich criminal, whose wealth augments his crime, to rejoice in prison next to the poor prisoner whose poverty extenuates his fault.[33]

Assiduity to labor and good conduct in the prison do not procure for the prisoner any alleviation of punishment. Experience teaches us that the criminal who has committed the most hateful and audacious attacks in society is often the least rebellious in prison. He is more docile than others because he is more intelligent; and he knows to submit when it is not in his power to revolt. He is ordinarily more skillful and active in work, above all when one indicates to him an easily attained pleasure as the goal of his efforts; thus, if we accord privileges to the prisoners on the basis of their conduct in prison we risk greatly alleviating the rigors of imprisonment for that criminal who has most merited them, and depriving of every favor those who are most worthy of it.

Perhaps in the present state of our prisons it would be impossible to govern them without the assistance of incentives granted for the diligence, activity, and talent of the inmates. But in America, where prison discipline operates supported by fear of punishment, they have no need of a psychological influence to direct them.

The interest of the prisoners requires that they never be idle; that of society desires that they work in the most useful way. We see in the new penitentiaries none of those machines used in England that the prisoners set in motion without intelligence, and by means of which their physical activity alone is exercised.

Labor is not only good because it is the opposite of idleness; one desires even more that by working the convict learns a profession whose exercise will support him when he leaves prison.

Thus, the prisoners are only taught useful trades: and among these, care is taken to choose those that are most profitable and whose products are the easiest to sell (*s*).

The Philadelphia system has often been reproached with making labor impossible for the prisoners. It is certainly more economical and advantageous to make a limited number of laborers work in a common workshop than to give employment to each of them in a separate place. It is still more true to say that a great number of industries cannot be advantageously undertaken by a single worker in a very narrow place: however, the example of the Philadelphia penitentiary, where every inmate works, proves that professions that can be exercised by isolated men are numerous enough to be able to usefully occupy them.[34] The same difficulty is not encountered in the prisons where the convicts work in common. At Auburn and at Baltimore, a very large variety of professions are exercised. These two prisons offer the appearance of extensive factories that bring together all useful industries. At Boston and Singsing, the occupation of the inmates has been thus far more uniform. In these two prisons, most of the inmates are employed in cutting stone. Wethersfield presents on a small scale the same spectacle as Auburn.

In general, the labor of prisoners is awarded to a contractor, who gives a specified price for each day and receives in exchange whatever is manufactured by the inmate.

There exist crucial differences between this system and the one practiced in our prisons. In France, the same man undertakes the provision of food, clothing, labor, and healthcare for the prisoners, a system detrimental to the convict and to prison discipline.[35] To the convict, because the contractor, who sees in such a transaction only a matter of money, speculates on provisions like labor; if he loses on clothing, he cuts back on food; and if the labor produces less than he counted on, he compensates by spending less on the upkeep that is his responsibility. This system is equally disastrous to the order of the prison. The contractor sees in the inmate only a laboring machine, dreaming, in serving him, only of the profit that he wants to draw from him; everything appears good to him to stimulate his [the prisoner's] industry; and he worries very little if the expenses for the convict are made to the detriment of the order. The extent of his privileges give him, moreover, an importance in the prison that he should not have; there is therefore interest in removing him from the penitentiary as much as possible, and to combat his influence when one cannot neutralize it (*u*).³⁶

It seems to us that the evil that we point out at the moment was generally avoided in the United States in the new penitentiaries that we visited. In these establishments, they have not exclusively adopted either the system of governance or that of the contract.

The clothing and bedding of the inmates are usually provided by the superintendent, who himself makes all contracts concerning these objects; he avoids many purchases by making the prisoners themselves manufacture and craft the materials necessary for clothing within the prison. At Auburn, Singsing, and Boston, the prisoners are fed by the contractor, according to a contract that must not be made for more than a year. At Wethersfield, the prison itself provides for this expense. The contractor who, at Auburn, is responsible for feeding the prisoners is not the same one who makes them work.

There is also a different contractor for each type of industry; the contracts being thus multiplied, the same contractor can obtain only a circumscribed and transient influence in the prison.

At Wethersfield, not only does the administration of the prison nourish and maintain the prisoners without having recourse to contracts, but it also contended for the greatest part of the labor itself.³⁷

In each of these establishments the contractor cannot, under any pretext, interfere with the interior discipline of the prison or bring the slightest breach of its regulations. He must not sustain any conversation with the inmates, if it is not instructing them in the profession that he is responsible for teaching them; still, he must speak to them only in the presence and with the consent of one of the guards.³⁸

Despite these wise precautions, the presence of the contractor or his agents in the prisons is not exempt from disadvantages. Formerly, the Auburn prison was governed by it;³⁹ and when the principle of contract was admitted there, Mr. Elam Lynds, who was superintendent at the time, did not allow the contractor to approach the inmate. The contractor was committed to pay at the agreed price for the manufactured objects produced from the work of the prisoners, and these objects were delivered to him without his having overseen the execution thereof.

The discipline benefitted greatly from this order of things; if it is advantageous to restrict the relationships that were established between the contractors and the inmates, it is still better to put a stop to them entirely.

However, such a system of administration was difficult and costly.

The contractors, being deprived of the right to inspect the labor, imposed disadvantageous conditions on the prison; on the other hand, their exclusion from the workshops there necessitated the presence of guards capable of teaching the inmates their profession; and men gifted with the technical knowledge necessary for that purpose were not easy to find. Finally, the sale of manufactured objects was harder and less productive for the superintendent than it is for the contractors devoted exclusively to commercial operations. Thus, it has developed into the contract system we have just described; this system, surrounded by the safeguards that accompany it, possesses advantages that seem to negate most of its disadvantages. However, Mr. Elam Lynds always seems to fear that the tolerated presence of the contractors in prison will lead sooner or later to the complete ruin of the discipline.

We will soon see, in the article on expenses and income, that the labor of the prisoners is generally very productive. In touring these various establishments, we have been struck with the hard work and sometimes talent with which the convicts work; what makes their diligence completely surprising is that they act without [self] interest. In our prisons, like in most of the prisons of Europe, a part of the revenue belongs to the prisoners. This portion, called the *pécule,* is more or less substantial in various countries: in the United States, it is nonexistent. There they accept the principle that the criminal owes all his labor to society to indemnify it for the costs of his imprisonment. Thus, the whole time of their punishment, the convicts work without receiving the slightest salary; and when they leave the prison, no account is given to them of what they have done. They are given only a few pieces of money in order to be able to return to the site they intend to make their new residence.[40]

This system appears excessively severe to us. We do not dispute the right of society, which appears to us incontestable, to find in the work of the inmate the indemnity that it is due: we do not know for that matter at what point a considerable *pécule* is useful to the convict who, most often when he leaves the prison, sees in the money he has amassed only a way to satisfy passions all the more urgent because they have been contained for a longer period of time. But what would be the disadvantage in giving a small incentive to the diligence of the convict, a feeble recompense for his activity? Why would we not throw into his solitude, and into the midst of his sufferings, an interest in profit that, small as it was, would for him be nothing less than an immense sum? Besides, is it not necessary that on the day of his reentrance into society he has, if not substantial monies at his disposal, at least some livelihood in the meantime until he is given work?[41] Why not adopt the discipline of the Baltimore prison, where, though acknowledging the principle of other American penitentiaries, its rigor has been softened? In that prison, every convict has his determined task for the day: when he has finished he does not stop working, but he begins to work for himself; everything that he does after his task composes therefore his *pécule*; and since it is only delivered to him upon the expiration of his sentence, we are sure that the money that he has earned in this way will not be harmful to the rule of the establishment. There was a time when the prisoners of Baltimore could immediately spend the money composing their *pécule* on food. Their labor was then much more productive; but we have recognized the disadvantages of such an indulgence, destructive to any rule; and today their *pécule* remains intact until they leave prison.[42]

Such is the order established in the American penitentiaries. We have said that this discipline was applied to any individual subject to imprisonment in the state prison; however, until now, female convicts have not been subjected to this discipline, save perhaps in the State of Connecticut. In American prisons, they are generally found mixed together, like they are in ours; and there, like in ours, they are exposed to any vice that is born from mutual communication.

Some people believe that it would be very difficult to apply a system, the very basis of which is silence, to women: however, the experiment that was made of it at Wethersfield, where the women are subjected, like the other inmates, to every rigor of cellular isolation during the night and absolute silence during the day, proves that the difficulty is not insurmountable.[43] Moreover, it is not the difficulty of execution that has, on this point, hindered reform of prisons in the United States. If, in the application of the new penitentiary system, women have been omitted, this fact must above all be attributed to the small number of crimes that they commit; it is because they occupy such little space in prison that they have been neglected.[44] It is the same for most social wounds, whose remedy we seek with ardor when they are deep; when they are not serious, we do not think to heal them.

Third Section: Disciplinary Means

The necessity of distinguishing between the Philadelphia system and that of Auburn. The first, easier to put in force and to maintain. That of Auburn has corporal punishments as auxiliaries. — Tempered discipline at Wethersfield. — Discretionary power of the superintendents. — Question of corporal punishments. — What is their influence on the health of the prisoner.

Let us now examine by what disciplinary means the order of things that we have just described is established and supported.

How is silence so rigorously maintained among united criminals? How do we make them work without interest?

It is still necessary to distinguish here between the rule of Auburn and that of Philadelphia.

At Philadelphia, the discipline is as simple as the system itself. The only critical moment is that of the entrance into the prison. The solitary cell of the criminal is full of terrible phantoms for some days. Agitated by a thousand fears, prey to a thousand torments, he accuses society of injustice and cruelty, and in such a disposition of mind it sometimes happens that he defies the orders that are given to him and repels the consolations that are offered to him. The only punishment that the regulation of the prison allows to inflict on him is imprisonment in a dark cell and a reduction in food. It is rare that more than two days of such a discipline are necessary to submit the most rebellious inmate to the discipline. When the criminal has battled the first impressions of solitude; when he has triumphed over terrors that pushed him to insanity or despair; when, after having fought himself (or struggled) in his solitary cell, amidst his remorse, his conscience, and the agitation of his soul, he is overcome with loneliness and has sought in labor a distraction from his troubles; from that moment, he is tamed and henceforth submits to the rules of the prison. What contravention to order can one commit in solitude? The entire discipline is found in the fact of isolation and in the very impossibility of violating the established rule where the prisoners are. In other prisons, disciplinary punishments are inflicted on prisoners who break the law of silence or refuse to work. But silence is easy to those who are alone; and labor is not refused by those for whom it is unique consolation.[45] We have pointed out the disadvantage of complete isolation, the defect of which is to deprive the inmates' submission of its moral character; but we must at the same time acknowledge its advantages in respect to discipline; and the facility of governing an establishment of this nature without employing rigorous and repeated punishments is certainly an important benefit. There are some who see in the order established at Philadelphia a system that is complicated in its organization and maintained with difficulty. Those who think thus seem to us to commit a great error. The Philadelphia system is expensive, but not difficult to establish; and once constituted, it sustains itself. It is the discipline that presents the least trouble; each cell is a prison within the prison itself, and the convicts who are detained there cannot make themselves guilty of misdemeanors that are committed only in association; there is no punishment because there is no infraction.

The discipline of Auburn, Singsing, Boston, Wethersfield, and Baltimore do not have the same character of simplicity; these various establishments do not follow uniform procedures in this respect.

In Singsing, the sole punishment for those who violate the established order is the whip. The application of this disciplinary punishment is extremely frequent there; and the slightest mistake brings it on the delinquent. This punishment is preferred to any other for several reasons. It immediately produces submission from the delinquent; his labor is not interrupted a single instant; this punishment is painful, but not to health; thus, it is thought that no other punishment would produce the same result.[46] The same principle is admitted at Auburn, but it is singularly tempered in its execution. The penitentiaries of Boston and Baltimore, a little more severe than Auburn, are, however, much less than Singsing; Wethersfield differs from every other by its extreme mildness (*v*).

In this latter prison, the use of corporal punishments is not rejected, only its application has been avoided as much as possible; Mr. Pillsbury, superintendent of the establishment, has assured us that for three years there had been only a single time that it was necessary to inflict the punishment of the whip. It is a severity to which one has recourse only when it is very evident that every other milder method has been tried without success; before using it, the influence of complete solitude is attempted on the recalcitrant inmate; shut up in his cell day and night, without leaving him the resource of labor; if we believe the employees of the prison, nothing is more uncommon than to see a prisoner resist this first trial; he has scarcely suffered the severity of complete isolation than he requests the favor of returning to his place in the common workshop and graciously submits himself to all the demands of the discipline. However, if he is not tamed from the first moment, they add a few more hardships to his solitude, such as utter deprivation of daylight, reduction of his food; sometimes also his bed is taken, et cetera. If the inmate is obstinate in his resistance, then and only then one looks to the whip as a more efficacious means of submission. The directors of this establishment seem to have a marked aversion to corporal punishments; however, they would deeply regret it were they not legally endowed with the right to inflict them. They reject the application of a cruel punishment; but in it they find the power to pronounce an effective and powerful means of action on the inmates.

The tempered discipline of Wethersfield seems to suffice for the success of the establishment. However, it is thought in other prisons that their administration would be impossible without the auxiliary of the whip. This is the opinion of every practical man whom we have seen in the United States, and particularly that of Mr. Elam Lynds, of whom we have spoken above.[47] The legislatures of New York, Massachusetts, Connecticut, and Maryland have had the same conviction, since they have formally authorized the infliction of corporal punishments. These punishments have also received the sanction of judicial authority; and the country, through the organ of its jury, has made several verdicts of absolution in favor of guards who confessed to having struck inmates (*x*).[48]

We have pointed out the remarkable differences that exist in the discipline of these various establishments; however, all allow the theory of corporal punishments; and it is correct to say that there are in the individual situation of each of these prisons circumstances that tend to explain the mildness or severity of its discipline.

If we recall the nature of the labor performed at Singsing and the order established in that prison, we easily understand the insurmountable obstacles that the discipline there would meet if it was stripped of the most energetic means of repression. Auburn does not require the deployment of such great severity, because the same threats do not menace the order of the establishment. Wethersfield is found in this respect in a still more favorable position; it contains less than two hundred criminals, while Auburn contains six hundred fifty of them, and Singsing more than nine hundred. It is clear that the relatively considerable number of inmates and the nature of the labor makes the penitentiary more or less easy to govern.

Now, can the discipline of these various prisons dispense with the aid of corporal punishments? This is a question that we would not dare to solve. We believe we can only say that, deprived of this powerful auxiliary, it will be surrounded by obstacles which are very difficult to overcome. Its difficulties would be all the greater as it rests on a single foundation, absolute silence; and because, should this foundation fail, it would collapse entirely.

How to maintain among criminals a complete silence if they are not constantly dominated by the terror of a prompt and rigorous punishment? In American prisons, this discipline founded on blows is all the more powerful as it is exercised with more arbitrariness.[49] At Singsing and at Auburn there is no written regulation: the superintendents of these prisons must alone, in their administration, conform themselves to the verbal prescriptions that they receive from the inspectors and to a few principles written in the law; these principles are: solitary imprisonment of the convicts during the night and their labor in silence during the day. For the rest, they enjoy a discretionary power for any act of execution (*y*). At Singsing, the superintendent even has the right to delegate this discretionary power to any of his inferior agents; and, in fact, he has transmitted his authority to thirty guards who are invested, like himself, with the right to punish the inmates. At Auburn, the superintendent alone has the power to punish; however, the same authority belongs to the inferior guards in any case of urgent and absolute necessity. It is the same at Boston. At Wethersfield, the regulations of the prison are written;[50] the restricted employees cannot in any case exercise the right to punish, which the superintendent alone enjoys, and which he himself exercises. Some important debates were raised in the state of New York on the question of knowing whether the presence of an inspector was necessary in order to be able to inflict the punishment of the whip on an inmate: in terms of the law, this guaranty was indispensable; however, the obligation for inspectors to assist in the infliction of corporal punishments caused them such frequent interruptions and such painful emotions that they immediately asked to be absolved from this duty; and today they acknowledge the right of the employees to exercise the discipline without official witnesses.[51] The inspectors do not retain less of a great influence on the application of disciplinary punishments. Singsing is the only prison where their surveillance in this regard has appeared superficial to us. The administration of this vast penitentiary is so difficult that there seems to be no desire to dispute with the guards the smallest part of their absolute power.

    We will not elaborate here the question of whether society has the right to punish with corporal punishments the convict who neither submits to the obligation of labor nor to other demands of the penitentiary discipline.

    Such theoretical questions are rarely discussed to the profit of reason and truth.

We believe that society has the right to do whatever is necessary to its conservation and that of the order established in its midst: and we understand very well that an assemblage of criminals who have all broken the laws of the country, in whom every inclination is corrupt and every instinct vicious, cannot be governed in prison according to the same principles and with the same means as [one governs] free men whose inspirations are honest and whose every action conforms to the laws. We further hypothesize that the convict who wishes to do nothing would be violently obliged to work, and that severity is employed to reduce to silence those who do not observe it; the right of society in this regard does not appear questionable to us, at least if it cannot with the aid of milder means arrive at the same results; but in our eyes, it is not the question here.

At what point can the use of corporal punishments be reconciled with the object itself of the penitentiary system, which is the reformation of the guilty? If this punishment is ignominious, does it not directly counter the goal that is proposed, which is to raise the morality of a man fallen in his own eyes?

This question appears to us [to be] the sole one to examine: but we do not think that it must be solved in an absolute manner. It seems to us that it greatly depends on the sentiment that, in public opinion and in that of the inmates, is attached to corporal punishments.

The discretionary power, by virtue of which the lowest guard at Auburn and the lowest turnkey at Singsing whip the prisoners, is little contested in the United States.

"The right of the guards over the person of the inmates," says one, "is that of a father over his children, the teacher over his students, the master over his apprentice, and the captain of a ship over the men of his crew."[52]

The punishment of the whip is used in the American navy with no idea of infamy attached to it. In the origin of the penitentiary system it had not been allowed as a means of discipline. When they introduced it into the prisons as an auxiliary to the regulations, some voices were raised against it; but this opposition was more a philosophical dispute rather than a repugnance of mores.

Pennsylvania is perhaps the only State of the Union that continues to protest against the use of corporal punishments, and that has excluded them from the discipline of its prisons. The Quakers do not stop protesting the inhumanity of this punishment, and to their philanthropic grievances is joined the eloquent voice of Edward Livingston, who equally rejects this disciplinary means from his penitentiary code. It is above all in consideration of corporal punishments used at Auburn that he declares himself the adversary of the system in force in that prison.[53]

But their words find little echo in most of the United States, and today every new penitentiary except those of Philadelphia finds in the punishments in question a means of order and discipline; the laws of the country authorize the discipline that they have adopted and these laws have the sanction of public opinion.

There is certainly great exaggeration in the reproaches addressed to the Auburn discipline. First of all, corporal punishments are not as frequently applied as [the public] appears to believe; necessary to introduce the discipline of silence in a newly established prison, they are rarely used to maintain this discipline once put in force.

Now, is the entire discipline of these prisons, as is alleged, injurious to health, and are the rigors of isolation, like the cruelties of discipline, destructive to the life of the inmates? On this point, we can provide positive documents.

All the inmates that we have seen in the penitentiaries of the United States had the appearance of strength and health; and if we compare the number of whose who die there with mortality in the former prisons we will see that the new penitentiaries, despite their severe discipline and their barbaric rule, are much more favorable to the life of the inmates. Mr. Edward Livingston desires that the punishment of the whip be substituted, like disciplinary punishment, with solitary imprisonment by day and night, without labor, and with reduction of food; it does not appear that at Wethersfield this punishment, which they have customarily inflicted there in preference to blows, has produced bad effects. However, ten individuals are mentioned as having died from this kind of punishment in the prison of Lamberton (New-Jersey), while there is still no example of an inmate having been the victim of corporal punishment.[54]

In the former Walnut-Street prison, there was on average one death out of sixteen inmates each year, and in that of New York (Newgate) one death out of nineteen. In both prisons, the inmates were neither alone, nor forced to silence, nor subjected to corporal punishments.[55]

In the new penitentiaries that have silence, isolation, and bodily discipline for their foundation, deaths are in an infinitely smaller proportion.

At Singsing, one out of thirty-seven inmates die; at Wethersfield, one out of forty-four; at Baltimore, one out of forty-nine; at Auburn, one out of fifty-six; at Boston, one out of fifty-eight.

Furthermore: if we want to compare the mortality of the inmates in prison to that of free men in society, this comparison will be more favorable to penitentiaries. In fact, in Pennsylvania one individual out of thirty-nine dies each year, and in Maryland one out of forty-seven. Thus, in the former prisons where free communication exists and where discipline was mild one-half more died than in society; and in the new penitentiaries, under the austere discipline of isolation, silence, and blows, deaths are less numerous.[56]

These statistics are better answers than any possible arguments to the objections that have been made.

We have said nothing on the sanitary state of the new Philadelphia prison, which has been established for too short a time to have been able to judge its effects. Everything leads us to think that the system of perpetual and complete seclusion that is in force there will be less favorable to the health of the prisoners than the system of Auburn. However, the doctor of the establishment already believes himself able to declare that mortality there will be less considerable than in the former Walnut-Street prison.[57]

To sum up this point, it is necessary to acknowledge that the discipline of penitentiaries in America is severe. While society in the United States gives the example of the most extended liberty, the prisons of the same country offer the spectacle of the most complete despotism.[58] The citizens subject to the law are protected by it; they have ceased to be free only when they have become wicked.

Notes

1. *Houses of correction were one of two types of prison dedicated to prisoner labor, which was for state use only. Houses of correction were unique in that those sentenced to 1–10 years labored together, rather than in isolation. There were ten original houses of correction, and three additional prisons set aside for women.
2. We will apply ourselves exclusively to expand on the penitentiary system of the United States, because that has been the only object of our investigation. If one desires documents on the prisons of Europe, one can consult the very remarkable work that has been published last year by Messrs. Julius, Lagarmitte, and Mittermayer, titled *Lessons on Prisons*.
3. Kentucky, Tennessee, Maine and Vermont have also adopted the same system: but this innovation among themselves is too recent to furnish useful documents.

4. *We consistently translate "les mœurs" as "mores" throughout the text. Tocqueville later gave his own definition of "mores" in *Democracy in America*: "I understand here the expression *moeurs* in the sense the antients attached to the word *mores;* not only do I apply it to mores properly so-called, which one could call habits of the heart, but to the different notions that men possess, to the various opinions that are current in their midst, and to the sum of ideas of which the habits of the mind are formed. I therefore comprehend under this word the whole moral and intellectual state of a people" (2000, p. 275).
5. See the report from the commissioners-redactors of the Penal Code of Pennsylvania, 1828. —pag. 16 and especially pag. 22. — See the letter from Roberts Vaux to Roscoe, 1827. — pag. 9. — Ibid. the report made by the commission of the Baltimore Penitentiary to Governor Kent, 23 December 1818. — Ibid. Report serving as an Introduction to the Code of discipline of the prisons of Edward Livingston, pag. 21. And the letter from the same to Roberts Vaux, 1828. — Ibid. Report of John Spencer to the legislature of New York. Solitary imprisonment of the United States had many adversaries. Among its most celebrated antagonists one can mention William Roscoe of Liverpool and the General Lafayette: the first returned his opinion that he had formed on it as soon as he knew that labor was admitted into the solitary cells of Philadelphia. (See his letter to D. Hozack of New York, written on 13 July 1830, shortly before his death.) As for General Lafayette, he has always forcefully attacked the punishment of solitude. "This punishment," he says, "does not correct the guilty. I spent several years in isolation at Olimutz, where I was imprisoned for having made a revolution, and in my prison, I only dreamt of new revolutions." Moreover, Mr. de Lafayette's opinion, which was created before the former system of solitude without labor was first established in Philadelphia, is perhaps modified like that of W. Roscoe, since this system has subjected itself to serious changes.
6. *I translate "méchans" as "cruel" because the sense seems to be: "Qui désire provoquer, occasionnellement ou non, la souffrance physique ou morale d'autrui" (One who wishes to cause, occasionally or not, physical or psychological pain of others).
7. See Introduction to the Code of the Discipline of Prisons.
8. See Inquiry into the Philadelphia Penitentiary, [Appendix] no. 10.
9. Everyone said to us that Sunday, day of rest, was much longer for them than the whole week.
10. *It is interesting to note that, within the same paragraph, Tocqueville and Beaumont use three different words for "laziness:" "la paresse," "la fainéantise," and "l'oisiveté."

11. See Letter of Livingston to Roberts Vaux, 1828, pag. 7 and 8. There are certainly examples that prove the observation of silence in a few cases: that is so true that, in each of the prisons that we examined at hand, there were some punishments inflicted on those who had been surprised in fault on this point; it must be added that a certain number of contraventions remain always unknown. But the question is not whether there are some infractions; are these infractions of a nature to destroy the order of the establishment and to prevent the reform of prisoners? This is the point to examine.
12. *Introduction of the important idea of "association."
13. *Rather than translate "savings" or "wage," I keep the French word "pécule" throughout the translation to retain its meaning as the earnings of a French prisoner's labor, part of which could be saved, but part of which could be spent while still in prison. Lieber notes in a footnote of his translation that "the *pécule* is now always called in America, *over-stint*" (Beaumont and Tocqueville 1833, p. 37). Tocqueville and Beaumont later make the argument that this two-fold use of the *pécule* poses a problem to the discipline of the prison because it allows prisoners to spend money on luxury items.
14. He is indifferently called warden, keeper, agent, or superintendent.
15. It is generally thought advantageous that the inspectors not change too often, and that they should not be all renewed at the same time. (See Report of 20 December 1830 on the Maryland Penitentiary). At Boston, they are appointed for four years. (See the law of 11 March 1828). At Philadelphia, the inspectors of the penitentiary are exempt from service in the militia, and from the responsibility of juries, from arbitrating or from overseeing the poor. (See rules of the prison.) Until 1820, there were five inspectors for the Auburn prison: it was recognized that this number was too large; and since then it was reduced to three. (See Report of 1820, by Mr. Spencer).
16. *Tocqueville and Beaumont seem to refer here to the state legislature.
17. At Auburn, the guaranty is 25,000 dollars (132,503 fr.). See report of 1832. — Ibid. at Singsing.
18. Each inspector there receives 100 dollars (530 fr.). At Baltimore the surveillance committee annually receives 1,144 dollars (6063 fr. 20 c.). See Report of 1830.
19. "We have little confidence in any system of law, unless there is a committee that often provides, through personal investigation, enforcement of the rules." Excerpted from the report of the inspectors of Wethersfield, 1830.
20. Although the salaries of the employees in the prisons of the United States are rather high, it is much less than it appears to us. The various industries are, in that country, so profitable, that any man endowed with some capacity easily finds a more advantageous career than what they are offered by

the administration of prisons. And we would not see such men as Mr. Samuel Wood at the head of American penitentiaries if they were not under the influence of a nobler sentiment than the urge to make a fortune.
21. See Report on the prison of Connecticut from 1830, page 1st. *Note: There is a question of whether this is printed as *11* (in Lieber's translation) or *1er*.
22. See Statistical Tables, Financial part. — Salary of the employees, Appendix No. 19.
23. *Introduction of another major theme: the rule of public opinion in America.
24. "It is very desirable that citizens of the state and especially gentlemen honored with the power of making and administering the laws should frequently visit this prison." (See Report of Mr. Niles, 1819.) The new penitentiary establishments attract many curious persons who desire to visit it. In terms of the law, the superintendent can have the right to refuse them entrance; but he never makes use of this right; and all those who present themselves are admitted by paying 25 cents (1 f. 32 c.). These visits become a source of revenue for the prison, and the administration keeps account of the money that comes in. During the year 1830, the Auburn prison created, in this way alone, a total of 1,524 dollars 57 cents (8,084 f. 81 c.). See New Statutes of the State of New York. §64 art. 2 chap. 3 tit. 2 part 4, 2nd volume.
25. There were 239 in 1830 in the State of New York alone; and this number has increased still more the last two years. (See Williams Register 1831 page 36.).
26. Each cell is aerated by a ventilator and contains a latrine hole whose construction makes it perfectly odorless. It is necessary to have seen all the cells of the Philadelphia prison, to have passed whole days there, in order to form a precise idea of their cleanliness and the purity of the air that is breathed there.
27. The cells at Auburn are much smaller than the cells of the Philadelphia prison; they are seven feet long and three and a half feet wide. A salubrious air is brought in by a ventilator.
28. Furthermore, every kind of gambling is prohibited there: the regulations are uniform on this point, and faithfully executed.
29. *Lieber translates: "monotonous and dumb" (Beaumont and Tocqueville 1833, p. 32).
30. See Report of Mr. Gershom Powers, 1828, pag. 14.
31. See New Statutes of the State of New York, 2 vol., pag. 707, § 57. If one wishes to know in detail what composes the food of the inmates at Auburn, see the report of Judge Powers, 1818, pag. 43 and the handwritten note of the accounting agent (Clerk) of Auburn. — For the food at Wethersfield, see Report on that prison, 1828, pag. 19. — For the food at Boston, see

Law of 11 March 1828. — For Baltimore, see Rules and Regulations, pag. 6. 1829.
32. See Report on the Wethersfield prison, 1828, page. 19.
33. We indicate here only the most important points of which the order, discipline and administration of penitentiaries are composed. In order to know in detail the established rules in the new prisons, the division of hours in the day, the nature of the labors, the tasks of the employees, those of the prisoners, the nature of punishments allowed, the obligations imposed on contractors, etc. — it would be necessary to read the regulations of the Connecticut prison (Wethersfield) whose translation we give. See [Appendix] no. 13— see also the rules made for the prison of Boston by Mr. Austin the superintendent (1 January 1831). —And the two reports of Mr. Powers on Auburn, 1826 and 1828. —And finally the rules of the penitentiary of Philadelphia. We have also consulted, for this object, handwritten notes that had been delivered to us by the clerk of Auburn and by the Superintendent of Singsing (Mr. Wiltse).
34. The professions practiced by the inmates of Philadelphia are weaving, shoemaking, tailoring, carpentry, etc. See Annual Reports of the Inspectors of the Penitentiary of Pennsylvania (1831).
35. In the central house of detention of Melun, there is a very considerable library for the use of the inmates. It is furnished by the contractor, who the prisoners pay for the rental of each volume that they read. We can judge by this fact the nature of the books that constitute the library.
36. *There is no reference to alphabetical note (*t*) in the main text of the first edition, although there is a note in the appendix. Lieber puts (*t*) here instead of (*u*) (Beaumont and Tocqueville 1833, p. 35). Mayer's edition puts (*t*) a few paragraphs above, in the sentence: "At Boston and Singsing (*t*), the occupation of the inmates has been thus far more uniform."
37. See art. 4 of Section 1 of the Regulations of the Connecticut Prison, [Appendix] No. 13.
38. See Report of Gershom Powers, 1828, pag. 42 —For Boston, see Regulations, 1 January 1831.
39. See report of Gershom Powers, pag. 41, 1828.
40. The law of the State of New York does not permit the superintendent to give more than 3 dollars to convicts when leaving (15 f. 90 c.), but he must give them the belongings that they need to clothe themselves with, except the value of these belongings cannot exceed 10 dollars (53 f.). See New Statutes of the State of New York, Part 4, Chap. 3, Tit. 2 Art. 2 § 62. —At Philadelphia, the superintendent can give to freed criminals 4 dollars (21 f. 20 c.) — (art. 8 of the rules). See Report of 1831. —At Boston, he is authorized to give them 5 dollars, that is to say 26 f. 50 c., and also he must provide to each free prisoner a decent suite of clothes that equals, it is said, a sum of 20 dollars (106 f.). The inspectors of the Massachusetts prison appear to regret that they give so much to the prisoners leaving annually.

See their Report of 1830, pag. 4. — For Wethersfield see Report on the Prison of Connecticut of 1828.
41. In general, the most dangerous moment for the freed convict is when they leave the prison. It is not unusual that their entire *pécule* is spent in the twenty-four hours that follow their release. At Geneva, to remedy this evil, it is common to not give the convicts their *pécule* at the time of their leaving the prison. They make them wait a little longer until they return to the site of their new residence. For some time, they did the same in France for the convict who leaves the *bagnes* and the *maisons centrales*. It is a wise measure that is important to keep.
42. See report on the Maryland penitentiary of 23 December 1828, addressed to Governor Kent. And report — Id. — of 1830.
43. The difficulty is two-fold:

   1. It is generally thought that women are resigned with more difficulty than men to complete silence;
   2. There is a lack, in order to compel them, of a coercive means that is used to tame men. The laws of the United States, which authorize the punishment of the whip to punish male inmates, forbid the infliction of this disciplinary punishment for women.

44. See Statistical Observations, [Appendix] No.17 § 4-Proportion of crimes committed by males and females.
45. The prisoner would be so inclined to pick up work when it amuses him and exercises his body and to rest idle when he is tired. But we do not allow, and with reason, a similar arrangement; it is necessary that he work all the time or not at all. If he refuses to work consistently, he is placed in a dark dungeon. He has then to choose between continual idleness in the dark and uninterrupted labor in his cell. His choice is never long to come and he always prefers labor. See Report on Philadelphia 1831.
46. We have no register of disciplinary punishments. We have been told that at Singsing there are approximately five or six per day (among 1,000 prisoners). At Auburn, the punishments that in the beginning were very frequent are very rare today. One of the inspectors of this prison told us: "I remember having seen, in the beginning, nineteen prisoners whipped in less than an hour. Since the discipline is well established, I continued once four and a half months without giving a single lash." (See black handwritten inquiry on the Auburn discipline).
47. See our conversation with Mr. Elam Lynds at the end of the volume.
48. *No alphabetical note (*w*).
49. We will mention here a remarkable fact that proves the efficacy of this discipline. On 23 October 1828, a fire burst out in the Auburn prison; it

consumed a part of the buildings belonging to the prison. As it became dangerous even to the lives of the inmates, the latter were let out of their cells; but the order was not troubled a single instant among the prisoners; all were occupied with diligence in putting out the fire and not a single one attempted to profit from this circumstance in order to escape. (See report of 1829 from the Auburn inspectors).

50. At Boston, the regulations are also written and traces of the employees' duties are found there. However, these provisions are only indicative: the superintendent and the under-warden do not enjoy less discretionary power. Regulation of the New Prison, pag. 100.
51. See reports from the inspectors of Auburn, 26 January 1825.
52. Report of Gershom Powers, page. 11. 1827.
53. "The question to resolve," Mr. Livingston says, "is that of how to know if the whip is the most efficacious means to inculcate in the souls of the convicts religious and moral sentiments, the love of labor and science; and whether a man will love labor better because he has been coerced, by blows or by the terror of receiving them, to do the tasks each day that have been imposed on him." See letter from Livingston to Roberts Vaux, pag. 11, 1828. —Mr. Gershom Powers, director of Auburn, the discipline of which Mr. Livingston thus attacked, responded: "It is announced that at Philadelphia blows will not be tolerated in any case, and that the reduction of food will be the principal means, if not the only means, of maintaining discipline; in other terms, that by humane motives, to which the inmates are submitted, one will make them die by starvation." See report of 1828, pag. 97. Mr. Elam Lynds, with whom we have had numerous conversations on this subject, often told us that during the time when the inmates of Auburn were confined day and night in their cells without work a great number of them had passed half their time at the hospital.
54. See Fifth Report of the Boston Society of Prisons, pag. 92.
55. See Statistical Observations, [Appendix] no. 17. At Auburn, the inmates are treated more severely; at Philadelphia, they are more unhappy. At Auburn, where they are whipped, they die less than at Philadelphia, where by humanity one is put in a solitary and gloomy dungeon. —The superintendent of the Walnut Street prison, where the disciplinary punishments are mild, told us before the visit that we made there that it is necessary to punish the prisoners without ceasing for their infractions to the discipline. Thus, the disciplinary punishments of Walnut-Street, softer than those of Auburn, are all the more repeated and more destructive to the life of the prisoner than the severe punishments used in this latter prison.
56. See Statistical tables of the States of New York, Pennsylvania, Connecticut, Maryland and Massachusetts, at the end of this volume, [Appendix] no. 17.

57. See Reports on the penitentiary of Philadelphia by the inspectors, 1831, and Observations of Mr. Bache, doctor of the prison.
58. *The first use of the word "despotism."

REFERENCES

1830. *Fifth Annual Report of the Board of Managers of the Prison Discipline Society.* Boston: Perkins and Marvin.

1831. *Annual Report of the Board of Inspectors of the Eastern Penitentiary of Pennsylvania, to the Legislature.* Harrisburg: Henry Walsh.

Beaumont, Gustave de and Alexis de Tocqueville. 1833. *On the Penitentiary System in the United States and Its Application in France, with an Appendix on Penal Colonies and also Statistical Notes.* Translated by Francis Lieber. Philadelphia: Carey, Lea & Blanchard.

Julius, N. 1831. *Leçons sur les Prisons.* Translated by H. Lagarmitte and M. Mittermayer. Paris: F. G. Levrault.

Livingston, Edward. 1827. *Introductory Report to the Code of Prison Discipline: Explanatory of the Principles on which the Code is Founded, Being Part of the System of Penal Law Prepared for the State of Louisiana.* London: John Miller.

———. 1828. *Letter from Edward Livingston, Esq. to Roberts Vaux: On the Advantages of the Pennsylvania System of Prison Siscipline, For the Application of Which the New Penitentiary Has Been Constructed Near Philadelphia, Etc..* Philadelphia: Jesper Harding.

Powers, Gershom. 1828. *Report of Gershom Powers, Agent and Keeper of the State Prison at Auburn, Made to the Legislature, January 7, 1828.* Albany: Croswell and Van Benthuysen.

Tocqueville, Alexis de. 2000. *Democracy in America.* Translated and edited by Harvey Mansfield and Delba Winthrop. Chicago, IL: University of Chicago Press.

Vaux, Roberts. 1827. *Letter on the Penitentiary System of Pennsylvania Addressed to William Roscoe.* Philadelphia: Jesper Harding.

Williams, Edwin. 1831. *The New York Annual Register For the Year of Our Lord.* New York: Jonathan Leavitt and Collins & Hannay.

Chapter 3: Reform

Illusions of a few philanthropists on the penitentiary system. —In what consists its real advantages. —Prisoners cannot corrupt each other. —Means employed to effect their moral reform. —Primary and religious education. —Advantages and disadvantages of the Philadelphia System in this regard. —The Auburn system, less philosophical, depends more for its success on men responsible for its execution. —Influence of religious persons on reform. —Is this reform obtained? —Difference between radical and external reformation.

First Section

There are in America, like in Europe, respectable men whose minds are nourished with philosophical reveries and whose extreme sensibilities need illusions. These men, for whom philanthropy has become a need, find in the penitentiary system a remedy to this generous passion: taking their point of departure from such abstractions that deviate more or less from reality, they consider man, however far advanced he is in crime, as capable of being always brought back to virtue. They think that the most infamous being can in every case recover the sentiment of honor, and following the consequences of this opinion they anticipate a time when, every criminal being radically reformed, prisons will be entirely empty and justice will no longer have crimes to punish (z).

Others, perhaps without having such a deep conviction, march nevertheless along the same path; they occupy themselves continually with prisons; it is the subject to which the labor of their whole life bears reference. Philanthropy has become a kind of profession for them, and they have a monomania about the penitentiary system, which seems to them to be the remedy applicable to all of society's ills.

We believe that both parties are exaggerating the merit of this institution to themselves, whose real benefits can be recognized without attributing to it imaginary ones which cannot belong thereto.

There is first an incontestable advantage inherent in a penitentiary system of which isolation forms the principal basis. It is that criminals do not come out of the prison worse than when they entered it. In this, the system differs essentially from the discipline of our prisons, which not only does not render the prisoner better, but even corrupts them more. With us all great crimes have been, before their execution, formulated to some extent in the prisons, and deliberated in societies of assembled malefactors. Such is the disastrous influence of the wicked on one another, that one consummate villain suffices in a prison for all those who see and hear him to be modeled after him and in a little time borrow from him his vices and immorality (*aa*).

Nothing, certainly, is more detrimental to society than this mutual education in prisons; and it is very certain that we owe to this dangerous contagion a special population of malefactors who become each day more numerous and more threatening. It is an evil that the penitentiary system in the United States remedies completely.

It is evident that any moral contagion among the inmates is impossible, above all at Philadelphia where thick walls separate the prisoners day and night. This first result is serious, and we must be careful not to overlook its importance. Theories on the reform of inmates are vague and uncertain.[1] It is not yet known to what degree the villain can be regenerated and by what means this regeneration can be obtained: but if the efficacy of the prison to make prisoners better is unknown, we know, because experience has revealed it, its power to make them worse. The new penitentiaries in which this contagious influence is avoided have thus gained a critical advantage; and as long as that prison has not yet been found whose discipline is evidently regenerative, perhaps we can be permitted to say that the best prison is the one that does not corrupt.

We perceive, however, that this result, however serious it may be, does not satisfy the authors of the system; and it is natural that, after having preserved the inmates from the corruption that threatened them, they aspire to make them better still. Let us see by what means they endeavor to arrive at this goal. We will then examine the success of their efforts.

Moral and religious instruction forms in this respect the whole basis of the system.[2] In every penitentiary establishment, those prisoners who do not know how learn to read. These schools are voluntary. Although no convict is required to attend it, each considers it an honor to be admitted to it: and when it is impossible to receive all who present themselves there, they choose those among the prisoners for whom the benefit of the instruction is most necessary.[3] The liberty accorded to the prisoners to attend the study makes those who go there voluntarily much more zealous and more docile: this school is held every Sunday. It precedes the morning religious service; almost always, the minister who performs this service accompanies it with a sermon in which he abstains from any discussion on dogma in order to address only religious morals; in this way the instruction of the minister is equally suitable for Catholics and Protestants, for the Unitarian as well as for the Presbyterian. The meals of the prisoners are always preceded by a prayer made by the chaplain attached to the establishment; each of them has a Bible in his cell, given to him by the State, which he can read the whole time that is not set aside for labor.

This order of things exists in all the penitentiaries; but we would be very deceived if we believed that uniformity exists on this point in those same prisons. Some attach much more importance to religious instruction than others. Some persons neglect the moral reformation of the inmates, while others make it the object of particular care. At Singsing, for example, where the nature of things requires the development of such a rigorous discipline, the direction of the establishment seems to have only the maintenance of the external order and the passive obedience of convicts in mind. There they disdain the help of moral influences; they indeed take a little trouble for the primary and religious education of the prisoners; but it is clear that this objective is only secondary. In the prisons of Auburn, Wethersfield, Philadelphia, and Boston, reform occupies a much greater place.

In Philadelphia, the moral situation in which the inmates find themselves is eminently proper to facilitate their regeneration. We have more than once noted with astonishment the serious turn that the ideas of the convict take in this prison. We have seen some inmates who from their disposition and their lightness were led to crime, and whose mind had contracted in solitude habits of meditation and reasoning altogether extraordinary. The discipline of this penitentiary appeared to us above all powerful on souls gifted with some elevation and on the persons whom education had polished. Intellectual men are naturally those whose souls are most troubled by isolation and who suffer the most from being separated from any society.

We can say, however, that this complete solitude produces the liveliest impression on every prisoner. We find in general their hearts prompt to open themselves, and this ease of receiving emotions disposes them even more to reform. They are especially accessible to religious sentiments, and memories of their family have an extreme power over their souls. Perhaps the man who is free and enjoys social communications is incapable of feeling the whole worth of a religious thought thrown into the cell of the convict.

At Philadelphia, nothing distracts the inmates from their meditations; and since they are always isolated, the presence of a person who comes to converse with them is an immense kindness, which they appreciate to its fullest extent. During our visit to this penitentiary, one of the prisoners said to us: "It is with joy that I perceive the figure of the inspectors who visit my cell. This summer a cricket entered my yard; it seemed to me I found in him a companion (it looked like company). When a butterfly or any other animal enters my cell, I never hurt it."[4] In this disposition of the soul, one perceives the full value that is attached to moral communications and the influence that wise counsels and pious exhortations can have on their mind.

The superintendent visits each of them at least once a day. The inspectors make the same visit to them at least two times per week, and a chaplain is especially responsible for care of their moral reformation. Before and after these visits, they are not entirely alone. The books that are put at their disposal are for them a kind of companionship that never leaves them. The Bible, and sometimes loose leaf pages containing edifying anecdotes, form their library. When they are not working, they read; and several of them seem to find a great consolation in this reading. There are some there who, knowing only the letters of the alphabet, have taught themselves to read. Others, less ingenious or persevering, managed only with the help of the superintendent or inspectors.[5]

Such are the means employed at Philadelphia to enlighten the convicts and make them better.

Is there a combination more powerful for reformation than that of a prison that hands over the criminal to all the hardship of isolation, leads him through reflection to remorse, through religion to hope, makes him laborious by the burden of idleness, and that, while inflicting on him the torture of solitude and isolation, makes him find an extreme charm in the conversation of pious men, whom formerly he would have seen with indifference and heard without pleasure?

The impression made by such a system on the criminal is certainly profound; experience alone will show whether this impression is durable. We have said that his entrance into the penitentiary was a critical moment; that of leaving the prison is even more critical. He passes suddenly from complete solitude to the ordinary state of society: is it not to be feared that at the expiration of his punishment he will greedily search for the social pleasures that he has been deprived of so completely? He was dead to the world, and after a loss of several years he re-appears in society, where he brings, it is true, good resolutions, but perhaps also very lively passions, and more impetuous from their being longer repressed.

Such is, perhaps, in respect to reformation, the gravest disadvantage of complete isolation. This system possesses, however, one last advantage that we must not pass over in silence: it is that the prisoners undergoing this discipline do not know each other.[6] This fact avoids serious disadvantages and leads to happy results. There always exists more or less a close link between criminals who have met in the common prison; and when they return to society after having undergone their punishment they are in mutual dependence. Compromised by each other, if one wants to commit an offence, the other is almost forced to give him assistance; it would be necessary to have become virtuous to not become a criminal again. This pitfall, generally so disastrous to freed convicts, is in truth half avoided in the Auburn prison, where the inmates, seeing without knowing each other, mutually contract no intimate liaison. Yet we are still more certain of avoiding this danger in the Philadelphia prison, where the convicts never see each other.

He who at the expiration of his punishment leaves this prison to return to society cannot find in other freed criminals, whom he does not know, any assistance in doing evil; and if he wants to enter into a good path he encounters no-one who diverts him. Desiring to commit new offences, he is left to himself; and in this respect, he is still as isolated in the world as he was in prison; if, on the contrary, he wants to begin a new life, he possesses the plenitude of his liberty.

This system of reform is certainly, in its entirety, a concept that belongs to the highest philosophy: in general, it is simple and easy to put in practice;

it presents, however, in its execution a rather serious difficulty. The first rule of the system being that the inmates cannot communicate together, nor even see each other, consequently one cannot have any religious instruction or school in common there; so that the instructor and the chaplain can instruct or exhort only a single person at a time; this incurs an immense loss of time.[7] If the prisoners could be united and participate in the benefit of the same lesson, moral and religious instruction would be much easier to circulate; but the principles of the system oppose it.

In the prisons of Auburn, Wethersfield, Singsing, and Boston, the system of reform does not rest on as philosophical a theory as at Philadelphia.[8] In this latter prison, the system seems to operate by itself, by the sole force of its principles; at Auburn, on the contrary, and in prisons of the same nature, its efficiency depends much more on the persons responsible for its execution; we see then concurring in the success of the former some exterior efforts that are not perceived as much in the other.

The Auburn plan, which allows the assembling of inmates during the day, seems in truth less conducive than that of Philadelphia to produce reflection and repentance; but it is more favorable to the inmates' education; in every prison subject to the same discipline the instructor and the chaplain can, in their lessons or sermons, address the entire prison. At Auburn, there is a chaplain (Mr. Smith) exclusively attached to the establishment. It is the same at Wethersfield, where Mr. Barrett, a Presbyterian minister, devotes himself entirely to care of the penitentiary.[9] After school, the service, and the Sunday sermon, the inmates return to their solitary cells, where the chaplain goes to visit them: he makes similar visits to them during the other days of the week[10] and strives to touch their hearts by enlightening their consciences: the inmates feel a sentiment of joy in seeing him enter their cell. He is the only friend who remains to them; he receives the confidence of all their sentiments; if they have complaints against the employees of the prison or some favor to solicit, it is he who is charged with their complaint. In giving them tokens of his interest, he tries to increasingly win their confidence. He soon becomes initiated into every secret of their previous life, and, knowing the morality of all, he endeavors to apply to each the proper remedy for his evil. The minister does not interfere with the rest of the discipline in the prison. When the inmates are in their workshops he never distracts them from their work; and if he receives a complaint, it does not belong to him to make it right; he merely solicits in favor of the unfortunate persons whose interpreter he is. It would be difficult to paint the zeal that animates Mr. Barrett and

Mr. Smith in the exercise of their pious functions, who perhaps sometimes have illusions on the results of their efforts, but are very certain at least of attracting the veneration of any who know them.

They are, besides, admirably seconded in their ministry by several persons who are strangers to the establishment. The Sunday school is almost entirely managed by inhabitants of the region residing near the prison. These persons, guided by a sentiment of humanity that is mixed with a deep sentiment of religious duty, spend two or three hours each Sunday in the prison, where they exercise the functions of primary instructors. They are not content sometimes with teaching the prisoners to read; they also focus on explaining to them the most remarkable passages of the gospel. At Auburn, it is Presbyterian seminary students who fulfill this gratuitous and religious ministry. School is also held at Singsing, Baltimore, and Boston.[11] In this latter city, we saw men of the highest distinction charge themselves with these obscure functions; they made several criminals assembled around them repeat the lesson; sometimes they mingled their observations with counsels so touching that the convicts shed tears of emotion. Certainly, if the reformation of a criminal is possible, it is by such means and with such men that it can be obtained.

Now, at what point is this reformation brought about by the different systems that we examined?

Before answering this question, it will be necessary to agree on the meaning attached to the word "reformation."

Do we mean by this expression the radical reformation that makes a wicked person into an honest man and gives virtues to him who had only vices?

Such regeneration, if it ever takes place, must be very rare; what would it be in fact?

To give back primitive purity to a soul that crime has defiled. Still, the difficulty is immense. It would have been much easier for the guilty to remain honest than for him to rise again after his fall. In vain society pardons him: his conscience does not give grace. Whatever his efforts, he will never regain that delicacy of honor that alone gives an unblemished life. Even when he takes the part of living honestly, he cannot forget that he has been a criminal; and this memory, which deprives him of self-esteem, also deprives his virtue of reward and guarantee.

However, when we think[12] of all the means that are employed in the prisons of the United States to obtain this complete regeneration of the wicked, it is difficult to think that it sometimes might not be the reward of so many efforts. It can be the work of religion and pious men who dedicate their time, their care, and their whole life to this important object. If society is powerless to reprieve consciences, religion has the power to do so. When society pardons, it puts the man in liberty; that is all: it is only a material fact. When God pardons, he pardons the soul. With this moral pardon, the criminal regains self-respect, without which honesty is impossible. It is a result that society can never claim because human institutions, powerful on the actions and the will, have no power over consciences.

We have seen in the United States some persons who have a great faith in this reformation and in the means put in practice to obtain it. Mr. Smith told us at Auburn during our visit that, out of the six hundred fifty prisoners in that prison, they already had at least fifty who were radically reformed, and that he considered them as good Christians. Mr. Barrett, at Wethersfield, estimated that of the one hundred eighty inmates in that penitentiary, fifteen or twenty were already in a state of complete regeneration.[13]

It would be useless to discuss here the question of whether Mr. Smith and Mr. Barrett deceive themselves in their estimate: it seems to us that we can admit with them the existence of radical reform.[14] Only it is permissible to believe that the cases are still rarer than they themselves think. This is at least the opinion of almost every enlightened man with whom we came into contact in the United States. Mr. Elam Lynds, who has great experience with prisons, goes much further and considers the integral reform of the criminal as a chimera which is not reasonable to pursue. Perhaps he falls into the other extreme, and an opinion as discouraging as his own would need, in order to be adopted, to be founded on an incontrovertible truth. There does not exist any human means of proving this complete reformation: how to demonstrate by statistics the purity of the soul, the delicacy of sentiments, and the innocence of intentions? Society, powerless to effect this radical regeneration, is no more capable of proving it when it exists. It is in both cases an affair of the heart of hearts: in the first case, God alone can act; in the second, God alone can judge. However, he who on earth is the minister of God sometimes also has the privilege of reading into the conscience; and it is thus that the two ministers whom we have just mentioned believe to know the morality of the prisoners and what passes in the depth of their souls. They are, no doubt, better placed than any other to obtain the confidence of these unfortunate beings, and we are persuaded that they often receive disinterested confessions of sincere repentance. But also how they risk being deceived by hypocritical protests! The convict, regardless of his crime, always hopes to be pardoned. This hope exists above all in the prisons of the United States, where for a long time the use of pardoning has been abused.[15] The criminal therefore is interested in showing to the chaplain, who alone maintains moral communications with him, a deep remorse for his crime and a lively desire to return to virtue. When these sentiments are not sincere, he does not express them any less. On the other hand, the good man who dedicates his whole existence to the pursuit of an honorable goal is himself under the influence of a passion that must engender errors. Since he ardently desires the reformation of the prisoners, he believes them easily. Must he be accused of naiveté? No, for the success in which he has confidence encourages him to renewed attempts; illusions of this nature become grievous only if, on the faith of similar regenerations, pardons would be multiplied. For this would encourage hypocrisy, and we will soon see the criminals reform themselves by calculation.[16] We must say that in general this danger seems keenly felt and that pardons are becoming rarer and rarer: if the desire of public opinion was completely satisfied, the governors would use their right to pardon only in favor of convicts whose guilt has become doubtful because of circumstances coming after the judgement. However, we must also add that the disadvantage of too many pardons accorded to convicts is not yet entirely avoided; and at Auburn, out of the total number of pardons, one-third is granted on the presumption of reformation.

In resuming this point, we say above all if the penitentiary system cannot propose to itself an end other than radical reformation of which we have spoken, then the legislature should perhaps abandon this system; not because the goal is not admirable to pursue, but because it is too rarely attained. Moral reform of a single individual, which is a great thing for the religious man, is a little thing for the politician; or, to say it better, an institution is political only if it is made in the interest of the masses; it loses this character if it profits only a small number.

But if it is true that radical reformation of the depraved man is only an accident of the penitentiary system, instead of being a rational consequence of it, it is equally certain that there is another kind of reformation, shallower than the first, but nevertheless useful for society, and that seems to be produced naturally by the system with which we are concerned.

Thus, we do not doubt that the habits of order that the prisoner undergoes for several years greatly influence his moral conduct after his return to society.

The necessity of labor that masters his penchant for idleness; the obligation of silence that makes him reflect; isolation that places him alone in the presence of his crime and his punishment; religious instruction that enlightens and consoles him; obedience at each instant to inflexible rules; the regularity of a uniform life; in a word, all the circumstances belonging to this severe discipline are of a nature to produce a deep impression on his mind.

Perhaps in leaving the prison he is not an honest man; but he has contracted honest habits. He was lazy; now he knows how to work. His ignorance prevented him from exercising an industry; now he knows how to read and to write, and the trade that he learned in prison furnishes him with a means of existence that he previously lacked. Without loving the good, he can detest crime, whose cruel consequences he felt; and if he is not more virtuous, he is at least more reasonable: his morality is not honor, but interest. Perhaps his religious faith is neither lively nor deep; but even if religion has not touched his heart, it gave his mind habits of order and his life rules of conduct; without having a great religious conviction, he acquired a taste for the moral principles that religion teaches; finally, if he has not in truth become better, he is at least more obedient to the laws, and that is all that society has the right to ask of him.

Considered from this point of view, the reformation of convicts seems to us to be frequently obtained with the aid of the system that occupies us; and the men who in the United States have the least confidence in the radical regeneration of criminals fervently believe in the existence of a reformation reduced to these simpler terms.

We will note here that the zeal of the religious man, who is often ineffectual to operate radical reform, has a great influence on this reform of the second order that we have just defined. It is because his goal is great that he pursues it with passion; and the nobleness of his enterprise elevates simultaneously his ministry and the functions of all those who, in concert with him, work for the reformation of criminals; it gives thus to the whole penitentiary establishment a greater interest and a much higher morality. Thus, though the religious man does not often arrive at the goal, it is important that he does not stop pursuing it; and perhaps the point that we have just indicated is obtained only because the aim taken is much higher.

The advantages of the penitentiary system in the United States can therefore be classified thus:

First: Impossibility of corruption for the inmates in the prison;
Second: Great probability for them to be given the habits of obedience and industry that make them useful citizens;
Third: Possibility of a radical reformation.

Although each of the establishments that we have examined tends towards these three results, still, in this respect some nuances distinguish the Auburn system from that of Philadelphia.

First, as we have already observed, Philadelphia has, on the first point, the advantage over Auburn: essentially, the inmates, separated by thick walls, can communicate still less with each other than those who are isolated only by silence. The Auburn discipline guarantees well the certitude that silence is not violated; but this is only a moral certitude subject to contradiction; while at Philadelphia the communication among convicts is physically impossible.

The Philadelphia system, being equally the one that produces the deepest impressions on the soul of the convict, must effect more reformation than that of Auburn. Perhaps, however, this latter system, with the aid of its discipline, conforms more than that of Philadelphia to the habits of men in society, producing the greater number of so-called legal reformations because they produce the external fulfillment of social obligations.

If it was thus, the Philadelphia system would make more honest men and that of New York more citizens subject to the laws.

Second Section

The goodness of the system proved by statistics. —Is the number of crimes in the United States increasing? — Influence of black persons and foreigners. — What is the effect of education in this respect? — Necessary distinction between the number of crimes and that of convictions. — The penitentiary system is most often foreign to the increase of crimes. — Its influence, limited to prisoners, is revealed by recidivism: it can be appreciated only after several years. — Comparison between the former prisons and the new penitentiaries. — Impossibility of comparing the number of crimes and recidivism in the United States and in France. — Different elements of the two societies: diversity of penal laws and of powers of judicial police in the two countries. — America can be compared only with herself.

After having exposed the consequences of the penitentiary system such as we understand them, can we find in statistics the proof of those facts that we believe can be attributed to it?

When one seeks to know the influence of the penitentiary system on society, it is customary to pose the question thus:

Has the number of crimes increased or diminished since the penitentiary system has been established (*bb*)?

The answer to every question of this kind is extremely difficult in the United States because it requires statistical documents that are almost impossible to procure. There does not exist in the Union, or in the individual States, any central authority that possesses them. One obtains with difficulty the statistics of a city, of a county, never of the entire State.[17]

Pennsylvania is the only one where we have been able to know the total number of crimes. During the year 1830, there were two thousand eighty-four individuals sentenced to imprisonment in Pennsylvania; which, compared to a population of one million three hundred forty-seven thousand six hundred seventy-two (1,347,672) inhabitants, gives one sentenced to imprisonment out of six hundred fifty-three (653) inhabitants.[18]

In the other States, we obtained very precise information on the number of certain crimes, but never of the totality of offences; thus, we know only the number of offences that, in the States of New York, Massachusetts, Connecticut, and Maryland, sentenced the criminals to the central prison (state prison).[19]

If we take those especially sentenced as the basis of our observations, we see that in the States of New York, Massachusetts, and Maryland, the number of criminals as compared to the population is decreasing; in the State of Connecticut it is increasing; while it is stationary in Pennsylvania.[20]

Shall we conclude from this exposition that the Connecticut prison is very bad; that those of New York, Massachusetts, and Maryland are the only good ones; and that those of Pennsylvania are better than the first and worse than the second?

This result would be strange, because it is an incontestable fact that the Connecticut penitentiary is better than the prisons of Maryland and Pennsylvania.[21]

If we want to carefully examine the situation of these different States and the political circumstances in which they are placed, we will see that the more or less considerable number of crimes, even their decrease and increase, can be held to causes totally foreign to the penitentiary system.

First, it is necessary to distinguish the number of crimes from their growth: in the State of New York there are more crimes than in Pennsylvania; yet the number of crimes is stationary in the latter State, while it diminishes in the first. In Connecticut, where crimes are increasing, there are in sum half of the crimes than in every other State.[22]

We will add that, in order to establish between the various States some well-founded points of comparison, it would be necessary to subtract the foreigners among them from the population of each and to compare only the crimes committed by the stationary population; in proceeding thus, one would find that Maryland is of all States the one whose stationary population commits the most crimes. This fact is explained by a cause unique to the southern States, the presence of the black race. In general, it has been observed that in the States where there is one black man for every thirty white persons, the prisons contain one black man for every four white persons.[23]

The states that have many black men must therefore furnish more crimes. This reason alone would suffice to explain the high statistic of crimes in Maryland: it is not, however, applicable to every southern State; it touches only those where the emancipation of blacks is permitted: for we would deceive ourselves greatly were we to believe that crimes of black persons are avoided in giving them liberty; experience teaches, on the contrary, that in the South the number of crimes is magnified more by those who are freed than by those who are slaves; thus, precisely because slavery seems to march to its ruin, the number of newly freed persons will be seen to increase for a long time in the South, and with them the number of criminals (*cc*).

While the South of the United States contains in its midst this fruitful principle for the increase of offences, in the States of the North, on the contrary, such as New York and Massachusetts, several political causes tend to diminish crimes.

On the one hand, the black population there decreases each day, compared to the white population that continually increases.

On the other hand, in these same states, foreigners who arrive from Europe each year without livelihood are a cause of crimes that is continually weakening.

In fact, in the same proportion as the population becomes more considerable, the number of immigrants, although not diminishing, is less in relation to the totality of the inhabitants. The population doubles in thirty years; but the number of immigrants is approximately always the same.

This cause of increase of crimes in the North, however mobile in appearance, loses its force each year; the figure that represents it, considered alone, is always the same; but it becomes smaller compared to another figure that each day becomes larger.

Some persons[24] in the United States think also that the lights of education, so widespread in the northern States, tend to diminish crimes.

In the State of New York, out of a population of two million inhabitants, five hundred fifty thousand children are instructed in schools and the State alone spends for this object about six million francs each year. It seems that an enlightened population that lacks none of the markets that agriculture, commerce, and manufacturing industry can offer must commit fewer crimes than the one that possesses these latter advantages without having the same enlightenment to exploit them; nevertheless, we do not think that this diminishment of crimes in the North must be attributed to education, because in Connecticut, where it is still more widespread than in the State of New York, one sees crimes increase with extreme rapidity; and if we cannot blame knowledge for this prodigious increase, we are at least forced to acknowledge that it does not have the power to stop it;[25] besides, we do not pretend to explain these strange anomalies offered by the States whose political institutions are approximately similar, and in which, however, the proportion of crimes to the population is so different; these difficulties belong to the number of those that never fail to lead to all kinds of statistical work.[26] But the considerations that we have just presented have at least served to prove how many serious causes, independent of the penitentiary system, influence the growth or diminishment of crimes.

Sometimes an industrial crisis, the disbanding of an army, et cetera, suffices to raise the number of offences during a year.

It is thus that during the year 1816 one sees the number of criminals increase extraordinarily in every prison of America: was the penitentiary system the cause of such things? No, it was simply a consequence of the United States' war with England; this war, being finished, has given place to a host of military persons returning to their homes whom peace had deprived of their profession.

There is another difficulty; even if we agree on the cause of crimes, we do not know exactly the cause of their increase.

How can we prove the number of crimes? By that of convictions; but several causes can make convictions more frequent without the number of crimes increasing (*dd*).

For example, the judicial police could pursue crimes with more zeal and activity, which ordinarily happens if public attention is directed to that object. The number of crimes committed is not increased; there are only more crimes proven. It is the same when the repression of criminal tribunals is more severe; this always happens when the penal law is softened. Then, the number of acquittals diminishes: there are more convictions, although the number of crimes has not varied. The penitentiary system itself, which must diminish the number of crimes, has for its first result from its origin increased the number of convictions. Consequently, in the same degree as judges often feel repugnant to sentence the guilty, because they know the corrupting influence of the prison that must receive them; the same thus are much more willing to pronounce a sentence when they know that the prison, far from being a school of crime, is a place of penitence and reform (*ee*).

In any event, it clearly results from what precedes that the augmentation of crimes or their diminishment is produced by causes sometimes general, sometimes accidental, but that have no direct relationship with the penitentiary system.

If we want to consider the object of the penitentiary system and its natural scope, we will see that it cannot have the general influence that we attribute to it; and that the question is badly posed when one asks it to account in absolute terms for the progression of crimes: the good or bad discipline of a prison can exercise influence only on those who have been imprisoned. Prisons can be very good in a country where there are many crimes and very bad in another where the crimes are very rare. It is thus that in Massachusetts, where there are fewer convicts, the prisons are defective; while they are good in the State of New York, where crimes are more numerous.[27] One bad prison cannot further deprave those who have not been exposed to its corrupting influence any more than one good penitentiary can reform the individuals who do not know its beneficial discipline.[28]

Institutions, mores, political circumstances, these influence the morality of men in society; prisons act only on the morality of men in prison.[29]

The penitentiary system does not therefore have the scope of action that is sometimes attributed to it. Reduced as it must be to the prison population, its direct influence is relatively important, so that one does not attempt to attribute to it what does not belong to it; and, in fact, if that part of the social body on which the penitentiary discipline is exercised is limited, it is at least the most gangrenous,[30] and the one whose wound is simultaneously the most contagious and the most essential to cure.

When, therefore, we want to appreciate the merit of a prison and system that has been put in force, it is necessary to observe, not the morality of society in general, but only that of individuals who, having been imprisoned in this prison, returned to society: if they commit no new offence, one can believe that the influence of imprisonment on them has been healthy; and if they fall into recidivism, it is proof that the discipline of the prison has not made them better.

If it is true that the large or small number of recidivism alone proves the defect or goodness of a prison, it must be added that it is impossible to obtain a perfectly precise statement on this point.

On the one hand, it is very difficult to obtain proof that the liberated convicts took an honest path; and on the other hand, we do not always have knowledge of the new crimes that they commit.

To these considerations, which appear necessary for us to reduce the question to its true terms, we will add one last consideration that seems to us equally important not to lose sight of: that is, to assess the effects of the penitentiary system it is not necessary to consider the time of its creation, but better the time that follows it. This truth, which seems obvious to announce, has, however, been forgotten by writers of a very great merit; we will mention an example.

We have already said that in 1790 a new system of imprisonment was established at Philadelphia: consequently, the Walnut Street prison was organized on the plan that we have recognized as totally defective; however, by a fortunate circumstance, or at least one whose cause is unknown, the number of crimes in Pennsylvania during the years 1790, 1791, 1792, and 1793 was much less considerable that it had been during the preceding years. Mr. Livingston and Mr. Roberts Vaux in the United States; among us, the Duke de La Rochefoucauld-Liancourt and Mr. Charles Lucas, have drawn from this decrease of crimes proof of the efficacy of the system;[31] but their reasoning appeared to us to be founded on a badly appreciated fact. To ascribe this result to the new discipline of prisons, it would have been necessary to prove that the individuals leaving the Walnut Street prison had not committed any new crimes: but this proof could not be made. In fact, the system commenced in 1790; and already in the years 1791, 1792, and 1793 the effects were sought, that is, before most of those who had been confined in the prison left it (*gg*).

It is easy to understand that the effect of the penitentiary system cannot be assessed until after a certain number of years, and only after the convicts who have been put in liberty at the expiration of their punishment have had time to commit new crimes or give example of an honest life.

We must for this reason disregard the results obtained by the new penitentiaries of Philadelphia, Singsing, Boston, and Baltimore: in giving up the arguments that we could draw from these different prisons, we will infinitely narrow the circle of discussion; but we will find at least the advantage of giving to our arguments only solid bases.

Let us then compare the effects produced by the former prisons of the United States with those resulting from the new system in place in the penitentiaries of Auburn and Wethersfield, the only ones that may have been established long enough for us to already judge their influence.

In the former prison of New York (Newgate), the total number of recommitted convicts was in proportion to the inmates one out of nine; in the prison of Maryland, one out of seven; in that of Walnut-Street, one out of six; and in the former Connecticut prison, one in four.[32] At Boston, one-sixth of the individuals released from prison returned there after having committed new crimes.[33]

The number of recommitted individuals is much lower in the new prisons of Auburn and Wethersfield. In the first, recidivists form one-nineteenth of the whole number; and out of one hundred individuals who left the second time since its creation, only five returned there for new offenses; that gives the proportion of one out of twenty.[34]

At Auburn, not only those criminals are noted who, after having been imprisoned in the penitentiary, have been brought back there by a new offence; but an attempt has also been made to state the conduct of freed prisoners who, not having committed new crimes, remain in society. Out of one hundred sixty individuals with respect to which some information has been obtained, one hundred and twelve have held good conduct; the others returned to bad or questionable habits (*hh*).

These figures, however conclusive they may appear, are the result of too small a number of years for one to be able to draw from it invincible proof of the efficacy of the system; one is nevertheless forced to acknowledge that they are extremely favorable to the new penitentiary prisons, and the presumption that these results bear in their favor is even stronger as the effect obtained perfectly accords here with what was promised in theory: it is necessary to add that, in spite of the impossibility of drawing any evidence from the too-new penitentiaries of Singsing, Boston, and any prison of the same nature, one cannot however contest that the success of Auburn and Wethersfield does not make those establishments that are established completely on the same model very probable.

In presenting these statistical documents, we have not compared the number of crimes and recidivists in the United States and in France, persuaded as we are that the basis of a parallel comparison would be imperfect.

The two countries have conditions of existence that are not similar and are composed of elements that are essentially different.

A young society, exempt from political embarrassment, as rich from the soil as from industry, must seem to furnish fewer criminals than a country where the ground is disputed foot by foot and where the crises that birth political divisions tend to augment the number of offences, because they increase poverty by disturbing industries.

However, if the statistical documents that we possess on Pennsylvania can be applied to the rest of the Union, there are in this country more crimes than in France in proportion to the population.[35] Various causes of another nature explain this result: on the one hand, the black population composes one-sixth of the inhabitants of the United States and half of the inmates in prison; and on the other hand, foreigners who come from Europe each year and who form one-fifth and sometimes a quarter of the number of convicts.

These two facts, which explain the high figure of crimes in the United States, make it incomparable with the number of offences in a country where similar facts are not encountered.

If we would subtract from the total number of crimes those committed by black persons and foreigners, we would find no doubt that the white American population commits fewer offences than ours; but in proceeding thus, we would fall into another error; in fact, to separate black persons from the population of the United States, is as if among us one would abstract from a part of the poor class, that is, those who commit the crimes. One evades one pitfall only to fall into another; in this respect, the only certain, incontestable fact that we have remarked in the United States and that can give place to a comparison is the completely extraordinary morality of women belonging to the white race. Thus, only four females out of one hundred inmates are found in the prisons of the United States; while with us there are twenty out of a hundred.[36] Now, this morality of the women must influence the whole society, because on them chiefly rests the morality of the family.

Nevertheless, the elements of comparison are otherwise so different we can on the whole only hazard probabilities.

Difficulties abound if we want to make approximations of this kind between the two nations. The difference that exists between the penal laws of America and ours adds to the obstacles.

There are, in the United States, some things punished as crimes that among us the laws do not reach; and, on the other hand, our code punishes offences that in the United States are not considered as such. Thus, many offences against religion and mores, such as blasphemy, incest, fornication, drunkenness, et cetera,[37] are reprimanded by severe punishments in the United States; while with us they are unpunished. There also exist in our laws infractions that are not provided for by the American laws. Hence, our code punishes bankruptcy, against which the laws of the United States have no punishment.

How then can we compare the number of crimes in countries whose legislation is so different? Let us add that, were this comparison made exactly, it would still be difficult to draw conclusive results from the statistics obtained: thus, it can well be said in general that the relatively great number of convicted criminals in a country proves its corruption or its morality. Yet there exist exceptions to this rule that throw a great incertitude on the calculations: thus, in one of the most religious and moral states of the American Union (Connecticut), there are more convictions for attacking mores than in any other State.[38] To understand this result, it is necessary to remember that crimes of this nature are punished only where they are rare: in societies where adultery is common, it is not punished. In the United States, bankrupt persons cannot be seen in the prisons; can we conclude that the crime of bankruptcy is never committed there? This would be to fall into a great error, because it is perhaps of all countries that in which bankruptcies are most frequent: it is necessary, therefore, in order to not admire the commercial morality of the United States in this respect, to know whether it is a matter of a crime that the law does not punish. On the other hand, if we know there are ten counterfeiters for every one hundred criminals in the United States,[39] we cannot take it as proof of that country's corruption relative to ours, where forgery is among other crimes only in the proportion of two out of one hundred.[40] In the United States the entire population is addicted to commerce, and in addition there are three hundred fifty banks that all issue paper money; the industry of the forger has then, in order to be exercised in this country, a material beginning that is not the same in countries where commerce is the attribute of a single class and where the number of banks is more restrained.

There is, finally, one last obstacle to comparing the crimes committed in the two countries; it is that in the cases even where the legislation of both punishes a common crime, they give for its repression different punishments; but, as the comparison of crimes is made by that of punishments, it follows that two analogous results are compared, obtained from two different bases: that is a new source of error.

If it is difficult to fruitfully compare the number and nature of crimes committed in the United States and in France, it is perhaps still more disadvantageous to compare the number of criminal re-committals and to find in this comparison proof of the relative merit of the prisons in these two countries.

In general, only the re-committals of those who return a second time to the same prison where they had already been imprisoned are counted in the United States.[41] His return to the prison where he is recognized is in fact the only means that one possesses to note his state of recidivism. In that country, where the requirement of passports does not exist, nothing is easier than to change one's name; if therefore a freed prisoner commits a new crime under an assumed name, he very easily hides his recidivism, at least if he is not brought back to the prison where he underwent his first punishment. There are besides a thousand means to evade this chance of recognition. Nothing is easier than to pass from one State into another, and it is in the criminal's interest to emigrate in this way, whether he desires to commit new crimes or whether he has resolved to live honestly. Thus, out of one hundred convicted criminals in one State, there are, on average, thirty who belong to a neighboring state.[42] Now, this emigration suffices to make proof of their recidivism impossible. The link that ties the United States together is purely political; there exists no central power to which the police officers might address themselves to obtain information on the past life of the indicted, so that criminal courts almost always sentence without knowing the true name and still less the history of the guilty. We judge, by this state of things, that the number of known recidivists is never the exact number of existing recidivists, but only that of noted recidivism (*ii*). It is not the same with us. There are a thousand ways in France to prove the individuality of the indicted and convicted; by the aid of mutual relationships that every agent of the judicial police maintains among themselves, a royal court of the North has the sentences pronounced by a court of the South; and justice possesses in this respect every means of investigation that is lacking in the United States. While, therefore, there are not more recidivists in France than in the United States, we know a greater quantity of them; and it is because the means of proving them in the two countries are so different that it would be useless to compare the number.

Any comparison of this kind between America and Europe cannot then lead to any result. America can be compared only with herself; this comparison suffices, moreover, to shed abundant light on the question that we are occupied with; and we have acknowledged the superiority of the new penitentiary system over the former, when comparing the effects of the one and the other we saw the recommitted prisoners who, in the former prisons, were on average in proportion of one to six, and in the new penitentiaries only in the proportion of one to twenty.

Notes

1. "... But from a closer and more intimate view of the subject, I have rather abandoned a hope I once entertained, of the *general reformation of offenders* through the penitentiary System. I now think that its chief good is in the prevention of crime, by the confinement of criminals." (Mr. Niles, ex-commissioner of the Maryland penitentiary, 22 December 1829). *Note: the first French edition included this note in English.
2. *Note the differentiation between moral and religious instruction; they form the basis of reforming prisoners, rather than merely preventing them from further corruption (of which silence is the basis).
3. At Boston, all those who present themselves are admitted (See Report of Mr. Gray, pag. 10 and 11).
4. See Inquiry on the Penitentiary of Philadelphia, [Appendix] no. 10.
5. There is no school regularly kept at Philadelphia; but when the inspectors or the superintendent sees in one of the prisoners a good aptitude, or for any reason feels interested in his favor, they give him more care than to others and begin by procuring for him the first elements of education. One of the inspectors of the penitentiary, Mr. Bradford, dedicates much of his time to this good work.
6. See 2nd Report on the penitentiary of Philadelphia 1831.
7. At Philadelphia, every inmate who is in the same hall of the building is made to participate in the same sermon: but since the penitentiary will have seven very distinct parts, seven consecutive religious instructions will be required to be given by the same minister or seven ministers occupied simultaneously with the same object.

8. The adversaries of Auburn say and write that in this prison, the system of reformation has obtained so little success that it has been entirely abandoned. —The argument that the efforts to regenerate the criminals are not always successful is admitted: but it would be imprecise to say that reformation is no longer sought at Auburn. We can attest on the contrary that the men who direct the establishment pursue this goal with extreme ardor. One can see among others Mr. Gershom Powers' response on this point to Mr. Livingston. (Letter of Gershom Powers to Edward Livingston 1829).
9. Mr. Barrett receives a salary of 200 dollars (1,060 f.).
10. In the evening, after their work when they have returned to their cells.
11. See Report of Mr. Niles 1829, 22 December. We must say that at Singsing, the school, although done with care, appeared to us limited to too small a number of prisoners. The number of convicts admitted to the Sunday school varies from 60 to 80; feeble proportion out of 1,000. (See Report of 1832 on Singsing.) The direction of this establishment is too material, which no doubt results from the fact that its superintendent and his inferior agents are uniquely preoccupied with maintaining the exterior order whose existence is ceaselessly threatened. We were witnesses of a fact that proves what could be the success of the school at Singsing if it received greater development. A poor black man, who had taught himself to read in prison, recited by heart to us two pages of the Bible that he had studied during his recreation of the week, and he did not commit the least fault of memory.
12. *It is interesting that Tocqueville and Beaumont use the word *songer*, which can also mean "to dream," considering their criticisms of those who fall under illusions. The authors, too, have dreams and are educating readers in how to properly use the imagination.
13. See Letter of Mr. Barrett, [Appendix] no. 14.
14. See Conversation with Mr. Elam Lynds, [Appendix] no. 11
15. See Statistical Notes, no. 16. We explain there the various causes that have, in the United States, contributed to the abuse of the right to pardon.
16. Mr. Smith himself told us that he guarded himself against exterior demonstrations of repentance: he added that in his eyes the best proof of the sincerity of a prisoner was that he did not desire to leave the prison.
17. We have nevertheless found in the authorities of the different States a very particular benevolence and an extreme readiness to procure for us the information that we desired. Mr. Flagg, Secretary of State at Albany, Mr. Riker, recorder at New York, Messrs. Me. Ilvaine and Roberts Vaux at Philadelphia, Mr. Gray at Boston, and all the inspectors of the new prisons, furnished us a great quantity of precious documents. Mr. Riker obtained for us the general statement of crimes committed in the entire State of

New York during the year 1830. This is a very interesting document; but we possess only the information for one year.
18. See Statistical Notes, [Appendix] no. 16.
19. See Statistical Observations and Comparisons, No. 17.
20. See Statistical Observations and Comparisons, No. 17.
21. We intend to speak here only of the former prisons of Pennsylvania and Maryland. The new penitentiaries of these States are still too recent to occupy us here with their effects.
22. See Statistical Observations and Comparisons, No. 17.
23. See Statistical Observations and Comparisons, No. 17.
24. Among others, Mr. Edward Livingston. See his writings, notably his letter to Roberts Vaux, 1828, pages 14 and 15. — Judge Powers considers ignorance and intemperance as the two principle sources of crime. (See Report of Gershom Powers of 1828, page 50).
25. Education, even if not separated from religious beliefs, creates a host of new needs, that, if they are not satisfied, turn those who feel them to crime. It multiplies social relations: it is the soul of commerce and industry; it thus creates among individuals a thousand occasions for fraud or bad faith that do not exist in the bosom of an ignorant and rude population. It is then in its nature to augment rather than diminish the number of crimes. This point seems to remain today rather generally acknowledged: because in Europe it has been observed that crimes are increasing in countries where education is most widespread. Meanwhile, we will state on this occasion our entire opinion on the influence of education. Its advantages seem to us infinitely superior to its disadvantages. It develops the intelligence and supports all industries. It also protects the moral strength and the material well-being of peoples. The passions that it excites, disastrous to society when nothing satisfies them, become fertile in advantages when they can attain the goal they pursue. Thus, instruction spreads, it is true, a few seeds of corruption among men; but it is also the case that it makes peoples richer and stronger. Within a nation surrounded by enlightened neighbors it is not solely a benefit, but even a political necessity. — See Note on Public Education in the United States, Appendix No. 5.
26. In order to know all the advantages of statistics and to learn the art of their use, it is necessary to read the excellent work that was just published by Mr. Guerry under the title *Essai sur la Statistique Morale de la France*. Paris, 1832.
27. We say that in Massachusetts, where there are fewer convictions, the prisons are defective: they were defective and are no longer; we are obliged to speak of the past in order to appreciate their effects.
28. Great efforts in the United States are necessary to correct a vice that is very common, intemperance. See Note on Temperance Societies, Appendix no. 9

29. Mr. Livingston has more than once proclaimed this truth, which is found energetically expressed in his letter to Roberts Vaux, pages 14 and 15, 1828. See in what terms he speaks, note (*ff*).
30. *Tocqueville's and Beaumont's use of the specific disease "gangrene" seems important, since "gangrener" means "to corrupt" in a figural sense.
31. See Introductory report to the code of prison discipline explanatory of the principles on which the code is founded. By Edward Livingston, pag. 7. — See also *Notices of the Original, and Successive Efforts, To Improve the Discipline of the Prison at Philadelphia, and to Reform the Criminal Code of Pennsylvania: With a Few Observations on the Penitentiary System* by Roberts Vaux, pag. 53 and 54. — See *Du Système Pénitentiaire en Europe et aux États-Unis*, by Mr. Charles Lucas.
32. See Statistical Observations and Comparisons, Appendix no. 17.
33. See Statistical Notes, Appendix no. 16.
34. See Statistical Observations and Comparisons, Appendix no. 17.
35. There are more serious crimes in France; but the total number of offences is lower than in America. See Statistical Observations and Comparisons, Appendix no. 17.
36. See Some Points of Comparison Between France and America, Appendix no. 18.
37. The crime of bestiality, attacking without violence the person of a child, pederasty, etc.
38. See Statistical Observations and Comparisons, Appendix no. 17.
39. See Statistical Observations and Comparisons, Appendix no. 17.
40. See Comparison between France and America, Appendix no. 18.
41. In using the term "first conviction" above, we mean as it respects this prison only; there are nearly twenty who have been in other prisons. (See Report on the Prison of Auburn, of the 1st January 1824, pag. 127). *Note: The first French edition included this footnote in English; I translated only the citation.
42. See Statistical Observations and Summaries, Appendix no. 17.

References

Guerry, André-Michel. 1833. *Essai sur la Statistique Morale de la France*. Paris: Crochard.
Livingston, Edward. 1827. *Introductory Report to the Code of Prison Discipline: Explanatory of the Principles on which the Code is Founded, Being Part of the System of Penal Law Prepared for the State of Louisiana*. London: John Miller.
———. 1828. *Letter from Edward Livingston, Esq. to Roberts Vaux: On the Advantages of the Pennsylvania System of Prison Siscipline, For the Application of*

Which the New Penitentiary Has Been Constructed Near Philadelphia, Etc.. Philadelphia: Jesper Harding.

Lucas, Charles. 1828–1830. *Du Système Pénitentiaire en Europe et aux États-Unis.* 2 vols. Paris: Bossange.

Powers, Gershom. 1828. *Report of Gershom Powers, Agent and Keeper of the State Prison at Auburn, Made to the Legislature, January 7, 1828.* Albany: Croswell and Van Benthuysen.

———. 1829. *Letter of Gershom Powers to Hon. Edward Livingston: Read in the Legislature January 23, 1829.* Albany: Croswell and Van Benthuysen.

Vaux, Roberts. 1826. *Notices of the Original, and Successive Efforts, To Improve the Discipline of the Prison at Philadelphia, and to Reform the Criminal Code of Pennsylvania: With a Few Observations on the Penitentiary System.* Philadelphia: Kimber and Sharpless.

Chapter 4: Financial Part

FIRST SECTION

Distinction between the Philadelphia system and that of Auburn. — The first requires more expensive construction. — The second very favorable to the economy. — Pitfalls to avoid. — Plans. — Estimate by Judge Welles. —Is it advantageous to build prisons by prisoners?

Finally, after identifying the principles and consequences of the penitentiary system in America from the point of view of criminal reformation, it remains only for us to speak of its results in a financial aspect.

This latter point includes the mode of constructing prisons and the maintenance costs of the prisoners compared to the product of their labors.

Construction of the prisons

It is necessary in this respect to distinguish between the Philadelphia system and that of Auburn.

The Philadelphia penitentiary (Cherry-Hill), when it is finished, will have cost 432,000 dollars (2,289,000 fr.); bringing the price of each cell to 1,624 dollars (8,607 fr. 51 c.).[1]

It is true that they have made enormous expenses for its construction that were not necessary. The greatest part of the cost had no other object than the ornament of the building. Gigantic walls, gothic towers, a large iron door, give to this prison the appearance of a fortified castle from the Middle Ages without it resulting in any real advantage for the establishment.[2]

Meanwhile, even if these luxurious expenses had been wisely avoided, there is a considerable amount that is inherent to the Philadelphia system and that would have been impossible to avoid. The convict being, according to this system, always confined, it is necessary that his cell be spacious, well ventilated, equipped with everything that is necessary in a place he never leaves, and large enough to permit him to work without too much inconvenience. It is finally necessary that a small yard be adjoined to this cell, surrounded by walls, in which he can each day, at hours fixed by the rules, breathe the outside air. Now, whatever pains one can take to build this cell and its outbuildings in the most economical manner, it will necessarily be much more expensive than a narrower cell, without a separate yard, and intended only to receive convicts during the night.

The prisons built on the Auburn plan are infinitely less expensive. There are, however, some very great differences in the respective prices of their construction.

This disparity seems at first difficult to explain; but, in deepening the causes, we recognize that the construction of new penitentiaries is expensive or cheap according to the means of implementation that are employed.

The penitentiary at Washington for the District of Columbia will have cost, when it is finished, 188,000 dollars (954,000 fr.). It contains only one hundred sixty cells, each of which will return the sum of 1,125 dollars (5,962 fr. 50 c.); while the penitentiary of Wethersfield, established on the same plan, has cost for two hundred thirty-two cells only 35,000 dollars (185,000 fr.): so that each cell of this prison costs only 150 dollars 86 cents (799 fr. 74 c.).[3]

Since every public expense is made with great thrift in the small State of Connecticut, we could believe that the result that has been obtained is the consequence of extraordinary efforts of which a larger society would not be capable, occupied as it is with other interests.

But the penitentiaries of Singsing and Blackwell Island, built at the same price as that of Wethersfield in the State of New York, the most significant of every State of the Union, prove that Connecticut has done nothing supernatural; the Baltimore penitentiary (Maryland) has not, for its construction, caused more spending.

What increases or diminishes the cost of the construction expenses is the care that some States take to avoid, in this matter, every kind of useless luxury; while others have not the same spirit of economy in this respect.

The Washington penitentiary was built on a sumptuous basis that is more appropriate for a palace than a prison.

The most difficult pitfall to avoid, in similar constructions, is the conceit of the architect, who always aspires to create a building of grand proportions and who is difficultly resigned to erecting a simple and strictly useful building. Some States have, however, triumphed over this reef against which Philadelphia, Pittsburgh, and Washington have crashed.

Of all the establishments founded on the Auburn plan, the construction of the Washington penitentiary was the most expensive.

It seems to us that the reason can be found in the nature of the authority itself that directed the work of this construction.

In general, the individual States of the Union adopt, for the construction of their prisons, the simplest plans: they monitor their execution with zeal and aim at strict economy in the littlest details. On the other hand, the high administration that resides at Washington, more elevated in its views, accepts grand conceptions more easily; and since it is absorbed by a host of general interests, it is obliged to rely for everything that belongs to the execution of the plan on agents who have neither time nor power to monitor it.

Furthermore, every practical man of the United States thinks that the penitentiary system of Auburn presents all conditions of economy for the construction of prisons.

In the houses of detention where the whole discipline consists in the strength of walls and solidity of bolts, thick walls and strong locks are necessary to gain control over the inmates.

In the new penitentiary prisons, these obstacles do not need to be as powerful, because it is not against those that the inmates have to combat each day: it is above all against psychological surveillance, of which they are the object, that they have to struggle continually. Isolated from others by the cell or silence, they are reduced to their individual force. It is therefore unnecessary, to tame them, to have a material force as large as if they were free to associate their efforts.

In truth, the necessity of a cell for each prisoner multiplies the walls and requires a larger area for the prison. But this augmentation is compensated for by a circumstance favorable to economy.

Since the inmates have no communication in the penitentiary, every classification becomes useless, and it is no longer necessary to have in the prison one [living] quarter for the young convicts, another for the criminals more advanced in age, a third for recommitted inmates, et cetera; finally, the principles of the penitentiary system being opposed to any conversation among the prisoners, there is no yard for recreation in modern penitentiaries. Much is economized in the buildings and walls that, in the system of our prisons, exists or should exist.

In sum, it can be said that, managed with attention to economy, the construction of a modern penitentiary must be made less expensively.

Mr. Welles, one of the inspectors of the Wethersfield prison, whose wisdom and experience we have constantly appreciated, often told us that in this matter everything depended on economy in the littlest details. He thinks moreover that one penitentiary of five hundred cells could be constructed using 40,000 dollars (212,000 f.), which would put the expense for each cell at 80 dollars (424 f.).[4]

It would be no doubt impossible to estimate exactly the price of a prison in France by what it costs in the United States. However, we are permitted to think that this price would be approximately the same in France as in America. Because if it is true that among us raw materials are more expensive than in the United States, it is also incontestable that the price of the workforce is much higher in America than in France.[5]

We have seen that in the United States the inmates are sometimes employed to build the prisons. It is thus that the penitentiaries of Singsing, Blackwell Island, and Baltimore have been constructed; however, many persons in America think that this mode of construction is not the most economical and that it is more profitable to build the prison by free laborers. This opinion seems at first in opposition to the nature of things. In fact, the work of free laborers is so expensive that it seems that one would have a clear interest in constructing the prisons by the inmates. But one responds that for the same reason, the high price of the workshops, manufactured articles are sold at a high price. Hence, it follows that the labor of the inmates applied to productive industries yields more for the State than it spends for the work of free laborers.

Nevertheless, this question must be decided according to place and circumstances; its solution, says Judge Welles of Wethersfield, also depends on the situation of the inmates; it is better to leave in the workshops those who are experienced in such industrial work, whose products are considerable; but the prisoners who are useless can be utilized with advantage for the construction of the penitentiary, in serving to transport materials and for other rough work that only requires the maneuvering of material force.[6]

In France, the construction of prisons by the inmates would be even more favorable than it is in America. We envisage the question only under the economic point of view and abstract from the difficulties that the surveillance of prisoners occupied in building their own residence can present.

The sale of manufactured things does not present the same chances of profit in France as in the United States, such that only by employing inmates in the construction of the prison can their work be utilized without running the risk of a depreciation in its products.

We are very sure that the walls that are raised will be profitable, since they have received their intended use even before being constructed: while nothing is more accidental and uncertain than future profit from the sale of merchandise.

If we employ free laborers to build, we pay their salary without diminution, while prisoners occupied in another industry work with every chance of loss and depreciation that is attached to manufactured production. If, on the contrary, the prison is made by the prisoners themselves, the fruit of their labor is immediately gathered; this labor does not procure a profit properly speaking; but it dispenses with an unavoidable burden.

We are well aware that it is not the same in America where, because markets are open to industry, manufacturing production has favorable chances: the object there is to profit, while we only aim to not lose. Finally, it is a great advantage in France to be able to employ the prisoners in a useful and sometimes necessary labor without injuring, by competition, the factories of free laborers.[7]

Second Section

Expensive maintenance of former prisons. — The new are a source of revenue for the State. —Daily expense of the new prisons. — Expense of food only. — Cost of surveillance. — Contract and Regulations. — Combination of these two systems of administration.

Annual Expense of the Prisons[8]

The new system in force in the United States also promises great advantages in relation to annual maintenance expenses; already its effects have, in this regard, surpassed the expectations that were conceived for it.

As long as the former discipline of prisons was in force, the maintenance of inmates was in every State a source of considerable expense. We will mention only two examples: from 1790 until 1826 the State of Connecticut has paid for the support of its prison (Newgate) 204,711 dollars (1,084,968 fr. 30 cent) (*see* Statistical tables, financial part), and the State of New York has paid for the support of the former Newgate prison over twenty-three years, from 1797 until 1819, 646,912 dollars (3,428,633 fr.). In 1819, in the State of New York, in 1827 in Connecticut, the new system is established; the charges diminished immediately in the first of these States, and in the second they changed immediately in an annual review. (*See* Statistical Tables, Financial Part, No. 19).

At Auburn for the last two years the income proves labor exceeded maintenance expenses, and the time is already foreseen when, the construction of Singing being achieved, the labor of prisoners applied entirely to productive industries will cover the expenses of the prison.

From the first year of its institution, the new Connecticut prison (Wethersfield) brought in 1,017 dollars 16 cents (5,390 fr. 95 cent.), expenses deducted; each year the revenue has increased; finally, the profit for the year 1831 was 7,824 dollars 02 cents (41,467 fr. and 30 cent.).

In sum, for three and a half years the new penitentiary that cost so much has, expenses of all kinds deducted, produced for the State a net benefit of 17,139 dollars 53 cents (90,839 fr. 50 cent.)

For three years, from the day of its establishment, the Baltimore penitentiary reported to the State of Maryland 44,344 dollars 45 cents (235,025 fr. 58 cent.) all costs deducted.

Assuredly, all these results cannot be attributed to the penitentiary system alone: and what proves it is that the Baltimore prison was productive even before a penitentiary system had been established there; we think moreover that the best penitentiary is not the one that yields the most; because the hard work and talent of prisoners in the workshops can be stimulated to the detriment of discipline. However, we are forced to acknowledge that this system, once admitted into the prison, is powerful in maintaining its order and regularity; it rests on surveillance at all times.

The labor of the prisoners is then simultaneously more hard-working and productive there.

In any case, in the presence of the numbers that we have just presented, it would be unreasonable to reject the penitentiary system as expensive, since this discipline that is established in the United States at so little cost sustains itself in some States and becomes in still others a source of revenue (*jj*).

In the new prisons each prisoner costs, on average, for his maintenance, his food, his clothing, and the surveillance of which he is the object, 80 cent. (15 cents); the prisons in which this expense is cheaper are those of Wethersfield and Baltimore; it is the most expensive at Auburn: in the various penitentiaries, the food of each prisoner costs per day on average 27 cent. (5 cents 10). It costs only 25 cent. (4 cents 70) at Wethersfield, and returns to 31 cent. (5 cents 85) at Singsing.[9]

In general, the costs of clothing and bedding are almost nothing due to the care to have all things relating to this object made by the prisoners themselves. The cost of surveillance is raised, on average, to 34 cent. (6 cents 41) per day for each prisoner. At Auburn they are the least, and at Singsing they cost the most.

In every new prison it is a greater expense to monitor the prisoners than to feed and clothe them;[10] every saving on this point would be destructive to a system that rests entirely on discipline and consequently on the good choice of employees.

We see that in each of the new prisons the total expense of maintenance, though different in some points, is however approximately always the same; and it is clear that as long as the administration of these establishments will be directed by upright men, and in the same economic view, the number of expenses will not vary much each year: there is a minimum beneath which it cannot descend without the well-being of the prisoners suffering from it, and a maximum beyond which it must not rise without luxury in the administration or embezzlement on the part of employees.

The same is not the case with the number of products that in its nature is as variable as the causes on which it depends. No doubt we must presume that the prison that yields the most is the one where the prisoners work the most. However, the difficulty of selling the objects generated from their work often contradicts this presumption. The things made by them are really produced only by the output that is in place: and even in the United States, where labor of the worker is so expensive, the demand of manufactured products undergoes numerous variations that raise and reduce the price of labor day by day.[11]

In sum, the financial administration of Auburn, Wethersfield, Singsing, and Baltimore appeared to us very cleverly directed; and perhaps the discretionary power with which the superintendents are invested is one of the principal causes of economy. They govern at their will the prison with which they are entrusted, under the surveillance of inspectors; they are responsible, but they act freely.

The administration of these prisons, which combines local control and contract, seems to us very favorable to economy.

There are many things in our prisons for which a high price is paid to the contractor and that are made for very little cost in a prison that governs itself.

At Auburn (in 1830),[12] out of six hundred twenty prisoners, there are one hundred sixty who are occupied for the account and service of the prison: they make everything that serves for the clothing, shoes, laundering, propriety, and order of the prison; four hundred sixty-two alone work for the contractor.

At Wethersfield, the number of prisoners who work for the contractor is proportionately still smaller. In America, they think that it is more profitable to employ a large number of contractors because they can stipulate the fairest conditions for each industry.

Particular care is taken to never make contracts for a long time; the contractors cannot, for this reason, justify their demands under the pretext of disastrous chance such as the possible depreciation of manufactured objects that they risk; often, the duration of the contracts does not exceed one year; it is sometimes less for the labor, and ordinarily six months only for the food contract.

The contractor pays for the day of an inmate approximately half of what he would pay a free worker (*kk*).

The continual renewal of leases allows the administration to seize any chance of economy and profit; it profits by the low rate of commodities in order to cheaply obtain food for the inmates; and if the price of manufactured objects is high, it obtains better conditions from the contractors to whom it hires out the labor of the prisoners; it makes these calculations for each contract, and must for this reason be acquainted with the movement of all industries; often the one prospers to the disadvantage of another; in this case, the prison will regain from one contractor the loss it has suffered with another.

It is perceived that such an order of things requires a perpetual vigilance from the superintendent, a great knowledge of affairs, and a perfect probity that merits him the confidence of the State and of all those who have business with him. The superintendent is not only the director of a prison, he is also a leader of manufacturing who, attentive to the movements of commerce, must incessantly watch in order to put in force the most productive industries in his establishment, and, when he has created value, work towards its most advantageous distribution and sale. This system, which combines the contract with local control, carries with it a rather complicated accounting system; and, in this respect, it will not please those who in every administration aim to see only a single person, in the accounts a single column, and in this column a single number; this simplicity is not seen in the bookkeeping of American prisons. It demands from superintendents a continual activity, from inspectors a meticulous surveillance, and from State Comptrollers a detailed examination.

Let us remark, in closing, that this variety of duties, this faculty of governing the prison or of putting contracts under his responsibility, this vast administration that is both moral and material, serves then to explain why the duties of the superintendent are sought after by men simultaneously intelligent and honorable.

Notes

1. The wall surrounding the Philadelphia prison alone cost almost 200,000 dollars (1,060,000 fr.). It is, however, of all the penitentiaries the one that has the least need of high surrounding walls, since each prisoner is isolated in his cell, which he never leaves. (See Report of the Boston Society and Report of Judge Powers, 1828, pag. 86).
2. In comparing the Philadelphia penitentiary to a castle from the Middle Ages, we only reproduce an image presented by the society of prisons of Philadelphia that drew attention to this resemblance with praise: "This penitentiary," they said, "is the only building in this country, which is calculated to convey to our citizens the external appearance of those magnificent and picturesque castles of the Middle Ages, which contribute so eminently to embellish the scenery of Europe." (See Description of the Eastern Penitentiary).
3. For the price of construction of other penitentiaries, see Financial Part, Appendix no. 19.
4. See Letter of Mr. Welles of Wethersfield, in which is shown the estimate of a prison for five hundred prisoners. This estimate is probably incomplete,

because the most experienced architects always omit some things in their provisions. But even if that would double the cost of his estimation, the construction of the penitentiary would still be half the cost per cell of our prisons. See Appendix no. 12.
5. See note *oo* at the end of the volume.
6. See Letter of Judge Welles, Appendix no. 12
7. See note *s* at the end of the volume.
8. See Statistics, Financial Part, section II, Appendix no. 19, at the end of the volume.
9. *In this paragraph, there seems to be some confusion regarding the numbers. Until this point, Tocqueville and Beaumont have placed American currency in-text, with corresponding French currency in parenthesis. Lieber, however, did not translate the French currency and here puts the number of French currency into his translation as American currency. Thus, Lieber translates: "Every prisoner in the new penitentiaries costs, on an average, for his support, food, clothing, and *surveillance,* fifteen cents; in Wethersfield and Baltimore, the support of the prisoner is the cheapest; at Auburn the dearest: the food costs in the various penitentiaries, on an average, five cents a day per head. At Wethersfield it costs but 4 cents, and at Sing-Sing, five cents" (Beaumont and Tocqueville 1833, p. 79).
10. Surveillance for each prisoner costs six cents more than food per day. See Statistics, Financial Part, Section II, Appendix no. 19.
11. These are those accidental causes that explain why the work day in the prison yields at Baltimore, on average, 1 fr. 39 c. (26 cents 31), while at Auburn it produces only 77 c. (14 cents 59). See Report of 21 December 1829, on the Maryland prison, pages 6 and 7, and financial part at the end of the volume, section II. The sale of manufactured things sometimes proves just as difficult in Connecticut. See Report of 1830, from the inspectors to the legislature. Among us the workday of seventeen thousand five-hundred convicted prisoners in the *maisons centrales* produces, on average, only 23 cents (4 cents 34).
12. See Report on Auburn, 1831.

Reference

Beaumont, Gustave de and Alexis de Tocqueville. 1833. *On the Penitentiary System in the United States and Its Application in France, with an Appendix on Penal Colonies and also Statistical Notes.* Translated by Francis Lieber. Philadelphia: Carey, Lea & Blanchard.

Part II

Chapter 1

Expensiveness of maintaining our prisons: reason for this fact. — They do not correct prisoners, but corrupt them; cause of this corruption; communication of the prisoners among themselves. —Misuse of the *pécule*. —The discipline of our prisons is disastrous to the life of convicts.

During the years 1827, 1828, 1829, and 1830, the State has paid more than 3,300,000 francs each year for the maintenance of eighteen thousand prisoners in the State prisons. Thus, the prisons that yield an income in the United States are in our country a burden on the public treasury. This difference is due to several causes.

The rule of our prisons is less severe, and the labor of the prisoners inevitably suffers from any relaxation in the rule.

The *pécule* of the prisoners absorbs, with us, two-thirds of the products of their labor, while in America it is nothing.

Finally, manufactured articles are sold in France with more difficulty and less profit than in the United States.

The object of the sentence[1] is to punish the guilty and to make them better; in reality, it punishes little, and instead of reforming it corrupts still more. We would expand on this sad truth if we thought that it could be contested. Out of sixteen thousand prisoners who are found in the State prisons at this moment, there are four thousand in a state of reported recidivism:[2] and the government itself now[3] admits that the number of prisoners in recidivism is constantly increasing.[4] The same was formerly the case in America; but since the new penitentiary system has been established, the number of recidivists has been diminishing.

The corruption in our prisons is due to two principal causes. First of all, and most important, is the free communication of the prisoners with each other day and night. How can the moral reformation of prisoners arise in the midst of this assemblage of all crimes, all vices, and all shameful deeds? The convict who arrives in the prison half-depraved leaves there with a complete corruption, and we can say that in the midst of so much infamy, it would be impossible to not become wicked.

The second cause of the depravation of prisoners is found in the misuse that they make of their *pécule*. They spend the part of the *pécule* that is handed to them in prison on excessive food or superfluities, and thus contract disastrous habits. Every expenditure in prison is destructive to order and incompatible with a uniform discipline, without which there is no equality in punishments. The *pécule* is good and really profitable to the convict only when it is given at the moment of his departure from prison. Let us add that, in the present state of things, the part of the *pécule* given to the convict at the time of his release is hardly more useful to him than the part he has spent in the State prison. If, during his imprisonment, he had contracted habits of order and a few principles of morality, the sum, sometimes very considerable, of which he is found the possessor, could be used by him in a wise manner and for his future profit. But, corrupted as he is by imprisonment itself, no sooner is he at liberty than he hastens to spend the fruit of his labors in debaucheries of every kind; and he continues this kind of life until the necessity of recurring to crime brings him back to court and thence to prison.

The prison, whose discipline is corrupting, is at the same time disastrous to the life of prisoners. Among us, the prisoners contained in our State prisons die in the proportion of one to fourteen.[5] In the American penitentiaries one out of forty-nine die, on average.[6]

In these prisons, where death is so rare, the discipline is austere; the law of silence has been imposed on the prisoners; all are subject to a uniform discipline, and the product of their labor cannot be wasted either in debaucheries or superfluous expenditures; the most rigorous punishments strike without pity those who contravene the order; not one hour of rest is accorded them during the day; and every night they are alone.

In our prisons, where death wreaks havoc, the prisoners chat freely together; nothing separates them day and night; rigorous punishments are not inflicted on them; each of them can, by means of his labor, alleviate for himself the rigors of imprisonment; finally, there are, for resting, recreation hours . . .

This severe rule of the American penitentiaries, this complete silence that is imposed on the prisoners there, this perpetual isolation which separates them, and this inflexible uniformity of discipline which cannot become milder for one without injustice to others, are they not in sum rigors full of humanity?

The contagion of mutual communications which corrupt the prisoners in our prisons is not deadlier to their soul than to their body.[7]

We point out here the principal defects that have struck our glance in our central prisons. It is easy to see that we do not present a complete picture of them; for that matter, we say nothing of the houses of arrest and justice, of other departmental prisons, and of the *bagnes*; we speak only of the central prisons intended for great criminals because they are the only ones that contain a population analogous to the one that the American penitentiaries contain.

NOTES

1. *The French word is *la peine*, which translates as either "punishment" or "[prison] sentence."
2. This number has been furnished to us in the office of the Minister of Public Works, thanks to the division of which Mr. Labiche is chief: we have drawn from this source all the documents that we possess on the French prisons.
3. *Or, "today."
4. See Report of the Seals Keeper on Criminal Justice, 1830. Page 16.
5. Documents provided in the office of the Minister.
6. See Statistical Tables, end of volume.
7. The defect of our State prisons is not in their administration, but in the principle itself of their organization. Perhaps it would be impossible to draw a better part of the present system. We have recently seen a central prison (that of Melun) where we have admired the order of labor and the external maintenance of the rule. The direction of central prisons is among others confided, by the Minister of the Interior, to very capable men. But, whatever may be done, one will not render better and one will not prevent the mutual corruption of criminals who do not cease communicating together.

Chapter 2

Application of the penitentiary system to France. —Examination of the objections made against this system. —Theoretically it seems preferable to any other. —What obstacles it would have to conquer to be established among us. These obstacles are in things, in mores, and in the laws. —In things: the existence of badly constructed prisons which must be replaced. —In mores: repugnance of public opinion to corporal punishments; and difficulty of giving the assistance of religious influence to the system. —In the laws: degrading punishments, variety of the modes of imprisonment, and administrative centralization. —Indication of a system of local administration. The penitentiary system, even if established in France, would not product all the effects that have been obtained in the United States. —Situation of the freed convicts. —Surveillance of the high police. —Agricultural colonies. —Even if the system were not adopted entirely, some of its advantages can be borrowed. —Model penitentiary. —Summary.

Could the system of American penitentiaries be established among us?

It seems to us that, considered theoretically and abstracted from the particular obstacles that its execution would encounter in France, this system is good and very practicable in its nature.

It is rejected with various objections that we must examine.

Many persons see in the penitentiary system a philanthropic design that has no other object than to ameliorate the material well-being of prisoners; and since they think that criminals are not too severely punished in their prison, they do not desire a system that would make their condition more comfortable. This opinion rests on a true fact; for a long time, those in France who raised their voices to ask for reforms in the prison discipline called public attention only to clothing, food, and to everything that can be added to the comfort of the convict.[1] So that, in the eyes of many, the adoption of a penitentiary system that necessitates such innovations tends only to ameliorate the material discipline of the prison.

Others, engaged in a way entirely opposite, think that the condition of the prisoners in a prison is so unfortunate that one must fear aggravating it; and if one tells them of a system of which isolation and silence form the base, they say that society does not have the right to treat men with such severity.

Finally, there is a third class of persons who, without pronouncing on the advantages or disadvantages of the penitentiary system, consider it as a utopia coming from the mind of philosophers and intended to enlarge the number of human aberrations. The sentiment of the latter has been, it must be admitted, favored sometimes by the writings of the most distinguished publicists, whose errors in this matter have been received like their sanest opinions.[2]

Thus, Bentham wishes in his panoptic prison that there was always music to help soften the passions of the criminals. Mr. Livingston requests for the young prisoners, and for the convicts themselves, a system of instruction almost as complete as the one that is established in free academies; and Mr. Charles Lucas indicates, as a mode of executing the punishment of imprisonment, a penitentiary system that would be difficult to reconcile with essential principles in criminal matters.[3]

Is it just to blame the severe or extremely mild discipline of penitentiary prisons? Must we condemn this system based on the exaggerations committed by writers who, too preoccupied with philosophical doctrines, have not guarded themselves against the dangers of a theory carried to its furthest consequences?

The new system seems to us, on the contrary, to have been conceived for the very object of avoiding the excess with which it is reproached: freed from severities that are not necessary for its success, unencumbered from indulgences that are sought for only by a badly understood philanthropy.

Finally, its execution is presented to our eyes with all the advantages of an extremely simple practice.

One thinks that two perverse beings united in the same place must corrupt each other: one separates them. The voice of their passions or the turbulence of the world dazed and misguided them; they are isolated and brought thus to reflection. Their communications with the wicked perverted them; they are sentenced to silence. Laziness depraved them; they are made to work. Poverty led them to crime; they are taught a profession. They violated the laws of the country; a punishment is inflicted on them, their life is protected, their body is safe and healthy: but nothing equals their psychological suffering. They are unhappy and deserve to be so; having become better, they will be happy in the society whose laws they will respect. Here is the whole system of the American penitentiaries.

But, it is said, this system, attempted in Europe, has not succeeded: and in order to prove it, the examples of Geneva and Lausanne are cited, where penitentiary prisons have been established at great cost without producing the results that were expected from it for the reformation of convicts.

We think that the example of what has been done in Switzerland must not, under any report, influence what France could do in this respect. Indeed, Switzerland has fallen into the same mistake, in respect to the construction of prisons, that has not always been avoided in the United States, that is in the manner of raising architectural monuments instead of simply constructing some useful establishments. The expense of the Swiss penitentiaries must not, then, in any way be prized as the basis for calculating the probable costs in France for prisons of the same nature. On the other hand, if the discipline of these penitentiaries has not been efficacious in respect to the reformation of prisoners, it is not necessary to lash out at the system in the United States: it is an error to believe that the discipline of the prisons of Geneva and Lausanne is the same as that of the American prisons. The only common point between the prisons of the two countries is that in the one and the other the inmates pass the night in solitary cells. But what establishes a critical difference between the penitentiary system of these two peoples is that in the United States the discipline rests essentially on isolation and silence, while in Switzerland the relations of the inmates among themselves during the day are not prohibited.

It is certain that the liberty of communication accorded to prisoners entirely denatures the American system, or to speak more correctly it births a new system that has no resemblance with the latter.

As for us, as much as we are given to believe that the system founded on isolation and silence is favorable to the reformation of criminals, we are equally inclined to think that the reformation of convicts who communicate together is impossible.

It seems to us therefore that, abstractly speaking, the penitentiary system in the United States, whose superiority over any other prison discipline appears incontestable to us, presents itself to France with all the conditions of success that a theory can offer whose first experiments succeeded. In giving this opinion, we are not blind to the obstacles that this system would have to conquer in order to be established among us.

The obstacles are in things, in mores, and in laws.

First of all, there is the existence of another order of things, established on a different basis and on diametrically opposed principles. The American system has for its foundation the separation of prisoners, and for this reason there are in each penitentiary as many cells as there are convicts. In France, on the contrary, the cellular system established in a general manner is unknown: and in all our prisons most of the prisoners are mixed together during the night in common dormitories. This point suffices to make impracticable among us, for the present, a system that rests entirely on the isolation of criminals. It would be necessary then, in order to put the system into practice, that new prisons be constructed on the model of modern penitentiaries; but here a grave difficulty presents itself resulting from the costs of first construction.

We are far from believing that the expense incurred by this object would be as considerable as is generally calculated. Those who see a model prison at Paris, intended for four hundred convicts, costing 4 million francs,[4] conclude from this with a kind of reason that to accommodate thirty-two thousand prisoners according to the same system it would be necessary to spend 320 million, that is, 10,000 francs for each inmate. The outcome is logical, but the basis of reasoning is defective; in fact, the exaggerated price of the prison to which we allude is only a consequence of the deplorable luxury that presided at its construction.

The elegance, the regularity of its proportions, and every ornament with which its architecture is decorated, are of no use for the discipline of the establishment: they are ruinous for the public treasury and will profit only the architect, who, to transmit his name to posterity, desired to raise a monument.

We will nevertheless remark here that it is necessary, when discussing construction expenses, to distinguish between the Philadelphia system and that of Auburn: we recognized great advantages in the system of complete isolation adopted in Pennsylvania, and if it was only a theoretical question to judge perhaps we would prefer it over the Auburn system; but the price of penitentiaries constructed on the model of Philadelphia is so considerable that it seems to us imprudent to propose the adoption of this plan. It would pose an enormous burden to society, for which the most successful results of the system would be hardly equivalent. Yet the Auburn system, whose theoretical merit is not less incontestable, is, as we have established above, much cheaper in its execution; it is then this system that we would ask to be applied to our prisons if it were a question of only choosing between the two.

But the discipline of Auburn itself would not be entirely established in France without great cost: this cost can certainly not be analogous to those incurred in the erection of the prison model that we just mentioned; we nevertheless believe that, all things considered, the construction (wisely directed) of a modern penitentiary would not cost much more in France than it has cost in the United States (*mm*). Meanwhile, whatever the economy was that presided over this enterprise, it is certain that over 30 million would be necessary for the general establishment of the system: and it will be easily conceived that France will not burden its budget by such an expense in the middle of political circumstances that require from her still more urgent sacrifices.

Is it also not to be feared that the serious interests which absorb the money of France harm the reform of prisons in another way? Do not political events cause such preoccupation that even the most important questions of interior improvement but feebly excite public attention? Every capacity, all intelligence is pointed towards a single object, the life of political society. Any other interest finds indifferent imaginations. Accordingly, men most distinguished by their talents, remarkable writers, capable administrators, in a word all those who exercise some power over opinion, spend their intellectual energy in discussions useful to the government but sterile for social benefit. Must we not fear the consequence of this general disposition for the penitentiary system, and fear to see welcomed with some warmth this institution that, in order to be established, has however need of attention and public favor?

But then, even if the political and pecuniary difficulties that we have just indicated did not exist, and supposing that nothing in the actual state of things would be opposed to internal reforms, the establishment of the penitentiary system in France would still meet with serious difficulties.

The American discipline has, as we have seen, corporal punishments for primary support. Thus, is it not to be feared that a system of which these punishments are the most powerful auxiliary would be badly welcomed by public opinion? If it was true that among us an idea of infamy was attached to this punishment, how can it be inflicted on those persons whose morality we desire to raise? The difficulty is real, and it appears more serious still when we consider the nature itself of the discipline that must be maintained. Silence is the basis of the system: this obligation of a complete silence, which is in no way incompatible with American gravity, would it be so easily reconcilable with the French character? If we believe Mr. Elam Lynds, the French are of any people those who submit most easily to every requirement of the penitentiary system: however, the question appears still new to us and we do not know to what point Mr. Elam Lynds has been able to judge the docility of French convicts in general by observations that he has made in American prisons, where he has seen only a small number of French dispersed amid a multitude of Americans.[5]

As for ourselves, without resolving this problem we believe that the law of silence would be infinitely more difficult to the French than to the American, whose character is taciturn and reflective; and for this reason, it seems to us that it would be even more difficult among us than in America to maintain the penitentiary discipline whose foundation is silence without the aid of corporal punishments. We are especially driven to think thus because the discipline of the American prisons is favored by another circumstance on which we ought not depend. There is in general in the United States a spirit of obedience to the law that is found even in the prisons; without having need to indicate here the political reasons for this fact, we state it; but this spirit of submission to the established order does not exist among us to the same extent. On the contrary, there is in the spirit of the masses in France an unfortunate tendency to break the law; and this penchant for insubordination appears to us of a nature to hinder even the discipline of prisons.

The penitentiary system, to which it would be difficult to give the material support of blows in France, which however seem more necessary to us than others, would perhaps also be deprived of a psychological auxiliary which, in the United States, contributes much to its success.

In America, the movement that has determined the reform of prisons has been essentially religious. It is religious men who have designed and accomplished everything that has been undertaken; they did not act alone; but it is they who, by their zeal, gave impulsion to all and thus excited in every mind the ardor that animated themselves; thus, religion is still one of the fundamental elements of discipline and reform in every new prison today: it is its influence alone that produces complete regeneration; and even in regard to shallower reformations we have seen that it contributes much to obtain them.

It is to be feared that, in France, this religious assistance is lacking in the penitentiary system.

Would there not exist some tepidity on the part of the clergy for this new institution, which the philanthropic among us seem to have seized?

And, on the other hand, if the French clergy should exhibit zeal for the moral reform of criminals, would public opinion view the persons responsible for this mission with favor?

There are among us, in great number, passions against religion and its ministers that do not exist in the United States, and our clergy also undergo perceptions unknown to the religious sects of America.

In France, where for a long time the altar struggled in concert with the throne to defend royal power, we are still not habituated to separate religion from authority, and the passions directed against the latter usually extend to the former.

It happens that, in general, [public] opinion shows itself unfavorable to what is protected by religious zeal; and on their side members of the clergy experience little sympathy for anything presented under the auspices of popular favor.

In America, on the contrary, the State and religion have always been perfectly separated from each other; and one can see political passions rise against the government there without ever addressing religion. This is why religion there is always outside debate: and it is what explains the absence of any hostility between the people and ministers of every sect.

We must add to this point one last observation: it is that in the United States, should the help of men devoted to the church fail, prison reform would not thereby be deprived of help from religious influence.

Accordingly, the society of the United States is itself eminently religious, and this fact still has a great influence on the direction of penitentiary establishments: a crowd of charitable persons, who are engaged in no religious ministry, nevertheless devote a part of their existence to the moral reformation of criminals; since their beliefs are strongly rooted in mores, there is not the lowest employee of the prison who does not have religious principles. For this reason, they never utter a word that is not in harmony with the sermons of the chaplain. The inmate in the United

States thus breathes a religious atmosphere in the penitentiary that comes to him from every part, and he is more susceptible to this influence because his primary education has disposed him to it and he has always lived in a society where great respect for religion is professed.

In general, the convicts among us do not have such favorable dispositions, and outside of prison the ardor of religious zeal is hardly encountered except in ministers of the church.

If they are away from the penitentiary, the influence of religion will disappear: philanthropy will remain for the reformation of criminals. It cannot be contested that there are among us some generous persons who, gifted with a deep sensibility, are ardent to relieve any misery and to heal every wound of humanity: until the present their attention, exclusively occupied with the material lot of the prisoners, has neglected a more precious interest, that of their moral reformation; we see very well, however, that called to this field, their beneficence would not wait: and some success would no doubt arise from their efforts. But these sincerely philanthropic men are rare: most often philanthropy is, among us, only an affair of the imagination. One reads the life of Howard, whose philanthropic virtues are admired, and one finds that it is beautiful to love humanity as he did; but this passion that is born in the head never arrives at the heart, and often evaporates in a journal article.

There are thus in our mores, and in the actual state of minds in France, some psychological obstacles against which the penitentiary system would have to struggle if it was established such as it exists in the United States. These obstacles that we point out certainly cannot always exist. A durable hostility of public opinion against religion and its ministers is not a natural thing; and we do not know at what point a society can conduct itself for a long time without the help of religious beliefs. But here we must not outdistance the present; and among the obstacles actually existing which would harm the penitentiary system in France, what we have just noted is without contradiction one of the gravest.

Our legislation also presents obstacles.

The first results from the very nature of certain penal laws.

At the time when the brand was written in our code, the penitentiary system could not have been established in a uniform manner; because it would have been contradictory to pursue the moral reformation of criminals who had already been branded with an indelible infamy. This punishment has disappeared from our laws, and its abolition, which reason and humanity imperiously demanded, is one less impediment to the efficacy of a good prison discipline. But there still exist in the penal code some provisions that are not less irreconcilable with a complete system of reform. We wish to speak of the infamy attached to most of the punishments and of the variety of punishments.

There are eight punishments in our laws that are expressly called infamous, without counting exposure, which is considered only as the accessory to certain punishments, and that of the ball, which figures in the law only as a mode of implementing work forces (art. 6, 7, 8, 15, and 22 of the penal code).

If we attach infamy to a perpetual punishment, we see little disadvantage to it once the principle of the perpetuity of the punishment is admitted. But is it not an inconsistency to declare infamous by judgement a man who later must reappear in society? To be logical, the law ought to say also that at the expiration of his punishment his honor is given with his liberty. It does not, because infamy, so easy to imprint on the forehead of the guilty, cannot be effaced in the same way. Even if this is the case, perpetual dishonor attached to a temporary punishment seems to us incompatible with the object of the penitentiary system, and we do not know how it would be possible to awaken sentiments of honor and virtue in souls which the law itself has taken care to degrade and debase. To put criminal legislation on this point in harmony with the essential principles of the penitentiary system, a few changes would be necessary; it would suffice to not call infamous the punishments pronounced by the code, and in every case to spare the convict from the transient shame of the pillory and the continuous humiliation of public labor.

It would finally be necessary to abolish from the penal code, if not the variety of punishments, at least the differences that exist in the manner of undergoing them.

The variety of punishments and the disciplines of imprisonment prescribed for each of them have made a great number of different prisons necessary. Since there are criminals of various degrees, and since the inmates are crowded pell-mell into our prisons, it is thought with reason that it would be immoral to mix them and to place under the same roof, in the same workshop, in the same bed, one who has incurred the punishment of twenty years of forced labor and one convicted to one year of imprisonment. There is, then, one prison for galley slaves, another for prisoners with longer sentences; and if the hope of the law was fulfilled, there would be a third prison for those persons correctionally convicted to more than a year [of imprisonment] and a fourth for those whose imprisonment is less than a year. These classifications, whose grounds are understood when one admits in principle the mixture of inmates in the prisons, become clearly useless when the system of isolation during the night and silence during the day is introduced. This system having been established, the least guilty among the convicts can be found placed alongside the most consummate criminal without having to fear the slightest contamination.

There is at the same time every interest to unite criminals of different kinds in establishments of the same nature: all are subject to a uniform discipline; punishment varies only by its duration. We lose thus the exceptional discipline of the *bagnes*, and see the administration of French prisons purged of this strange anomaly that places one third of those convicted in criminal matters under the responsibility of the Minister of the Navy.

It would then be necessary, to put our legislation in this regard in harmony with the penitentiary system, to abolish the provisions of the penal code that prescribe distinct prisons for each kind of convict, each subject to a special discipline.[6]

The second obstacle that our laws contain is found in the too great extent that, among us, the principle of centralization has received, forming the basis of our political society.

There are no doubt general interests for the conservation of which the central power must retain its strength and its unity of action.

Every time that it is necessary to defend the country, to secure its foreign dignity and its tranquility at home, the government must give a uniform impulse to all parts of the social body; this is a right that one cannot rob from it without compromising public safety and national independence.

But however necessary this central direction imprinted on objects of general interest is to the political strength of a country such as ours, as this same centralization is applied to objects of local interest it seems to us contrary to the development of internal prosperity.

It has appeared to us that the success of new prisons in the United States is principally due to the system of local administration, under whose influence they are formed.

In general, the first expenses of construction are made with economy, because those who execute the plan are the same who pay the expenses. There is little embezzlement to dread on the part of inferior agents, because those who do the act are near to those who guard them; finally, when the building is constructed and the establishment instituted, the same men who have put a lively interest in its creation are occupied with ardor at putting it into action; and even after the system that they have introduced there is in force they do not cease to monitor its execution. They are preoccupied with it as with a thing that is their own work and in whose success their honor is interested.

Once a State has thus founded a useful establishment, all others, animated by a happy spirit of emulation, show themselves zealous to imitate it.

Would our laws and our mores, which in France leave everything to the central power, give to the penitentiary system the same ease for its foundation and maintenance among us? We do not think so.

If it was a matter of creating a law, this centralization would be far from being an obstacle; in fact, it would be much easier for our government to obtain from the chambers the adoption of the penitentiary system for all of France than it has been in America for the governors of the diverse States to direct the same principle by the different legislatures to which it had to make request.

But after this principle is written into law it must still be executed: it is here that the difficulties begin among us.

Is it to be feared that the buildings which the government will construct for this object may not be established on an economical plan, and that the costs of construction, monitored by secondary agents, will greatly exceed the quotes that will have been presented? And yet, if the first attempts are too expensive, they will discourage public opinion and the most zealous partisans of the penitentiary system. Supposing these first obstacles overcome, should we not fear the indifference of the locality for the success of an establishment that will not be its work, and yet will not prosper if it is only the protégé of the administrative zeal of employees of the prison? Finally, how can the central power, whose action is uniform, subject the penitentiary system to the modifications that are necessary because of mores and local needs?

It seems to us difficult to hope for the success of the penitentiary system in France and to expect great results if its establishment and direction are the work of the government, and if for those central houses of detention that exist at this moment we are limited to substituting others for them, built only on a better plan.

Would not the chances of success be greater, if one were to confer to the departments, at their expense and direction, according to certain general principles written in a law common to all, the care of constructing their own prisons of every kind, not excepting those intended for great criminals?

The laws of 1791 posed in principle that the surveillance of prisons belonged essentially to the municipal authority, and their direction to the administrative authority of the department.[7] These same laws prescribed, for the discipline of prisons, a great number of important innovations, and contained the same germ of the penitentiary system since adopted in the United States.[8]

But the principles that they proclaimed received only an incomplete execution. Upon his accession to the consulate, Bonaparte decreed the establishment of central houses of detention without taking the trouble to abolish by constitutional powers the laws contrary to his decree. This institution was destructive to any direction and local surveillance. Consequently, most of the central prisons presently existing are none other than ancient convents, scattered here and there in all of France, some near cities, others in the middle of fields.

However, Bonaparte recognized in 1810 that each department must have, besides the houses of justice and arrest, a prison intended to receive prisoners convicted for minor offences.

If, therefore, the system of a general prison for each department were adopted, we would return to the principle of the laws of 1791 and would only extend to every criminal the local imprisonment that Bonaparte himself desired to establish for those convicted of minor offences.

This extension would be without disadvantages regarding the discipline of the prison, since we always reason under the hypothesis of a change in the penitentiary discipline, founded on the silence and isolation of the inmates.

The State, in stripping itself of the right to direct the central prisons, would abandon a prerogative that is only onerous for it without being beneficial for the departments. It would conserve a right of impulse, control, and surveillance; but instead of acting itself, it would make others act.

We hasten to say that we present here only the draft of a system that, in order to be adopted, must be matured; we are certain that those which exist are bad, but the remedy does not appear as sure as the existence of the evil.

Our prisons, created and governed entirely by the central power, are expensive and powerless to reform the inmates; we have seen in America cheap prisons raised in small States under the influence of localities, in which every corruption has been avoided: it is under the impression of this contrast that we write.

We are not ignorant of the fact that the situation of the various American states and that of our departments cannot be compared. Our departments possess no political individuality; their circumscription has been purely administrative until now. Accustomed to the yoke of centralization, they have no local life; and it is not, we must agree, the care of governing a prison that will give them the taste and habits of individual administration; however, it is permitted to hope that political life will enter further into the mores of the department and that the interests of administration will be more and more localized.

If our hopes in this respect were realized, the system that we indicate would become practicable and the penitentiary discipline in France would find itself surrounded by a great party of favorable circumstances which have determined its success in the United States.

Each department, having its central prison, would contribute only to the maintenance of its own convicts; while today the wealthy and populated department, whose inhabitants commit few crimes, pays more for the maintenance of central prisons than the poor department, whose smaller population furnishes more criminals.

If the department constructed its own prison, it would vote with less repugnance for the funds which it would itself employ. The construction that would be its work would be no doubt less elegant and less regular than if it had been built by the central power assisted by its architects . . . but the beauty of the building adds little to the merit of the establishment. The great advantage of a local construction would be to strongly excite the interest of its founders. The French government, acknowledging how necessary local direction and surveillance are to the prosperity of prisons, has tried at several times to interest the departments in the administration of their prisons;[9] but its attempts in this respect always remain without success. Whatever the government may do, the localities will never assume interest in what they have not made themselves.

Would not this constant surveillance, this continual and meticulous care, this constant solicitude and zeal, necessary to the success of a penitentiary prison, be attached to the kind of establishment created by the department that would be witness of its birth, development, and progress?

Among the obstacles which would impede the execution of this system are some which are perhaps less serious than one thinks and which we believe we must indicate. It is feared, with reason, that in multiplying the number of central prisons, the price of their construction does not proportionally increase at all. Consequently, eighty prisons intended to contain thirty-two thousand prisoners would cost more to build than twenty prisons fitted to contain the same number of individuals. But we will remark that if the advantage of economy belongs to great constructions, on the other hand the merit of a better discipline is unique to smaller establishments.

It is certain that, in order to be well directed, a prison must not contain too great a number of criminals; the personal safety of the employees and the order of the discipline are perpetually threatened in establishments where two or three thousand malefactors are assembled (as in the *bagnes*). It is the small number of inmates at Wethersfield that forms one of the principal advantages of the penitentiary; there, the superintendent and the chaplain have an in-depth knowledge of the morality of each inmate, and after having studied the evil, they endeavor to cure it. At Singsing, where there are one thousand prisoners, a similar study is impossible: thus, it is not even attempted. Supposing that the thirty-two thousand prisoners that are in France were divided into eighty-six departmental prisons, there would be on average about four hundred in each of them. Indeed, there are departments whose large and corrupted population furnishes many criminals, while others, whose inhabitants are less numerous and more honest, send few convicts to the prisons; but what would result from this fact? The departments in which the most crimes are committed would construct the larger prisons, while the others would erect smaller penitentiaries. In this respect, our departments would find themselves in the exact same position as the different States of the American Union.

The State of New York, which counts two million inhabitants, has two State prisons, of which one alone contains a thousand prisoners. Connecticut, which has only two hundred sixty thousand inhabitants, possesses a single prison where only two hundred criminals are contained.

Few departments would have a prison as populated as that of Singsing, whose principle defect is in the excessive number of its inhabitants. Conversely, many departments whose population is analogous to that of Connecticut would not have more criminals in their prisons than there are at Wethersfield; and it is permitted to think that this limitation on the number would be an advantage, since Wethersfield, which is the smallest penitentiary in America, is also the best. Finally, the example of this penitentiary that, albeit less considerable, has cost less to build than all the others, would it not prove only that one can, with the help of an economical mind and local surveillance, regain most of the expense incurred by a construction made on a small scale?

One perceives with what reserve we have been indicating these ideas. To proceed safely and steadily on a similar path, it would be necessary to possess some administrative knowledge that we lack, and to be supported by documents that are not at our disposal.

In the absence of the lights we need to guide us, we do not present a system; we have only raised a question whose solution is of vital interest to society, and on which we call the lights of all enlightened men.

Now, supposing the penitentiary system established and prospering in France, perhaps we ought not to expect from it all the positive results that it produced in the United States.

Thus, we doubt that the labor of inmates in the prison would be as productive for the State as it is in America, even admitting that one fully eliminated the *pécule* of the convicts. It is in fact incontestable that manufactured articles do not find among us the markets that are open to them in the United States; it is necessary, to estimate the revenue of the prison, to take account of productions whose output would not take place.

The penitentiary prison, which will be less productive among us, will be for an analogous reason less efficacious in respect to the reformation of the convicts.

In America, where wages are so high, the convicts easily find labor when they leave the prison; and this circumstance singularly favors their good conduct at the time of their return into society:[10] in France, the position of freed convicts is infinitely less favorable; and even when they have resolved to lead an honest life, they are often brought back to crime by a disastrous necessity. In the United States, the freed criminal ordinarily leaves the State where his conviction is known; he changes his name and moves to a neighboring State where he can begin a new existence: among us, everything is obstacle and embarrassment for the convict who leaves prison. The police surveillance which he undergoes chains him to a fixed residence that he cannot leave without becoming guilty of a new infraction; he is condemned to live in the place where his first crime is officially known; and everything contributes to deprive him of the livelihood that is necessary to him. The defect of such a state of things is such that everybody feels it: and we doubt that it will be maintained for a long time.

The surveillance of the high police, such as it is exercised today, is less useful to society than disastrous to the freed convict. It would be only advantageous if, by its influence, society, informed of the real situation of each free criminal, had some way to procure work for those who have none and aide for those who have need of it. Would not the government be able to find these means in the foundation of agricultural colonies such as those that flourish in Belgium and Holland today?[11] If such colonies were founded in France on the still uncultivated parts of our soil, no idler would complain of lacking work without the government offering it to him; beggars, vagabonds, paupers, and all free prisoners whose number, always growing, incessantly threatens the safety of individuals and even the tranquility of the State would find a place in the colony, where they would work to augment the wealth of the country.

Perhaps we can also place there those sentenced to short terms of imprisonment. There would be an incontestable advantage in introducing there the greatest number of prisoners possible. In fact, one of the principal advantages of agricultural colonies is that it does not harm individual industries:[12] they consequently avoid one of the greatest dangers presented by the establishment of factories in prisons.[13] The system of agricultural colonies therefore deserves serious attention on the part of political men; it seems that after having admitted the principle of it, it ought to be extended as much as possible, and that one can easily reconcile its application with the principles of the penitentiary system. Finally, the establishment of agricultural colonies would have among other advantages that of deriving successful results from that administrative surveillance whose consequences are almost all disastrous; and it would thus make one of the obstacles that damage the establishment of the penitentiary system disappear.

We have pointed out the difficulties that the penitentiary system would encounter in France, and we have not disguised the gravity of them. We do not deny that we see very great obstacles to the establishment of this system among us, such as it exists in the United States, and surrounded by all the circumstances that accompany it. We are, however, far from thinking that nothing can be done for the improvement of our prisons.

We have never had the idea that France could suddenly attempt a general revolution in its prison system, raze the old establishments, suddenly build new ones, and consecrate to this single goal, in a single moment, enormous sums, for a share of which interests of another nature present themselves. But we can reasonably ask for progressive reforms in the system of our prisons; and if it was true that it would be impossible to found in France a discipline supported by the assistance of the whip; if it was true that we lack the assistance of local influence for the success of the establishment and the aid of religion for the progress of moral reformation; it is also certain that, without adopting in its entirety the system of American prisons, a part of its principles and advantages can be borrowed from it. Thus, every new prison that would be constructed according to the cellular system would have an incontestable superiority over the present prisons. Separation of prisoners during the night would stop the most dangerous communications and destroy one of the most active elements of corruption; we cannot imagine what would be the objection to the cellular system if, as we have every reason to think, the prisons constructed according to this system do not cost more than others.[14] We have said that it seems to us difficult to maintain an inviolable silence between convicts without the aid of corporal punishments. However, this is only one opinion on our part; and the example of Wethersfield, where for several years the prisoners were managed without the whip, does it not tend to prove that this severe means of discipline is not absolutely necessary? It seems to us that the chance of success would be well worth a trial on the part of the government; this trial seems to us much more reasonable, so that if one were not entirely successful, one would be sure of a way to arrive very close to the goal; thus, even if public opinion shows itself completely hostile to corporal punishments, in order to establish the law of silence one would be reduced to disciplinary punishments of another nature, such as absolute solitude without work and reduction of food; there is good ground to think that with the aid of these latter punishments, less rigorous than the first but nevertheless efficacious, silence would be obtained well enough to almost avoid the disadvantage of moral communications among the inmates; the most important point would be first to proclaim the principle of isolation and silence as regulating the discipline of the new prisons; the application of the principle would perhaps meet with more obstacles among us, because it would not be aided by such energetic auxiliaries; but we do not doubt that in seeing this goal, a great good would be already attained.[15] By means of this incomplete system, one would perhaps not attain radical reformations, but great corruptions would be avoided and we would thus borrow from the American system those of its advantages that are most incontestable.

We think that the government would do a useful thing in establishing a model penitentiary, constructed on the plan of the American prisons and governed, as much as possible, according to the disciplinary rules that are used in these prisons. It would be necessary that this construction, designed according to all the simplicity of the plans that we made, were executed without any architectural luxury. Care should be taken to place in the penitentiary only the newly convicted; for if the nucleus of an old prison were introduced suddenly, individuals accustomed to the tolerant discipline of our central prisons would undergo the severity of the new discipline with difficulty.

In summary, we have pointed out in the first two parts of this report the advantages of the penitentiary system in the United States. The inflexible severity of a uniform discipline, equality of punishments, religious instruction and labor, are substituted for the discipline of violence and laziness; liberty of communications is replaced by isolation or silence; reformation of criminals succeeds their corruption; in the place of jailers, honorable men to direct the penitentiaries; economy in expenditure instead of disorder and embezzlement: such are the characteristics that we have recognized in the new American system.

For France, the necessity of reform in the discipline of its prisons is urgent and acknowledged by everyone; the ever-rising number of recommitted criminals is a fact that strikes every mind. The freed convicts, who are only criminals further corrupted by their sojourn in prisons, become wherever they show themselves a proper object of fear. In our inability to correct the guilty, will society take part in deporting them? Let France cast her eyes on England; let her judge if it would be wise to imitate her.[16]

There are defects in our prisons, infected by a frightful corruption; but this wound, which is extended each day, can it then be healed? And do we not see prisons efficacious for the reformation of the wicked in a country whose prisons, for fifteen years, were worse than ours?

Do not declare incurable an evil that others have healed: do not condemn the prison discipline; labor to reform it.

To arrive at this end, the combination of many efforts is necessary. First of all, it is necessary that every writer who by their talent exerts some influence on public opinion strive to imprint on it a new direction, and to succeed so far that the moral part of the discipline is not more neglected than the improvement of the material discipline of the prison. It is necessary that interest in reform preoccupies the mind and passes into every conviction. A controversy, even, would be desirable between the diverse organs of opinion, in order to state what are the disciplinary punishments that can be allowed without injuring public sentiment and those that are incompatible with our civilization and our mores.

It would be necessary, finally, that the government put our legislation in harmony with the principles of the penitentiary system, and above all that it provoke the deliberation of the most enlightened men on these serious matters.

The future success of the penitentiary system depends much on its debut among us. It is important, therefore, that every precaution is made to secure the success of the first establishment that will be created in France. It is above all necessary, for this establishment to succeed, that public opinion is occupied with it, welcoming it favorably, the protégé of its vote, and instead of throwing up barriers surrounds it with that moral assistance without which no institution can prosper in a free country.

Notes

1. The prisons have for a long time deserved most of the reproaches addressed to their material discipline: it is thus with reason that the abuse and defects infecting the prisons were attacked; we are consequently very far from blaming the efforts of those who have managed to correct the evil; except alongside wise and measured philanthropy are found those whose zeal exceeds the goal; there are in France some prisons that one can no doubt desire to change respecting their cleanliness; but it can be said in general that in our prisons the prisoners are clothed and nourished as well as they must be; any amelioration on this point would effect a contrary abuse that would not be less deplorable than the defect it was intended to remedy. The task of those who justly call for better clothes and better bread for the prisoners seems at an end; however, the work of men who believe that there is a psychological [or: moral] part that must not be neglected in the discipline of a prison must begin.
2. *The division and classification of forms of thought, particularly into groups of three, is a peculiarly Tocquevillian trait in *Democracy in America*.
3. See *Du système pénal et répressif*. Mr. Lucas has seen the whole penal legislation in the penitentiary system. He said: "It is not just a matter of reforming the wicked; once this reformation is effected, the criminal must return to society." There are some true things in this system; but it is incomplete. The first object of punishment is not to reform the convict, but rather to give society a useful and moral example: this is obtained by inflicting on the guilty a punishment commensurate to his crime. Every punishment that is not in harmony with the offence shocks public equity, and is immoral whether from its severity or by its indulgence. But it is also important for society that those who are punished as an example are corrected in prison: here is the second object of punishment, less serious than the first, because

its consequences are less extensive. The system of Mr. Charles Lucas is defective in that it considers only the second point and entirely neglects the first. He always puts punishments as a means of reformation for the guilty and not as a means of example for society. It is for this reason that he wishes that liberty be restored to the criminal as soon as there is a presumption of his regeneration. Seeing in imprisonment only a time of trial, during which the convict shows himself relatively quick in repentance and correction, he makes the duration of the sentence depend on conduct in prison. However, conduct in prison proves absolutely nothing; we have since recognized that it is an indication more contrary than favorable (See Chapter II, Section II, §7). Besides, who will judge the conversion of convicts? We can judge a fact: but who will descend into the conscience of the prisoner in order to see his repentance? —And where is the reparation due to society? And how to prove to society that the criminal has become an honest man and that this change is worth expiation?

4. The prison of the Rue de la Roquette near Père-Lachaise.
5. See our conversation with Mr. Elam Lynds, end of the volume.
6. While establishing a single and similar discipline of detention for all convicts, we can conceive very well that there would be, according to the gravity of the punishments assessed by their title or by their duration, some differences in the discipline: thus, prisoners for police offences might be accorded a more considerable *pécule* than that accorded to the criminals stricken by a more severe punishment, etc., etc. If we ask for a uniform discipline, we only wish to reclaim the application of the fundamental principles of the penitentiary system, isolation at night and silence during the day, and we assert that once these two principles are allowed, the variety of houses of detention becomes useless.
7. See Laws of 22 July, 29 September, and 6 October 1791.
8. Article 16 of the law of 6 October 1791 reads: "Every person sentenced to confinement alone in an enlightened place, without chains or attachments; cannot have for the duration of his punishment any communication with the other convicts, or with outside persons." Here is exactly the theory of solitary imprisonment: it is the system of Cherry Hill (Philadelphia).
9. See: Circular of the Minister of the Interior of 22 March 1816; ordinance of 9 April 1819.
10. "It must not be concealed, that one great reason why crimes are so infrequent is the full employment the whole country offers to those who are willing to labor, while at the same time the ordinary rate of wages for a healthy man is sufficient to support him and a family. This is a point which you will not lose sight of in comparing the institutions of America with those of Europe." (Letter of the Attorney General of the State of Maryland,

30 January 1832). *Note: Since the paragraph is originally included in English in the French edition, we simply translate the French citation.
11. See: Note on Agricultural Colonies, Appendix no. 4.
12. *Lieber translates: "the industry of citizens" (Beaumont and Tocqueville 1833, p. 104).
13. See alphabetical note *s*.
14. See alphabetical note *mm*.
15. *The longest sentence in the book.
16. See Appendix on Penal Colonies, no. 2

References

Beaumont, Gustave de and Alexis de Tocqueville. 1833. *On the Penitentiary System in the United States and Its Application in France, with an Appendix on Penal Colonies and also Statistical Notes*. Translated by Francis Lieber. Philadelphia: Carey, Lea & Blanchard.

Lucas, Charles. 1827. *Du système pénal et du système répressif en général, de la peine de mort en particulier*. Paris: Charles-Béchet.

Part III: On Houses of Refuge

Chapter 1

Origin of the houses of refuge in the United States. —System of their organization. —Elements of which they are composed. —The establishment has all the rights of a guardian over juvenile delinquents. —The house of refuge is a medium between the prison and college. —Discipline of these establishments. —Houses of refuge of New York, Philadelphia, and Boston. —How the time of the children is divided between labor in the workshop and school. —Contract. —Disciplinary means. —Remarkable theory of discipline established in the Boston House of Refuge. —Those of New York and Philadelphia, less elevated, but preferable. What causes the children of the refuge to leave? —Effects of houses of refuge in respect to reformation.

Governor Clinton, whose name is forever celebrated in the State of New York, said: "The houses of refuge are the best penitentiary establishments that have been conceived by the genius of man and instituted by his beneficence." We will finish our work with an examination of them, as we announced in the beginning.

The first house of refuge was created in the city of New York in 1825; Boston in 1826, and Philadelphia in 1828, have seen similar establishments raise their walls; and there is every indication that Baltimore will soon have an analogous one. It is possible, at this occasion, to judge how great the power of association is in the United States.

Touched by the dreadful fate of young delinquents who were indiscriminately mixed with hardened criminals in the prisons, some individuals of New York conceived an idea of remedying the evil; they united their efforts, labored first to enlighten public opinion, and then, giving the example of generosity, to establish a house of refuge they made pecuniary sacrifices that have been followed by a multitude of subscriptions.

The houses of refuge, arising thus from the assembly of several charitable individuals, are therefore in their origin a private institution: yet they received the sanction of public authority; any individual who is contained there is in legal custody; but in approving the houses of refuge, the law does not interfere at all in their direction and surveillance, which it leaves to the individuals who are its founders.

Each year the State gives pecuniary help to aide in the expense of their maintenance; and yet it takes no part in their administration.

The governmental authority for the houses of refuge resides in the entire body of subscribers, who contributed to the erection of the buildings or who contribute still each day to the annual maintenance expenses. The subscribers meet and nominate directors (managers), to whom they confer the power of governing the establishment in the manner that they judge most advantageous. These directors choose employees and make any administrative regulations that are necessary. There is a permanent active committee in their midst, responsible for superintending the execution of every proceeding: this is the executive power of the institution. The employees of the house of refuge are the immediate agents of the acting committee, to whom they submit all their actions. They do not have to give an account to the government, which does not ask it of them.

Among the employees, the superintendent is the one whose choice attracts the attention of the directors, because he is the soul of the administration.

Thus abandoned to themselves, and subject to the control of public opinion alone, the houses of refuge prosper; the efforts and aide that they support are all the more powerful as they are spontaneous and free. The expenses that they entail are without trouble or regret because they are voluntary, and the least subscriber has his part in the administration and consequently in the success of the establishment. Although the costs of construction and maintenance are not paid by the State, they are not less a responsibility of society; but at least they burden those who, because of their wealth, can best support them and who find a moral indemnity in the sacrifice that they have had the merit of imposing on themselves.

Houses of refuge are composed of two distinct elements: they receive young people of both sexes, under the age of twenty, stricken by a conviction for crime or offence; and those who, without having incurred any conviction or judgement, are sent there as a precautionary measure.

Nobody contests the necessity of houses of refuge for young convicts. In any time and in any country, we have recognized the disadvantage of placing in the same room and subjecting to the same discipline young delinquents and the guilty whom age has hardened in crime; the prisoner whose age is still tender has most often committed only a slight fault; how to associate him in the prison with those who have hideous crimes to expiate? This defect is so serious that judges hesitate to prosecute juvenile delinquents, and the jury to convict them. But then another danger presents itself. Encouraged by impunity, they give themselves up to new disorders, from which a punishment proportional to their fault might have forever saved them.

The house of refuge, whose discipline is neither too severe for a child nor too mild for a guilty person, has then for its object simultaneously withdrawing the young delinquent from the severity of punishment and from the dangers of impunity.

The individuals not convicted but sent to the refuge are young boys and girls who, without having committed any crime, are found in a position alarming for society and for themselves: orphans whose misery has led them to vagabondage or beggary; children abandoned by their parents, who lead a disordered life; all those in a word who, by their fault, or that of their parents, or by the fault of fortune alone, are fallen into a state so close to crime that they would become infallibly guilty if they retained their liberty.[1]

It has therefore been thought that houses of refuge must simultaneously contain young criminals and those who were on the point of becoming one; one avoids the infamy of judgement for the latter; for all, the defilement of prison. And finally, that no shame be attached to the presence of this juvenile delinquent in the house of refuge, this establishment has been given a name that awakens only the idea of misfortune. The house of refuge, though including in its care a certain number of convicts, is thus not a prison. Those who are inmates there do not submit to a punishment: and, in general, the decision by which the children are sent to the refuge has neither the solemnity nor the form of a judgment. It is here that we will point out a fact that seems to us to be characteristic of the institution. The magistrates who send children to the refuge never determine the duration of time that the juvenile delinquent must pass there; they simply place them in the house, which from that moment acquires over them all the rights of a guardian. This right of guardianship expires when the child attains his twentieth year; but even before he has reached this age, the directors of the establishment can make him leave it, if his interest requires it.

The house of refuge is a medium between college and prison; the young delinquents are received there less to punish them than to give them the education that their parents or fortune refused them; the magistrates cannot therefore establish the duration of their stay at the refuge because they cannot predict what time will be necessary to correct the children and reform their vicious tendencies.[2]

The care of this assessment is left to the directors of the establishment, who, seeing each day the children entrusted to their surveillance, judge their progress and designate to each the liberty that can be accorded without danger: meanwhile, even when a child leaves the house of refuge as a result of his good conduct, he does not cease to be under the patronage of the directors until he attains his twentieth year; and if he does not realize the expectations that he had been thought to have, the latter have the right to bring him back to the house of refuge and can, in order to compel him to return there, employ the severest means.

Some have, in Pennsylvania, raised some objections against the right attributed to the houses of refuge to receive individuals who have not committed any crime or incurred any conviction:[3] such a power, they said, is contrary to the Constitution of the United States: they added that the ability accorded to the directors of the establishment in diminishing or prolonging at their whim the duration of the detention was a source of arbitrariness that cannot be tolerated in a free society. Theoretically, it would have been difficult to answer these objections: however, it was understood that the houses of refuge alleviated the fate of young criminals instead of aggravating it, and those children not convicted who were contained there were not victims of persecution but only deprived of a disastrous liberty.

Nobody today raises his voice against houses of refuge. We understand, however, with what reserve the functions of those who have power to send children there must be exercised when we imagine that they have the right to take a child from his father and mother to place him in the establishment, and that they must exercise this authority every time the parents must blame themselves for the disorders of their child. The law has foreseen the possibility of abuse and has attempted to remedy it: the child has, under the law, the right to appeal to the ordinary judge against the decision of the functionary who sends him to the refuge. The parents have the same power; and it is not without example that this right has been exercised.

Besides, it is not persecution and tyranny that are to be feared in these establishments. However necessary it is that the house of refuge not present the severity and the wholly material discipline of a prison, it would be equally dangerous if it were to offer the too indulgent and wholly intellectual discipline of a school. But if these establishments in America deviate from the true goal of their institution, it would be less by inclining towards too much severity than by tending towards too much mildness.

The fundamental principles on which the houses of refuge rest are simple: at New York and Philadelphia, the children are separated during the night in solitary cells; during the day, they can communicate together. Separation at night seems urgently required by the interest of good mores; it is not necessary during the day; complete isolation would be fatal to children and silence cannot be maintained among them without punishments whose violence alone must make them repugnant. There would be, besides, the most serious disadvantages to depriving them of social relations, without which their intellectual progress cannot be developed.

At Boston, they are separated neither during the day or night: we have not noticed that the communications of night were disadvantageous in this house of refuge; but their danger is not less great in our eyes and it is avoided at Boston only by a zeal and vigilance altogether extraordinary, which would be wrong, in general, to expect from men most dedicated to their duties.

The time of the children is divided between education that they receive and material labors in which they are engaged: they are taught elementary knowledge that will be useful to them in the course of life, and they learn a trade whose exercise will furnish him with a livelihood. Their intellectual labors give to the establishment the appearance of a primary institution, and their labor in the workshop is the same as in a prison. These are the two different traits that are characteristic of the house of refuge.

They are not limited to exercising the skill of their hands and to developing their intelligence: above all, they attempt to form their hearts and to inculcate in them some principles of religious morals. Mr. Hart, superintendent of the House of Refuge at New York, often told us that without the aid of religion, he did not think the success of his efforts possible.

When the juvenile delinquent arrives at the refuge the superintendent acquaints him with the regulation of the establishment, and first gives him these two counsels as guides for his conduct, remarkable for their simplicity: 1. Never lie; 2. Do the best you can. The superintendent then inscribes the name of the newcomer in the great register of moralities. This register is intended to receive any information concerning the children. It contains, as much as possible, their previous life, their conduct during their stay in the house and after they leave the establishment. The child is then placed in the class that his age or his morality make known to be suitable. Mr. Hart, of New York, defines the first class as those children who never swear, never lie, never use any obscene or inappropriate expression in their language, and who are equally hard working at school and in the workshop. According to Mr. Welles, of Boston, this same class is composed of those who make positive, regular, and constant efforts towards the good.

At Boston, admission of the child into the refuge is accompanied by circumstances that appear to us worthy of being reported: the establishment forms a small society, mirror of the great. To be received into its midst, it is necessary not only to know the laws and to freely submit to them, but also to be accepted as a member of the society by all those who already compose it. The reception is consequently preceded by a proving time, after which the candidate is admitted or rejected by the majority of votes.[4]

In each of the houses of refuge the subjects are divided into good and bad classes. Conduct, according to whether it is good or bad, makes the juvenile delinquents pass from one to the other. The good classes enjoy privileges that are refused to the bad; and the latter are subject to privations that the first are not.[5]

Each day, at least eight hours are dedicated to labor in the workshops, where the children are occupied with some useful business, such as carpentry, the profession of shoemakers, those of the tailor and carpenter, et cetera. Four hours are given to study. Prayers are offered after rising and before going to bed. Three meals each take a half-hour; in sum, the day is about fifteen hours: there are nine hours at night for sleep. Such is, with little difference, the order established in the two houses of refuge of New York and Philadelphia. This order is the same each day, and varies only according to the change of seasons, which affects the hour of rising and sleeping; it is not completely similar at Boston, where the moral part of the education occupies a much greater place. In this latter house of refuge, only five and a half hours are dedicated to labor in the workshops; another four hours are passed in school; more than one hour is given to religious instruction; and all the children have, each day, two and a quarter hours of recreation. These hours of leisure are not the least profitable ones to the young inmates. Mr. Welles, the superintendent, takes part in all their games, and while their physical strength develops during bodily exercises, their moral character is formed under the influence of a superior man, who, though present to their eyes, is really masked in the middle of them, and whose authority is never greater than in the moment when he does not make them feel it.

In school, the children learn to read, to write, and to count; they are also given some knowledge in history and geography. The method used in each of these is that of Lancaster's mutual education. In general, the children show a very great facility to grasp the ideas offered them by the teacher. It has often been remarked in America that the houses of refuge are composed of a class of children more intelligent than any other; and the nature itself of these establishments explains this fact: they generally receive children abandoned by their family, or who have escaped from paternal homes, and who, for this reason, have been reduced to their own strength early on, and constrained to find the resources to exist in their intelligence and natural means. Therefore, the progress that they make in education is not surprising. Most of them have, besides, a restless mind, adventurous, avid to know. This disposition, which first pushed them to their ruin, becomes for them a powerful source of success in school. No useful books that they desire to instruct themselves are withheld from them. There exists at Philadelphia, in the library of the establishment, more than fifteen hundred volumes that are wholly for use by the children.

The hours of labor are invariably established for all, and no-one has the right to be excused from them. Each has a fixed task, after the accomplishment of which the young inmate who is more active than the others can begin recreation.

The surveillance, of which the children are the object in the school and workshop, does not cease during the leisure hours. They play freely with each other, but gambling is strictly forbidden.

Everything in their discipline is favorable to health. Each day they are required to wash their feet and hands. They are always properly dressed; and their food, although disgusting, is abundant and healthy. No one can eat anything other than what is prescribed by the ordinary discipline of the establishment; and water is the only beverage there. There is no cafeteria where the children can go to obtain additional food or drink; and one watches with care that they do not procure it by communication with outside persons.

Food, clothing, and bedding for the young inmates is supplied by the administration. The labor alone of the children is let out by contract; and then the restrictions that on this point abound in the contract are such that the contractor cannot have any kind of influence in the establishment.

In New York and Philadelphia, eight hours a day are given to the contractor for labor; at Boston, five and a half hours only. The contractor or his agents come into the house of refuge to teach various professions that are exercised there. Still, they cannot maintain any conversation with the children, nor keep them in the workshops one minute longer than the fixed time. One understands that with such conditions, one cannot stipulate markets with the contractors that are advantageous from a financial sense; but the children are not made to work to take a profit from their labors; the only object in view is to give them habits of industry and to teach them a useful profession.[6]

It is therefore not surprising if the maintenance of the houses of refuge costs more than other penitentiary establishments. On the one hand, the young inmate is better nourished, better clothed than those convicted for crimes, and a greater expense is incurred for their education; and on the other hand, their labor cannot yield as much as that of criminals who are sent into the prisons for a long time. Thus, as we will soon see, the young inmate leaves the establishment as soon as he can be advantageously placed elsewhere. He is put in liberty as soon as he knows a trade, that is, the instant his work begins to produce something for the establishment.

The administration of houses of refuge in the United States is almost entirely locally governed; it is reasonably thought that the contract system, applied to all branches of administration, would be irreconcilable with the moral direction that the establishment must receive.

Although in sum maintaining the young inmates is expensive, everything seems calculated in a manner to avoid costs. The houses of refuge simultaneously contain boys and girls who, although united under the same roof, are perfectly separated. But this proximity allows for entrusting to the girls much of the work that, done by others, would be to the charge of the house. Thus, they wash clothes, mend the effects, and make most of the clothes that are worn by the children or by themselves; they also make food for the whole house; in this way, not only do they avoid expenses for the establishment, but they also usefully occupy the young girls for whom it would be difficult to find productive work in another way.

This order of things is established and maintained by the aid of disciplinary means that we must examine. Two motives are employed: punishment and rewards. But, in applying this principle, it is necessary to distinguish between the houses of refuge of New York and Philadelphia, and that of Boston.

In the first two establishments, the punishments inflicted on the children who contravene the discipline are:

1. Privation of recreation;
2. Solitary confinement in a cell;
3. Reduction of food to bread and water;
4. And in serious cases, corporal punishment, that is to say, blows of the whip.

In New York, the regulation expressly authorizes the application of blows. That of Philadelphia does not dare to expressly permit it, but merely does not prohibit them: the distribution of punishments belongs to the superintendent who enjoys a discretionary power in the establishment.

While the disobedient young prisoners are subjected to various punishments, according to the gravity of their fault, some honorific distinctions are accorded to the children whose conduct is good: besides the honor of belonging to the first classes, those who distinguish themselves from the others are given a mark of honor that makes them recognized among all; finally, the superintendent designates among the best subjects a certain number of monitors, to whom he confides a part of the surveillance for which he is responsible: and this testimony of confidence is, for those whom he has chosen, a distinction to which the elected attach great value.

In Boston, corporal punishments are excluded from the house of refuge; the discipline of this establishment is wholly psychological and rests on principles that belong to the highest philosophy.

Everything there tends to relieve the soul of the young inmates and to make them jealous of their own respect and that of their equals: to achieve this, they are treated as if they were men and like members of a free society.

We treat this theory under the point of view of discipline, because it seems to us that the high opinion that is inspired in the child of his morality and social condition is not only proper to effect his reformation, but is also the cleverest means to obtain a complete submission from him.

It is above all a principle well established in the house that no one can be punished for a fault not prescribed by the laws of God, be it by those of the country or by the laws of the establishment. Here is the first principle in criminal matters proclaimed in the house of refuge. The regulation also contains the following principle:

> "Since it is outside the power of man to punish disrespect towards the Divinity, it suffices to forbid any participation in religious offices to those who will be rendered guilty, thus leaving the criminal to the justice of God that attends him in the future."

In the Boston House of Refuge, the child withdrawn from religious service incurs, in the eyes of his comrades and in his own opinion, the most terrible of any punishment.

It is said elsewhere that the children will not be allowed to denounce the faults of one another; and in the article which follows it is added that no one will be punished for a fault sincerely confessed. We know of public establishments in France where denunciation is encouraged, and where it is exercised by the good subjects of the house.

A register of moralities also exists at Boston, where each has his account of good or bad marks: but what distinguishes this register from those found in other houses of refuge is that at Boston, each child gives himself the marks that concern him. Every night, the young inmates are consecutively questioned; each is asked to judge his conduct of the day: and it is on his declaration that the mark concerning him is written. Experience teaches that he always judges himself more severely than he would be judged by others. It is also often necessary to reform the severity, the injustice itself, of the sentence.

When difficulties are presented on the classification of moralities, or some young inmates have committed infractions to the discipline, a trial takes place. A dozen judges taken from among the children of the establishment are gathered, and they pronounce either the conviction or the acquittal of the accused.

Each time that it is necessary to elect from among them a judge or a monitor the community assembles itself, proceeds to the elections, and the candidate who obtains the majority of votes is proclaimed by the president. Nothing is more serious than the manner in which these electors and jurors exercise their functions of ten years.

One will forgive us for entering into the explanation of this system and for having pointed out the smallest details. We do not need to say that we do not take these child citizens seriously. But we believed ourselves obliged to analyze a system remarkable for its originality. Moreover, there is more depth than is thought in these political plays that accord so well with the institutions of the country. Perhaps these impressions of childhood and this precocious use of liberty contribute more strongly to make the young delinquents more obedient to the laws. And without preoccupying ourselves with this political result, such a system is at least powerful as a means of moral education.

Indeed, one understands the elasticity of which these young souls are capable when one excites therein all the proper sentiments to elevate them above themselves.

However, discipline has other weapons that it uses when the psychological means just mentioned are insufficient.

The children whose conduct is good enjoy great privileges.

They alone participate in the elections and are alone eligible; the voice of those who belong to the first class counts for two: a kind of double vote of which the others cannot be jealous, because it depends only on themselves to obtain the same favor. The good [children] are depositaries of the most important keys of the house; they freely go out of the establishment and leave their spots in the places of assembly without having need of permission; they are believed on their word in every occasion, and their birthday is celebrated. Not all the good children enjoy these privileges; but whoever belongs to a good class has the right to a few of these prerogatives.

The punishments imposed on the class of the bad [children] are: privation of the electoral right, of the right of eligibility; for most, they cannot go in to the room of the superintendent nor speak to him without his permission, and they are not allowed to converse with the other young inmates; finally, when this is necessary, a punishment is inflicted on the delinquent which materially affects him. Sometimes he is made to wear handcuffs; sometimes a band is put on his eyes; or, finally, he is confined in a solitary cell.

Such is the system of the Boston House of Refuge.[7]

Those establishments of New York and Philadelphia, although infinitely less remarkable, are perhaps better: not that the Boston House of Refuge does not appear to us admirably directed and superior to the other two; but its success seems to us much less a consequence of the system itself than of the distinguished man who puts it in practice.

We have already said that the mixing of the children during the night is the serious defect of this house of refuge: the system that is established rests therefore on an elevated theory that risks not always being perfectly understood; and its being put into force would lead to great difficulties if the superintendent does not find in his spirit immense resources to triumph over them.

At New York and Philadelphia, on the contrary, the theory is simple. Isolation at night, classification during the day, labor, education, all in such an order of things is easily conceived and executed; it is not necessary to have a profound genius to invent this system, nor a continual effort to maintain it.

In summarizing this point, the discipline of Boston belongs to an order of ideas much more elevated than that of New York and Philadelphia; but it is difficult to practice.

The system of these latter establishments, founded on a simpler theory, has the merit of being within reach of the whole world. It is possible to find superintendents who agree with the Philadelphia system: but we must not hope to encounter men such as Mr. Welles.

Despite the well-marked difference between the two systems, of which one can be practiced only by superior minds, while the other is up to the standard of ordinary intelligences, we must acknowledge that, in the end, both in the one and the other case, the success of the houses of refuge essentially depends on the superintendent. It is he who puts into action the principles on which the system rests, and he must, in order to arrive at them, unite in his person a great number of qualities whose assemblage is as necessary as they are rare.

If a model of a superintendent for the houses of refuge were required, it would perhaps be impossible to find a better one than what is offered by Mr. Welles and Mr. Hart, who are at the head of the houses of refuge of Boston and New York. A constant zeal and an indefatigable vigilance are their lesser qualities; to a distinguished mind they join an equal character whose firmness does not exclude indulgence. They have faith in the religious principles that they teach and confidence in their efforts. Gifted with a deep sensibility, they obtain still more from the children by touching their hearts than by addressing their intelligence. Finally, they consider each young delinquent as their child; it is not a profession that they perform, it is a duty that they are happy to fulfill.

We have seen how the young inmate enters the refuge and what discipline he undergoes.

Let us now examine what causes the child to leave and try to follow him into the society where he re-enters.

The principle stated above, that the prisoner in the house of refuge does not undergo a punishment, finds here its application. Since he has been sent to the refuge only in his interest, the child leaves as soon as his interest requires.

When, therefore, he has learned a profession; when, having acquired moral and industrious habits over one or several years, it is thought that he can become a useful member of society; at this time, he is not released purely and simply; for, what would become of him in the world, alone, without support, unknown by anyone? He would find himself exactly in the situation where he was before having entered the house of refuge. This disastrous pitfall is avoided: the superintendent attempts to make the exit from the establishment an occasion to put each in apprenticeship to some artisan, or to place him as a servant to some honest family; he avoids sending him to a city where he would rediscover bad habits and companions of his first disorders; and anytime he has the occasion, he prefers to give him employment among farmers.

In the moment when he leaves the establishment, they give him a paper whose style is touching and that contains advice for his future conduct; the gift of a Bible is added to it.

In general, they have recognized the disadvantages of giving the young inmate his liberty before at least one year of staying in the house has given him habits of order.

In leaving the refuge, he does not cease to belong to the establishment that, in putting him in an apprenticeship, reserves over him all the rights of a tutor over his student; and if he leaves the master with whom he has been placed, he is, according to the law, brought back to the refuge, where he remains under the discipline of the house until a new trial once again proves him to be judged worthy of his liberty. Therefore, he can be thus consecutively brought back to the establishment and restored to liberty as often as the directors judge appropriate; and their power, in this respect, ceases only the day the inmate attains the age of eighteen, if it is a girl, and twenty, if it is a boy.

During his apprenticeship, the child is always the object of attention of the house of refuge. The superintendent corresponds with him and strives, by his counsels, to keep him on a good path; the child writes on his part to the superintendent, and more than once the latter has received from young delinquents letters full of touching expressions of their gratitude.

Now, what results have been obtained? Does the discipline of these establishments really reform? And can we support the theory by statistics?

If we consider only the system itself, it seems very difficult not to admit its efficacy. If it is possible to obtain the moral reformation of some human beings, it seems that it must be hoped for from these young inmates, among whom there has been less crime than inexperience, and in whom all the generous passions of youth can be excited. With a criminal, whose corruption is old and entrenched, honest sentiment is not awakened because the sentiment is extinct in him; in the child, this sentiment exists; only it has not yet been excited. It seems to us, then, that a system that is applied to correct vicious tendencies in order to birth only good inspirations gives a protector to those who had none, a profession to those who were deprived, habits of order and labor to the vagrant and beggar whom idleness had corrupted, elementary education and religious principles to the child whose education had been neglected; it seems to us, speaking among ourselves, that a similar system must be fertile in benefits.

There are, however, cases when the reform of juvenile delinquents is almost impossible to obtain; thus, the experience of the superintendents whom we have seen taught them that reform of young girls who had evil mores is a kind of chimera that is useless to pursue. For the boys, the most difficult to correct are those who have acquired habits of theft and drunkenness; their regeneration, however, is not as desperate as that of girls who have been seduced or are prostitutes.

It is generally thought in the United States that it is necessary to avoid receiving young boys older than sixteen and girls older than fourteen years into the refuge; after this age, their reformation is difficult to obtain through the discipline of these establishments, which is less fit for them than the severe discipline of prisons.

At Philadelphia, it is estimated that more than half of the children who left the refuge have good conduct.[8]

Desiring to verify for ourselves the effects produced by the House of Refuge of New York, we made a complete analysis of the great register of moralities, and examined separately the article of each child entering the refuge, we researched what has been his conduct since re-entering society.⁹

Out of four hundred twenty-seven young male delinquents who left the refuge, eighty-five held good conduct, and forty-one an excellent conduct. There are thirty-four of whom the information obtained is bad, and twenty-four of whom it is very bad. For thirty-seven of them, the information is doubtful or contradictory; for twenty-four, they are more good than bad; and for fourteen, more bad than good.

Out of eighty-six young girls who left the refuge, thirty-seven have had good conduct; eleven, excellent conduct; twenty-two, bad conduct; sixteen, very bad. For ten the information is doubtful; three appear to have held conduct more good than bad, and three others [appear to have held] conduct more bad than good.

Thus, out of the five hundred thirteen children who, after having been confined in the New York House of Refuge, returned to society, more than two hundred have been saved from infallible ruin and have abandoned a life of disorder and crime for an honest and harmonious existence.

Notes

1. We found, when visiting the House of Refuge of New York, that more than half the children who have been received there until this day are there because of evils that would have been imputed to them. Thus, out of five hundred thirteen children, one hundred thirty-five lost their father, forty their mother, sixty-seven were orphans, fifty-one had been pushed into crime by notorious misconduct or lack of care by their parents; there are forty-seven whose mother had remarried.
2. The various authorities who can send children to the house of refuge are:

    1. The courts of criminal justice;
    2. Police officers;
    3. Commissioners of the hospital of the poor (Almshouse).

    See §17 of title 7 (chapter 1) 4th part of the revised statutes of the State of New York: "Whenever any person under the age of sixteen will be convicted of a felony, the Court, instead of sentencing to imprisonment in a state prison, can order his detention in the House of Refuge established in the city of New York by the society instituted for the reformation of juvenile delinquents, unless the court has been informed by the so-called society that the House of Refuge has no available space."

3. *Lieber inserts a footnote: "This seems a mistake. Children cannot be sent there who have not committed a crime: for poor children, who have none to take care of them, and become a charge on the public, and consequently vagrants, are considered, technically, criminal: vagrancy is a crime, though the result often of misfortune. The constitutional doubt was, as to the legality of confining children, merely charged with a crime, and not convicted of it" (Beaumont and Tocqueville 1833, p. 113).
4. See Regulation of the Boston House of Refuge, by Mr. Welles [Appendix No. 13, bis].
5. See Various Regulations of the Houses of Refuge in Boston, New York, and Philadelphia.
6. We see that in the United States there is nothing that resembles what is practiced among us. In the Madelonettes prison, consecrated for young prisoners at Paris, the discipline is entirely invaded by the contractor. He considers each child as his personal property; and if one intends to give instruction to the young prisoners, the contractor does not permit it. "*We waste*," he says, "*the time that is mine.*" He cares only for his material interest; that of the children does not touch him. Thus, he thinks only to draw the most money possible from their labor. Since a trade takes a long time to learn, he rarely takes the trouble to teach the children; he prefers occupying them with certain manual labors that necessitate neither skill nor cleverness, such as cardboard packaging, fastening, etc., etc. These labors, productive for him, are in no way useful for the children, who in leaving the house will have no profession to exercise. *Note: "Adresse" and "habileté," as they are used in this sentence, really mean the same thing: "skill." "Habile" generally means "clever," indicating the activity of intelligence. The use of two interchangeable words emphasizes the attribute of work that should be a priority in reforming individuals: the intelligent use and development of skill, rather than simply physical or habitual labor.
7. See the translation that we give of this regulation at the end of the volume.
8. See Conversation with the Director of the House of Refuge of Philadelphia, [Appendix] No. 15.
9. Any information that was necessary for us to make this verification has been put at our disposal with an extreme alacrity, and as we found ourselves thus in possession of original documents we have been able to form for ourselves a precise opinion of the conduct of all the children after their time in the refuge. Our examination focused on all children admitted into the refuge from 1 January 1825 until 1 January 1829. Since this latter year, many subjects have been received into the House of Refuge of New York and several have left; but those who passed into society have had very little time, so that their conduct proves nothing in their favor; to be decisive, the proof must be longer.

Reference

Beaumont, Gustave de and Alexis de Tocqueville. 1833. *On the Penitentiary System in the United States and Its Application in France, with an Appendix on Penal Colonies and also Statistical Notes.* Translated by Francis Lieber. Philadelphia: Carey, Lea & Blanchard.

Chapter 2

Application of the system of houses of refuge to our houses of correction. —State of our penal legislation relative to children under sixteen years old and detained for crimes or offences, or as a precautionary measure. —They are corrupted in the prisons. —Modifications to make in penal legislation and in the discipline of the houses of correction.

If France borrowed from the American houses of refuge some of the principles on which these establishments rest, she would remedy one of the principal defects of its prisons.

According to our laws, criminals less than sixteen years old must not be mixed with older convicts; and the law gives the name "house of correction" to the place that must contain them. However, with few exceptions, juvenile delinquents and old criminals are found intermingled in our prisons. There is more: one knows that the child less than sixteen years old, who, since he lacks discernment, was acquitted, must nevertheless, depending on the circumstances, be sent back to his parents or to a house of correction to be brought up and detained for such a number of years as the judgement will determine and that will not exceed the period wherein he will have completed his twentieth year.

Thus, when a child who has been accused of a crime is acquitted, the tribunals are the masters either to give him to his parents or send him into a house of correction. This alternative makes the intention of the law easy to grasp. If the parents produce character references as to suitability,[1] the child will be returned into their hands so that they can correct his depraved tendencies and reform his bad habits. On the contrary, if the judges have fair grounds[2] for thinking that the disorders of the child are due to the unfortunate examples of his family, they will keep themselves from returning him to his parents, near whom he would complete his corruption, and they will send him to a house of correction that serves him less as a prison than as a school; he will be brought up and detained, says the law. However, we ask, is the intention of the legislature fulfilled? And do the young prisoners receive the education that the law intended to procure for them?

One can say that, in general, the prisons that contain the juvenile delinquents among us are only schools of crime; thus, any judge who knows the corrupting discipline of these prisons is reluctant to condemn an indicted youth, whatever evidence of his fault; they prefer to absolve him and free him rather than to contribute to his corruption by sending him to a prison; but this indulgence, whose motive is understood so easily, is not less disastrous for the guilty, who finds in impunity an encouragement to crime.

There is also a right sanctioned by our civil laws, and whose exercise is in some way suspended by the defect of our prisons; we would like to speak of the power belonging to the parents to imprison those of their minor children whose conduct is reprehensible.

What parents will want to use their authority if they know into what den of corruption their child will be thrown when leaving the paternal house?

There is then, a void in our prison discipline which is important to fill.

We can accomplish this by establishing houses of refuge or of correction, based on the imitation of those whose picture we have presented.

It will, nevertheless, be difficult to entirely adopt the American system among us; for example, the power given to every police officer in the United States to send children whose conduct is suspicious to the house of refuge, even if no offence can be imputed to them; the exorbitant right they also have of taking a child from his parents when they do not sufficiently take care of his education; would they not be as contradictory to our mores as to our laws?

But the discipline of the American houses of refuge would have great advantages in France, applied only to young convicts or to those who, without being declared guilty, must be imprisoned for a determined time in execution of a judgement.

If our houses of correction, whose weakness frightens every court, experienced reform, the judges would without reluctance send there a crowd of juvenile delinquents, vagrants, beggars, et cetera, who abound in every city and whose errant life and lazy conduct infallibly lead to crime. This reform can be made by establishing solitary cells in houses of correction that would stop communication at night, and adopting a system of instruction and labor analogous to that which is in force at New York and Philadelphia.

It would be necessary, however, for the success of the houses of correction in France, to make an important change in our legislation.

Most of the happy effects that are produced in the houses of refuge in the United States are due principally to the discretionary power that the directors of these establishments have to retain or release according to their will the children whose guardianship is entrusted to them; they use this right in the sole interest of the juvenile delinquent, for whom they take care to procure an advantageous place, either as a domestic worker or as an apprentice: and each time that a favorable occasion presents itself, they can grasp it because they have the entire disposal of the children contained in the refuge.

According to our laws, the director of a house of correction cannot do anything similar; he would be obliged, to release a young prisoner, to wait for the expiration of the time established by the ruling. What would result from it? Only that after leaving the house of correction, the child finds himself as humiliated respecting his fate as before entering there: he would be no doubt full of good resolutions and good principles, but incapable of putting them into practice.

It seems to us that a single modification to article 66 of the penal code would remedy this disadvantage in great part.

Juvenile delinquents younger than sixteen years old are of two kinds: those who, having acted with discernment, are declared guilty and convicted; and those who, having acted without discernment, are acquitted, and imprisoned only in the interest of their education. Regarding the first, their fate is entirely fixed by the ruling and must be so; they have committed a crime, and they must suffer the punishment. The one is correlative to the other. The courts alone can pronounce and determine the duration of this punishment; when it is fixed, it must be undergone in its entire extent according to the terms of the ruling: in this case, the interest of the child is of little importance; it is not only for the purpose of correction that he is imprisoned: it is above all in the interest of society and for the sake of an example that a punishment is inflicted.

But the child, acquitted as lacking discernment, is in a different position: he is retained in a house of correction not in order to secure his person, but because we think that he will be better there than with his family; we want to give him a good education that he would not find elsewhere; he is judged only unfortunate, and society is responsible to give him what has been denied by fortune; it is not for public retribution, but more in his personal interest that he is placed in the house of correction; since he has committed no crime, no punishment is to be inflicted.

Regarding the young prisoners who are found in this position, it seems to us that the duration of their stay in the house of correction must not be fixed by the courts. We understand well that the power to send them there is left to the judicial authority alone, according to the circumstances of which it would have appraisal: but why burden them at the same time, as the law does, with determining the number of years during which the education of the child will be provided? As if it were possible to foresee for each child the time that will be necessary to correct his vices and reform his bad habits!

Would it not be better to give to the inspectors and the director of the house the guardianship of the child whose education is confided to them, and to invest them with any right that guardianship carries?

If it were thus, the directors of these establishments would study the dispositions of the children placed under their authority; they would be more able to seize the proper moment to effectually put them in liberty; the time of the stay in the houses of correction would thus be determined in a much more rational way. And if a good opportunity presented itself for someone among them, either to be an apprentice or another advantageous circumstance, the directors would benefit for the placement.

Even if any of the advantages that it promises do not result from this change, there would already be a greater good by effacing from our laws the provision that is in question. This provision is in fact the source of the gravest abuse: it will surprise us little if we consider that it confers to the courts a power that it does not also give them the right to regulate. Thus, it allows them to directly send into the house of correction, for a certain number of years (at their discretion), children acquitted for lack of discernment: but on what will they fundamentally build to decide the number of years during which the child will remain in the house of correction? The law is silent on this point: it is what they themselves cannot know.

When a court pronounces a punishment, it measures it by the offence; but on what to measure the stay at the refuge, when it is important to the education of a child whose intellectual state is unknown by the court, and whose progress, whether more or less rapid, the court cannot foresee?

This impossibility of finding a basis for the sentence has led to a completely arbitrary execution of the law on the part of the court. Judges will condemn a child to be imprisoned until his fifteenth or twentieth year without having any kind of motive for choosing one term longer than another: note that this badly defined authority often leads to the most shocking decisions.

Does a child less than sixteen years old appear before a tribunal? The first question that is examined is that of discernment: if it is judged that he acted with discernment, he is sentenced to be imprisoned in the house of correction; since it is a punishment pronounced by the court in proportion to the offence, it appears not very serious considering the youth of the guilty. The latter then incurs a condemnation to several months of imprisonment only.

However, let us consider a second accused youth of the same age; his crime has no gravity, and the tribunal recognizes that he acted without discernment. Very well, the latter will be sent for several years into the house of correction, in truth to be brought up and imprisoned, but in fact to be locked up in the same prison as the first, with this difference: that he remains there a very long time, while the one who will have been declared guilty stays there only a very short time.

Thus, it can be said with reason that for children less than sixteen years old it would be better to be declared guilty than acquitted. Whoever has experience in criminal justice will acknowledge the existence of the defect that we point out; this defect is not imputable to the judge, it belongs entirely to the law and to the mode of its execution. This evil would be remedied in great part if, in every case where children are imprisoned without being convicted, the courts ordered their entrance into the house of correction without irrevocably fixing the duration of their imprisonment; by the judgement, the directors of the house would be authorized to keep the child until a finished time; but it would be permissible for them, according to the circumstances, to lengthen it before the expiration of the term.

They would not be able to detain him for a longer time than the established period, but they would be free to keep him less.

It seems to us, then, that there would be great advantages in changing the provision of the law with which we are concerned. Houses of correction would then become, in the true sense of the word, houses of refuge, and they would be able to exercise a beneficial influence on the soul of the juvenile delinquent that, in the present state of our legislation, does not belong to them. Besides, we indicate here only the principal changes that would need to be executed to arrive at this goal; many questions connected with this subject will have to be discussed and dealt with in-depth if we want to produce a reform that is fertile with successful results. Thus, it will first be necessary to examine what would be the best way to interest the public in the success of this reform; to determine the elements of which the houses of refuge must be composed; to fix the principles of their organization, and to discuss the question in what place and in what number these establishments must be founded, et cetera. All these questions, and many others that we pass over silently, need to be submitted to the examination of enlightened men and those versed simultaneously in the knowledge of our laws, our mores, and the present state of our prisons.

If this discipline was introduced among us, we must strive to remove anything that is of a nature to compromise its success.

We have already pointed out the pitfall that is most important to avoid in this matter, that is to say, the difficulty of maintaining the house of refuge at equal distance from the school and the prison. In the United States, one is too close to the first, and this fault can become disastrous to the houses of refuge where the children, excited by their parents themselves, will want, without necessity, to search for advantages that they would not find amidst their families. We must not ignore that these establishments, to fulfill their true object, must, although different from the prison, conserve a part of its harshness; and that the material wellbeing as well as the moral instruction the children find in houses of refuge must not make their fate enviable by children whose life is irreproachable.

Let us be reminded on this occasion of a truth that cannot be ignored without danger, which is that the abuse of philanthropic institutions is as disastrous to society as the evil they are intended to cure.

Notes

1. *The literal translation is: "present guarantees of morality."
2. *Or, "just motives."

Part IV: Appendices

Appendix: On Penal Colonies

Preface

We believe we ought to treat with some development the question of penal colonies, because we have observed that in France the most widespread opinion is favorable to the system of deportation. A great number of general councils[1] have pronounced in favor of this punishment, and some clever writers have touted its effects; if public opinion should go further in this direction, and should finally be able to entice the government to follow it, France would find herself engaged in an enterprise with immense costs and very uncertain success.

Such, at least, is our conviction; and it is because we are deeply aware of these dangers that you will forgive us if we report them with some detail.

The system of deportation presents some advantages that we must acknowledge at the outset.

Of all punishments, that of deportation is the only one that, without being cruel, nevertheless frees society from the presence of the guilty.

The imprisoned criminal can break his chains; once freed, at the expiration of his sentence, he becomes an object of well-founded fear for any who surround him; the deported person reappears only rarely on the native soil; with him departs a fertile seed of disorders and new crimes.

This advantage is no doubt great; and it could not fail to strike the minds of a nation where the number of criminals is increasing, and in whose midst a whole population of malefactors is already arising.

The system of deportation therefore rests on a true idea, very proper, by its simplicity, to descend into the masses, which never have the time to investigate the subject. We do not know what to do with criminals in the bosom of the fatherland; export them under another sky.

Our goal here is to indicate that this measure, so simple in appearance, is surrounded, in its execution, with difficulties that are always very great, often insurmountable; and that it does not even attain, as a result, the principal goal that is proposed by those adopting it.

Chapter 1: Difficulties That the System of Deportation Presents as Legal Theory

The first difficulties are encountered in the legislation itself.

To which criminals shall one apply the punishment of deportation?

Shall it be only to those sentenced for life? But then the utility of the measure is very limited. Those convicted for life are always in small number; they are already rendered harmless. Regarding them, the political question becomes a philanthropic question, and nothing more.

The criminals whom society has a real interest in exiling far from it are those convicted for time, who, after the expiration of their sentence, recover the use of liberty. But to those the system of deportation cannot be applied without reserve.

Let us suppose that any individual who will be deported to a penal colony is prohibited, regardless of the gravity of his crime, from ever reappearing on the territory of the mother country: in this way we would have attained, no doubt, the principal goal that the legislator proposes to himself; but the punishment of deportation, thus understood, will present, in its application, a great number of obstacles.

Its greatest defect will consist in its being entirely disproportionate to the nature of certain crimes, and in striking guilty persons who are essentially different in a similar way. Assuredly, the individual sentenced for life cannot be placed on the same level as one whom the law destines only to a detention of five years. Both, however, will have to be called to end their days far from their family and their country. For the one, deportation will be an alleviation of his punishment; for the other, an enormous aggravation. And by this new penal scale, the least guilty will be the most severely punished.

After having kept the criminals in the site of deportation until the expiration of their punishment, shall one provide them on the contrary a way to return to their country? But then we will fail to achieve the most important goal of the penal colonies, which is to dry up little by little the source of crimes in the mother country by making their authors disappear each day. One certainly cannot believe that the convict returns to his region an honest man simply because he has been to the antipodes or has been forced to make a voyage around the world. Penal colonies do not correct, as do penitentiaries, by reforming[2] the individual who is sent there. They change him by giving him interests other than those of crime, by creating a future for him; he will not be corrected if he nourishes the idea of returning.

The English give to the freed convict the oft-illusory possibility of returning to the native soil; but they do not furnish them money with which to pay passage.

This system has still other disadvantages: first, it does not prevent a great number of criminals, the most adroit and dangerous of all, from reappearing in the midst of the society that has banished them;[3] and, in addition, it creates in the colony a class of men who, having preserved, during the time they are undergoing their punishment, the desire to return to Europe, have not been reformed; after the expiration of their sentence, these men are not connected to their new country by anything; they burn with the desire to leave it; they have no future, consequently no industry; their presence threatens the repose of the colony a hundred times more than that of the prisoners themselves, whose passions they share without being restrained by the same chains.[4]

The system of deportation presents, therefore, as a legal theory, a problem that is difficult to solve.

But its application gives birth to even more insurmountable difficulties.

CHAPTER 2: DIFFICULTIES THAT ARE PRESENTED TO THE ESTABLISHMENT OF A PENAL COLONY

Choice of a proper site to found it. —Cost of the first establishment. — Difficulties and dangers that surround the infancy of the colony. —Results obtained by the penal colony; it does not save any money in the charges of the treasury; it augments the number of criminals. —Budget of the Australian colonies. —Increase of crimes in England. —Deportation, envisaged as a means of colonization. —It creates colonies hostile to the mother country. —Colonies founded in this way always resent their first origin. —Example of Australia.

It is certainly not a small enterprise to establish a colony, even when one intends to compose it of healthy elements, and when one has in his power all the desirable means of execution.

The history of the Europeans in the two Indies proves very well what the difficulties and dangers are that always surround the birth of such establishments.

All these difficulties present themselves in the foundation of a penal colony, and many others still that are peculiar to these types of colonies.

First, it is extremely difficult to find a suitable site to found it; the considerations that determine this choice are of an entirely special nature; it is necessary that the region be healthy; and, in general, an uninhabited land is not so before the first twenty-five years of its clearing; then, if its climate differs essentially from that of Europe, the life of the Europeans there will always run great dangers.

It is thus desirable that the land which is sought for be located precisely between certain degrees of latitude and not beyond.

We say that it is important that the soil of a colony should be healthy and that it should be such from the first days; this necessity is much more felt for prisoners than for free colonists.

The convict is a man already weakened by the vices that eventually brought him to crime. He has been subjected, before arriving at the site of his destination, to privations and fatigues which, almost always, have damaged his health more or less; finally, at the site itself of his exile, it is rare to find in him that psychological energy, that physical and intellectual activity that, even in an unhealthy climate, sustains the health of the free colonist and often allows him to brave with impunity the dangers that surround him.

There are many statesmen, and perhaps even some philanthropists can be found, who would not be stopped by this difficulty, and who would respond to us from the depths of their souls: what does it matter, after all, that these guilty men go to die far from our eyes? Society, which rejects them, will not call for an account of their fate. This answer does not satisfy us. We are not systematically opposed to the death penalty, but we think that it must be inflicted fairly; and we do not believe that men's lives can be thus removed by detour and deception.

For an ordinary colony, it is certainly an advantage to be situated near the mother country; this can be understood without any commentary.

The first condition of a penal colony is to be separated from the mother country by an immense expanse. It is necessary that the prisoner should feel himself cast into another world; that he should be obliged to create an entirely new future for himself in the place that he inhabits, and that the hope of returning should appear to his eyes as a chimera. And how much even then will this chimera not trouble the imagination of the exile? The deported person of Botany Bay, separated from England by the entire diameter of the globe, still tries to make a path to his [former] country through insurmountable perils.[5] In vain his new land offers him tranquility and ease in its midst; he dreams only of diving once again into the miseries of the old world. To be able to return to the shores of Europe, a great number subject themselves to the hardest conditions; several commit new crimes to procure a means of transport that they lack.

Penal colonies differ so essentially from ordinary colonies that the natural fertility of the soil can become one of the greatest obstacles to their establishment.

The deported, it is easy to conceive, cannot be subjected to the same discipline as the inmates of our prisons. They could not possibly be locked up within four walls; for then, we might as well keep them in the mother country. It is thought sufficient to regulate their actions, but not to completely shackle their liberty.

If the land on which the penal establishment is founded presents natural resources to the isolated man; if it offers some means of existence, as is generally the case in the tropics; if the climate there is continually mild, wild fruits abundant, hunting easy; it is easy to imagine that a great number of criminals will profit from the semi-liberty left to them, in order to flee into the desert, and will exchange with joy the tranquility of slavery for the perils of an independence full of struggles. They will form just as many dangerous enemies for the nascent establishment; on an uninhabited land, it will be necessary from the first days to have weapons in hand.

If the continent, where the penal colony is located, were peopled by semi-civilized tribes, the danger would be even greater.

The European race has received from heaven, or has acquired by its own efforts, such an incontestable superiority over all other races that compose the great human family, that the man placed among us, because of his vices and his ignorance, on the last rung of the social ladder, is still the first among savages.⁶

The convicts will emigrate in great numbers to the Indians; they will become their allies against the whites, and most often [they will become] their chiefs.

We are not reasoning here based on a vague hypothesis; the danger that we are pointing out has made itself already strongly felt on the island of Van-Diemen. From the earliest days of the British establishment, a great number of convicts have fled into the woods; there, they formed associations of marauders; they have allied with the savages, married their daughters, and adopted, in part, their mores. From this crossbreeding was born a race of half-breeds, more barbarous than the Europeans, more civilized than the savages, whose hostility has always disturbed the colony and sometimes caused it to run the greatest dangers.

We have just indicated the difficulties that present themselves, from the first, when the choice is made of a proper site to establish a penal colony. These difficulties are not of an insurmountable nature, since the site that we describe has been found by England. If they existed alone, perhaps it would be wrong to spend any time discussing them; but there are several others that likewise deserve to attract public attention.

Let us suppose the place has been found; the land where the penal colony is to be established is on the other side of the world; it is uncultivated and uninhabited. It is necessary, then, to carry everything there and to take care of everything at once. What immense costs are required for an establishment of this nature? There is no question here of counting on the zeal and industry of the colonist to make up for the lack of useful things whose absence will always be felt, whatever is done. Here, the colonist takes so little interest in the enterprise that it is necessary to force him by rigor to sow the grain that is to nourish him. He would almost resign himself to die of starvation in order to disappoint the hopes of the society that punishes him. Great calamities must therefore accompany the beginning of a similar colony.

It suffices to read the history of the British establishments in Australia to be convinced of the truth of this remark. Famine and disease almost destroyed the young colony of Botany Bay three times. And it was only by rationing that its inhabitants, like the sailors of a shipwrecked vessel, were able to wait for aide from the mother country.

Perhaps there was apathy and negligence on the part of the British government; but in a similar enterprise, and when it is necessary to operate from so far away, can we flatter ourselves that we will be able to avoid all faults and errors?

Amid a region where everything has to be created at the same time, where the free population is isolated, without support, in the midst of a population of malefactors, it is understandable that it is difficult to maintain order and prevent revolts. This difficulty presents itself particularly in the first moments, when the guards, like the prisoners, are preoccupied with the care of providing for their own needs. The historians of Australia tell us, in fact, of constantly renewed conspiracies, always frustrated by the wisdom and firmness of the three first governors of the colony: Philip, Hunter, and King.

The character and talents of these three men must account for much of the success of England. And when the British government is accused of ineptitude in directing the affairs of the colony, it must not be forgotten that it at least fulfills the most difficult task and the most important perhaps of any government, that of choosing its agents well.

We have supposed just now that the place of deportation was found; we are also accepting, now, that the first difficulties are conquered. The penal colony exists; we must now examine its consequences.

The first question that presents itself is this:

Is it economical for the State to adopt the system of penal colonies?

If, abstracting from the facts, we consult only reason, we may be allowed to doubt it; for, while admitting that the maintenance of a penal colony costs less for the State than that of prisons, without a doubt its founding requires more considerable expenses; and if it is economical to feed, maintain, and guard the convict in the place of his exile, it is very costly to transport him there.[7] Besides, not every kind of convict can be sent to the penal colony; the system of deportation does not make the need to build prisons disappear altogether.

Writers who, until the present, have shown themselves the most favorable to the colonization of criminals have had no difficulty recognizing that the creation of a penal establishment of this nature was extremely onerous for the State. The reasons for this fact are easily understood, without it being necessary to develop them.

It has not yet been possible to determine with exactitude how much it cost to create the Australian colonies; we only know that from 1786 to 1819, that is to say for thirty-two years, Great Britain spent, for its penal colony, 5,301,623 pounds sterling, or approximately 133,600,000 francs.[8] It is certain, moreover, that today the costs of maintenance are much less than in the first years of the establishment; but do we know at what price this result has been obtained?

When the prisoners arrive in Australia,[9] the government chooses from among them not the men who have committed the greatest crimes, but those who have a profession and know how to work in an industry. It seizes the latter and occupies them with the public works of the colony. The criminals thus reserved for the service of the State form only one-eighth of the totality of the convicts,[10] and their number tends to continually decrease, as public needs themselves diminish. To these prisoners are applied the discipline of British prisons, very nearly, and their maintenance is a heavy charge upon the treasury.

The rest of the criminals, immediately after disembarking in the penal colony, are distributed among the free farmers. The latter, independently of the necessities of life that they are obliged to furnish for the convicts, must still pay for their services at a fixed price.

Transported to Australia, the criminal, from having been a prisoner, really becomes thus a hired servant. This system, at first, seems economical for the State; we will later see its bad consequences.

Various calculations, whose basis we give in a note,[11] lead us to believe that in 1829 (last known year) the maintenance of each of the fifteen thousand convicts to be found in Australia cost the State at least 12 pounds sterling, or 302 francs.[12]

If we add to this sum the annual interest on the money spent founding the colony; if we then take into account the progressive increase of the number of criminals who get themselves sent to Australia, we will be led to think that the savings that one can reasonably expect from the system of deportation reduces itself in sum to very little, if it even exists.

For the rest, we willingly acknowledge that the question of saving money comes here only in second place. The main question is whether, in the final analysis, the system of deportation diminishes the number of criminals. If that were the case, we could imagine that a great nation should impose on itself a financial sacrifice whose result would be to assure its well-being and peace.

But the example of England tends to prove that if deportation makes great crimes disappear, it noticeably augments the number of ordinary offences; and thus, the decrease of re-committals is more than outweighed by the augmentation of first offenses.

The punishment of deportation intimidates nobody, and emboldens several in the path of crime.

To avoid the immense costs which the guarding of the prisoners in Australia entails, Great Britain, as we have seen, gives liberty to the greater number as soon as they have set foot in the penal colony.

To give them a future and secure them in the new land by means of personal and lasting ties,[13] it facilitates with all its power the emigration of their families.

After their sentences have been served, they are given farmland so that idleness and vagrancy do not lead them back to crime.

From this combination of efforts, it sometimes results, it is true, that the man cast aside by the mother country[14] becomes a useful and respectful citizen in the colony; but it is even more often seen that those whom the fear of punishments would have forced to lead a regular life in England violate the laws that they would have respected, because the punishment with which he is threatened has nothing that frightens him, and often encourages him in his imagination rather than restraining him.

A great number of convicts, says Mr. Bigge in his report to Lord Bathurst, are held back much more by the ease of subsistence in Australia than by the possibility of making money there, and by the easy-going mores that prevail there than by the vigilance of the police. What a singular punishment, this one the convict fears to escape from!

To tell the truth, for many of the British deportation is nothing but immigration to Australia undertaken at the expense of the State.

This consideration could not fail to strike the mind of a people so justly renowned for its intelligence in the art of governing society.

Thus, from 1819 (6 January) we find in an official letter written by Lord Bathurst this enunciation: the terror that deportation at first inspired gradually diminishes, and crimes increase in the same proportion. (*They have increased beyond all calculations*).[15]

The number of convicts sentenced to deportation, which was 662 in 1812, in fact rose each year until 1819, the year of Lord Bathurst's letter, to the figure of 3,130; during the years 1828 and 1829, it attained 4,500.[16]

Partisans of the system of deportation cannot deny such facts: but they say that this system has, at least, the consequence of rapidly founding a colony that gives back to the mother country in wealth and power more than it cost her.

Thus envisaged, deportation is no longer a penal system, but is rather a method of colonization. From this point of view, it not only deserves the attention of the friends of humanity, but also of statesmen and all those who exert some influence on the destiny of nations.

For ourselves, we will not hesitate to say, the system of deportation appears to us as inappropriate for forming a colony as for the repression of crimes in the mother country. No doubt it quickly transports to the land one wants to colonize a population that would not perhaps have gone thither of itself; but the State gains little from gathering these early fruits, and it would have been desirable that it let things follow their natural course.

And first, if the colony actually grows rapidly, it soon becomes difficult to maintain there the penal establishment at little cost: in 1819, the population of New South Wales was composed only of around 29,000 inhabitants, and already surveillance was becoming difficult; by now, the idea of erecting prisons to contain the convicts was being suggested to the government: it is the European system with its flaws, transported 5,000 leagues from Europe.[17]

The more the colony grows in population, the less it will be disposed to become the receptacle of the mother country's vices. It is known what indignation was excited in America by the presence of criminals deported there by the mother country.

In Australia itself, among this people still in its infancy, composed in great part of malefactors, the same murmurs are already heard, and it may be thought that as soon as the colony has the strength to do so, it will energetically refuse the disastrous presents of the mother country. Thus, the investment Great Britain made in its penal establishment will have been for naught.

The Australian colonies will attempt all the sooner to free themselves from the onerous obligations imposed by England, given that their inhabitants harbor little kindness for her in their hearts.

And this is one of the most disastrous effects of the system of deportation applied to colonies.

Nothing is tenderer in general than the sentiment that binds colonists to the soil on which they were born. Recollections, habits, interests, prejudices, everything still unites them to the mother country despite the ocean that separates them. Several nations of Europe have found and still find a great source of power and glory in these ties of distant fraternity. One year before the American Revolution, the colonists whose fathers had a century and a half ago left the coasts of Great Britain still called it home, in speaking of England.

But the name of the mother country recalls to the memory of the deported only the recollection of misery, sometimes unmerited. It is there that he was unfortunate, persecuted, guilty, dishonored. What ties unite him to a region where, most often, he has left no-one who is interested in his fate? How could he ever wish to establish commercial or friendly relationships with the mother country? Of all points of the globe, the place where he was born appears to him the most odious. It is the only place where his history is known and where his shame has been divulged.

It can hardly be doubted that these hostile sentiments of the colonist perpetuate themselves in his race; in the United States, among this rival people of England, the Irish can still be recognized by the hatred they have vowed against their former masters.

The system of deportation is therefore disastrous to the mother-countries in that it weakens the natural ties that must unite them to their colonies; further, it prepares for these young States themselves a future full of storm and misery.

Partisans of the penal colonies have not failed to cite the example of the Romans, who began with robbery and ended with the conquest of the world.

But these facts that are spoken of are very far from us; there are other, more conclusive facts that have passed almost before our eyes, and we cannot believe that it is necessary to recur to examples given three thousand years ago when the present speaks so loudly.

A handful of sectarians land around the beginning of the seventeenth century on the coasts of North America; there, they establish almost in secret a society to which they give liberty and religion as the foundation. This band of pious adventurers has since become a great people, and the nation created by them has remained the freest and most religious in the world. On an island off the same continent, and almost at the same moment, a band of pirates, the scum of Europe, seek an asylum. These depraved but intelligent men also established a society there that soon abandoned the predatory habits of its founders. It became rich and enlightened, but remained the most corrupted of the globe, and its vices led to the bloody catastrophe that terminated its existence.

We need not turn to New England or St. Domingo for examples; we need only, to make our thought better understood, expose what is occurring in Australia itself.

Society,[18] in Australia, is divided into diverse classes as separate from and hostile to each other as the different castes of the Middle Ages. The convict is exposed to the contempt of those who have obtained freedom; the latter to the insults of his own son, who was born in liberty; and all to the haughtiness of the colonist whose origin is without stain. They are like four enemy nations meeting on the same soil.

We can gain an idea of the sentiments that animate these different members of the same people by the following passage that is found in the report of Mr. Bigge: "As long as these sentiments of jealousy and enmity subsist, he says, it would be wrong to introduce the institution of the jury into the colony. In the present state of things, a jury composed of former convicts will not fail to unite against an accused person belonging to the class of free colonists; just as juries taken from among the free colonists will always believe they are manifesting the purity of their class by condemning the former prisoner against whom a second accusation is directed."

In 1820, only one-eighth of children received instruction in Australia. The government of the colony, however, opened public schools at its own cost; it knew, as Mr. Bigge says in his report, that education alone could combat the disastrous influence of the parents' vices.

What is essentially lacking, in fact, in the Australian society, is mores. And how could it be otherwise? Scarcely in a society composed of pure elements does the power of example and the influence of public opinion manage to restrain human passions; out of thirty-six thousand inhabitants that Australia counted in 1828, twenty-three thousand, or nearly two-thirds, belonged to the class of convicts. Thus, Australia still found itself in this unique position, where vice obtained the support of the majority. Hence the women there had lost those traditions of modesty and virtue that characterize their sex in the mother country and most of its free colonies; although the government encouraged marriage with all its power, often even at the expense of order, bastards still formed one-fourth of the children.

There is, moreover, a material cause, as it were, that is opposed to the establishment of good mores in penal colonies, and on the contrary, facilitates disorders and prostitution there.

In all countries of the world, women commit infinitely fewer crimes than men. In France, women form only one-fifth of the convicts; in America, one-tenth. A colony founded with the help of deportation will thus necessarily present a great disproportion in the number of the two sexes. In 1828, out of thirty-six thousand inhabitants contained in Australia, only eight thousand women were counted, or less than a quarter of the total population. But, as can be easily imagined, and experience proves it moreover, for the mores of a people to be pure the two sexes must exist in an approximately equal proportion.

But not only are infractions to moral precepts frequent in Australia; crimes against the positive laws of society are committed there more than in any other region of the world.

The annual number of executions in England is around sixty, while in the Australian colonies, which are ruled by the same legislation, peopled by the same race, and which still have only forty thousand inhabitants, one counts, it is said, fifteen to twenty executions each year.[19]

Finally, of all the British colonies, Australia is the only one that is deprived of those precious civil liberties that have been the glory of England and the strength of her children in all parts of the world. How to entrust the functions of the jury to men who come themselves from the benches of the *court of assizes*?[20] And can the direction of public affairs be left without danger to a population tormented by its vices and divided by deep animosities?

It is necessary to acknowledge, deportation can contribute to rapidly populating an uninhabited land; it can form free colonies, but not strong and peaceful societies.[21] The vices that we thus remove from Europe are not destroyed; they are only transplanted to another soil, and England discharges herself of a part of its miseries only to bequeath them to its children in the lands south of the equator.

Chapter 3: Difficulties Peculiar to Our Time and France

> Where can France hope to find a place fit to found a penal colony? —The genius of the nation is not favorable to overseas enterprises. —Facilities that Great Britain encountered in the founding of Botany-Bay and that are lacking in France. —Expenses that would be entailed in the creation of a similar colony. —Possibility of a maritime war.

We have shown in the preceding chapter the reasons leading us to believe that the system of deportation is useful neither as a repressive measure nor as a method of colonization. The difficulties that we have exposed seem to us bound to occur in all times and in all nations; but at certain moments, and for certain peoples, they become insurmountable.

First, where will France at present look for the site that is to contain her penal colony? To start by knowing whether that place exists is certainly to follow the natural order of ideas; and, on this occasion, we cannot abstain from making a remark.

Speak to a partisan of the system of penal colonies: you will first hear a summary of the advantages of deportation; then general and often ingenious considerations regarding the good that France might derive from it are developed; then some hopes for its adoption are expressed; some details on the colonization of Australia are added in closing. Meanwhile, the means of execution draw little attention; and as to the choice of the location for a French colony, the conversation will finish without a single word on this point. But if we hazard a question on this point, they will hasten to pass on to another subject; or else they will limit themselves to saying that the world is very large and that the little piece of land we need must exist somewhere. It is as though the universe is still divided by the imaginary line that the Popes had once drawn, and as though beyond it unknown continents extend where the imagination can go lose itself in liberty.

It is, however, on this very limited matter that we would like to see the partisans of deportation come pronounce themselves; it is on this wholly factual question that we would like the most enlightenment.

As for ourselves, we confess without difficulty that we do not perceive anywhere the spot that France could seize for the purpose. The world seems to us no longer vacant; all locations on it appear to us to be occupied.

Keep in mind what we said above on the choice to be made of selecting a site appropriate for establishing a penal colony; which, I believe, is incontestable.

Now, let us ask the question here in precise terms: in what part of the world is such a site to be encountered today?

Fortune pointed out such a site to England fifty years ago. A continent that was immense, and consequently having a limitless future, spacious harbors, safe anchorages, a fertile and inhabited land, the climate of Europe, everything is found united there and the privileged spot was placed in the antipodes.

Why, it will be said, abandon to the English the free possession of a region ten times larger than England? Cannot two peoples make use of this immense territory? And will a population of 50,000 English be straightened if, 900 leagues from there, on the western coast, we desire to establish a French colony? Those who ask this question are no doubt unaware that England, alerted through what occurred in America to the danger of having neighbors, has repeatedly declared that she would not allow a single European establishment to be founded in Australia.

To be sure, we feel as much as others the haughtiness and insolence of such a declaration; but do the partisans of deportation want us to start a maritime war with England, just so we can found a penal colony?

An author who has written with talent on the penitentiary system, Mr. Charles Lucas, points out, indeed, for the government's consideration two small islands of the Antilles and the colony of Cayenne that could serve, he says, as places of detention for certain convicts. It would contain recidivist murderers as well as those who have infringed on the liberty of the press and religion. But deportation, restricted to those two kinds of criminals, is not a generally felt utility, and one can doubt, moreover, that the place indicated is well chosen. The author of whom we speak, who contests the right of society to remove life, even from the parricide, surely would not want to leave to the insalubrity of the climate the burden of doing what justice cannot ordain.

Nobody so far, to our knowledge, has seriously concerned himself with answering the question we have posed above. And yet should we not concentrate our attention on this first point above all?

We must, moreover, hasten to say: we are not maintaining that it is impossible to find a site appropriate for founding a penal colony, simply because our research has not revealed it to us.

But even if this site were discovered, there still remain the difficulties of execution; they have been great for England; they appear insurmountable for France.

The first of all [difficulties], it must be admitted, is encountered in the character of the nation, which until the present has shown itself unfavorable to overseas enterprises.

France, through its geographical position, its size, and its fertility, has always been placed in the first rank of continental powers. It is the land that is the natural theater of her power and glory; maritime commerce is only an appendix to its existence. The sea has never excited in us, and will never excite, no doubt, those profound sympathies, that sort of filial respect that navigating and commercial peoples have for it. Hence it has often been seen among us that the most powerful minds are suddenly obscured when it is a question of assembling and directing naval expeditions. The people, on the other hand, have little confidence in the success of these distant enterprises. Private individuals only reluctantly invest their money in such schemes; the men who in our country volunteer to go found a colony are most often from the number of those to whom the mediocrity of their talent, the decline of their fortune, or the recollections of their former life deny the hope of a future in their country. And yet, if there is any undertaking in the world whose success depends on the leaders who direct it, it is no doubt the establishment of a penal colony.

When England, in 1785, conceived the project of deporting its convicts to New South Wales it had already approximately acquired that immense commercial development we see in our day. Her preponderance on the seas was even then an acknowledged fact.

She profited greatly from these two advantages; the extensiveness of her commerce made it easy for her to procure the sailors that she planned to make the voyage to Australia. Private industry came to the aid of the State; ships with large tonnage[22] presented themselves in great number to transport the convicts at a cheap rate to the penal colony. Thanks to the great number of vessels and to the immense resources of the Royal Navy, the government could provide for all the new needs without difficulty.

Since then, the power of England has not ceased growing: the Isle of St. Helena, the Cape of Good Hope, and the Isle of France have fallen into her hands, and provide today for her vessels so many ports where they can conveniently put in, sheltered by the British flag.

The empire of the sea is acquired slowly; but it is less subject than any other kind of empire to the sudden vicissitudes of fortune. Everything indicates that for a long time England will still tranquilly enjoy its advantages and that war itself could not pose an obstacle to her doing so.

England was then of all nations in the world the one who could found a penal colony the most easily and with least expense.

The infancy of the colony of Botany-Bay was, however, very painful, and we have seen what immense sums England had to spend to found it.

These results are self-explanatory. A nation, regardless of its advantages, cannot, at little expense, create a penal establishment three or four thousand leagues from the center of its power; especially when everything must be carried there, and nothing can be expected from the efforts or industry of the colonists.

In imitating our neighbors, we cannot hope to enjoy any of the advantages that they encountered in their enterprise.

The French navy cannot, without considerably augmenting its budget, each year send ships so far afield; and French commerce, for its part, presents few resources for expeditions of this kind.

Once departed from our ports, it would be necessary for us to run half the circumference of the globe without encountering a single anchorage where our ships could be sure of finding support and efficacious assistance.

These difficulties can be expressed in just a few words, but they are very great; and the more we examine the subject, the more we are convinced of this fact.

If we should happen to surmount similar obstacles, it would be only by the cost of sacrifices and money.

It is inconceivable that, in the present state of finances, we could desire to increase at this point the burdens on the treasury. Even if the undertaking should have a fortunate outcome, even if money were to be saved as a result, France does not seem to us capable of affording the first expense. The result by no means seems to warrant such sacrifices.

And besides, are we sure of collecting the fruits of such a costly enterprise for a long time?

Those who are occupied with penal colonies avoid, in general, dwelling on the risks to which a maritime war would necessarily expose the new colony; or if they speak of the subject, it is to repel far from their thoughts the idea that France could dread a conflict and not have the strength to make at all times the justice of its rights respected.

We will not follow this example: true greatness, in a people as in a man, has always appeared to us to consist in undertaking not all that one desires but all that one is capable of. Wisdom, like true courage, is in knowing ourselves and in judging ourselves without weakness, all the while preserving the correct confidence of our powers.

The geographical position, colonial establishments, maritime glory, and commercial spirit of England have given her an incontestable preponderance over the seas. In the present state of things, France can sustain a glorious struggle against her; she can triumph in individual battles; she can even effectively defend some small possessions not very far from the center of the empire; but history teaches us that her distant colonies almost always ended up succumbing under the blows of her rival.

England has establishments started and harbors prepared on all the coasts; France can hardly find a point of support for its fleets except on its territory, or in the Antilles. England can disseminate its forces into all parts of the globe without running the chances of unequal success; France cannot fight except by uniting all of hers in the sea that surrounds her.

After having made long efforts to found its colony at great cost, France would see herself in almost certain danger of having it taken away by its enemy.

"But such a colony will tempt the cupidity of England very little." Nothing authorizes us to believe it. England will always have an interest in destroying a French colonial establishment, whatever it is. England, moreover, by seizing the penal colony, will hasten no doubt to give it another purpose, and will endeavor to people it with other elements.

But suppose that, the colony having had the time to make considerable growth, England neither wants to nor can seize it; she has no need to do so to harm France; it suffices for her to isolate the colony and to stop its communications with the mother country. A colony, and especially a penal colony, at least if it has not arrived at a high degree of development, endures a complete isolation from the civilized world only with difficulty. Deprived of its connections with the mother country, we should soon see her decay. On her side, if France can no longer transport its convicts across the sea, what would be the results of deportation, so dearly bought? Its colony, instead of being useful to her, will stir up difficulties for her and necessitate expenses that did not previously exist. What is to be done with the prisoners who were destined to go to the penal colony? It will be necessary to keep them on the continental territory of France; but nothing is prepared to receive them; during each maritime war, it will be necessary then to create provisional *bagnes* that can contain the criminals.

Such are, in the present state of things, the almost certain results of a war with England. Now, if we open the annals of our history, we can be convinced that the peace that subsists today is one of longest that has existed between England and ourselves in the past four hundred years.

Notes

1. *The *conseils généraux* are part of the governance of the different departments throughout France, created around 1800 as a deliberative or legislative body which worked alongside the prefect and council of prefecture, both executive branches of each department. The *conseils généraux* thus function as part of the intermediary governmental institution between local (city, town, village) governments and the national government, but represent the interests of the national government rather than local interests.
2. *The French reads: "en moralisant."
3. From the report of Mr. Bigge it is seen that, each year, there arrives at New South Wales a certain number of convicts who have already been deported there a first time.

4. See *Histoire des Colonies Pénales*, by Mr. Ernest de Blosseville. In all that follows, we have often had recourse to the book by Mr. de Blosseville. This work, whose author appears moreover favorable to the system of deportation, abounds in interesting facts and curious researches. It forms the most complete document that has been published in our language on the British establishments of Australia.
5. During the first years of the colony, the very general belief was widespread among the prisoners that New Holland touches the Asian continent. Several convicts tried to escape on that side. Most of them died in poverty in the woods, or were obliged to retrace their footsteps. It was very difficult to convince these unfortunate persons that they were in error.
6. *Important sentence for Tocqueville's and Beaumont's understanding of the progress of human nature and race. Note that the elements that drive progress are either heaven (divine providence) or human effort.
7. During the years 1828 and 1829, each prisoner sent to Australia cost the State for transport approximately 26 pounds sterling (655 fr.). *Legislative Document sent by the British parliament*, vol. 23, pag. 25.
8. The pound sterling is worth 25 fr. 20 c., the shilling 1 fr. 24 c.
9. Inquiries made by order of the British parliament in 1812 and 1819. These inquiries are found in a number of legislative documents brought by the British parliament, volume entitled: *Committees Reports*, tom. 90 and 91. Report made by Mr. Biggs of the commission charged to examine the budget of the colonies, 1830, same collection.
10. In 1828, out of 15,668 convicts, 1,918 were employed by the government. *Legislative Documents brought by the British parliament*, vol. 23.
11. See the note placed at the end of the alphabetical notes. *Translator is not sure what note is referred to here.
12. Each prisoner in the hulks, a kind of floating *bagnes* established in several ports of Great Britain, costs annually, deduction made for the price of his labor, only 6 pounds sterling (about 165 fr.). It is true to say that, by another note, the maintenance of each individual detainee in the penitentiary of Milbank returns annually to about 35 sterling pounds, or 882 fr. See Inquiry made by order of the British parliament in 1832.
13. *The French is: "les fixer sans retour par des liens moraux et durables;" a literal translation would be: "fix them without return by moral and durable links."
14. *In the French, *la métropole* designates a particular city or nation considered in relation to colonies which it has founded, on whom those colonies depend. See the definition provided in TLFi. The word is consistently translated "mother country" in the text.
15. *The text in parentheses is in English in the original French edition.

16. In 1832, the British parliament appointed a commission to examine what was the best way to render efficacious the application of punishments other than the death penalty. The commission made its report on 22 June 1832. From this precious document, we draw the following extracts; we ought to say, however, that the commission was not unanimous, and that its conclusions express only the majority opinions. This is at least what a very distinguished member of the British parliament who was part of the commission assured us.

> "According to some testimonies received by it, the commission has reason to believe that there often exists in the minds of some individuals belonging to the lower classes of the people, the idea that it is very advantageous to be deported to Botany-Bay. It is thought that some examples of crimes have been committed with the sole view of being sent to Australia. It seems, therefore, necessary to inflict on the convicts a real punishment either before their departure from England, or immediately after their arrival in Australia and before placing them as domestics among farmers." Page 12.
>
> "The commission thinks that the punishment of deportation to Australia, reduced to itself, does not suffice to divert from crime; and as no means has been indicated so far to make individuals once deported undergo the punishment called for by society, without considerably augmenting the charges to the public treasury, consequently it is necessary to inflict this punishment before their departure to New South Wales." Page 14.
>
> "The punishment of deportation, such as it is put into practice in England, and if inflicted alone, appears to the commission an insufficient punishment. But it could become useful, combined with other punishments." Page 16.
>
> "It results from the declaration of witnesses, that the impression produced on minds by deportation depends essentially on the situation of the convicts. Laborers who have a family fear to the last point of being sent to the penal colony, while for the unmarried men, the workers who are sure to obtain very elevated wages in Australia, and in general for all those who feel the need to change their position and conceive the vague desire to ameliorate it, to accomplish the latter, deportation is not at all formidable. All reports that are sent from New South Wales and the earth of Van Diemen, the commission have proof, are in fact very favorable. They represent the situation of the convicts in Australia as very happy, and the chances of fortune that are opened to them very certain, if they conduct themselves with prudence. It is natural, therefore, that deportation would be considered by many individuals rather as an advantage than as a punishment." Page 17.

"It is not surprising that in a region with a superabundant population, where a crowd of men suffer great privations, and consequently where great attraction to crime exists, those whose education has been abandoned, and who are left exposed to needs, yield without pain to the temptation of bad conduct. On the one hand, they rely on the incertitude of legislation and on the probability of acquittal that it presents; if this chance of salvation were to fail them, they know that the worst that can happen to them is to experience a change of condition that renders them scarcely worse than they already were." Page 30.

"The rapid and progressive increase of criminals in this region (England and the Gallic regions) has for some time excited the alarms and foiled all efforts of philanthropists and statesmen. In vain has it been attempted to stop this increase, either by amending our penal laws, or by establishing more efficacious police. All these means could neither retard the progress of evil nor diminish the frightful catalogue that the monument of jurisprudence offers each year. Without recurring to distant periods, it can be shown by the official documents furnished to the commission that the number of persons accused, jailed, and sentenced for crimes and offenses in England and in the Gallic regions constantly increases.

Number of individuals indicted or jailed.
From 1810 to 1817 — 56,308.
1817 to 1824 — 92,848.
1814 to 1831 — 121,518.

Number of convicted individuals.
From 1810 to 1817 — 35,259.
1817 to 1824 — 62,412.
1824 to 1831 — 85,257"

(Report of the select committee appointed to inquire into the best mode of giving efficacy to secondary punishments and to report their observations to the House of Commons 22 June 1832).

17. In 1816 (27 February), the governor of New South Wales established a new prison independent of what already existed at Sidney. Several establishments had already been created in various parts of the colonial territory, to hold the most indocile of the deported. See the documents printed by order of the Chamber of commons of the English, and among others the ordinance of Governor Darling, in 1826, and the *Regulations on Penal Settlements* printed in 1832.

18. Inquiry of 1812 and 1819. Report of Mr. Bigge. Report of the commission on the budget in 1830. See legislative documents sent by the British parliament.

19. We have confirmed this fact by a dignified person of the law, who has lived for more than two years in New South Wales.
20. *The *cour d'assises* was created in the wake of the French Revolution in 1810; it was a departmental court that included the innovation of a jury composed of citizens who could decide upon the guilt of the indicted, but not the punishment. See: Perrot 2008.
21. *It is interesting that Tocqueville and Beaumont suggest that the formation of society occurs from a different source or at a different time from the initial legal establishment of a community.
22. Vessels under 500 tons are hardly employed.

REFERENCES

1968. *British Parliamentary Papers: Australia 1800–1900, Vol. 1.* Portland, OR: Irish University Press.

Blosseville, Ernest de. 1831. *Histoire des Colonies Pénales de l'Angleterre dans l'Australie.* Paris: Adrien le Clere.

Governor of New South Wales. 1832. *Instructions Issued by the Governor of New South Wales for the Regulation of the Penal Settlements.* London: House of Commons.

Perrot, Roger. 2017. *Institutions Judiciaires*, 16th ed. Paris: LGDJ.

Appendix: Alphabetical Notes

(*a*) It was in 1804 that the erection of the first penitentiary of Baltimore (Maryland) was decreed; and in 1809, the general reform of criminal laws took place in combination with a new system of imprisonment.

"Any person (says article 28 of the law), convicted of a crime punished with imprisonment in the penitentiary will be placed in a solitary cell, where he will receive course and scanty food, and where he will remain for the whole time determined by the court; provided the entire time spent in the cell does not exceed half the total punishment of imprisonment and is not less than one-twentieth part of that punishment; on the condition also that the directors of the penitentiary will have the power to make [him] undergo isolation in the manner and intervals that they judge appropriate."

See Act of Assembly, Baltimore 1819, page 24.

Article 30 of the same law prescribes labor for the inmates in the penitentiary except in the case of imprisonment in the cells; and article 40 authorizes the punishment of the whip as a disciplinary means. The law of Maryland differs in this point from that of New York.

The system of absolute isolation in certain determined cases was not adopted in the Boston prison (Massachusetts) until 21 June 1811.

(See Rules and regulations for the government of the Massachusetts state prison. Boston 1823).

It has been implemented in New Jersey since the year 1797.

See 5th Report of the Boston Society of Prisons, p. 422.

In 1820, New Jersey made a law that authorized the courts of justice to pronounce, in the case of arson, murder, rape, blasphemy, lying under oath, burglary or theft with violence, forgery, et cetera, against the guilty, the punishment of solitary imprisonment in a cell for a time that cannot exceed one quarter of the time they could have been sentenced to imprisonment with labor. (See Letter from Mr. Southard of New Jersey, from 27 December 1831).

(*b*) On 2 April 1821, the New York legislature issued a decree by which the directors of Auburn were charged with choosing a class of the convicts composed of the most hardened criminals, and to confine them day and night without the least interruption in their solitary cells, where they would not be permitted to work. On 25 December 1831, a sufficient number of cells being completed, they chose eighty convicts that they placed in the cells. (See report from Gershom Powers, superintendent of Auburn in 1828, page 80, and handwritten note from Elam Lynds that he handed to us.)

This decree of the legislature was made on the report of an investigatory committee of which Mr. J. Spencer of Canandaigua was a member, one of the most distinguished criminalists of the State of New York:

"The prisoners," he said in his report, "ought to be classed according to their morality; the scoundrels hardened to crime will be subject to an uninterrupted solitary imprisonment; those who come after in the scale of crime will be for part of the time subject to the same punishment; and during the rest of their imprisonment they will have permission to work; the least criminal and depraved will have the ability to work all day." (See Report to the legislature of the year 1821).

(*c*) This was during the year 1822, which immediately followed the experiment of solitary cells without labor. Here is how Mr. Gershom Powers, the director of Auburn, recounts what happened in this circumstance:

"During the year 1822, he says, there were, on average, two hundred twenty inmates in the prison. From the physician's report to the inspectors, it appeared that the number of sick in the hospital each day was, on average, seven or eight. There were ten deaths, of which seven had been caused by pulmonary consumption; and out of these seven, five belonged to solitary cells. In his report, the doctor discusses sick convicts leaving the cells and arriving at the hospital with irregular respiration and chest pains."

Here are the terms with which the doctor of whom Mr. Gershom Powers spoke concluded:

"It is henceforth acknowledged that sedentary life, regardless of the circumstances that accompany it, has the effect of weakening the body, and consequently disposes it to sickness; this effect can be noted in schools as in prisons, and everywhere the exercise of the body does not receive its complete development. If we review the psychological causes of human illnesses, we will probably come to recognize that the sedentary life in prison, which calls to its aid every debilitating passion such as melancholy, chagrin, et cetera, must singularly hasten towards the progress of pulmonary consumption."

See Report of Gershom Powers 1828, page 81. We will see later that labor added to the prison discipline entirely changes the physician's conclusions.

(*d*) This prison is today in a sort of abandonment; the solitary cells, each one intended to receive one convict, are open to all inmates, who can communicate between themselves; we found sixty-four of them in the prison; the only thing that was kept in the system was that which was defective, that is, the absence of labor. The inmates, with the exception of a very small number, are entirely idle because they do not have a workshop to unite them. Despite the material defects of the establishment, it seems to us that a better part can be taken away; but the administration is disgusted by the bad arrangement of the place; and the system not having had the success that was expected, public attention has ceased to focus on this point. In a government where coercion and follow-up have no part, we succeed only in the undertakings that deeply interest public opinion and that consequently give glory or profit to the individuals who get involved. The Philadelphia penitentiary is directed by men of great merit; that of Pittsburg, already forgotten, finds for its direction only agents of an ordinary capacity.

(*e*) The Boston Prison Society dates from the year 1826. From that time until today, that is, during a space of six years, it spent 17,498 dollars 19 cents (97,740 fr. 40 c.), of which $15,681 (85,111 fr. 31 c.) were given by charitable persons. It is with the help of such resources that its members have been laboring successfully in the work of prison reform: one of the society's greatest assets includes the zeal of Mr. L. Dwight, its secretary, whom we see research with indefatigable ardor any document appropriate to enlighten public opinion; neglecting no journey, however difficult it is, when he pursues the truth; visiting the good as well as the bad prisons; pointing out the defects of some, the advantages of others; indicating the improvements obtained and what is still to be done. He labors tirelessly at the work of reform.

The reports published under the auspices of the society are like a genuine book in which every abuse and error of the penitentiary system are registered, while we find there all the favorable innovations.

The Boston society, which thinks religious instruction must be the basis of the entire system of prison reform, has for six years maintained some ministers of the church in the prisons of Auburn, Singsing, Wethersfield, Lamberton (New Jersey), and Charlestown near Boston on its own funds. The sums spent by it for this object amounted to 4,727 dollars 29 cents (25,654 f. 63 c.). See the six reports published by this society."

(*f*) The law that prescribes labor in solitary cells is from 23 April 1829: See section 3 of the law entitled "*An Act to reform the penal laws of this commonwealth*.

It frequently happens, even in the United States, that the true character of the new Philadelphia penitentiary is misunderstood; some, believing that this prison is nothing other than that of the former Walnut [Street Prison] touted in spite of all its defects, praise or blame it according to their judgement of its reputation, where they have a personal knowledge; others, informed of the existence of the new prison, but thinking that labor is prohibited in it in conformity with the intention of its founders, condemn this prison and its discipline in the belief that they do not allow labor, which, however, is in force there.

(*g*) It is rather remarkable that the penal law and that which regulates the mode of its execution, that is to say the system of imprisonment, forms only a single context. This manner of proceeding is simultaneously logical and wise. Consequently, any sanction of a punishment is in its execution. The judgment that convicts a criminal is only a principle, an idea, if it does not take material form by its execution. The law that regulates this execution is therefore as important as what decrees the principle; this is why any law that gives the punishment of imprisonment ought to state with care how this punishment will be administered. This is what the Pennsylvania legislature has done.

(*h*) The Massachusetts penitentiary was organized in 1829; that of Maryland in 1 January 1830; those of Tennessee and Kentucky were constructed at the same time. The Vermont prison has not yet been entirely completed today; but it is continuing right now and is executed on the Auburn plan. As to the Maine prison, we consider it as having been established on the same system, although in principle it was intended for solitary imprisonment without labor in special cases determined by the law; indeed, it has been consistent for some years, the number of cells having been increased and the workshops having been formed for the inmates to be able to labor; this penitentiary that had some similarities with Pittsburg and Walnut in its origin, today belongs entirely to the Auburn system.

(*i*) The plan for a house of refuge has already been adopted there; and a committee is formed to pursue its execution.

We can, among the bad prisons, mention that of Lamberton (New-Jersey).

Children and the elderly are mixed together there. Every principle of discipline is unknown; the prisoners and employees of the prison agree to break the regulations. The conversation of the prisoners turns uniquely on the crimes that they have committed, on those that they will commit one day, and on their plans for escape. Since the establishment of the prison, one thousand two hundred six individuals have been confined therein, of whom one hundred and eight escaped. The discipline is defective, but it is severe: ten prisoners are mentioned who died because of harsh punishments. The prisoners' labor is unproductive and their maintenance is very expensive. See 5th Report of the Boston Prison Society.

(*j*) We have seen prisons that contain those convicted for crimes infected with the greatest corruption; and a remedy was applied where the greatest trouble appeared: the houses of arrest, where the same trouble exists, but where it has a less devastating effect, have been forgotten; meanwhile, to neglect the least guilty in order to work to reform only the greatest criminals is as if one is occupied only with the most sick in a hospital, and if, in order to heal some perhaps incurable illnesses, all those who could be easily brought back to health are left without care. The defect that we point out here is felt in America by the most distinguished men.

Mr. Edward Livingston attacks it with great strength in his writings:

"In prisons that contain convicts, he says, only the guilty are mixed with the guilty; but in cells where the defendants [who were] arrested provisionally are found, crime is mixed up with innocence."

(See his Introduction to the Disciplinary Code of Prisons, page 31.)

To make all the disadvantages of a bad system of imprisonment for the indicted better felt, Mr. Livingston presents a table of individuals arrested, tried, acquitted, or convicted at New York from 1822 until 1826 inclusively. It therefore follows from this table that four-fifths of persons arrested in New York as defendants of crimes or offences and thrown as such into a prison in the meantime for the trial day, are ultimately recognized to be innocent, whether by police officers, by the grand jury, or finally by the final judgement. See this Table, at the end of the volume. We have not encountered anyone who is more sincerely grieved at the evil state of houses of arrest in America than Mr. Riker, recorder of the city of New York, public servant of a rare worth and a high virtue who adds to much knowledge significant experience in criminal affairs.

(*k*) In the United States, the head of society is always in front in the path of reform: the rest of the social body, who comprises the mass of the population, usually follows the movement but from a distance; and if one wants to lead it too far, it stops quite short. It is thus that in Pennsylvania the Quakers have not been able to entirely abolish the death penalty: its abolition in the case of assassination repulsed the feelings of the masses: it would be the same in the other most enlightened States of the Union if the attempt is made to abolish it in cases where general opinion judged it necessary. The legislators of the various States can only do what is pleasing to the greatest number: and if, surpassing public opinion, they were to attempt an innovation whose need was not yet felt, they would expose themselves not only to lose popular favor, but also to see their work destroyed the following year by their successors.

(*l*) Solitary imprisonment has sometimes been reproached for unequally punishing the criminals who undergo it. It is very certain that this punishment makes the prisoners feel very diverse impressions; it affects the man whose mind has been cultivated more vividly than the brute whose senses have not been developed by education: solitude becomes more painful in proportion to the greater needs of sociability.

But this inequality in the effects of the punishment is not specific to solitary imprisonment. Any degrading punishment is crueler for the man whose social position is elevated than for those who, to undergo it, are of an obscure condition. The criminal whose imagination is fervent and vivid suffers more from a few hours of imprisonment, even if not solitary, than the convict whose mind is naturally tranquil. We have noticed that the Indian cannot support the privation of his liberty for a long time; is this a reason to abolish imprisonment, of whatever nature, in any society where there are Indians?

(See Report of Commissioners-redactors of the Penal Code of Pennsylvania.)

(*m*) Without speaking of the monstrous relationships that the inmates have between themselves during the night, it suffices to say that the conversation of two criminals contained in a prison revolves uniquely around the crimes that they have committed and on those that they hope to commit when they will be in liberty. In such conversations, each boasts of his evil doing and everyone disputes for the privilege of infamy. Those less advanced in the career of crime listen to the discourse of the more experienced; and the most corrupt among the prisoners is a type on which all moralities are soon modeled.

Everyone who has visited the prisons of France acknowledges the truth of this picture. Mr. Louis Dwight, in the reports of the Boston society, points out a multitude of facts that prove that in this painting we are still below reality.

Moreover, the contagion of prisons and the uselessness of classifications are now two points acknowledged in the United States. Mr. Livingston speaks on this point in terms that merit quoting:

"It became evident that we must not hope for any reform among the prisoners while this confusion exists.

It has been attempted in England and even among us to remedy this evil by the classification of the convicts; but it was recognized as an insufficient means. For the system to be good, it was necessary to bring about the individual separation of each prisoner. Consequently, even when the classes of individuals put together was reduced to two, it was always found that one had the power of corrupting the other; and if it happened by chance that two persons arrived at the same time and in the same degree of depravation; if, by an even greater chance, there was a guard whose discernment was such that he could perceive this conformity of two similar moralities that is so difficult to know, their union would still be disastrous because it would augment for each of them shared resources of crime (the common stock of guilt)." Letter from Livingston to Roberts Vaux. 1828.

(*n*) The Baltimore system is that of Geneva. In this latter city, silence was thought so cruel that man does not have the right to impose it on his equal. Consequently, prisoners are permitted to chat with each other. Because of this, they do not have a penitentiary system. The Genevans' conscience finds its source in a very praiseworthy sentiment of humanity, but that seems to us to be misunderstood. In order to not cause a difficult privation for the prisoners, they are left a disastrous liberty. To save them from psychological suffering, they are left prey to the most frightful of all evils, the corruption of the prison.

The right of society is contested: and why! Society has the right to enchain the guilty whose arm committed homicide, and it cannot smother a voice that makes itself heard only to corrupt! They speak also of the rights of man! But can the right to liberty be spoken of after having put him in prison?

(*o*) For the visit to this penitentiary, we were introduced to every possible facility. Mr. Samuel Wood, superintendent of the prison, man of rare merit, gave orders so that we were allowed at all hours into the establishment, whether he was present or not. At the same time, he instructed every employee of the house to open all the cells for us, according to our fancy, and to allow us to communicate with the prisoners without witness. Mr. Wood often told us: "We have no other interest than that of the truth. If there is anything defective in the prison that I direct, it is important that we know it."

We have carefully noted all the conversations that we have had with the prisoners. They form, under the title of *Inquiry on the Philadelphia Penitentiary*, an interesting document that shows the successive impressions that the prisoners feel in solitude.

See: Inquiry on the Philadelphia Penitentiary, [Appendix] number 10.

(*p*) See how Mr. Elam Lynds speaks on this subject in a note that he gave us himself:

"Obedience to the laws of society is all that is required of a good citizen. This is what is necessary to teach to the criminal: and you will teach him much better by practice than by theory. If you contain a man convicted of a crime in a cell, you have no control over his person: you act only on his body. Instead of that, put him to work and force him to do everything that he is ordered; you teach him to obey and give him habits of industry; now I ask, is there anything more powerful over us than the force of habit? When you have given habits of obedience and work to a man, there is a smaller chance that he will ever become a thief.

The criminals confined in absolute solitude who ask to work, they do not do so because they like to work but because they are bored of their isolation."

(*q*) One cannot see the prison of Singsing and the system of labor established there without being struck with astonishment and fear.

Although the order is perfect, one feels that it rests on a fragile basis: it is due to a power which acts constantly but that must be reproduced each day under threat of compromising the entire discipline. The safety of the guards is incessantly threatened. In the presence of such dangers, so cleverly but so difficultly evaded, it seems to us impossible not to doubt some catastrophe in the future. Moreover, the risks that the employees run in the prison are, for the present, one of the surest guaranties of maintaining order; each of them understands that the preservation of his life depends on it.

(*r*) See report of Judge Powers from 1828, page 108.

We cannot attach too much importance to the choice of employees: the discipline established in these penitentiaries is sustained only by a constant zeal and uninterrupted vigilance.

See what Mr. Powers says on this point, page 25, report of 1828, and Mr. Barrett in his letter [in Appendix] No. 14. See also the various reports of the Boston society.

This necessity of having good employees to monitor the prisoners must be made to avoid badly understood thrift. In 1829, the salary of the employees of the Baltimore prison was increased to keep them; without this increase they would have retired and perhaps been replaced by men without talent or morality. (See Report to Governor Martin of 21 December 1829.)

It is important to have capable and honest employees, not only in the interest of the prison discipline, but also in respect even to financial economy.

Until 1817, the Maryland penitentiary had been expensive to the State; since that time, it was more or less productive; this sudden change is operated without having substituted another discipline of imprisonment for the former system. There was simply a better administration due to more honest and intelligent employees. See Mr. Niles' brochure from 22 December 1828.

See also what the inspectors of the Auburn prison say on this question, who in 1826 requested the increase of the salary of employees of this prison. Report of 28 January 1826, page 3.

(*s*) The American prison system, which makes the labor of the prisoners as productive as possible, is perfectly suitable to this country where the workforce is extremely expensive due to lack of manpower.

One does not fear, in establishing factories in the prisons, compromising the situation of free workers. In truth, a nation is generally interested in always increasing mass production because prices fall in proportion to their increased quantity; and the consumer, paying less for each, is enriched. Nevertheless, in countries where abundance of production has reduced the value of manufactured objects to its lowest rate, production cannot be increased without putting the existence of the entire working class at risk. It can be said that products have their price at the lowest rate when the earnings of the worker barely give him what he needs to live. When the wages of the free worker descend to this point, the establishment of factories in prisons is even more dangerous than the creation of new free factories. In fact, it is not only competition that the particular establishments have to maintain. Between the factories of free workers and those of prisons, the portion is not equal. The prison manufactures not for profit, but to diminish its charges; it consequently lowers the price of its product as it pleases, and its existence is never threatened. If the manufactured articles depreciate, the entrepreneur pays less for each of the prisoners' labor, and it is necessary for the State to pay more for maintenance costs. On the other hand, the ordinary manufacturer can only sustain himself if he profits; the workers that he employs need to find livelihood in their work; and if the yields become so modest that there is profit for neither one nor the either, the factory collapses.

When, therefore, factories are established in prisons, competition is raised against all free industries which becomes fatal if, due to the price of the work force, they find themselves reduced to either ceasing their rate [of production] or working at a loss. In summarizing this point, free factories fall if they do not profit because they have a limited capital; prison factories, sustained by the State, are always maintained, whether they produce little or much, because they are not intended to profit but to lose as little as possible, and because they have a capital that is infinitely renewed to sustain them.

These are doubtless the considerations which are the cause of the English government's having already interrupted the labor of the inmates in prison several times. That is why they invented these machines (treadmill) that make labor without generating profit.

Envisioned merely regarding the interest of the prisoner, these machines fulfill only half the goal that is proposed in making them labor. It is true that they occupy the inmate and preserve him against the dangers of laziness; but what will he do after being released from prison? And how will the art of turning the tread-mill serve him? Therefore, in view only of the interest of the convict, we must never make him labor in this way. But in society we ought not consider only the advantage of individuals in prison; the government's trouble on this point is easily understood. It is a great difficulty to determine the moment when factories can be established in prisons without danger to particular industries; at the same time, it is a delicate question of morality and equity to know at what point the imprisoned criminal can be protected without oppressing the honest and free worker. Absolute theories on these questions cannot be presented: their solution is dependent on a perfect knowledge of facts and of the state of things in each country.

There is, however, a case where the tread-mill appears to us bad without any restriction; it is when it is established in a manner to create products, as sometimes happens. In this case, it unites the double inconvenience of not teaching the prisoner any profession and increasing the sum of manufactured products to the detriment of free workers.

Be that as it may, the particular question of the tread-mill, and that of labor in general, which are serious for several countries in Europe, presents no difficulty in the United States; and it is obvious that in this country, given the price of manufactured objects, the tread-mill in prisons will not meet any need.

There are, on the contrary, interests for society in general, as for the prisoners, that the latter exercise a useful profession in their prison. For society: because production in the United States is still below the needs of consumption. For prisoners: because it is important for them to learn a trade whose exercise will furnish them with a livelihood later on.

(t) It is probable that when the Singsing prison is finished, a great variety of professions will be introduced into the establishment. In truth, the beautiful marble quarries that exist on the same place where the prison is built, and whose exploitation is made easy by the location of the Hudson, will provide sufficient occupation for the prisoners for a long time; but will the danger that a thousand sentenced criminals are left to work in liberty outside the walls of the prison never be a cause of fear?

At Auburn and Baltimore, the most occupied workshops are those of weavers, carpenters, coopers, shoemakers, locksmiths. (For details, see Annual Reports on the Prisons of Auburn and Baltimore.)

(u) See notebook of charges for the general contract of service to the state prisons. Besides food, clothing, and bedding for the inmates, the cleanliness, health of the prison, laundry, et cetera, is included in the contract. It is the contractor who shaves the prisoners and cuts their hair; he is responsible for heating and lighting for the inmates and guards; he is also responsible for stocking office supplies such as paper, ink, wax, et cetera. He looks after the necessary religious things to see to the burial of the prisoners; all things relating to health, life, religion, death, are given in the contract.

For fear of forgetting anything, they say at the end of the notebook of charges that the contractor will provide any general supplies, approved or not.

The cafeteria is exploited by the contractor interested in selling the most wine possible; interested consequently that discipline be violated; a more dangerous provision, as the inmate can spend half his *pécule* in the prison, which is two thirds of the product of his labor.

Consequently, the contractor, being responsible for everything, is the most important man in the prison. The overseers of the workrooms, masters, cooks, bakers, caterers, laundry workers, barbers, nurses, pharmacy boys, servants, executioners, and all others whose functions are not subject to a simple surveillance are chosen by the contractor, who must simply be approved of by the prison administration.

Hence, the prison and its discipline are at the mercy of the contractor and his agents.

The contractor has, moreover, an immense business to conduct: everything depends on him, the greatest operations as well as the smallest details.

There is no doubt a great simplicity in accountability when all affairs are given to a single man. But it is evident that this man must be extremely exigent; as he does everything, he must profit the most. Add to this fact that his very complicated position is in some respects very unfavorable; in cases of dispute, the process between him and the administration is judged by the council of prefectures, that is by the administration, in other words by the opposing party. It is understood that he does not engage in business without almost certain chance of great profit.

If one desires to imprint a moral direction to the discipline in our present prisons, the contractor would be an obstacle thereto. The universality of duties vested in him make most of the employees of the prison his personal agents; elected, salaried by him, they are directly dependent upon him; and it is thus that he finds himself in possession of the most important parts of the discipline.

When we blame the disadvantages of the contract, we by no means claim to approve the discipline of every prison where it is not in force. Thus, we are far from being partisans of the Walnut Street prison, whose administration is governed internally; we even think that the principle of contracting, applied wisely, is in essence more useful than disastrous.

(*v*) In the course of the year 1828, a revolt broke out in the Newgate prison (New York) and became of such a serious nature that the sentinels were obliged to fire upon the inmates. They ended, however, by subduing the rebels, but after being subjected to force, one hundred of the most stubborn[1] refused to work; there was not, to compel them to obey, any other means than imprisonment in solitary cells with bread and water. This means was employed: but for seventy days it was inefficacious; and thus the insubordinate prisoners remained more than two months without working.

See Report from 20 January 1819.

The superintendent of the former prison of New York (Newgate), in which solitary imprisonment in the cells with reduction of food was the only disciplinary punishment in force, said on this subject:

"The current mode of punishment, whatever its duration, weakens the prisoners without, however, taming them at all."

(See Report from 31 December 1818.)

(*x*) The law of the State of New York stated once, in express terms, the quantity of blows (it was thirty-nine) that the guards were authorized to give to delinquents; the revised statutes were limited to saying that employees of the prison will use any means suitable to execute the rules of discipline. "The officers of the prison shall use all suitable means to defend themselves, to enforce the observance of discipline, et cetera."

See Revised statutes of the State of New York, tit. 2, ch. 3, 4 part, art. 2, §59.

The Connecticut law authorizes the infliction of blows in formal terms, but it limits them to a maximum of ten: moderate whipping (it says there) not exceeding ten stripes for any one offence. It moreover follows from this that one can give twenty blows of the whip to the detainee who has committed two infractions.

See law of 31 May 1827, page 163, section 3.

The law of Maryland also expressly permits the usage of whips, of which the maximum must not, it says, exceed thirteen.

See article 40 of the penal Code of 1809.

In a trial of an assistant guard at Auburn, accused of having struck inmates, Mr. Walworth, chancellor of the State of New York, and responsible for presiding over the proceeding, expresses thus in his summary addressed to the jury:

"There is nothing in imprisonment with labor that inspires terror for the prisoners; the forced labor that the convict undergoes during his imprisonment is hardly more painful than that of the honest class of free workers who labor to sustain their families. In order to reform the guilty and to restrain the wicked by the terror of punishment, it is absolutely necessary that the convict is made to understand the state of corruption into which he has fallen; he must be made to understand that he is in prison to atone for his infraction of the laws of the country; it is necessary that he appreciate for himself the difference that must exist between the condition of the good man who works in society to profit his life and that of the wretch who, by acts of fraud or violence, has deprived the honest man of the fruit of his labor; the misdirected sympathy that one feels for such scoundrels is truly an injustice against the healthy part of society. The system of discipline adopted by the inspectors of the prison, under the sanction of the laws, is perfectly suited to the way of reforming the less vicious among the convicts and driving away others from crime by the severity of punishments. In this system, corporal punishments play only a secondary role. The rigor of the punishment is mostly a psychological rigor; but it is by terror of corporal punishments that this moral [psychological] impression reaches the souls of the inmates; and it is for this reason that the regulation of the prison is without power if the inmate who refuses to submit to the regulations of the prison is not immediately and rigorously punished by the application of a corporal chastisement."

See Report from Mr. Gershom Powers, 1828, page 121.[2]

(*y*) See how Messrs. Allen, Hopkins, and Tibbits, inspectors of the Auburn prison, explain the necessity of investing the superintendent with discretionary power:

"No doubt the power to punish the prisoners must be exercised within the limits of the law; but we also consider as a principle of right common among us, even as it is a principle of reason and good sense, that every prison guard must personally have the right to punish.

Prisoners have the strength of numbers: if the power to punish them is not absolute, their submission will itself be incomplete.

We are unanimous on this system of discipline, and we do not hesitate to explain before the legislature our very fixed opinion that the administration of a prison filled with criminals must be absolute. The principal guard must be firm, discreet, vigilant; he must be accountable for everything that concerns the conduct and the safety of the inmates. Without this, there is neither discipline nor economy.

Everything works together to require this perfect control of the master: the lives of the employees of the prison is as interested as that of the prisoners themselves; economy also calls for it; another point of useful work."

(Report of Allen, Hopkins and Tibbits of 1825. See Gershom Powers, page 109, report of 1828.)

The question is often discussed in America of whether employees ought to be restricted, for inflicting chastisement, in referring to the superintendent, or rather if they ought to enjoy some right to instantly punish (on the spot) the infractions that are committed under their eyes. The inspectors of the Auburn prison have treated this question in one of their reports and they issue the opinion that inferior employees ought to be invested with the right that is in question here. "The danger of abuse," they say, "is a lesser evil than the relaxation of discipline produced by lack of authority." This opinion has prevailed.

See Report of the commission of which Mr. John Spencer was the organ. 1820.

(*z*) Among a number of these respectable philanthropists, who appeared to us to make some illusions on this point, we will mention Mr. Tukerman of Boston, who hopes that a day will come when, every wicked person having been regenerated, there will be no need of prisons. It is certain that if there were many more men as passionate as he for the cause of humanity, his hope would not be chimerical. The name of Mr. Tukerman must be pronounced only with respect; he is the living image of beneficence and virtue. A disciple of Howard, he passes his life in doing good works and aspires to relieve every human misery; weak of body, pale, and almost extinct, he has only a breath of life; but in the presence of a good deed to be done, we see this kind of phantom human take life and become full of energy. Mr. Tukerman, who perhaps deceives himself on some questions, does not render less immense services to society. His charity towards the poor people of Boston has given him the right to be their guardian; and if his kindness for them is extreme, it is also necessary to say that nothing equals his severity in their regard: the latter like to say that he is their benefactor; but they respect and fear him, because they know the austerity of his virtue. They know that his interest for them depends on their good conduct... Mr. Tukerman does more for the law and order of Boston than all the aldermen and justices of the peace combined.

(*aa*) The inspectors of the Philadelphia prison point out one of the advantages of solitary imprisonment in these terms:
"Pride, which so often leads the criminal to judge his own merit by the high opinion that his prison companions arouse in him, ceases to influence him because he has no one to applaud and admire him." Excerpted from the report of Philadelphia 1831.

(*bb*) It is a rather common opinion in the United States, among the people, that the number of crimes is increasing more rapidly than the population, even in northern States: this is an error. This error rests on a misunderstood fact, the ever-increasing crowding of inmates in the prisons. It is certain that on 30 January 1832 there were six hundred forty-six criminals at Auburn, which is ninety-six more than there were cells; and at Singsing, at the same time, the cells, which are a thousand in number, did not suffice for all the inmates: in each of these prisons it was necessary to double a certain number of cells, which is destructive to the entire penitentiary system: however much haste one puts into building new prisons, the number of prisoners grows faster than the buildings that are being constructed. This increase of criminals in the prisons has three principal causes: 1. The population in the State of New York increases with an extreme rapidity; 2. The new laws of the State of New York (the revised statutes) have multiplied the cases in which criminals are sent to penitentiaries (State prisons). Finally, infinitely fewer pardons were granted of late than formerly. This latter cause alone suffices to explain the progressive accumulation of inmates in the prisons of Singsing and Auburn. See Statistical Observations, No. 17.

(*cc*) The emancipated person commits more crimes than slaves for a very simple reason; it is only in receiving his liberty that he is found responsible for the care of his existence that was provided by his master during his servitude. Raised in the ignorance and brutishness of his original condition, he has been habituated to act like a machine whose every movement is determined by an external impetus. Nothing has developed his intelligence, to which he has never been forced to have recourse to avoid difficulty. His life has been wholly passive and material. In this state of moral annihilation, he commits few crimes: why would he steal, since he can own nothing? The day when his liberty is given to him he receives an instrument that he does not know how to use, and with which he will wound himself, if he does not kill himself. His movements, which were constrained when he was enslaved, are almost always disordered when he is free; he has no foresight for the future because he has been habituated to plan nothing. He finds himself assailed in society by passions that have not been progressively developed and that suddenly impose a yoke on him. He is prey to needs that he cannot satisfy, reduced thus to steal or die of starvation. Thus, the penitentiary is filled with emancipated black people, while the number of black male slaves who commit crimes is very restrained; and free black persons die half as much as enslaved black persons. (See Statistical Notes, no.15). Must we conclude from the preceding that it is wrong to emancipate slaves? Certainly not; it would be as much as saying that when an evil exists it is necessary to conserve it in perpetuity. It seems to us that one must only acknowledge that the passage from servitude to liberty causes a transition more detrimental than favorable to the emancipated generation, and from which subsequent generations alone can receive the benefit.

(*dd*) In France, outside of the list of sentences pronounced, one also keeps track of the number of complaints lodged and the suits not followed by condemnation: one also knows almost exactly the proportion of crimes committed to condemnations. In the United States, it would be very difficult, if not impossible, to obtain a document of this nature; first, no magistrate is directed by the government to do the work, and on the other hand, it can be said that to a certain point, the basis itself of the document does not exist.

In our habits of judicial policing, we are accustomed, when a crime is committed, to first state it, and then to search for the author, who is convicted despite being absent. In the United States, another path is followed; nobody is convicted by default; and until the culprit has been seized, little attention is paid to the offence; among us, it seems to be the crime that we prosecute, while in the United States it is the criminal. This explains how we know better the number of crimes committed independently of the number of convictions handed down against their authors.

(*ee*) This is one of the causes to which, in Connecticut, the extraordinary increase of crimes is attributed. Consequently, it seems to us incontestable that the reputation merited by the excellent penitentiary of Wethersfield has contributed to multiply the number of convictions. But it is clear that this cause is not alone, since the increase of which we speak is progressive and precedes the founding of the penitentiary by twenty years.

(*ff*) "Whatever partial good can be obtained from penitentiary punishments, no radical reform can be effected in society if one does not begin (as the fairy tale says) at the *beginning*. Forcing education on the people instead of constraining them to labor for the expiation of crimes that ignorance alone made them commit; teaching religion, the sciences, and the elements of penal law in primary schools; adopting a system of criminal procedure that is prompt, free, easy to understand, and which removes from the guilty any chance of escaping the law by the defect of forms; assuring an existence to the poor who cannot labor, and labor to those who can.

But above all, do not soil the indicted who you put into prison, innocent or guilty, with corruption that you yourselves endeavor to wash from them after they have been acknowledged guilty. Remember that in Philadelphia, as well as in New York, more than two thousand five hundred individuals are annually put in prison, and that out of this number, less than a quarter are declared guilty; and that every year there are thus more than one thousand eight hundred persons, presumed innocent, who are placed in a school where vice and crime are taught by professors of the first order. We shut our eyes before an enormous evil; and by an incredible inconsistency, we are going to preach the necessity of isolation and labor for convicts as if the penitentiaries where convicts have been confined were the only places where corruption of communications was to be dreaded."

(*gg*) Those who maintain that the Walnut Street prison has in fact produced the effects generally ascribed to it respond to our objection, that the rigors of solitary imprisonment and everything that accompanies the discipline of isolation exercises a healthy influence not only on the inmates, but even on all free men who can fear being sent there. This influence may no doubt exist: but then it is not the influence of a penitentiary discipline that reforms the guilty; it is the effect of a punishment that acts by the terror that it inspires; under this point of view, the death penalty would be the better of the punishments; however, in the eyes of the excessive partisans of the penitentiary system, the merit of such a system is not to be cruel and terrible. It is therefore necessary, to judge the penitentiary system in its proper meaning, to consider only the influence that it exercises directly on the reform of the inmates. It is so remarkable that the system of Walnut Street is today acknowledged deficient by even those who attribute to it such fortunate efficacy.

(*hh*) See Gershom Powers, page 64, 1828 and Report of the inspectors of Auburn 1829. In 1826, they tried to obtain for the first time, by means of circular letters addressed to post-masters, sheriffs, and attorney generals, information on the morality and conduct of convicts freed from the Auburn prison, in order to judge the effect produced by their imprisonment. This correspondence was prolonged until 1829, the time when it stopped: it was judged to be too expensive and its results too uncertain.

The transportation of letters is very expensive in America: and this expense became very onerous for the prison administration. For it to continue to receive information of this kind, it would be necessary that the central government, in whom the responsibilities of the post is placed, give it relief from transporting letters; and this is not what took place. Moreover, it was Mr. Gershom Powers who had the idea of making these inquiries: the government of the State did nothing; when he who had conceived the thing abandoned it, it was not implemented. We do not know, for that matter, whether these documents merit full confidence. It sometimes happens that those who are consulted are influenced in their response by motives other than the interest of the truth; sometimes they give a good character out of a pure sentiment of benevolence and charity; sometimes out of fear of those on whose account one consults them. As he benevolently offers this information, he does not feel himself bound to give exact information when there is danger of compromising himself.

(*ii*) The superintendent of the prison of Columbus (Ohio) says in a report:
"Out of one hundred sixty-five convicts who are in the Ohio penitentiary, fifteen are in recidivism; and it is to my knowledge that fifteen or twenty individuals who left this prison are at this moment in prisons of Indiana, Kentucky, Virginia, and Pennsylvania."

Thus, we see that more than half of recommitted convicts do not return into the first prison where they were imprisoned; and yet generally, in the United States, the fact of recidivism can be proved only by returning the convict to the same prison. Note, however, that the Columbus prison that is in question here is one of the worst prisons in the United States.

See superintendent's report on the Columbus prison. 6th Report of the Boston Society, page 508.

(*jj*) We will demonstrate that the penitentiary system in question is less expensive than the former prison discipline. However, while the new system costs more for its establishment and maintenance, it would be perhaps definitively less expensive for society if it is true that it has the power to reform the wicked. A prison system, however economical, becomes very expensive when it does not correct the inmates. Mr. Livingston has thus said it very well, "To put in liberty a thief who has not been reformed in prison, is to strike all of society with a tax whose amount has not been determined."

(Livingston. Letter to Roberts Vaux, 1828, page 13.)

(*kk*) The reasons for this difference are: 1. That the contractor is obliged by his contract to pay the ignorant and clumsy prisoners as well as the one who works with skill and talent; 2. The contractor is not certain of selling what he has commissioned and yet he can never terminate the labor; 3. The workday in the prison is shorter than that of the free laborer: the latter work in winter from six in the morning until eight in the evening, while those in the prison work only from eight in the morning until four; 4. It appears that at this time the contractors, and especially those of Auburn, have obtained too favorable conditions. This is one of the reasons why Auburn produces less than Wethersfield and Baltimore. In France, the contractor pays for the inmates that he makes work a little less than half the salary paid to workers in free workshops. But this contractor has a general contract for the long term.

(*ll*) The *pécule* is the part that is accorded to the inmate out of the product of his work. We understand that it is in the interest even of the administration to give to the inmates who work an appropriate salary to stimulate their zeal; and if this wage was moderate, the State itself would gain by paying it. It is thus that in the *bagnes*, where formerly the work of the chain gang was without recompense, at present a slight *pécule* is allowed that, in making them more industrious, has also made their labor more productive. The State gives to the convicts what it pleases. According to the law, it owes them nothing.

But in the central houses of detention and correction, two thirds of the products of labor belongs to the prisoners; one third is given to them in the prison to aid them in improving their lot, the other third is put in reserve and delivered to them at their release from prison; one third only is retained by the State. It can thus be said with reason that they work for their own gain. It seems to us that it would be more correct to admit the contrary principle, uncontested in the United States, which is that convicts work in prison for society, to which they must compensate some costs of their imprisonment. We have blamed the severity of American laws that give no *pécule* to the convict; what is granted to the criminals in France seems to us too considerable, and we think that it should be reduced. In any case, we will not criticize existing laws here; for the order of things that we blame is not prescribed by law, and, in some respects, is contrary to its provisions. The penal code, in accord with previous legislation, does not recognize for chain gangs any right to the *pécule*; however, the convicts in the work forces who are in the houses of detention receive, like the other inmates, two-thirds of the product of their labor. As to the prisoners with longer sentences, article 21 of the penal code says that they will be employed in labor whose product can be in part applied for their benefit, thus that it will be regulated by the government; but no part of the law imposes on the government the obligation to give them two-thirds of the profit. It leaves this point to its discretion. Thus, regarding the prisoners with longer sentences, the administration, in giving them such a considerable *pécule*, does not act illegally, but neither would it be illegal to act otherwise.

The correctional convicts are the ones to whom the law (article 41 of the penal code) recognizes this right to a *pécule* of two-thirds, which the administration gives to all convicts indiscriminately. But this right conferred expressly by the law to the convicts whose position is more favorable than that of chain gangs and prisoners with longer sentences, does it not suffice to prove that the legislator intended only the convicts in criminal and correctional matters to be treated in the same way? We doubt very much that the individuals correctionally convicted for more than one year merit the favor that article 41 of the penal Code grants them; and if we insist on this point, it is only to prove that in conceding them this favor, the law necessarily refuses it to all those who are still less worthy of it.

If the *pécule* of the prisoners serves to make them better, we would do well to guard ourselves from attacking it, however great it might be, persuaded as we are that the expenses with whose aid the wicked are reformed are advances from which society gathers fruits at a later time. But we see, on the contrary, that the *pécule* that causes such expense is itself one of the most fertile sources of corruption of prisons.

(*mm*) In France, the average price for a day's labor of any kind of work can be given at 2 francs 50 centimes; in the United States, it is double. This price that, in Paris, varies from 3 to 4 francs is less by two-thirds in other cities except for a few great cities, such as Lyon, Marseille, et cetera.

The workforce is therefore infinitely cheaper in France than in America. The price of raw materials is, in truth, a little higher.

In the United States, a cubic foot of hard stone costs 25 cents (1 franc 32 centimes); in France, it costs from 1 franc 50 c. to 2 francs (double in Paris).

In America, a thousand feet of lumber for carpentry costs from 60 to 80 francs, while in Paris their price is about 200 francs (including sawing, transporting, entrance fee, et cetera). It is less in the departments.

A pound of iron costs approximately the same in France and in the United States. It is from 14 to 17 centimes (melting) in France, and around 21 centimes in the United States (4 cents).

See, for the American prices, the note of Mr. Cartwright, very distinguished engineer of Singsing, and the estimate of Mr. Welles of Wethersfield, [Appendix] number 12.

We are beholden for information on the prices of France to the courtesy of Mr. Courtier, architect at Paris, who furnished us with a great number of useful documents.

(*nn*) The penal establishment of the British in Australia is at the same time a colonial establishment that has its own administration, magistrates, police. It is almost impossible to estimate the expenses that relate uniquely to the penal establishment as opposed to those that are applied to the colony.

Thus, for example, the deportation of prisoners in Australia requires the presence of a body of troops. But if there were no convicts in the colony, England would still be obliged to maintain a garrison there; only this garrison would be less numerous. These difficulties present themselves in each article of the budget for the Australian colonies.

It is therefore impossible to establish by pounds and cents what the penal establishment costs; but it is understood that the enlightened English can, with the aid of points of comparison furnished by other British colonies, arrive at an approximate result and present a rather precise idea of the cost of maintenance for the English deportation of criminals.

In 1829, the expense incurred by the penal colonies was raised in totality to 401,283 pounds sterling, or 10,112,331 francs.

The reporters of the budget, who announced this fact before the British parliament, remarked that it had been impossible for them to establish in a precise manner what was, in this expense, the portion applicable only to the penal establishment. But they add that the greatest part (the much greater proportion) must be attributed to the presence of convicts on the Australian soil.

Supposing that only half this sum, or 200,641 pounds sterling (5,056,153 francs), was in fact dispensed to guard and to maintain 15,688 convicts who were found last year in Australia, each prisoner would have cost around 12 pounds sterling, or 302 francs, to the State.[3]

It can be answered, no doubt, that one part of these expenses was covered by the product of the customs of the colony, that were raised the same year to 226,191 pounds sterling, or 5,700,013 francs. But these revenues belong to England, and if they were not intended to maintain its convicts in Australia, they would come to grow the treasury of the State. Perhaps, it is true, they would be less considerable if deportation did not exist, since then the colony would be less populated. It is this last consideration that leads us to attribute only half the totality of expenses to the support of the penal establishment; although in reality, two-thirds of the 400,000 pounds sterling has been probably employed for the transport, guard and maintenance of the prisoners.

Besides, it seems to be believed in England that it hardly costs more to deport the convicts to Australia than to guard them in the metropolis. We find in fact in a legislative document of 1816 this utterance:

Estimate of what it would cost to guard, maintain, and employ the convicts in England during the year 1817: 75,000 pounds sterling or 1,890,000 francs.

Estimate of probable expense to honor the bills drawn by the Governor of New South Wales on the treasury, during the same year: 80,000 pounds sterling or 2,016,000 francs.

See Report to the commission nominated to examine the Budget of the colonies, 1st November 1830. This report is found in the legislative documents sent by the British parliament, volume entitled: Commissioners Reports 1830–1831, page 69. For the above estimates, see the same collection, tome 37, page 297.

NOTES

1. *Alternatively translated as: opinionated.
2. *It might be useful to compare the French to the original text in the report which Tocqueville and Beaumont reference (Powers 1828). The excerpt from Judge Walworth's charge to the jury begins on page 118 of that report.
3. We find, in the deposition of a witness heard on 18 March 1832, by the nominating commission in the midst of British parliament, to the effect of discovering what was the efficacy of the punishments, the following announcement: The annual costs incurred by a deportation into New South Wales was raised to 13 pounds sterling without counting the expenses entailed in their transport to Australia. See inquiry of 1832.

REFERENCES

Allen, Stephen, Samuel M. Hopkins and George Tibbits. "Report of Allen, Hopkins and Tibbits of 1825." In *Journal of the Senate of the State of New York; at their Fiftieth Session.* 59–63. Albany: E. Croswell.

Livingston, Edward. 1828. *Letter from Edward Livingston, Esq. to Roberts Vaux: On the Advantages of the Pennsylvania System of Prison Siscipline, For the Application of Which the New Penitentiary Has Been Constructed Near Philadelphia, Etc..* Philadelphia: Jesper Harding.

Powers, Gershom. 1828. *Report of Gershom Powers, Agent and Keeper of the State Prison at Auburn, Made to the Legislature, January 7, 1828.* Albany: Croswell and Van Benthuysen.

Appendix No. 4: Agricultural Colonies

In any European State, not excepting those of the same where the art of agriculture has been the most perfected, one still comes across very large extents of territory whose arid soil has deterred industry, and that have remained available to all, for lack of having found a master who desired to take the trouble to fertilize them.

Alongside these useless fields is often found placed a population of proletariats who at once lack soil and livelihood. In France, almost 2,000,000 poor are counted, and the uncultivated earth forms more than one seventh of the area of the kingdom.

Experience, meanwhile, has shown that most of these lands, thus abandoned by man, can become productive when sufficient capital and continuous efforts are dedicated to their cultivation.

---

*The appendices are labeled idiosyncratically in the first edition of the text. In the original Table of Contents for the first edition, the main text was labeled "No. 1," Appendix on Penal Colonies "No.2," Alphabetical Notes "No.3," which makes Agricultural Colonies "No.4," and so forth. Neither of the first two appendices (On Penal Colonies and Alphabetical Notes) are marked by "No." in the French edition. The numbering in the original Table of Contents suggests that Tocqueville and Beaumont considered the main text as equally weighty to the appendices, and thus elevates the importance of the appendices.

Thus, the idea of agricultural colonies was born: it was understood that it was perhaps easy to settle the poor person on these fields neglected by the industry of the rich person, and that one could, by advancing the necessary money to him and subjecting him to useful regulations, enable him to make the soil that was delivered to him fertile.

If this experiment succeeded, one obtained a favorable result both for the poor, who exchanged his misery for the comfort of a farmer, and for the whole society, that saw its resources and well-being augmented without being obliged to impose on itself any new sacrifice.

It was in Holland that one attempted to reduce these theories to practice for the first time; and, until the present, it could be said that the success has exceeded expectations.

The society that attempted this good venture was formed at The Hague in 1818 with the approval, but not under the direction, of the government; its example was followed in Belgium in 1822.

According to the statutes of association, any private person who furnished the sum of 3 florins (6 fr. 12 cent.) becomes a member of it; and, as such, he contributes to the direction of its affairs and to the nomination of its administrators.

With the aid of funds that the voluntary donations of its members provided to it, the society acquired a vast extent of uncultivated land, which it then divided into lots of three and a half acres. 1300 florins (2743 fr.) was expected to be sufficient to purchase, clear, and sow these three acres. It placed there the poor person and his family, being able to form in all eight individuals.

We feel that such farmers must appear in a great state of destitution; they are often unhabituated to work, they do not possess the necessary instruments; finally, the earth on which they are confined produces little during the years that follow the clearing [of the land].

The society of beneficence, that has given shelter to the poor, has guarded against abandoning him to his own resources; it furnishes him on the contrary all that can be useful to him, instruments, livestock, clothing, food; but it furnishes it to him as an advance only; sixteen years is the time judged necessary for the new arrival to be able to habituate himself to his duties, make the terrain entirely productive, and completely pay back the advances that society has made in his favor.

In return for the benefits accorded to him, and which cannot degrade him, since in reality they constitute only a loan, the colonist is required to follow the direction of the administrators of the establishment, to submit to certain moral prescriptions, and finally to deliver each year the greatest part of the products of his harvest, which are used to acquit him towards society. Once the advances of the latter are covered, (and we have seen that it was calculated that they should be covered within sixteen years), the colonist returns to the exercise of all his rights; he becomes a true farmer, and his relationship with the colony differs in no way from that of another farmer with his master. The price of each farm is valued at 50 florins (105 f.) per year.

Annuities that come thus [to] the society, and the surplus of money provided by the donations of its members, must be used to purchase new lands and to gratuitously found new farms.

It is seen by this exposition that the society of beneficence from the Netherlands had in view only a purely philanthropic and charitable goal; it took care to stimulate the ardor of its members, in according them privileges: every man, as we have remarked, had a chance, in paying the sum of 6 francs, to become a member of the association of beneficence; but all members did not enjoy the same benefits.

Those who gave to the society 1,600 florins (3,376 fr.), once paid, acquired in perpetuity the right to designate the poor family that it pleased them to allow into one of the lots. The same right was accorded to those who, for sixteen years, annually paid the sum of 23 florins for each pauper that he placed on the colony (48 fr. 53 cent.), the amount of annual aid reputed necessary for the new colonist for sixteen years to make the terrain that was entrusted to him productive and to cultivate it without help.

The success of agricultural colonies in Holland was soon noted by the experiment. Many of the townships and public administrations were not slow to achieve the right to send indigents there for life; and the government finally devised the idea of dealing with the society itself, to discharge on it a part of the maintenance of vagabonds and foundlings that the laws put into its charge.

It is this agreement between the government and the association that gave birth to compulsory agricultural colonies.

We feel that the original plan of the society was not applicable to children, to whom the cultivation of the earth cannot be entrusted; and even less perhaps to the ex-convict, whom vice, more than misfortune, had ordinarily driven into workhouses.

And first, it was natural to fear that their labors would be less productive than that of grown men and free paupers. Consequently, society demanded that one pay it for sixteen years the annual sum of 45 florins

(94 fr. 95 cent.) to take care of a child, and that of 35 florins (73 fr. 85 cent.) in order to allow into its establishments a pauper who would come from the workhouses.

The administration of the forced colony must also rest on different bases than those of the free colony: in order to watch the new colonists more easily, they were united in a single location; they were given particular clothing in order to make flight less easy; they were made to work under the direction of guards and to undergo a severe discipline: instead of handing over an entire farm to them, they were treated only as workers of the task,[1] whose fair compensation encouraged efforts, and who returned to the midst of society when their conduct at the colony had furnished to the State sufficient safeguards.

Forced colonies did not prosper less than free colonies; their success, in a few places, appeared even greater and more rapid. It was easier, in fact, to constrain a prisoner to work than to persuade a free colonist to stop his idle habits, and to combat his ignorance.

The agricultural colonies of Holland and Belgium already contained in 1829 more than 9,000 prisoners, foundlings, or free colonists.

In the space of ten years, a vast extent of territory had for the first time been given over to agriculture and to the development of the kingdom's population. The State had found in this revolution some wages of peace, the public treasury a new source of revenue and an even greater source of saving; in fact, the child and the beggar cost simultaneously less in the agricultural colony than in hospitals and workhouses; and the government, in paying this already reduced sum for sixteen years, acquired the right to free itself forever.

In the brief picture that we desire to trace of agricultural colonies, our goal has been only to make comprehensible the bases of the system on which they rest. For those who desire to know in detail this good institution, we cannot do better than to refer them to the excellent work that Mr. Huerne de Pommeuse has just published on this subject.

Note

1. *Can also be translated as "piece workers."

Reference

Pommeuse, Huerne de. 1832. *Des Colonies Agricoles et de leurs Avantages*. Paris: Imprimerie de Madame Huzard.

Appendix No. 5: On Public Education

It seems to us that the system of public education was based, in every State of the Union, on analogous principles that were easy to make known.

Schools are divided, in the United States as elsewhere, into colleges dedicated to higher studies and into elementary schools.

At the head of the first are found placed, generally, a certain number of establishments high in cost or subsidized by the munificence of the State, which takes an indirect part in their administration.

Most of the elementary schools are equally subject to the supervision of public authority. Each municipality, in terms of the law, must be provided with a primary school open to any child of its inhabitants. This school is usually under the direction of local authorities; sometimes, however, the government has retained the right to inspect it.

Outside this system of national education reins a complete liberty. Each is master of establishing competition with the State in matters of public education, and the personal interest of families is the only judge. In certain parts of the Union, they believe only that their duty requires, as guaranty against the abuse of this liberty, a certificate of a good life and mores delivered to the new instructor by the local authorities and pastor of the municipality.

In the United States, the power to direct public education is not therefore abandoned; but it is not monopolized. Moreover, to make this theory better understood, we will present a picture of what happens in the State of New York, whose extent, population, and wealth place it at the head of the whole Union.

In the State of New York, the legislature has created two special funds, one called *the literature fund*, and the other *the common school fund;* the first is intended to support higher studies; the second, elementary studies. We will see more of the basis on which these funds are composed.

At the head of higher education is placed an administrative body called the State University of New York.[1]

Twenty-one members, called regents, form this body. The governor and deputy governor of the State are part of the governance of it. The legislature elects the nineteen other members.

Any time that an individual establishment wishes to obtain a charter from the State that permits it to exist by itself in perpetuity, to act and contract in its name, in a word, to become a kind of public establishment, it must address itself to the regents of the university; and it is only after having taken their advice that the legislature concedes the charter requested of it. Once this legal existence is recognized, numerous relationships are established between the college and the State. Each year, the regents of the university distribute aide to all establishments of public education thus recognized, furnished by one of the funds of which we have spoken above. In return for this benefit, the subsidized colleges undergo the inspection of the regents, who report the results of their investigations to the legislature annually. To the regents also belongs the right to give diplomas in science and literature.

The funds for primary schools are infinitely more considerable than those designated to support higher studies; likewise, society takes a more direct part in the governance of these schools.

A public servant is placed at the head of primary education in the State of New York, called the Superintendent of the schools. It is he who is called when some difficulties arise in the execution of the laws relating to public education; it is he who is responsible for distributing the annual aid of the State between the counties.

Each town (*township*) is required to have a school and to consecrate to it a sum at least equal to that which the State grants.

Several public servants are placed at the head of the schools of each township, called the commissioners of the schools. These commissioners distribute to each of the municipalities that compose the township the portion given to it by the State's liberality. They examine the teachers, choose, inspect, and revoke them; but one can appeal their verdicts to the superintendent of the schools.

The latter receives each year an account given of the state of education in every township of the republic, and he places summaries of these reports under the eyes of the legislature, with accompanying observations.[2]

Apart from the subsidized colleges and the communal schools, there are in the State of New York a very great number of establishments dedicated to public education that receive nothing from the State and that live entirely outside political society.

STATISTICAL DETAILS ON THE MONEY DEDICATED BY THE INHABITANTS OF THE STATE OF NEW YORK TO PUBLIC EDUCATION, ON THE NUMBER OF SCHOOLS AND THAT OF SCHOOLCHILDREN IN 1829

To provide for the needs of public schools, there are two simple systems: in one, the State gives nothing and the municipalities are responsible for every expense; in the other, the State alone is faced with every expense.

These two systems have [different] supporters and implementations in America.

The system in the State of New York is mixed: the legislature annually furnishes to each township a certain sum to support the costs of primary education; and, on the other hand, the township is required to impose at least an equal sum. The results of this system are greatly praised. If the township was responsible to meet all the costs of public education by itself alone, would it perhaps halt at such an expense? If, on the contrary, it received from the public treasury the entire sum necessary, it would stop closely monitoring employment. But here, the generosity of the State stimulates its zeal and furnishes it with resources without, however, preventing it from giving the school the interest that one always has for one's own work.

There are certain States of the Union, Pennsylvania for example, where primary schools, established at the expense of society, are intended only for the poor, which they receive gratuitously.

In the municipalities of the State of New York and New England,[3] they have only a single subsidized primary school. The rich as well as the poor meet there, and contribute to it according to their means. The inhabitants of the State of New York claim that the poor person puts more effort into obtaining the means of education which are less costly, but which he thinks he can purchase, than to receive what they supply to him for nothing and under the title of charity; they add, and they have reason, that this mixture of all the children in the same schools is more in harmony with the democratic and republican institutions of their country.

See, then, in what way the townships gather the necessary sums to maintain the primary schools:

1. The State or nation, acting in its highest political capacity, annually grants a certain sum to each township;
2. The township raises one [sum], on the other hand, that is at least equal. Until now, it is society that, in totality or in part, acts for a political goal. It is the body of citizens who establish schools and who furnish part of their maintenance, although many of them do not have a direct and present interest in spreading public education.
3. But the money thus obtained is far from sufficient; it forms only an incentive given to parents, just as the subsidy of the State was only an incentive given to municipalities. In order to take his part in the national and municipal liberality, each student is required to pay a certain sum that serves to cover the surplus of the expenses.

These will be better understood from the following table:[4]

In 1829, the State gave to the different townships a sum of 100,000 dollars or 530,000 fr.

This sum formed the annual earning of funds intended for the primary schools, which itself was 1,696,743 dollars or 8,992,737 fr.

This same year, the townships taxed themselves for a sum of 124,556 dollars or 660,146 fr. 80 c.

Further, this same year a municipal fund, specially applied to primary schools, produced 14,095 dollars 32 cents or 74,705 fr. 20 c.

Thus, society in 1829 gave to primary schools in the State of New York a subsidy of 238,651 dollars 33 cents or 1,264,852 fr.

Every citizen took part in this liberality, even those who have no direct interest in contributing to it. Following is a review of interested persons.

Independently of the 1,264,852 fr. furnished by the State or townships, primary schools in 1829 still cost for their maintenance a sum of 821,986 dollars or 4,356,525 fr., which had to be furnished by the students' parents.

The total sum spent in 1829 by the inhabitants of the State of New York for primary education was about[5] 1,060,637 dollars or 5,621,377 fr.; bringing the portion furnished by each inhabitant to 2 fr. 94 c.

It must not be forgotten that the greatest part of this money has been voluntarily furnished. The tax relating to primary education in reality amounts to only 66 cents per person.

The funds intended to encourage higher studies consist of a capital of 256,002 dollars, or 1,356,810 fr.

This capital produced, in 1829, an income of 10,000 dollars or 53,000 francs that the regents of the university have distributed between the different colleges under their supervision.

Each year, the income from the funds intended to encourage higher studies are distributed in the same way; but, independently of this liberality, it frequently happens that the legislature grants a considerable sum to create or support an establishment of education which appears useful. It is thus that in 1814 it dedicated 70,000 dollars or 371,000 francs to the acquisition of a botanical garden.

In 1829, the primary schools created by the municipalities and subsidized by the State numbered one thousand eight hundred forty-six. In 1829, there were in the State of New York two medical colleges, four colleges dedicated to the sciences, and fifty-five establishments of education of inferior rank called *Academies,* to which the State granted a subsidy.

We do not know the number of schools that support themselves and are independent of the government; but it cannot fail to be considerable, as we will see now by the number of schoolchildren.

In 1829, in only the primary schools subsidized by the State, education has been provided to four hundred ninety-nine thousand four hundred twenty-four (499,424) children.

That same year, the entirety of schoolchildren admitted into the colleges and academies that we mentioned above was three thousand eight hundred thirty-five.

We estimate approximately forty-five thousand as the number of children who have procured means of education by another way.

Thus, in the State of New York in 1829 about five hundred fifty thousand children frequented schools; which number, compared to those of the population during the same year, gives one school out of 3 48/100 inhabitants.[6]

We see that in the State of New York almost all children receive a more or less complete education. The superintendent of schools, in his report of

1850, still complains, however, of the lack of enthusiasm certain persons have for procuring the means of education that have been given to them for their children. The inspectors of schools, he says, have taken great care to strongly represent to families what are their duties on this point, and to engage them in instructing their children.

For that matter, it is not in our day alone that American society has taken every interest in spreading education among its members. Here is what can be read in the laws of New Haven from the year 1665:

> "Parents and teachers must ensure that their children and apprentices, in proportion to their advancement in age, acquire, with the grace of God, a degree of education that can at least enable them to know for themselves the Holy Scriptures and be instructed in reading other useful books published in English.
>
> Parents and teachers who neglect this duty will be sentenced, the first time, to pay a fine of 10 shillings. If, three months after this first conviction, they are convicted a second time for the same fault, the fine will be 20 shillings. If they commit anew the same fault, they can be convicted for an even stronger fine, or better their supervision of their children or apprentice can be taken away and given to others."

Notes

1. Revised Statutes, vol. 1, pages 456–466.
2. Revised Statutes, vol. 1, pag. 466–488.
3. There are six States in New England. They are situated east of the Hudson. New England is the output of American civilization.
4. The table is excerpted from a legislative document entitled: *Report of the superintendent of the common schools of the State of New-York*, 1831.
5. Here is the detailed use of this money:
    Interest at 6 p. 100 of the sum of 1,928,230 dollars or 10,219,650 fr.

    1. Used to establish schools, 115,694 dollars or 613,178 fr.
    2. Annual expenses for books, 249,717 dollars or 1,323,500 fr.
    3. Heating the schools, 88,460 dollars or 468,838 fr.
    4. Payment of teachers, 606,766 dollars or 3,215,861 fr.

    Total: 1,060,637 dollars or 5,621,377 fr.
6. This great number of children compared to the total population of the State is perhaps surprising. But it is necessary to note that in America the average human life is not longer than others, perhaps less, and that families there are, in general, much more numerous than in Europe.

Appendix No. 6: Pauperism in America

The Americans have borrowed most of their institutions relating to the poor from England.

In America, as in England, any man in need has an open right against the State. Charity has become a political institution.

Aide is accorded to the poor in two ways: in each great city, as well as in the greatest number of counties, some establishments are placed that bear the name of *alms-houses,* houses of charity, or *poor-houses,* houses of the poor. These establishments can be considered simultaneously as places of refuge and as prisons. The neediest paupers who depend on the public are received and supported there. Vagrants sent by the justices of the peace are contained and made to work there. Thus, the houses of the poor simultaneously contain indigents who cannot and those who do not want to profit their life by honest work.

Independently of the help provided in the houses of charity, the administration responsible for the surveillance of the poor in fact reaches as far as the household.

Each year, the townships levy a tax to support public charity at its own costs, and trustees are nominated to investigate the use of funds thus collected.

It is a generally allowed principle that in providing for the needs of the poor, the State can only advance money which the latter must repay by work. But it is evident in America, as in England, that it is almost impossible to arrive at the rigorous application of this principle in practice. A great number of poor persons are incapable of any work; it is this incapacity itself that puts them in the care of the State. The true pauper has almost always contracted habits of sloth that are difficult to change. Besides, the poor person who is confined in a house of charity is considered unfortunate, not guilty; he contests the right of society to force him by violence to a fruitless labor and to hold him against his will. The government, for its part, feels helpless in this respect; the discipline of a house of charity cannot be that of a prison; even in the case of a man whose habits are not free, he nevertheless cannot be treated as a criminal.

Extreme difficulties arise from this, and one can consider them as inherited from the system of English legislation on the poor; difficulties whose number have been able to be diminished by more or less ideal administrative proceedings, but that we must despair of seeing completely disappear.

Thus, in Maryland it is established that the poor person, in entering the house of charity, enters into the obligation to remain there until the costs caused by his presence are entirely paid. Such is the theory posed: but we understand without difficulty that its application in every case will be very onerous to the public treasury that we want to protect; most of the poor are incapable of procuring the money that is asked of them by their work; condemning them to remain in the house of charity until they have compensated the State will be, most often, condemning them to a perpetual confinement as injurious for the public as for themselves. It was therefore necessary, in decreeing the law, to allow the administrators of the poor to ceaselessly violate it in the ordinary exercise of their functions, and to don judges with an unlimited discretionary power. Let us add that the administration, whatever care the legislator has taken to furnish it with weapons, is still powerless to retain against their wishes the indigents who desire to recover their liberty; for, we repeat, a poor house is not and cannot be a prison.

It cannot be doubted, however, that the principles of welfare [poor] legislation in Maryland have produced a notable decrease in the budget of public expenses in this State; not, perhaps, that they have consequently had an increase of products from the work of the poor, but they have made public charities less desirable to them, and they have thus prevented the poor from making use of public charities without the most extreme necessity.

For the remaining, is a regular system of public charity injurious or useful? It is the one great question that we are not in a position to discuss in detail or to resolve.

It seems to us that in such matters it is necessary to carefully distinguish the poverty that is born from a physical and material incapacity from the one that comes from other causes. As for the first, the State can ameliorate it, without it resulting in a great injury to society. No-one assuredly will expose themselves to lose a limb to be fed at the expense of the public. But we are led to believe that any law which comes, in a regular and assured way, to aid the poverty of the people, will result almost certainly in ceaselessly augmenting the number of poor persons. Such a law, for that matter, always depraves the population that it is expected to relieve. We know how much money has already been raised in England by the poor tax; however, the present state of things still lasts half a century, and it can be fairly stated that, in that country, the proletariats enjoy the soil and that the proprietors are their farmers. There are few indigents in America; but this fact seems to us owing to reasons foreign to the object which occupies us; and it can be believed that it is thus, not because of the law, but on the contrary despite the law. We have remarked in the United States that legislation on pauperism is a source of administrative abuse of every kind, of very great expense, and of innumerable difficulties in execution. It appeared to us that the lower classes of people in America indulged in ordinary habits and acted with a lack of foresight that was often due to the certainty of being rescued from need. The Irishman from the great cities spends the summer in abundance and the winter in the poor house; public charity has lost its cachet of ignominy for him, because some thousands of men there have daily use of it. We have observed, for that matter, in Europe, that when the superior classes of society undertake to relieve the miseries of the poor, they almost always exceed the goal which they desire to attain, because their imagination exaggerates for them the sufferings of the needy caused by hardships that they have never endured themselves. It is thus in America; the houses of charity which we have had opportunity to visit generally offer to the poor a refuge not only healthy, but agreeable; they find there a well-being and pleasures which an honest worker cannot procure outside [of the refuge].

We will add to these preliminary reflections the statistical table of the number of poor in the State of New York in 1830, and some sums that have been expended for their maintenance: this table will serve to give a very precise idea of pauperism in America; the State of New York is, as is known, the greatest of the Union; and nothing indicates that the number of needy there must be less than others.

The State of New York was, in 1830, divided into fifty-five administrative districts, called *counties;* in each of these counties resided three or five administrators called *Superintendents of the Poor*. These magistrates see to it that aid is provided to the needy, to build and maintain the house of charity of the county, and to preside over its direction. Each year, the funds necessary to this object are raised after the vote of an elective body, called the board of supervisors, which represents the county. The superintendents of the poor must, in terms of the law, send an annual account of their administration to the central government of the State. We are going to present excerpts from these different annual reports.

Forty-four districts alone, containing one million six hundred forty-three thousand eight hundred forty-five inhabitants, sent their reports in 1830.[1]

As a result of these documents, in the forty-four counties, fifteen thousand five hundred and six poor were helped in 1830; that gives one pauper out of one hundred seven inhabitants.[2] Among the fifteen thousand five hundred and six poor were found two thousand three hundred sixty-six foreign individuals in the State of New York: there thus remained one pauper of the State of New York out of every one hundred eighty-six inhabitants.

The work of these fifteen thousand five hundred and six individuals has spared the State an expense that can be estimated at 10,674 dollars in 1830.

Each pauper thus profited the State during this year only 70 cents, or 3f. 71 c.

The maintenance of these fifteen thousand five hundred and six poor cost the State, deductions made for the product of their work, around 216,535 dollars or less;[3] which gives for the maintenance of each pauper during the year an expense of 14 dollars, or 74 fr.

The costs of administration and justice alone stood at 27,981 dollars or 158,299 fr.

Thus, in the year 1830, the tax relating to the maintenance of the poor, in the State of New York, stood at 13 cents or 69 c. per inhabitant.

Independently of these annual expenses, the lands and buildings that the State dedicates to food and to contain the poor form a considerable capital.

They recently applied the system of agricultural colonies to sustain the poor in the State of New York.[4] In the forty-four counties of which we have spoken, they have allocated for their use three thousand eight hundred sixty-six acres of good land. These lands, in general, belonged to the State or had been acquired by it at little cost. In dedicating them to the needy, the charges on the public treasury are very much diminished and the poor are occupied with the only work that is wholly appropriate for them. It is, then, one of the greatest advantages that the United States has over England.

They estimated in 1830 the property thus promised by the State of New York at 757,257 dollars or 4,013,409 fr.

Notes

1. The Secretary of State, in his Report to the Legislative Body, pointed out this important omission on the part of the local administrations of eleven counties. But he established the fact without accompanying any observations. In America, the central authority exists only by tolerance, and it hides itself as much as it can. In the state of New York, the only place where a shadow of centralization can be found already complains very loudly of the power accorded to the government.
2. Some evaluations whose basis is, it is true, very uncertain, give the number of poor in France at around one out of sixteen inhabitants.
3. We say "at least" because, in effect, several counties have not spoken in their reports of the cost of administration, which, however, is very considerable.
4. When we say that the system of agricultural colonies has been applied for relief from poverty, we do not want to intonate that it can imitate the example of Holland. In both countries, the poor are employed to cultivate the earth; but for the rest, there is almost no analogy between the two systems.

Appendix No. 7: Imprisonment for Debts in the United States

The former American laws on imprisonment for debts were extremely severe. Like every British institution, they were above all hard for the poor person; they gave short shrift to his liberty.

Thus, imprisonment for debts took place whatever the amount of the debt. It preceded the judgement and struck the debtor before his obligation had been proved. The security was sufficient for the creditor to bring it about. In general, it must be noted with surprise that the English have been, of all modern peoples, those who have put the most liberty into their political laws and who have made the greatest use of prison in their civil laws.

For approximately the last ten years, this oppressive legislation has begun to be the object of violent attacks in America; several States of the Union have already modified or repealed it. It is thus that in the States of Kentucky, Ohio, and New York, imprisonment for debts has been entirely abolished in cases where the debtor seems not to have been dishonest.

In many others, women have been exempted from bodily constraint; in still others, such as New Hampshire and Maryland, a rather high minimum has been fixed to the debt, below which the debtor cannot be subject to imprisonment.

But in the majority of States the former law is still in force. It is thus that in Philadelphia one encounters a great number of prisoners whose debt is not higher, in capital, than 1 dollar (5 fr. 30 c.). In 1830, a man was arrested for a debt of 19 cents (approximately 1 fr.); he spent nine days in prison, and was finally released by paying, independently of the original debt, 8 fr. of fees. Such a law does not come to the aid of creditors; it only sanctions violence and private vengeance.

It is thought that in Pennsylvania the number of individuals arrested for debt is annually seven thousand. If we add this figure to that of those convicted for crime and misdemeanor, which we have estimated to have risen in 1830 to two thousand seventy-four, we will find that in Pennsylvania, out of one hundred forty-four inhabitants, there is approximately one who lives in prison each year.

See *Fifth and sixth annual Reports of the Prison Society of Boston.*

Appendix No. 8: Imprisonment of Witnesses

In the United States, when a witness cannot give bail he is put in prison, and he remains there, mixed with those convicted and sentenced, until the [judicial] procedure is complete and the criminal court hears his case.[1]

At Philadelphia, we were told the history of two young Irishmen who, having arrived in the country too recently to find some guarantors and too poor to give bail, had thus been imprisoned for an entire year, always waiting for the courts to want to[2] receive their testimony.

A foreign merchant is robbed in a Baltimore inn; he gives complaint; but, since the thief did not leave anything for him to give security, he is arrested. Thus, to discover who robbed him of a part of his fortune, he is forced to await justice in prison and to abandon affairs which urgently call him into the West.

We mention these examples out of thousands.

One often complains in Europe of onerous obligations that the laws sometimes impose on the destitute, and of the obstacles that surround him when he seeks his right.

In America, the condition of the poor person is even harder: if chance makes him witness of a crime, he must hurry not to be seen; and if he is the victim himself, his only recourse is to flee, out of fear that justice does not undertake to avenge him.

However monstrous such legislation may seem, habit there has so familiarized minds that our remarks on this subject have been understood only by a small number of enlightened men.[3] The mass of lawyers do not see in the same type of procedure anything that appears to them contrary to the ideas of justice and injustice, nor even to the principles of the democratic constitution that rules them.

The Americans, sons of the English, have wholly provided for the convenience of the rich, and [have provided] almost nothing for the security of the poor. In the same country where the plaintiff is put in prison, the thief remains in liberty if he can give bail. Murder is the only crime whose authors the law does not protect.

NOTES

1. *Literally: "[is] in [the]state of hearing [his case]."
2. *The combination of "voulussent bien" indicates a meaning of "to want to do the right thing."
3. *Another complaint of the negative effects of habit.

Appendix No. 9: Temperance Societies

There is no country in the world where one has benefitted more from association than in America. It is association that, in the midst of a country where equality of fortunes rules, creates enormous assets, and with them support for the greatest commercial and industrial movement that exists. It is by association that, in politics, minorities unite to repel a tyrannical majority, to take ground little by little in public opinion, and to reign in turn. In America, they are united in goals of pleasure, science, religion. The support that an association lends to the weakest of individuals is so well known that a great number of men have finally conceived the idea of associating to combat a wholly intellectual enemy, a passion whose effects in the United States are more disastrous than elsewhere: intemperance.

The inhabitants of the same township or of the same county, who desire to form a temperance society, assemble in a convenient place; there they commit each other, in writing, to abstain from any strong liquor (ardent minds), and to make sure that their subordinates abstain. All those who are engaged in this way become members of the new society. They nominate administrators who are charged with receiving the newly aggregated. These administrators have researched the annual consumption of strong liquors in the township or the county where the association is formed. They strive to know the influence that the abuse of strong liquors exercises on the morality and wellbeing of the inhabitants, and they strive to state the results already known by establishing the society, or those that ought to be expected. Each year, the result of these studies is recorded in a report that is sent to the assembled societies.

A central society is usually placed above all the lower societies of a State, which is responsible for analyzing and publishing the generally obtained results.

In America, the most influential men are eager to take part in temperance societies. They hope to lead public opinion with them, to engage vanity in the moral cause, and to thereby activate a revolution in the habits of their compatriots.

It is impossible to know exactly to what point these efforts have succeeded; what we cannot doubt is that a great good has already been produced. In the State of New York, the temperance society counts more than a hundred thousand members, and we have reason to believe that the consumption of strong liquors has already diminished by half. In Pennsylvania, the number of societies is unknown; but it is estimated that the consumption of strong liquors has already been reduced by five hundred thousand gallons each year.

In 1831, there were one hundred forty temperance societies in Maine; one hundred ninety-six in New Hampshire; one hundred thirty-one in Vermont; two hundred nine in Massachusetts; two hundred two in Connecticut; twenty in Rhode Island; seven hundred twenty-seven in the State of New York; sixty-one in New Jersey; one hundred twenty-four in Pennsylvania; five in Delaware; thirty-eight in Maryland; ten in the District of Colombia; thirty in Virginia; thirty-one in North Carolina; sixteen in South Carolina; sixty in Georgia; one in Florida; ten in Alabama; nineteen in Mississippi; three in Louisiana; fourteen in Tennessee; twenty-three in Kentucky; one hundred four in Ohio; twenty-five in Indiana; twelve in Illinois; four in Missouri; thirteen in Michigan; total: two thousand two hundred. The members of these societies numbered two hundred seventy thousand. It ought to be noted that here it is only a matter of societies that publish an account of their operations (returns). It is thought that the totality of temperance societies in the United States could be higher than three thousand.

Reports of the temperance Societies of the States of New-York and Pennsylvania 1831. Letter to the Mechanics of Boston.

Appendix No. 10: Inquiry into the Philadelphia Penitentiary

(October 1831)

No. 28. The prisoner can read and write; he was sentenced for murder. He says that his health, without being bad, is inferior to what it was outside the prison. He strongly denies having committed the crime that was the reason for his conviction; he easily confesses that he was a drunkard, turbulent, and irreligious. But now, he adds, his soul is changed: he finds a kind of pleasure in solitude, and is tormented only by the desire to return to his family and give a moral and Christian education to his children; things that he had never thought of before.

D. Do you think that you can live here without labor? — R. Labor seems to me absolutely necessary for existence; I believe that I would die without it.[1]

D. Do you often see the guards? — R. About six times a day. — D. Is it a consolation for you to see them? — Yes, sir: it is with a kind of joy that we perceive their figure. This summer, a cricket entered my yard; it seemed to me that I found in him a companion. *It looked like company for me.*[2] When a butterfly or any other animal enters my cell, I never harm it.

No. 36. The prisoner has already undergone a first punishment in the Walnut Street prison; he claims to prefer the stay in the penitentiary to that of the former prison. His health is very good, and solitude does not seem insupportable to him.

When asked if he is forced to work, he responds negatively. But labor, he adds, must be regarded here as a great benefit. Sunday is the day of the week whose length appears the most unending because it is the day when labor is forbidden.

D. What is, in your opinion, the principal advantage of the new system of imprisonment to which you are subjected? —R. Here the prisoner does not know any of his companions and is not known by any. It is a friend from prison who, after leaving Walnut Street, drove me anew to commit a theft.

D. Is the food that they give you sufficient? —R. Yes, sir.

D. Do you think the yard attached to your cell [is] necessary to your health? —R. I am convinced that one cannot do without it.

No. 41. This prisoner is a young man; he confesses that he is a criminal; he sheds tears during the entire course of our meeting, often when he speaks of his family. Happily, he says, no one can see me here; he hopes therefore to be able to return unashamedly into the world and to not be repulsed by society.

D. Do you find solitude difficult to endure? —R. Ah! sir, it is the most frightful torture that can be imagined. — D. But your health does not suffer from it? —R. No, it is very good; but the soul is very ill. — D. What do you think of most often? — R. Religion; religious ideas are my greatest consolation. — D. Do you sometimes see a minister of the church? — Yes, every Sunday. — D. Does it give you pleasure to be with him? — R. It is a great happiness to be able to talk with him. Last Sunday we spent an hour together; he promised to bring me some news of my father and mother tomorrow. I hope they are alive; during the year that I have been here I have not spoken with them. —D. Do you consider labor to be an alleviation of solitude? —R. One cannot live here without labor. Sunday is a very long day to pass, I assure you. —D. Do you believe that, without threatening the health of the prisoners, it is possible to remove the yard attached to the cell? —R. Yes, by establishing in the cell a continual current of air. —D. What idea have you formed of the usefulness of the system of imprisonment to which you are subject? —R. If there is one that can allow men to turn into themselves and to correct themselves, it is this one.

No. 56. This prisoner has already been convicted three times. He is of a feeble constitution; he has been suffering during the first months of his stay in the penitentiary, which he attributes to the absence of exercise and to the lack of a current of sufficient air. He has been brought to the penitentiary at his own request; he loves, he says, solitude; he wants to lose his former companions from view and not make any new ones: he shows us his Bible and assures us that it gives him his greatest consolations in this life.

D. You appear to work here without difficulty: you have said that it was not the same in other prisons where you were confined; where do you see the difference?

— R. Labor is a pleasure here; it would be a great aggravation of our troubles if we lost it: I believe that while in this severity, I could not go without it.

No. 46. This prisoner is fifty-two years old. He was sentenced for burglary; he enjoys good health: solitude appears to him an extremely hard punishment: the presence even of guards is a pleasure for him, and he regards it as a good that a minister of the church sometimes comes to visit: he considers labor as his greatest consolation. He denies having committed the crime that was the reason for his conviction.

No. 61. This prisoner was sentenced for horse stealing; he says he is innocent. No one, according to him, can understand what terrors there are in continual solitude. When asked how he manages to pass the time, he responds that he has only two pleasures: labor, and reading his Bible. The Bible, he says, is his greatest consolation. This prisoner appears very agitated with ideas and even religious passions; his conversation is animated; he cannot speak for a long time without being emotional and having tears in his eyes. (We have made the same remark of all those we have seen up to this point.) He is German in origin, lost his father early, was badly raised. He has spent a year in prison. Good health. According to him, the courtyard attached to the cell is absolutely necessary to the health of the prisoners.

No. 65. This prisoner is thirty years old, without family, convicted of forgery: has been in prison for seven months; very well supported. This convict communicates little; he complains of the troubles that solitude causes, from which, he says, labor is the only relief. He appears little preoccupied with religious ideas.

No. 32. This prisoner is a black man, twenty years old; he has received no education and has no family; he was sentenced for burglary; he has already spent fourteen months in the penitentiary: his health is excellent; he declares that labor and the visits of the chaplain are the only pleasures which he knows. This young man, who appears to have a very thick mind, hardly knew the letters of the alphabet before entering prison; he is, however, able to read his Bible fluently by his own efforts.

No. 20. This prisoner was convicted for the murder of his wife; he has spent eighteen months in the penitentiary, and his health is excellent; he has a very intelligent air; solitude, he says, is insufferable at first, but one is accustomed to it by degrees; labor becomes a distraction and reading the Bible a pleasure; isolation from others is tempered by the daily visits of the guards. He has learned to weave in prison. The turn of ideas in this prisoner is singularly serious and religious: it is a remark that we have already had occasion to make of almost all those whom we have visited.

No. 72. This prisoner is a twenty-four-year-old black man, convicted for the second time as a thief; he seems full of intelligence.

D. You have been imprisoned in the Walnut Street prison. What distinction do you make between that prison and the penitentiary where you are?

R. —The prisoners were much less unhappy in the Walnut Street prison than here, because there they could communicate freely among each other.

D. You seem to work with pleasure: was it the same in the Walnut Street prison?

R. No. Labor was a punishment from which one tried by all means to escape; here, it is a great consolation. — D. Do you read the Bible sometimes? —R. Yes, very often. —D. Did you do so in the Walnut Street prison? — R. No: I have never found more pleasure in reading the Bible and hearing religious discourse than here.

The prisoner has been in the prison for six months: excellent health.

No. 83. This prisoner is thirty years old; he is in a state of recidivism. In the Baltimore prison, where he has already been detained, the discipline was very hard, and the tasks imposed on each prisoner very considerable. —D. Do you prefer being imprisoned here? —R. No: I would like very much to return to Baltimore, because there is no solitude there.

The prisoner has been in the penitentiary for only two months; he had the fever, but his health is completely restored.

No. 64. This prisoner is a twenty-six-year-old black man; he was convicted for burglary; his intelligence appears very limited; he has learned to weave in the prison.

No. 00. This prisoner was convicted for attempted murder; he is fifty-two years old, and has seven children: he appears to have received a distinguished education. Before his trial, he was imprisoned in the Walnut Street prison; he makes a frightful picture of the defects that reign in that prison; he believes, however, that most of the convicts would prefer to return there than to enter into the penitentiary, since they fear solitude.

Interrogated on his opinion touching the system of imprisonment followed in the penitentiary where he is found, he responds that it cannot fail to make a deep impression on the souls of prisoners.

No. 15. This prisoner is twenty-eight years old; he was convicted for homicide (*manslaughter*); he has been at the penitentiary for approximately two years; his health is excellent; he has learned to weave in his cell. Solitude, he says, appeared in the first moments insufferable; but one is later accustomed to it.

No. 54. This prisoner is thirty-five years old: he was convicted for the murder of his wife; he has been in the penitentiary for a year and is doing well.

The reflections made by this man on the troubles caused by solitude prove how he has suffered it; but he begins to be habituated to the kind of life that it imposes on him and does not find it so hard.

No. 22. This prisoner is a thirty-four-year-old black man; he has already been convicted a first time for theft; he has inhabited the penitentiary for eighteen months; his health is rather good.

D. Do you find the discipline of the prison where you are right now as rigorous as it is represented?

R. No; but that depends on the mental disposition of those who are contained here. If the convict thinks solitary imprisonment bad, he falls into irritation and despair; if, on the contrary, he perceives any kind of advantage that it can give him in his position, is does not appear insufferable to him.

D. You have already been imprisoned in the Walnut Street prison?

R. Yes, sir, and I cannot imagine a greater repository of vices and crimes. There, it requires only a few days for a person not very guilty to become a consummate scoundrel.

D. Thus, you believe that the penitentiary is superior to the former prison?

R. It is as if you ask me whether the sun is brighter than the moon.[3]

No. 68. This individual is twenty-three years old; he was convicted for theft; he has been in the penitentiary for six months; his health is excellent; this young man is cold and not very communicative; he is animated only in speaking of the troubles of solitude; he sets to work with ardor; the presence even of a visitor does not interrupt him.

No. 85. This individual has inhabited the penitentiary for only two months; he was convicted for theft. His health is good, but his mind appears to bear great agitation. When he spoke of his wife and child, he burst into tears. In sum, the impression produced on him by the prison appears very profound.

No. 67. The prisoner is thirty-eight years old. He was convicted of theft; he has inhabited the penitentiary for eight months. His health is good. He learned shoemaking in the prison and makes six pairs of shoes per week.

This man appears to have received a serious and meditative mind by nature. The stay in prison has singularly augmented this natural disposition. His reflections are drawn into a very elevated order of ideas. He seems preoccupied with philosophical and Christian thoughts.

No. 52. This convict is thirty-nine years old. He is in recidivism. He has previously been imprisoned in the Walnut Street prison. That prison, he says, is a horrible place; one cannot leave it honest. If I had been in a prison such as this one from the beginning, I would not have been convicted a second time.

D. Were you easily habituated to solitude?

R. —Solitude seemed frightful to me in the beginning; I am little by little habituated to it; but I believe that I cannot live here without labor. Without labor, there is no sleep here.

This man has spent nearly a year in prison. He is doing very well.

No. 1. This prisoner, the first who was sent to the penitentiary, is a black man. He has inhabited the prison for more than two years. His health is very good.

This man works with ardor; he makes ten pairs of shoes per week. His mind seems very tranquil and his dispositions excellent. He seems to regard his arrival in the penitentiary as a benefit signaled by Providence. In general, his thoughts are religious. He read to us the parable of the good shepherd from the Gospel, whose meaning, which had penetrated him, vividly touched him; he who was born from a degraded and oppressed race and had never felt anything but the indifference or hardness of men.

No. 17. The prisoner is a mulatto convicted of theft. He has inhabited the penitentiary for twenty months and has never been ill there. Some charitable men came to teach him to read. He also learned shoemaking in the prison. The need that he felt to labor was such that within eight days he was already able to make a crude form of shoes.

No. 50. This convict, thirty-seven years old, is a recidivist. He makes an energetic portrait of the defects that reign in the Walnut Street prison, where he has already been imprisoned.

If they had put me here, he says, after my first crime, I would never have committed a second; but one always leaves the Walnut Street prison more corrupt than when you entered. It is only here that one can reflect and repent of oneself.

D. But the penitentiary discipline is very severe?

R. —Yes, sir; especially in the beginning. During the first two months, little was needed for me to fall into despair. But reading and labor have little by little consoled me.

The prisoner has been in the prison for twenty months. He is in perfect health.

No. 62. This prisoner is a very stately man, thirty-two years old. He was a doctor. Solitary imprisonment appeared to have made a deep impression on this young man. He spoke of the first time of his imprisonment only with terror; this memory led him to tears. For two months, he says, he lived in despair; but this impression softened with time. At present, he is resigned to his fate, however austere it may be. He was granted the liberty to do nothing; but laziness in solitude is such a horrible thing that he works constantly. Since he knows no craft, he occupies himself with cutting the leather that serves to make shoes. His greatest regret is not being able to communicate with his family. He ended the conversation by saying: solitary imprisonment is very hard to endure, but I do not regard it less as an eminently useful institution to society.

The health of the prisoner is good. He does not complain of the physical discipline that he undergoes.

No. 4. This man, twenty years old, has already been imprisoned in the Walnut Street prison. He attributes his recidivism to the pernicious influence of that place. One is much happier here, he says: it is not, however, because the penitentiary discipline is soft; far from it, the first moments that are passed here are above all frightful; I believed that I would die here of despair. However, I have never been sick here and it is already two years that I have been confined here.

No. 35. This prisoner is more than eighty years old. When we entered his cell, he was occupied with reading the Bible.

No. 73. This cell is occupied by a twenty-year-old black woman, who is found in a state of recidivism. The penitentiary, she says, is very superior to the Walnut Street prison.
D. Why is that? — R. Because it makes one reflect.
This woman has inhabited her cell for seven months. She bears it very well.

No. 63. This prisoner, twenty-two years old, was sentenced to thirteen months in prison for *fornication*. He has inhabited his cell for nine months. His health is excellent. His dispositions appear good. He congratulates himself on having been imprisoned in the penitentiary.

No. 6. This individual has spent two years in prison. He arrived there sick and has reestablished his health there.

No. 69. This individual is thirty years old. He was convicted for theft. He has spent five months in prison. His health appears very good, but his mind is very afflicted. I do not believe, he said, that I will ever leave here alive: solitude is disastrous to the constitution of man, and it will kill me.
D. What are your consolations?
R. — I have only two: labor, and reading my Bible.

No. 51. This prisoner, forty-four years old, has already been convicted a first time. He bitterly regrets having been imprisoned in the Walnut Street prison. It is only here, he says, that one can reflect.
He has been in his cell for ten months, and has never been better.

No. 47. This man has already spent one year in the penitentiary; he appears to enjoy excellent health.
His dispositions seem good; but it is difficult to attach great importance to his words, since he hopes to obtain his pardon soon.

No. 66. This convict is twenty-one years old. Atypically, he at first refused to work, and a long fast was necessary to reduce him to it. However, he appears completely submissive; he has felt the utility of labor in solitude and reads with ardor. He learned shoemaking in little time and now makes eight or nine pairs of shoes per week.
He has inhabited his cell for eight months. Excellent health.

No. 00. This prisoner is forty years old; he was convicted for armed robbery on a public road. He appears full of intelligence. Here is, in his own words, the account of his history:
I was fourteen or fifteen years old when I arrived at Philadelphia. I was the boy of a poor farmer from the West, and I came in search of profiting my life by working in a great city. I was not recommended by anyone, I did not find work; and from the first day I was reduced, to take refuge, to go

to bed on the deck of a port vessel. This was where they discovered me in the morning; the constable arrested me and the mayor sentenced me to one month in prison, as a vagrant. Mixed in for months of imprisonment with a host of malefactors of all ages, I lost the honest principles that my father had given me; and in leaving the prison one of my first acts was to join several young delinquents of my age and help them commit various thefts. I was arrested, tried, and acquitted. I believed myself now free from the efforts of justice, and, full of confidence in my ability, I committed other offences that led me again before the courts. This time, I was sentenced to imprisonment for nine years in the Walnut Street prison.

D. Did this punishment make you feel the necessity of correcting yourself?

R. —Yes, sir; it was not, however, that the Walnut Street prison gave me regret for the criminal actions that I had committed. I admit that I could have never repented there, nor even that I had the idea of doing it during my entire stay in that place. But I soon noticed that the same individuals constantly reappeared there, and that, whatever the skill, force, or courage of their theft, they always ended up being caught. This brought me back seriously on myself, and I made the firm resolution to forever stop, when I left the prison, such a dangerous kind of life. This resolution made, my conduct became better, and after seven years of imprisonment I obtained my pardon. I was taught the trade of the tailor in prison, and I soon found favorable employment for myself. I married; and I began to profit my life rather easily; but Philadelphia was full of men whom I had known in prison; I ceaselessly feared being betrayed by them. One day, in fact, two of my former roommates presented themselves to my master and asked to speak to me. I first pretended not to recognize them; but they soon forced me to acknowledge who I was. They then asked me to give them a considerable sum; and, on my refusal, they threatened to reveal the history of my life to my master. I promised then to satisfy them, and I suggested that they return the next day.

After they left, I left myself; and embarking immediately with my wife I quit Philadelphia and went to Baltimore. I very easily found employment for myself in that city, and for a long time I lived a very comfortable existence there; when one day my master received a letter from one of the Philadelphia constables which advertised that he had a former prisoner of Walnut among his workers. I do not know who was able to bring this man to such an act. It is to him that I owe being here. As soon as he received the letter of which I speak, my master dismissed me with disgrace.

I went to every other tailor in Baltimore, but they were warned and refused to receive me. Poverty compelled me to go work in the silver mines established between Baltimore and Ohio. Grief and fatigue from a dangerous kind of life were not long in giving me a violent fever. I was sick for a long time, and used up my resources. Barely recovered, I took myself to Philadelphia, where the fever resumed. When I began to recover, I saw myself without resources, without bread for myself and my family; I thought of all the obstacles that I had found to honestly profiting my life and of every unjust persecution that I had suffered; I fell into a state of inexpressible exasperation. I told myself: Oh well! Since I am reduced to it, I will go back to being a thief; and if there is still a single dollar in the United States, were it in the pocket of the President, I will have it. I called my wife; I ordered her to sell all the clothes that were not necessary to us; and with the money, I went to buy a pistol. Armed with this weapon, and in a time when I was still too weak to walk without crutches, I went into the middle of the city; I arrested the first passerby and forced him to give me his wallet. But I was discovered the same night. I had been followed from afar by the person whom I had robbed; and my weakness had forced me to stop in the neighborhood; it was no trouble to take hold of me. I acknowledged my crime without difficulty and was sent here.

D. What are your present resolutions for the future?

R. I feel disposed, I tell you frankly, neither to blame myself for what I did, nor to become what is called "a good Christian;" but I am determined not to steal, and I see the possibility of succeeding. When I leave here in nine years, nobody will recognize me in the entire world; no one will know that I have been in prison; I will have no dangerous acquaintance. I will be free to improve my life in peace. This is the great advantage that I find in this penitentiary, and that is why, despite the harshness of the discipline that is in force here, I prefer a hundred times over finding myself here than inhabiting the Walnut Street prison again.

In prison for a year. Very good health.

No. 00. This prisoner is forty years old. He has been in the penitentiary only eight days. I found him reading the Gospel. He appeared calm and almost satisfied. He tells me that during the first days, solitude seemed insupportable to him. He was not allowed to read or work.

But yesterday he was given books; and from there he found his condition completely changed. He showed me that he had already read almost an entire volume which contains the gospels. This book provides him with several religious and moral reflections. He could not conceive that he had not had the idea of reading them sooner.

No. 00. This prisoner has spent two years in the penitentiary. His punishment was to expire after a few days. His health was excellent. There reigned on his physiognomy an air of hope and joy that was pleasing to see. He greatly praised the treatment that he had undergone in the prison. He assured us of having made the firm resolution to not commit any faults in the future. Everything announced that the intentions of the young man are in fact good, and that he will follow them. He was sentenced for an act of violence. His conduct in the prison has always been exemplary.

No. 00 and 00. These two individuals are insane. The director of the penitentiary assured us that they arrived as such into the prison. Their madness is very tranquil. Amid the incoherence of their discourse, nothing can be grasped which allows attributing the illness that afflicts them to their imprisonment.[4]

No. 00. This prisoner is sixty-two years old; he arrived in the last stage of pulmonary consumption. He is preoccupied only with thoughts of the next life.

No. 00. This prisoner was a doctor before his conviction. He is responsible for care of the pharmacy in the penitentiary. He converses intelligently, and speaks of the various systems of imprisonment with a liberty of mind that his position renders rather extraordinary. The discipline of the penitentiary appears to him, in his case, mild and reformatory. For a very elevated man, he says, it is better to live in absolute solitude than to be found mixed with the miserable of all kinds. For everyone, isolation favors reflection and is useful for reform.

D. But have you not noticed that solitary imprisonment is harmful to health? In your capacity as prisoner and doctor, you are better able to judge this question than any other.

R. I have not noticed that overall there is more illness here than in society. I do not believe that people here feel worse.

No. 00. The individual confined in this cell is fifty-five years old. Before his conviction he enjoyed a comfortable fortune, and he was justice of the peace in his county. He was sentenced for having killed his wife's lover.

This prisoner, who speaks French, seems preoccupied only with a fixed idea: that of obtaining his pardon. We were never able to speak of anything other than his trial and the causes leading up to it. He is writing a memo to the governor; we were made to hear him read a part of it and to examine with him the pieces of the trial. He is sentenced to a long imprisonment;

he feels old, and lives only on the hope of a further extension. This man appears to us to believe in the efficacy of the kind of imprisonment to which he has been submitted. He finds it singularly proper to correct the guilty, among which, moreover, he is very careful not to rank himself.

Very good health.

No. 00. This prisoner is a young man of twenty years. He is English by birth, and arrived in America a little while ago. Sentenced for forgery. He appears intelligent, docile, and resigned. His health is excellent. His dispositions for the future appear good.

No. 00. This prisoner is the age of the preceding; English as well. He appears irritated and not subdued by the punishment. It seems he dislikes people coming to visit him; he does not interrupt his work to speak to us, and hardly responds to the questions we address to him. He does not testify of repenting and shows no preoccupation with religious ideas.

Good health.

No. 00. This prisoner is thirty-eight years old. He has not been in the penitentiary more than three weeks; thus, he is plunged into true despair. Solitude terrorizes me, he says; I can never endure the punishment that is inflicted on me until the end. I will die before becoming free.

D. Do you not find a consolation in your labor at least?

R. Yes, sir; solitude without labor is a thousand times more horrible still; but labor does not prevent me from thinking and being very unhappy. Here, I assure you, the soul is very sick.

This poor man sobbed in speaking of his wife and children, whom he did not believe he would see again. When we entered his cell, we found him crying and working at the same time.

No. 00. This prisoner is twenty-five years old; he belongs to the highest class of society. He speaks with warmth and ease. He was sentenced for falsely declaring bankruptcy.

This young man shows great pleasure in seeing us. It is easily seen that solitude is a frightful torment for him. The need of intellectual relationships with his equals seemed to preoccupy him even more vividly than those of his companions who have received a less careful education; he hastily recounted his history to us; he speaks of his crime, of his position in the world, of his friends, of his parents above all; the sentiments of family appear to have been extraordinarily developed in him. He cannot think of his parents without bursting into tears; he draws some letters from under his bed that his family managed to send him. These letters are almost tattered from the force of having been read; he relishes them again, comments on them, and is softened by the least expression of interest that they contain.

D. I see that the punishment which is inflicted on you appears extremely hard. Do you think, at least, of reforming?

R. Yes, sir; I think that overall this kind of imprisonment is better than any other. It would be even more painful for me to find myself mixed with the poor of all kinds than to live here alone. Besides, it is impossible that such a sentence would not make one think much.

D. But do you not think that its influence could be disastrous to reason?

R. I think that the danger that you warn of must sometimes exist. I remember, for my own part, that during the first months of my solitude I was often visited by strange visions. For several nights in a row, it seemed to me, among others, that I saw an eagle perched on the foot of my bed. But now I work, and am accustomed to the kind of life that I lead; I am not tormented by such ideas.

One year in prison. Good health.[5]

Notes

1. *The translator has carried over "D" and "R" as written in the French manuscript.
2. *This sentence is in English in the original French text.
3. We believed we must literally reproduce the responses of the prisoners.
4. In America, there are no insane asylums where one can recover freely from illness; it must often happen in the United States, as it does among us, that a fool is convicted to the prison for giving to his family the right to make him a prisoner at the expense of the State.
5. No one can visit the convicts during their imprisonment, except for the inspectors, guards, and chaplain. The judges of Philadelphia were kind enough to make an exception to this rule in our favor. We were then introduced successively into all the cells and left alone with the prisoners. We put here under the eyes of the reader the result of these conversations conducted over fourteen days. The number that precedes the article of each prisoner indicates his rank of seniority in the house. We often omitted making note of it, as will be seen by following the inquiry.

Appendix No. 11: Conversation with Mr. Elam Lynds

.........I have spent ten years of my life in prison administration, he said to us; I was witness of the abuses that prevailed in the former system for a long time; they were very great. The prisons were very expensive then, and the inmates completely lost their morality there. I think that this state of things might have ended by leading us back to barbarous laws of the former codes. The majority, at least, were beginning to be disgusted with any philanthropic idea whose execution experience seemed to demonstrate as impossible. It was in these circumstances that I began reform at Auburn. I first found in the legislature, and even in public opinion, great obstacles to overcome: they cried much of tyranny; it took nothing less than success to justify me.

D. Do you think that the system of discipline established by you can be used in places other than in America?
R. I am convinced that it can be used anywhere they follow the method that I have followed. As far as I can judge, I think that in France there are more chances of success than among us. It is said that in France the prisons are under the immediate direction of the government, which can lend a solid and durable support to its agents; here, we are slaves to a public opinion that changes incessantly. Thus, it is

necessary, in my opinion, that a director of the prison, above all when he is innovative, be coated with a complete and guaranteed authority; it is impossible to count on this in a democratic republic such as ours. Among us, it is necessary that the laborer simultaneously attract public favor and carry out his business; two things that are often irreconcilable. My principle has always been that to reform a prison, it was good to concentrate all power and responsibility in the same man simultaneously. When the inspectors wanted to force me to agree with them,[1] I told them: you are perfectly free to send me away; I depend on you; but as long as you keep me, I will follow the plan that I have conceived; it is up to you to choose.

D. We have heard it said of Americans, and we would not be far from believing it, that the success of the penitentiary system in the United States must be attributed, in part, to the habit that is contracted among your people to scrupulously obey the law.

R. I do not think so. At Singsing, one-fourth of the inmates are composed of men foreign to the Union. I have them all bend to the rule like the Americans of the United States. Those who were the most difficult to curb were the Spaniards from South America, a race that is more ferocious beast and savage than civilized man. The easiest to govern were the French; they were those who submitted most readily and with the best grace to their fate when they judged it inevitable. If I had the choice, I would prefer to direct a prison in France than in America.

D. What is, then, the secret of such a powerful rule that you have introduced at Singsing, and whose effects we have admired?

R. It would be very difficult for me to tell you: it is the result of a series of efforts and daily cares, which it would be necessary to witness. General regulations cannot be indicated. It is important to maintain continual work and silence; to accomplish this, it is necessary to be ceaselessly occupied in surveilling the guards as well as the prisoners; being simultaneously unmerciful and just.

D. Do you think that corporal punishments can be dispensed with?

R. I am convinced of the contrary. I regard the punishment of the whip as the most efficacious and at the same time the most humane that exists; it never hurts health and it forces inmates to lead an essentially healthy life. Solitary imprisonment, on the contrary, is often powerless and always dangerous. I have encountered in my life many inmates whom it was impossible to reduce in this manner, and who were put in a dungeon only to be taken to the hospital. I believe it is impossible to govern a large prison without the service of the whip. Only those who have learned about human nature in books can say the contrary.

D. Do you not think that they make a mistake at Singsing in leaving the prisoners to work in an open field?

R. For my part, I would prefer to direct a prison where such a state of things exists than another where it would be different. It is impossible in an enclosed prison to obtain the same surveillance or continual care from the guards. Once, for that matter, one has managed to completely subdue the prisoners to the yoke of discipline, one can without danger employ them in labor that one judges the most profitable and in the sites that one desires to choose. It is thus that the State utilizes criminals in a thousand ways, after it has improved the discipline of its prisons.

D. Do you believe that it would be completely impossible to establish a good discipline in a prison where the cellular system does not exist?

R. I think that we could maintain great order in such a prison and make labor productive there; but we could not prevent a crowd of abuses[2] from slipping in whose consequences are very serious.

D. Do you believe that one can establish cells in an old prison?

R. That depends entirely on their layout. I do not doubt that in many old prisons the cellular system can be introduced without great difficulties. It is always easy and inexpensive to establish wooden cells; but they have the disadvantage of retaining a bad odor, and consequently of sometimes becoming unhealthy.

D. Do you believe ultimately in the reform of a great number of prisoners?

R. It is necessary to hear each other [carefully]: I do not believe in complete reform, except for juvenile delinquents. Nothing is rarer, in my opinion, than to see a criminal of a mature age become a religious and virtuous man. I do not put faith in the saintliness of those who leave prison; and I do not believe that the guidance of the chaplain or the meditations of the prisoner can ever make him a good Christian. But my opinion is that a great number of former convicts do not fall into recidivism, and that they even become useful citizens, having learned an art in prison and having acquired the habit of constant labor there. Here is the only reform that I have ever hoped to produce, and I think that it is the only one that society can demand.

D. What do you think proves the future reform of the conduct of the prisoner in prison?
R. Nothing. If it would be necessary to give a prognosis, I would say that even the prisoner with good conduct in prison will probably return to his former habits when leaving the penitentiary. I have always noted that the worst citizens[3] make excellent prisoners. They generally have more skill and intelligence than others; they perceive more quickly and more completely that the only way to make their condition less intolerable is to avoid painful and repeated punishments that are the foolproof consequence of insubordination; they therefore behave well without being better for it. The result of this observation is that pardon must never be accorded to the prisoner merely on account of the conduct that he had in prison. We thereby only create hypocrites.
D. The system that you attack is that of almost every theorist.
R. In this, as in many other points, they are wrong, because they do not know well those things they speak of. If Mr. Livingston, for example, was responsible for applying his penitentiary theories to men born like himself, in a social position where intelligence is strongly developed and moral sensibility very excited, I easily think that he would happen to produce excellent results; but prisons are on the contrary filled with rough beings, whose education is nothing and who perceive ideas and often even sensations only with difficulty. That is what he continually forgets.
D. What do you think of the contract system?
R. I think that it is very useful to hire out the labor of inmates to the company; provided, however, that the director of the prison remains perfectly master of their person and time. When I was at the head of the Auburn penitentiary, I made contracts with different contractors that forbade them from entering the house. Their presence in the workshops can only be very harmful to the discipline.
D. In France, the price of work for the prisoner is estimated to be very low.
R. It would rise in the same degree as the discipline would become better. That is what we have experienced. Formerly, the prisons were very expensive to the State of New York; they are profitable today. The well-disciplined prisoner works more; he works better and never spoils the raw material that is entrusted to him, as would sometimes happen in the former prisons.

D. What is, in your opinion, the quality that one must look for the most in a director of prisons?
R. The practical art of leading men. It is above all necessary that he is profoundly convinced, as I have always been, that a dishonest man is always a coward. This persuasion, which he cannot fail to communicate soon to those who he must govern, will give him an irresistible ascendency over them, and will easily give him a crowd of things that can appear hazardous at first glance.[4]

During the entire course of this conversation, which lasted for several hours, Mr. Elam Lynds ceaselessly returned to this idea, that he had begun by taming the soul of the prisoner and convincing him of his weakness. This point obtained, everything became easy, regardless of the construction of the prison or the site of labor.

Notes

1. *Literally, "to enter into their views."
2. *Third-person singular imperfect subjunctive of *glisser*.
3. *Or, subjects.
4. In expressing this last thought, Mr. Elam Lynds probably alluded to a fact that we had heard recounted at Singsing a few days previously. One individual, confined in the penitentiary, had announced that at the first opportunity he would kill Mr. Elam Lynds, then director of the establishment. The latter, well educated in the dispositions of this man, sent for him, introduced himself in his chamber at his bed, and, without appearing to perceive his trouble, made him shave him. He then dismissed the convict, saying: I know that you desired to kill me; but I despise you too much to believe that you could ever have the audacity to execute your plan. Alone and without arms, I am always stronger than you all.

Appendix No. 12: Excerpts

FROM A LETTER ADDRESSED TO US BY MR. WELLES, JUDGE AT WETHERSFIELD, AND FORMER INSPECTOR OF THE CONNECTICUT STATE PRISON. OCT. 1831

...Although the Wethersfield prison has been built cheaply, I think that we could have raised it with much less expense. Useless expenses were incurred in its construction. Thus, for example, we have a slate roof, copper gutters, and cornices on the walls. With a climate like ours, it is better that water fall directly on the ground; it freezes in the gutters. On other points, we have done at great expense what did not require such expenditures.

...It seems to me that the architect of a prison is susceptible to committing two great errors. The first consists in not establishing a precise proportion of strength between different parts of the building. It is thus that we often see walls five or six feet thick composed of enormous stone blocks bound together by iron clamps; to these walls are joined doors and windows, whose strength only corresponds to a wall of one foot thick. Furthermore, a massive and expensive door is sometimes mounted on hinges that are weaker than those of a light gate.

The second error arises from the idea that the building that we raise is made to survive in centuries to come. We ought to think that many men of solid minds and consummate experience ceaselessly devote their time and talent to the construction of prisons. One improvement leads to another, and it is in the power of no man to foresee the result of these different efforts. With them, public opinion is modified; ultimately, society does not look with favor on an establishment that does not include all the improvements suggested by experience. In the space of twenty years, there is often a complete revolution in ideas; the old prisons no longer meet the needs of society, and they are abandoned. Such is the history of most of the prisons in the United States. It is therefore very important that these establishments be built cheaply, since they later become obstacles to improvements; obstacles all the more difficult to overcome the more expensive the building.

…The characteristic trait of the modern system is the substitution of vigilance for material force. In the new prisons, the eye and ear of the guard never rest a single instant. A perpetual silence is maintained day and night there.

This constant vigilance must contribute to make the construction of our penitentiaries more economical. Experience has, in effect, demonstrated that the only indispensable strength to such buildings is what they need to withstand the elements and to guarantee them a certain duration. It is useless to give them more strength than individual houses.

…The prison of Wethersfield is constructed from irregularly carved sandstone. The walls are three feet thick[1] at their base and two at their top.

2.5 feet at the base, 1.5 feet at the top would be sufficient. Further, the height of the walls would have had to be made level with the ceilings of the cells.

The walls, completely constructed, cost 10 cents (55 centimes) per square foot; knowing: 4 cents (21 centimes) per foot; 4 cents (21 centimes) for the workforce; 1 cent for the mortar; 1 cent for the scaffolding and other accidental expenses.

Our cells are in bricks; they cost us 20 cents (1 fr. 6 cent.) per square cube. Many of them have a floor made of a single stone. Each of these stones cost 4 dollars (21 fr. 20 cent.). The other floors are formed by a piece of wood that is three inches thick, on which we have set a row of bricks. The whole thing is covered with sealant and amounts to 2 dollars for each cell (10 fr. 60 cent.).

The door of the cells is made of oak planks three inches thick, closed by four bolts. This door, minus the ironwork, costs 2 dollars 50 cents (13 fr. 25 cent.). I have estimated that the total price of the cell came to

28 dollars (148 fr. 40 cents), everything included: masonry, hinges, locks, screens.

I have attached further down the estimate of a prison having 500 cells (see below).

...There is a question of whether it is more advantageous to employ inmates or free workers to build a prison. I will say that this depends on what the inmates are doing at the time when one wants to use them. If they are already profitable employees, it is better to leave them in their workshops. If, on the contrary, they are a little lazy, then they must be used for any labor that does not require special knowledge, or those with which they are already acquainted. Thus, they can be made to work the iron, to prepare and carry materials, to make mortar to aide in laying stones and bricks. The cost of the guard necessitated by the presence of prisoners outside the prison is, moreover, so considerable that it will always be less economical to use their labor thus.

Can the labor of the prisoners cover the costs of maintaining the prison? On this point, I will add only a single remark to what has already been said between us. We had as many reasons for supposing the labor of prisoners insufficient as the French themselves can have of it. The former Connecticut penitentiary did not stop incurring great expenses for us. Few persons thus dared to hope that the work of the prisoners in the new [penitentiary] could ever cover the total costs of the establishment, and nothing, even more so, could make us think that the difference in favor of the public treasury would be raised in a single year to 16,000 dollars (84,800 fr); this is what we have been witnesses to, however.

It is said that in France the free workers themselves cannot find employment as easily as in America, and that consequently it is harder to use the labor of prisoners there. But if the free worker can manage to sustain himself and his family, although it is very difficult, the worker in prison must certainly do equally, since his maintenance costs less; and with a successful construction the surveillance can be exercised by a small number of individuals and at little cost. If the work produces less, the expenses are smaller: these two things are correlative, and between them there necessarily exists an exact proportion.

I persist, then, in firmly believing that in a prison advantageously constructed, the well-directed labor of the prisoners must completely indemnify the State.

Estimation of Expenses Necessary to Build a Prison Able to Contain Five Hundred Prisoners

Main Building

1. Building length.   250 feet.
2. Width.   50 feet.
3. Bottom thickness   2 ½
4. Top thickness   1 ½
5. Average for full height   2
6. Length of walls in its foundations   3
7. Depth of foundations   3

The whole must be composed of 49,800 square feet of stone built in mortar, at 10 cents (53 centimes) per foot. The expense will amount to 4,980 dollars or 26,394 fr.

1. Slate roofs, 1,250 dollars (7,625 fr.)[2]
2. Five hundred cells, at 28 dollars each, 14,000 dollars (74,200 fr.)
3. Plastering and Ceiling, 600 dollars (3,180 fr.)
4. Brick floor, four and a half bricks per foot, 200 dollars (1,060 fr.)

Offices

Two buildings placed at each side of the court, 15 feet from the walls, intended to contain the workshops, food halls, schools, et cetera.

1. Width   270 feet.[3]
2. Length   30
3. Two floors, slate roof, cellar: 6,000 dollars (31,800 fr.).
4. Parameter walls: 18 feet high, based at 3 feet of depth, 2 feet thick at the base, 18 inches at the top, containing 31,500 cubic feet of stones, at 10 cents (53 cents) per foot.
5. Expense: 3,150 dollars (16,695 fr.)
6. Flying buttresses to hold the outside walls, 200 dollars (1060 fr.)
7. Patrol path established on top of the perimeter wall, 200 dollars (1,060 fr.)
8. Barred windows: 500 dollars (2,650 fr.)
9. House for superintendent, attached to the prison: 2,500 dollars (13,250 fr.)
10. Unforeseen expenses: 6,420 dollars (34,026 fr.)

Total: 40,000 dollars or 212,000 francs.
Expense for each prisoner: 80 dollars or 424 francs.

This estimate is made following the actual price of the raw material, which is as follows:

1. Stone: cubic foot, 4 cents (21 centimes).
2. Lumber (1,000 feet, 1 inch thick), 10 dollars (53 fr.).
3. Day of work: 1 dollar (5 fr. 30 cent.).
4. Iron, one pound, 4 cents (21 centimes).

In the construction of the prison, I am using sawn or hewn stones only for the top and base of different openings in the walls.

We should observe that, in the quote above, we have not considered doors or windows. In the estimate for the walls, I have abstracted from any opening that will be necessary to drill; I have considered them as if forming only a solid mass. The walls, in reality, will thus cost less than I have stated, and this deduction of cost will cover the expense of the doors and windows and even a part of the cost of fences.

At Wethersfield, the locks for the cells have been crafted by prisoners at the price of 2 dollars 25 cents each (12 fr. 92 cents). A single key opens a hundred doors.

ESTIMATE FOR THE EXPENSE THAT WOULD RESULT IN MAINTAINING AND GUARDING FIVE HUNDRED PRISONERS IN THE PRISON THAT IS IN QUESTION ABOVE

Expenses

1. Food, clothing, bedding for each prisoner. 22 dollars (116 fr. 60 c.)
2. Expenses for 500 prisoners. 11,000 dollars (58,300 fr.).
3. Expenses for 1 Superintendent. 800 dollars (4,240 fr.).
4. Expenses for 1 Under-Warden. 400 dollars (2,120 fr.).
5. Expenses for 8 monitors of the workshop. 2,800 dollars. (14,840 fr.).
6. Expenses for 8 guards.[4] 2,000 dollars (10,600 fr.).
7. Medicine and hospital expenses. 700 dollars (3,710 fr.)
8. Chaplain. 400 dollars (2,120 fr.)
9. Lighting, heating and incidental expenses. 1,000 dollars (5,300 fr.)

Total: 19,100 dollars (101,230 fr.).

Profits

Out of five hundred prisoners, I deduct fifty each day from them, those who are too old for work, sick, or unproductive employees; leaving four hundred and fifty who must each day make a total of 25 cents (1 fr. 32 cent.). In counting 300 days in the year, the total earnings should amount to 33,750 dollars or 178,875 fr.

Deducting from this number the cost of 19,100 dollars (101,230 fr.), there remains the net gain: 14,650 dollars or 76,645 fr.

This result will not appear exaggerated if one understands that during the last year the one hundred-sixty men confined in the Wethersfield prison have earned for the State more than half the sum given above, or 7,824 dollars (41,467 fr.).

I do not doubt that at Wethersfield one can easily cover all the expenses of a prison, containing five hundred prisoners, with 19,100 dollars (101,230 fr.); and I believe, on the contrary, to have estimated the profit obtained by a similar prison much too low. Consequently, when it came to expenses, I based it on the actual price of the Wethersfield prison; when I have spoken of profits, I took care, on the contrary, to evaluate the work of the prisoners less than what the same penitentiary yields. Thus, the price per day, on average, in my estimation, has been raised to 25 cents each day, while at Wethersfield the least paid prisoner earns 30 cents, and many of them bring 1 dollar to the State (5 fr. 30 cent.).

Notes

1. We must note here that anytime mention of *feet* and of *inches* is made in this letter, Mr. Welles intends to speak of *English* feet and inches. The English foot is about one-fifteenth smaller than the French foot. The French foot is composed of 324 millimeters, the English foot of 304 millimeters only.
2. *Here Lieber inserts a footnote: "The French had here *ardoise*, but the authors were mistaken. It is precisely the slate which Judge Welles considers unnecessary at the beginning of these extracts. The original, from which the authors translated, had shingle" (Beaumont and Tocqueville 1833, p. 206).
3. The bottom of each floor in these buildings has 8,100 feet of surface, which gives a total of 32,400 feet. 40 feet more than suffices for a man's labor. Those who are shoemakers only need 20 feet. Five hundred men will therefore occupy 20,000 feet; and there will remain 12,400 for the storerooms, offices that will substantially meet every need.

4. *In the original text, Tocqueville and Beaumont have a margin note indicating that the costs of the superintendent, under-director, surveillance, and guards together constitute "*Frais de garde.*"

REFERENCE

Beaumont, Gustave de and Alexis de Tocqueville. 1833. *On the Penitentiary System in the United States and Its Application in France, with an Appendix on Penal Colonies and also Statistical Notes.* Translated by Francis Lieber. Philadelphia: Carey, Lea & Blanchard.

Appendix No. 13: Regulations of the Connecticut Prison

Section 1

Duties of the warden

1. The warden will reside in the prison; he will visit the rooms and cells at least once each day and will see each of the inmates;
2. He cannot be absent for more than one night without giving notice of it to the directors;
3. He will have to make sure that the books and registers of the prison are maintained in a way to clearly show in what state the inmates are found, the number of those that are employed in each kind of industry, their earnings, the number of sick persons; these registers will show the prison accounts, receipts and payments, purchases and sales; he will have to put these books before the eyes of the directors when they meet quarterly, or anytime he will be required to do so. The reports will be presented four times a year by him; he will affirm them to be true and will specify there, in detail, the persons to whom money has been paid or who has received it, as well as the purpose of the payment.
4. The chief warden will be responsible for making all contracts, purchases, and sales for the prison account. He will command all lower

employees and will oversee them in the exercise of their functions; he will take care that they are conforming to the laws, as well as to the regulations prescribed by the directors. He will ensure that[1] prisoners are treated with kindness and humanity, and that inferior employees of the prison do not exert useless severity on them. But if the safety of the house was compromised, or if violent acts were feared, the chief warden and other employees ought to use any means that the law accords them to defend themselves and to seize the authors of disorder. In executing his duties, the chief warden must never lose the reformation of the criminals from view; he will carefully guard himself against movements of anger or resentment that could animate him against them. Any order that exudes from him will be given with mildness and dignity; he will execute them with firmness and promptitude.

5. The chief warden will politely receive any person who desires to visit the prison, and see to it that the inferior employees of the establishment use the same regard for them.
6. The law imposes on the directors the right to ascertain for themselves the position in which the convicts are found and what treatment they are made to undergo. Nothing must therefore prevent the inmates from freely discussing with the directors anytime that they are present in the prison: no one has the right to punish them for having talked to them. In filling this part of their functions, the directors will take care that the inmate who addresses himself to them does not speak in the presence of his companions or in such a way as to be heard of them.
7. The chief warden can, after having received the advice and consent of the directors in writing, choose a person to serve alongside him; he can in the same way remove him.

Section II

On the deputy-warden

1. The deputy warden will be present at the opening and closing of the doors of the prison; he will assist in the religious service, as well as everything that is done within the establishment;
2. Each day he will visit the hospital, the kitchen, the cells; he will see to it that cleanliness and order prevail everywhere.

3. He must, under the director of the warden, inspect and oversee the whole establishment as well as all its details; he will see to it that each inferior employee strictly fulfills the duties that are imposed on them; he will visit frequently, and without giving advance notice of his coming, the workshops and courts; he will see whether the inmates are engaging in labor with diligence and continuity; in a word, he will ensure that every regulation of the establishment is precisely followed and that every precaution is taken to maintain the order and safety of the prison.
4. He will oversee the clothing of the inmates; he will see whether anything is missing from it and whether the changes that cleanliness specifies have been made.

Section III

On [the] overseer

1. An overseer will be found in each workshop. This overseer will be nominated by the warden.
2. Each overseer, in entering his functions, must carefully take stock of all the furniture or instruments belonging to the workshop of which he is in charge; he will estimate the monetary value of them. Copies of this statement will be submitted by him into the hands of the warden; and every three months there will be added to the list new instruments that have been purchased in the interval, just as one takes note of everything that, during the same time, has been broken, damaged, or lost. He will take account of raw materials that have been furnished to his workshop, of objects that have been manufactured and sold there, and what each prisoner earns by day and by week. He will see to it that any furniture belonging to his workshop is treated with care and that the labor is done accurately. He will do everything that will depend on him to serve the interests of the State or those of the contractors who will be responsible for employing the inmates. It is specially urged that each overseer make the greatest order reign in his workshop.

He must not allow the slightest conversation to be established between the prisoners: he himself must not speak to the prisoner other than to direct him in his labor. If a convict shows himself to be lazy or intractable, the overseer will give an account of it to the warden or the

deputy-warden. Each overseer will have a book on which to record the name of those who are sick among the inmates: each day, before nine in the morning, this list with its date will be handed over to the warden or the under-warden and subsequently posted in the hospital.
3. Each overseer will be attendant at his turn in the night guard, as will be determined by the warden.

Section IV

On watchmen

1. The guards are responsible, under the direction of the warden, to watch night and day for the safety of the establishment. In the exercise of their functions, it is necessary for them to exert activity and a great vigilance; when they are not in service, or found united in the guard house, they must conduct themselves towards others and vis-à-vis everyone in a respectable and measured manner; they will have taken care to abstain from everything that distracts them from propriety; they will treat any person who desires to visit the establishment with an equal politeness, and will always remember that the reputation as well as the safety of the house essentially rests on them individually and collectively. They must show themselves always perfectly proper and neat in their person; it is necessary that their guard house always present the image of order and cleanliness. Their weapons must always be found in a good state and ready to be used. It is not permitted to any guard to speak with the inmates unless directing them in their labor. The guards will not give to the inmates or receive from them any object whatsoever without the warden or the deputy warden being notified of it.
2. The warden will choose one person whose functions will be to see to it each day that the rations determined by the present regulation, after having been weighed and measured with care according to the number of prisoners, are handed to the cook of the house. This attendant will keep an exact account of the number of rations thus delivered; this account, which he will write in his own hand, will be submitted by him every three months to the warden: he will affirm under oath the truth of its content and then the warden will make it pass under the eyes of the directors.

3. Everyone who will be nominated by the warden to fill a job in the prison, or that touches the prison, must be considered as committed to the establishment itself; so that if the warden desires to stop his functions, the employees that he has chosen must continue to perform their services to the prison for one month from death, dismissal, or resignation of the warden, unless of course his successor returns before then.

If the employee refuses or neglects to fulfill the duties of his place, he will owe the amount of his salary for the past three months. The recovery of this money must be pursued by the new warden. One will consider that this part of the regulation is known to anyone who accepts employment in the prison, and they will supposedly be subject to the conditions that it imposes on the contractor.

Section V

On the property

1. The cells and halls will be swept every day. The sweepings will be brought outside the prison; the floor of the great circular gallery will be washed every fourteen days. The cells will also be washed and bleached frequently.
2. The beds and everything that serves as a couch for the inmates will be carried outside the prison and exposed to the great air in the court once a week during the summer, and once a fortnight during the rest of the year, when the weather permits. The inmate will have to apply himself to making the greatest cleanliness reign in his cell, and to prevent the objects intended for his use from being found damaged. If he fails to observe these rules, anything that will serve as his bed will be taken from him until he will submit.
3. The utmost care must be taken that the inmates maintain a great cleanliness on their person. They will be furnished with anything that can be useful for them to attain this goal.
4. Night buckets will be cleaned with care and their content will be carried beyond the walls of the prison.
5. One will not allow any filth or harmful material to remain disposed of around the walls of the prison, the workshops, and the court. It is necessary, on the contrary, that the entire establishment present a model of good order, surveillance, and cleanliness.

Section VI

On the hospital and doctor

1. The warden, after having taken the advice of the directors, will designate the person fit to fulfill the functions of doctor in the prison. The doctor, thus chosen, will receive compensation which has been determined by the directors.
2. The hospital will be furnished with beds, tables, and everything that can be useful to the sick; it will always be ready to admit those inmates who the doctor believes must be sent there.
3. The doctor will give the necessary orders for procuring aid, provisions, and furniture that will be needed for sick persons. On seeing his application, the warden is authorized to procure them. The doctor will take note on a register of any requisitions of this kind, as well as of the nature and time of the requests. He will take care equally to take stock of everything that belongs to the hospital. The same register will show the number of his visits; the names of individuals who, each day, are given as ill, and among them the names of those who have left the hospital, of those that he has merely put on a diet in their cell, and finally those whom he has made return to their workshops. The doctor will visit the hospital every day, or more often if such became necessary or if he is required to do so. He will personally oversee all the inmates who are sick in the report journaled by the overseers. He will make note of the name of the sick people that leave the hospital and those who die there. He will record in a registry the fate of what illness they were suffering, what remedies have been prescribed, and will add in general any remarks that he will judge useful concerning the nature of afflictions and of the means used to treat them; he will log on the same register his observations relating to the health, discipline, labor of the prisoners, as well as the cleanliness of the house. The register that will contain these details will always remain at the establishments; it will always be available to the warden and the directors.

The doctor will obtain from the warden the assistance of a certain number of inmates to cure the ill persons, when this assistance becomes necessary. In general, the doctor and the warden must unite their efforts to make the condition of the sick prisoner as comfortable as his situation permits. If it is found that the inmate is not

sick enough to enter the hospital, the doctor can nevertheless order him to undergo a particular diet. In this case, everything that this diet includes will be drawn from the hospital or from the prison supply.
4. If it happens that the orders of the doctor are not successful, and that his prescriptions were left without execution, he must give account of this omission on his register, and in making known the cause, at the same time take steps so that such abuse will not take place again.

Section VII

General rules

1. It is expressly forbidden to the employees of the prison, as it is to everyone who is attached in some manner to the establishment, to buy or sell anything that is from the inmate; to contract any engagement with him; to employ his labor for their use and benefit; to grant him any special favor, and to treat him with more indulgence than the law permits. They are to abstain from receiving from an inmate, or in his interest, any compensation, gift, or reward. It will not be allowed to make them promises, to commit to render services for them, or to procure aide, even without an apparent goal. They are not to receive for their use or that of their family any right or liberality of any person committed to guard them from friends or acquaintances of the same persons, nor from any other individuals; those who fail in this part of the regulation will be immediately dismissed.
2. The compensation of each employee will be fixed by the directors before he enters upon his duties; and he will not receive more than the determined sum. He shall not be permitted to withdraw an indirect profit from the monies of the State or the prisoner's labor until he has received written authorization from the directors.
3. In no case can alcohol[2] be furnished to the inmates unless by order of the doctor. And it is instructed to the employees to completely abstain themselves when they are attached to the establishment. Those who contravene this obligation will be dismissed.
4. Only the warden has the right to inflict corporal punishments on the inmates. The other employees can strike an inmate only when they are reduced to the necessity of defending themselves.

5. The employee who is absent from the prison without legitimate cause will be deprived of his compensation until his return.
6. A Bible will be placed in each cell; the prisoners can be given other religious writings that the warden and the directors believe to be of a nature to bring a reform in his principles and in his conduct.
7. Any sums deposited as offerings by persons visiting the prison will be collected for the account of the State; they will be part of the prison revenue and will figure in the quarterly reports of the warden.

Section VIII

Obligations of the prisoners

1. The inmates must show themselves active, submissive, obedient. They will work in silence and with assiduity.
2. The inmates will not carry with them any hidden instrument or any object that can serve for their escape.
3. No inmate can write or receive letters, nor maintain relationships with those who are outside the prison, without permission from the warden.
4. The prisoners should abstain from breaking, damaging, or destroying the raw materials or the manufactured objects that belong to the State. They will not damage or spoil any part of the buildings.
5. They will always conduct themselves with deference and respect towards the employees of the house. They will maintain great cleanliness on their person, clothing, and bedding; when they are entering the refectory or workshops, they will march in lock steps with order and silence.
6. No prisoner can converse with another prisoner or stop his work without the permission of an overseer. He will not speak to those who desire to visit the establishment, and will not even look at them. He will leave the hospital only when he shall be allowed. At work, he will make only necessary sounds, and, in general in the cellular workshops, he will not engage in in any act of a nature to trouble the good order that must always reign in the house.

Section IX

On rations, on sleep

1. The ration of each day will be established according to the following: one pound of beef, one pound of bread made with corn and rye flour. There will be five bushels of potatoes per one hundred rations. At dinner, the inmates will be given a porridge composed of twenty pounds of corn and six quarts of peas, divided into one hundred rations. Each inmate will also have some salt and pepper at his disposal.
2. The bed will be composed of: one mattress filled with straw, three blankets in the winter, two in the summer, two sheets of a course cotton mill and a sufficient size. Everything will be maintained with the greatest cleanliness. The prisoners will not be allowed to sleep fully clothed, nor to stand or lie down before the bell has given its signal. They will take their meals in the cells.

Notes

1. *Literally: "take the hand."
2. *Or, spirituous liquors.

Appendix No. 13 Bis.: Regulations from Mr. Welles for the Boston House of Refuge

INITIATION

1. When a young boy is brought to the house of refuge, they examine him, make him take a bath, dress him as needed; and, if he is sick, medicinal relief is immediately given to him.
2. The chaplain questions him next; he seeks to know his history, his principles, his passions. He explains to him the cause that drove him into the house, the goal that it is necessary to hold there, the time that he must remain there, and the evidence of good conduct that will allow him to leave.
3. The young man is then introduced by name to the other members of the society. If he knows how to read, he is handed a copy of the regulations and is placed, according to the circumstances, in the second or third category of the second division. He remains there for a trial week. If, during this time, his conduct has been good, it is taken into account and the members of the society are called to decide by their vote whether the new arrival can or cannot rank among them. If, in the number of votes that are against him, there is found a member of the first category of the first division, two from the

---

*"Bis." in French means "second part."

© Translation by Emily Katherine Ferkaluk 2018
G. de Beaumont, A. de Tocqueville, *On the Penitentiary System in the United States and its Application to France*, Recovering Political Philosophy, https://doi.org/10.1007/978-3-319-70799-0_21

second, four from the third, or five in all, he is not allowed and must await another trial.

Division and Occupation of the Time

1. There will be three meals each day. At least one hour will be granted for the three. There will be three breaks per day; each will last three-quarters of an hour. There will be two times at the school and two times in the workshops, except Sunday.
2. The precise moment wherein each of these things must be done, as well as the hour of rising and sleeping, will be indicated by the sound of a bell. The rule in this regard can vary according to the seasons and with the approval of the Board.
3. It is the chaplain who regulates everything related to exercises of piety. Sunday, he must celebrate the divine service. Moreover, he will pray every day, morning and night.

Discipline

Discipline must rely particularly on a psychological bond.

1. No member of the society can be punished by the whip or by jail. For these punishments are substituted solitary rooms, headbands to prevent seeing, handcuffs, privation of company, games, work, some food or even an entire meal.
2. Punishments can be administered only for wrongdoing expressly forewarned by the laws of God and of country, or by the rules of the house; it is essential that the delinquent know the existence of these laws and regulations.
3. No one shall be forced to expose the offences of another; we will not even allow it when it will be obvious that it is the conscience alone which makes the informant act.
4. No-one shall be punished for an offence, no matter how large it is, if he comes to confess it with frankness and honesty, unless it appears that the offender has had recourse to a confession because he was suspected and in part discovered. No one will be punished for an offence that the confession of another revealed, unless whoever made the confession consents to it.

5. A record of moral accounting shall be kept for each member of the society. When one among them commits a minor offence, the letters D.R. (debt) will be recorded on the record. At the end of each day, all the members of the society will be called by their names. They must judge themselves and declare whether, according to them, their conduct has been good, acceptable, or bad. Nothing will be said to them that can suggest their response to them; but if they judge themselves with too much severity or favor, the masters or monitors will restore the truth. The member of the society, whose conduct shall have been good in fact, will receive the mark C.R. (credit) on the record.
6. Each day, after the morning or evening prayers, a court will examine and judge questions relating to the conduct held by members of the society.
7. Since it is outside the power of man to punish the lack of respect committed towards the Divinity, we will limit ourselves to forbidding those who are guilty of it from any participation in religious services, thus abandoning the criminal to the justice of God which awaits them in the future.
8. Every Saturday night, the accounts of moral accountability shall be settled. If, after having established the balance, there remains two bad points to a member of the society, one can move them to the account of the following week. But those who have more than two bad points will descend by one or two categories following the regulations that govern these categories. Only if the offender belongs to the first category of the second division can one then be limited to withdrawing the Sunday dinner from him, provided that he does not have more than four bad points.

If, after having established the balance, there remains to a member of the society several good points, one passes them to the current account and they are used by him to purchase books, papers, crayons, pens, handkerchiefs, and other useful or agreeable things.
9. The one who shall have extraordinarily reprehensible conduct, whether by nature of the offences that he will commit or by their frequency, can be excluded from the society. In that case, there will not be any relationship between him and the other members; and if, subsequently, he is made worthy to be admitted again, he will not be exempt from the ordinary course of testing.

10. The management of the house is, in part, committed to the monitors. The monitors shall be nominated at the beginning of each month. Their number and their functions will be regulated accordingly: there will be one chief monitor, who will manage the establishment in the absence of employees; two guardians of the keys, who must ring the bell, open and close the doors in the morning, night, and at other fixed times; a sheriff and his two chief mates, who will be responsible for keeping the disobedient in order; the sheriff will have to watch the second and third divisions at all times (the first during the break only); a steward assisted by an aide, who will be responsible for everything concerning the provisions and meals of the members of the society; an inspector, who will have under his command two or three assistants; he will be responsible for cleaning and organizing the part of the house inhabited by the young men, only excepting, however, the dormitories and the cafeteria; an inspector of the dormitories, who will see to it that they are cleaned and organized each day; an inspector of the wardrobe, who will see to it that the clothes are brushed and held in order; three guards of the doors who, according to needs, will be attendants to the guard of the doors. One can even nominate other monitors if they were deemed useful. The monitors responsible for the management of members from the first division (the proven ones) will be elected by the latter every month; they will march at their head and will see each day to whoever is last, always maintaining the greatest propriety on their persons.

Classification of the Members of the Society

The members of the society shall be ranked under two great divisions, according to the good or bad conduct that they hold in the house.

Division I

The members of the first division are divided still further into three categories.

First Category

The first category is composed of those who make positive, regular, and constant efforts towards the good.

Their offences are only the result of an error, or very rarely of carelessness.

The privileges of those who form part of this category are the same as the privileges of others, and furthermore they can swim without being accompanied by a monitor, leave their room without permission and go into the dining room when necessary; leave their seats in the assembly hall without permission; everything being equal, they have the right to choose first. They can use the break room. The most important keys are entrusted to them when this happens. Their word is authoritative in ordinary circumstances. Finally, their birthday is celebrated. They wear the small uniform.

Second Category

Those who make positive and regular efforts towards the good compose the second category.

Their offences arise from carelessness. They are not serious, at least in the intention of the one who commits them. A few bad points remaining after having established the balance on the book of moral accountability suffices to lower them from the first category into this one. It is the same for transgressions to the disciplinary regulations.

The privileges of the members of the second category are: the ability to go into the city without being accompanied by a monitor, provided, however, that their current account on the book of accountability presents twenty-five good points; to be responsible for keeping keys of a secondary importance; to be able to be nominated for responsibilities at the choice of the director; to take books in the library; to make use of papers that are found in the assembly room without asking permission. Everything being equal, to have the right to make a choice before the members of the lower categories.

Third Category

It is composed of those who make positive efforts toward the good. Their offences result from carelessness or a moment of error. These offences can be reprehensible in themselves; but the guilty has repented of it as soon as he has been able to reflect on it. Three bad points remaining on the book of accountability suffices to place a member of the society into this category.

The privileges of those who are part of it are: to go into city accompanied by a monitor, after having obtained twenty-five good points; to walk in the garden with a monitor; to go to the gymnasium and the library; to use, after having asked permission, books and papers that are found in the assembly room; to be able to be elected to the responsibilities of the house.

Division II

Composed of those whose conduct is bad.

The members of the second division are further divided into three categories.

First Category

In the first category are those who are *positively* inclined to the bad. Their offences are generally violations of the discipline. They have nothing reprehensible in themselves, or, if they have this character, it is at least very infrequent. Five bad points lower one into this category.

Those who are found there can play and converse only with members of their category, unless the kind of work which occupies them otherwise directs. They cannot enter the superintendent's room; they do not have the right to vote in elections. If they commit offences, they are punished by recording bad points in the book of moral accountability, or by sending them to lower categories.

Second Category

Those who form the second category show positive and regular inclinations to the bad. Their offences are either purely disciplinary or morally reprehensible. Ten bad points lower them into this category.

Those who form it can converse with no member of the society, except when their work requires it. They can speak to the superintendent only when the latter allows them; they are deprived of their ordinary seats; they occupy distinct ones under the inspection of a sheriff. Cake and any other extra food is taken away from them. If they commit offences, they are lowered into the last category unless, however, their offences are very slight; in which case, one merely inscribes some bad points in the book of accountability.

Third Category

Those who form the third category are positively, regularly, and continually inclined to evil. Their offences are infractions to moral laws, committed in great number. A single offence suffices, if it has been committed with the sole desire of doing wrong.

Those who form this category have only bread and water for food. One can make them wear handcuffs, put a band over their eyes, or best of all confine them in solitary chambers.

When an individual of this category commits an offence, or when a member of another category is sent to the latter for some serious offences, such as lying, dishonest action, profane words, or other infractions of similar nature, he is punished in the manner indicated above.

One can, as has been seen, rise from one category into another category according to one's conduct; but before leaving the category where one is found, a time of trial is necessary. Thus, members of the first division are obliged to remain four weeks in the second category after passing into the first, and two weeks in the third after passing into the second. Members of the second division cannot leave the first category before having passed one week there, and the second as well as the third before having passed at least a day there.

Appendix No. 14: Letter from Mr. Barrett, Chaplain of the Wethersfield Penitentiary

Wethersfield, this 7 October 1831.
To Messrs. de Beaumont and de Tocqueville.

Gentlemen,
The population of Connecticut is around 280,000 souls.
For thirty-six years, the mines located at Timesbury and known as Newgate served as the state prison. The new prison was inhabited only four years ago.
During the forty years leading up to July 1831, the number of individuals sent to these two prisons rose to 976. Their crimes were classified according to the following: 435 had committed burglary; 139 had stolen horses; 78 had used counterfeit money; 41 had committed acts of violence; 47 were guilty of attempted rape; 3 of attempted poisoning; 1 of murder (the punishment had been commuted); 11 of highway robbery; 1 of robbing the mail; 1 of the crime of bestiality; 60 of forgery; 25 of misdemeanors; 15 had been convicted for having attempted to free prisoners; 34 for arson; 9 for homicide; 4 for rape (the penalty had been commuted); 2 for cheating; 5 for bigamy; 23 for adultery; 16 for breaking fences; 3 for having attempted to escape from prison; 9 for theft committed to the injury of the prison; 4 for incest; 3 for perjury; finally, 5 for an unknown crime.

In the midst of the free population in Connecticut, there are 3 colored people for every 100 white people. In prison, black men are in the proportion of 33 to 100.

Out of the 182 convicts whom I have examined, 76 did not know how to write and 30 did not know how to read.

60 had been deprived of their parents before reaching 10 years old; and 36 others had the same loss before having reached their fifteenth year.

Out of 182, 116 were originally from Connecticut.

90 were twenty to thirty years old, and 18 were sentenced for life.

The prison contains 18 women at this time. Some are employed at cooking the food and washing the laundry of the prisoners, others at sewing shoes.

For one pair of shoes, they receive 4 cents (around 20 cent.); one woman can sew six to ten pairs in a day. During the night, they occupy separate cells.

Morning and evening prayers are made in the presence of the convicts; passages of the Bible are read and explained to them. The prisoners, on these occasions, show themselves attentive and meditative. Each finds a Bible furnished by the State in his cell, which he can read when it seems good to him. In general, they tend to indulge in this reading. The other day, passing in front of the cells, I noticed 23 out of 25 prisoners who were seriously occupied with reading.

On Sunday, a sermon is preached in their presence that they rarely fail to listen to with great attention. These are often followed by curious questions on the meaning of the words that they have just heard.

When the principles of the Holy Scriptures are etched in the heart of a convict, one can believe without doubt that his reform is complete; we have reasons to think that this result has sometimes been obtained. I am tempted to believe that out of the actual number of convicts, one can find among them 15 or 20 in this case. It is impossible, however, to establish, for the present, this point in a positive manner. It is necessary to wait until the state of liberty and resistance to temptations are achieved in order to prove reformation.

No one, at least among the prisoners, refuses religious instruction, and I have not yet encountered among them a single one who has shown me the least lack of respect when I came to visit him in his cell.

I noticed that ignorance, abandonment on the part of parents, and intemperance formed, in general, the three great causes to which we must attribute crimes.

Most of the prisoners show themselves eager for instruction. There are those who arrived without knowing the letters of their alphabet, [and] have learned to read in two months. They could not have recourse, however, to any other books than the Bible, and did not receive any other lessons than those that can be given to them through the grates of their cell.

The result that one can expect from a prison greatly depends on the character of the guards. It is necessary that they have moral habits, that they speak little, and are able to see all.

If the guards are what they ought to be; if the convicts, separated at night, work in silence during the day; if a continual surveillance is joined to frequent moral and religious instructions; a prison can become a place of reform for the convicts and a source of revenue for the State.

I am respectfully, et cetera.
G. Barrett, chaplain of the prison

Appendix No. 15: Conversation with the Director of the Philadelphia House of Refuge

(Nov. 1831)

D. Until what age, do you think, can the reformation of juvenile delinquents be obtained?
R. Experience has revealed to us that after fifteen or sixteen years there remains little hope of reform. Almost all the young people who had exceeded this age when they were sent to the house of refuge have had bad conduct in leaving it.
D. How many young prisoners have left the house since its founding?
R. One hundred boys and twenty-five girls.
D. Do you think that a great number of these delinquents had been reformed?
R. About two-thirds of them have so far behaved well, at least as far as I can judge by the reports that have been passed on to me by the individuals with whom these young people have been put in apprenticeship.
D. What vices, in your opinion, are corrected with the most difficulty?
R. The habit of theft among the boys; evil mores among the girls. One must almost renounce correcting a young woman who has lived in disorder.

D. Do you find that the children who you wish to instruct make rapid progress?
R. Yes; I believe even that they learn faster than honest children.
D. Don't the regulations permit loaning them books from the library each week?
R. Yes, sir.
D. Do you notice that they enjoy reading?
R. Out of 151 young prisoners, there are about 80 who appear to like reading very much.
D. What are the disciplinary punishments in use?
R. The whip, solitary imprisonment, and reduction of food to bread and water.
D. Do you believe that it is dangerous to allow the young prisoners to communicate freely with each other during recreation hours?
R. This tolerance can, no doubt, present some dangers, and one could, if one desired it, establish here, as in the large penitentiaries, complete silence; but I doubt that it is wise to do so; children have need of activity and merriment, because their bodies are developing and their character is forming.
D. What have been the expenses of first establishing the house of refuge?
R. Estimated 65, 230 dollars (345,719 fr.).
D. What are the annual expenses?
R. Estimated 12,000 dollars (63,600 fr.) all included. The salaries of the employees there amount to a sum of 2,953 dollars (15,650 fr.).
D. What is withdrawn each year from the labor of the prisoners?
R. About 2,000 dollars (10,600 fr.); this brings the annual expenses of the house, deductions made for the earnings of the prisoners, to 10,000 dollars (53,000 fr.).
D. How many books do you have in the library of the house?
R. 1,500 volumes. These books have been given by charitable persons. The State has not designated any funds for this object.

Appendix No. 16: Statistical Notes

No. I. Various documents relating to the sanitary state of the Auburn and Philadelphia penitentiaries. — II. Documents relating to the individuals who, from 1822 to 1831, received their pardon at Auburn and Singsing. Also, some observations on the exercise of the right to pardon in America. — III. Some penal laws of Maryland relating to slaves. — IV. Difference that one notices between the mortality of black and white persons, of the emancipated and slaves. — V. Total number of individuals sentenced to the punishment of imprisonment in the State of Pennsylvania in 1830. — VI. Number of executions that have taken place in Maryland from 1785 to 1832. — VII. Table of individuals who, from 1821 to 1827, have been confined in New York prisons, judged, acquitted, and convicted. — VIII. Influence of the city of New York on the criminality of the State of the same name. — IX. Total number of convictions pronounced in 1830 in the entire State of New York by ordinary courts.

No. I. — DOCUMENTS RELATING TO THE SANITARY STATE OF THE AUBURN AND PHILADELPHIA PENITENTIARIES

Annual reports of the doctor at Auburn

1826... The illnesses that reign in the penitentiary are the same as those that prevail in the vicinity. If they will maintain the discipline from the prisoners to which they are presently subjected, and as long as they will maintain the same cleanliness in the prison, they ought not be afraid to see an epidemic sickness settle there.

1827... The illnesses that reign in the prison continue to be the same as those that one notes in the surrounding countryside. We do not believe that the first cause of the illnesses should be attributed to the state of imprisonment where the convicts are found. Out of nine persons who have succumbed during the year, four had arrived sick to the penitentiary. However, we cannot deny that death, among them, has not been hastened by the action that imprisonment can never fail to exercise on the soul and body.

1828... We are happy to note that the sanitary state of the prisoners is at least as satisfying as it can be among a similar number of free men. For the majority of prisoners, imprisonment, work, and the rigors of discipline have had salutary results. Their health is strengthened when they cannot indulge in their disorderly habits. They encounter among themselves, it is true, some men who have lived so long under the influence of debilitating causes, such as intemperance and debauchery, that illness has entirely impaired their organs. For the latter, imprisonment is disastrous. This remark is mostly applicable in the case of pulmonary consumption. Subject to a moderate exercise, and to a discipline appropriate to their state, the person with pulmonary tuberculosis had resisted the progress of the illness for a long time; imprisonment aggravated it. One cannot deny, either, that imprisonment, when it is combined with sedentary work, predisposes one to certain illnesses. The free worker, whose work forces him to keep constantly bent on himself, is always exposed to organic lesions of the stomach, liver, and lung. It is thus, and with stronger reason, for the prisoner whose liberty is hampered, and who can take only a very limited exercise. Despite these adverse conditions, we have seen a great number of prisoners whose constitution has been enervated by a thousand excesses still find the strength to triumph over their illness in themselves, because they cannot surrender to the defects that it had given them. Several have thus recovered the health that over the years they had lost.

1829...One must attribute the sanitary state of this prison, which is without example, to the progress that the discipline has made there, to the simple and uniform discipline that the prisoners undergo, to the regular work that is imposed on them, to the propriety that reigns over them and in their cells, to the means of ventilation that one has introduced, and, above all, to the abstinence from alcohol.

One is mistaken when thinking that a man habituated to the use of strong drinks cannot be deprived of it without danger. The example of the prison proves the contrary. Among the 391 convicts who, during the past four years, have left the penitentiary, 211 have been freed from the passion for strong alcohol; it has been learned by themselves.

It was equally proven that the use of strong liquors is dispensable for sustaining the strength of men exposed to the sun, to fatigue, and to rough work. If what we say was contested, we could prove it beyond doubt by presenting the statement of work performed by the prisoners, who had in the middle of their toil no other drink than water.

1830...Among the 18 individuals who died this year, there were only two who were healthy upon entering the prison.

1831...The sanitary state continues to be very good. However, one cannot hide that imprisonment is injurious to those inmates whose occupations are entirely sedentary: it is notably the case with tailors and shoemakers. The position in which the nature of their work forces them to stand, and the little exercise that they take in going to the refectory and the cells, favors the development of illnesses when they are predisposed to them.

Some 15 individuals died in the year, 1 from suicide, and 10 were already sick when they entered the penitentiary.

(*Annual reports of the inspectors of the Auburn prison.*)

Translation of a piece removed from a brochure published by Dr. Bache on the penitentiary system in 1829[1]

It can be neither affirmed nor denied in an absolute manner that solitary imprisonment is hazardous to health. This kind of punishment can, according to the circumstances, be injurious or inoffensive. Do we understand by "health" that state of perfect wellbeing in which one conceives a man who lives in ease of all without abusing anything? I am actually of the opinion that solitary imprisonment must injure a health of this kind. Do we give, on the contrary, the name "health" to the state in which an individual is found who is not affected by any existing disease? Now then, I am prone to think that if you take a given number of prisoners belonging, as is ordinary, to the most debauched and intemperate classes of society, you will perceive yourself that after a certain time of solitary imprisonment their state of health will have become better; I am convinced, at least, that mortality will be infinitely less great among them than it would have been among the same number of individuals remaining in liberty.

Comparing the two systems of imprisonment between themselves and relative to the influence that they exert on the body, we will come no doubt to think that the former method in itself is less dangerous for health than solitary imprisonment. But if we contemplate every defect that experience shows us as inherent in the former system, we will tend to think that this system is, all things considered, more injurious to life than the new. The official reports published on the sanitary state of the Walnut Street prison show us that mortality in the penitentiary was, for six or eight years, in the proportion of six percent, on average. After careful consideration of it, I think that this mortality would have been less if the same number of inmates had been subjected to solitary imprisonment.[2]

There is much talk of the disastrous influence that solitary imprisonment must exercise on the reason of inmates.

For myself, who has continuously examined the effect produced by an imprisonment of this nature over the period of six months to a year, I think myself justified in thinking that these fears are exaggerated. Imprisonment tends no doubt to break down the body and the groin, and it can produce insanity among those who have a predisposition to this disease; but nothing can come to establish that this result is produced more by solitary imprisonment than by any other.

Excerpt from the report of Mr. Bache, Doctor of the Philadelphia prisons for the year 1831

It is difficult to have an idea, for the present, of what will be the cause of mortality in the new penitentiary of Philadelphia; the number of inmates contained in this prison having been, until now, too restrained for one to be able to draw a conclusive argument from the number of deaths that took place among them.

It cannot be said that one illness rather than another has prevailed in this penitentiary because of the discipline of imprisonment or the system of governance that has been followed there. There is no statement of mental affections there. The most frequent ailments have been colds, rheumatic disorders, and diarrhea.
(*Hazard's register 1832.*)

Summary of Mr. Bache's report from 1830

In sum, the doctor of the prison believes himself authorized by what he has already seen in the penitentiary to conclude that if the system of solitary imprisonment that is followed there sometimes affects the health of inmates, it is still, all things considered, much more favorable to their existence than the system in force in the former prisons.
(*First and second annual reports of the inspectors of the Eastern State Penitentiary of Philadelphia 1831.*)

No. II. — Documents relating to the individuals who from 1822 to 1831 received their pardon at Auburn and Singsing; as well as some observations on the exercise of the right to pardon in America

We thought that some details relating to the way in which the right of pardon is exercised in America, and particularly in the State of New York, would be read with interest.

From 1822 to 1831, both at Auburn and Singing, 130 individuals sentenced to 3 years of prison were pardoned.

Among these prisoners, those who remained the longest in prison before obtaining pardon were there for 2 years.[3]

The minimum stay of the pardoned in prison before obtaining pardon has been 17 days.

86, or more than half, have obtained their pardon before accomplishing half their punishment.

In the same period, 49 individuals sentenced to 5 years in prison were pardoned.

Maximum duration of stay in the prison before obtaining pardon: 4 years.

Minimum: 3 months.

27, or more than half, obtained their pardon before having completed half their punishment.

9 individuals sentenced to 6 years of prison were pardoned.

Maximum stay in the prison: 5 years.

Minimum: 1 year.

6 prisoners obtained their pardon before having undergone half their punishment.

83 individuals sentenced to 7 years of prison were pardoned.

Maximum stay in prison: 6 years.

Minimum: 4 months.

53, or close to two thirds, had not yet undergone half their punishment.

38 individuals sentenced to 10 years in prison were pardoned.

Maximum duration of the stay in prison: 9 years.

Minimum: 2 months.

28, or almost three quarters, were pardoned after having undergone half their punishment.

36 individuals sentenced to 14 years in prison were pardoned.

Maximum stay in prison: 10 years.

Minimum: 1 year.

22, or almost two thirds, have been pardoned before having undergone half their punishment.

Finally, 60 individuals sentenced for life were pardoned.

Everyone obtained their pardon before having passed 7 years in prison.

Several, after having passed two years, and one after being there less than 8 months.

We see, therefore, that anyone sentenced for life who has obtained their pardon in the courts during these 8 years spent less time in prison than the individuals sentenced to 14 years and even to 10 years.

It is easy to prove also that the choice of the authority who pardons falls more often on those than on the other prisoners.

Thus, those sentenced for life form about one-eighteenth of all convicts who have been sent each year to Auburn and Singsing from 1822 to 1831; it is therefore necessary to think that they also form approximately one-eighteenth of inmates.

Now, out of 447 pardoned individuals, 60 prisoners have been convicted for life, or one-seventh of the pardoned.

There is, then, one convicted for life out of 18 inmates, and one out of 7 pardoned convicts.

Those convicted for life find themselves thus doubly privileged, and it can be said without exaggeration that in the State of New York it is in the interest of the criminal to see the strongest punishment of imprisonment pronounced against him.

It is easy to indicate why the right of pardoning is exercised so frequently in America, and why it is so often made use of in favor of those convicted for life.

Without examining the question of how to know whether it is absolutely indispensable to the good of society to confine to one authority such a right of remitting punishments, it can be said, nevertheless, that the less this authority is elevated and independent, the greater will be the abuse of pardoning.

In America, it is the governor of each State alone who has, in general, the dangerous power of pardoning; he can even do what the most absolute sovereigns of Europe cannot: exemption from the requirement to be judged. In that, the Americans follow the traditions of the former colonial constitution more than the logical order of ideas. Now, despite the extent of these rights in specific matters, the governor of a State in America occupies a lower social position. Anyone can address him at any instant of the day; pressuring him at all times and in all places. Living thus without intermediary to the solicitations, can he always refuse?

He feels himself subject to the caprices of the public; he depends on the odds of an election and he needs to set aside partisans with care. Will he want to dissatisfy his political friends by refusing them a slight favor? Moreover, being coated in little power, he must love to make ample usage of the rights that are left to him. All these causes, added to the difficulty that they have for a long time needed to find prisons that can contain all the prisoners, explain why the executive power in America has made such great abuse of the right to pardon. It was only the excess of abuse that, some years ago, finally awoke public attention. Pardons, which are distributed still in much too large a number, are, however, much less frequent than formerly.

The same reasons explain in part why the prisoners convicted for life are treated more favorably than others.

First, among all the prisoners, these have the most interest in obtaining their pardon, because they are the most punished. Moreover, a man submits more easily to a punishment whose duration is fixed. We tend, further, to patiently wait for the term of a punishment whose exact duration is known. The imagination of the convict and his friends rests easily in limits fixed in advance; the authority, for its part, easily refuses to shorten a punishment that must end.

But the one sentenced for life has nothing that bears his hopes or his fears; he and his friends always have an interest in employing the most pressing pleas to obtain a pardon that can be delayed for years or be granted tomorrow.

The governor thus finds himself solicited more obstinately and with more ardor in favor of those sentenced for life than any other; and he grants much sooner what they ask him, because, not wanting to always refuse, he does not see clearly why he would give in one moment more than another.

That is how the guiltiest are precisely those who bring together the most chances for pardon in their favor.

Moreover, nothing better exposes the abuse that reigns in the exercise of the right of pardon in the United States than the following piece excerpted from an American work:

"It has been acknowledged by the commission of prisons of the State of New York that there are some men who have no other profession than to procure for the convict their pardon; this industry provides their livelihood. Their talent consists in obtaining signatures of recommendation within the executive power in favor of those who have use of their department. In general, they are successful. Few men have enough courage to not grant their signatures when they are asked to do it by some persons in respectable appearance; and few governors have enough energy to refuse pardons that are solicited with insistence. It is certain that the pardon does not at all depend on the character of the crime, but uniquely on the pecuniary resources that the convict can use to employ people who engage in this traffic. The individual, sentenced for murder accompanying the most aggravated circumstances, has ten times more chances of being pardoned if he has some powerful friends or deep pockets, than the impoverished inmate who has committed a simple theft." Carey, page 59.

Proportion of individuals who, after having been pardoned, fall into recidivism

Out of 641 prisoners who, from 1797 to 1811, received their pardon in the Newgate prison (New York), 54 committed new crimes and returned to the same prison. This makes one individual in recidivism out of 12 pardoned, approximately.

We have not been able to obtain the figure for the years following.
(*Excerpted from the old Newgate register*).

No. III. — Some penal laws from Maryland relating to the slaves

In Maryland, as well as in most of the southern States, the same penal dispositions are not applied to slaves and free black persons.

Free black persons submit to the same laws as white persons. The same punishments are inflicted on them; but slaves are found in a special position regarding punishment, unlike the rest.

When a black male slave is made guilty of a very serious offence, he is meted out the punishment of the whip, and the master pays compensation as if it were a matter of damage incurred by a domestic animal. They hang slaves who commit a great crime, and they sell out-of-state those whose offence, although serious, does not yet merit death.

This legislation is economical: it rests on simple ideas whose execution is easy and rapid; qualities particularly appreciated in democratic governments. We must not less consider it as one of the numerous anomalies that American society presents.

When the sale of a slave is thus ordered by the courts, the guilty is delivered to contractors whose industry is to sell slaves in the northern States where their number surpasses demand, to transport them into the southern States, where they are highly sought. The criminal slave is mixed amid others; his history is carefully covered; for if his morality were known, buyers would not be found. The State that thus sells a guilty slave does nothing other than save itself from a germ of crime in order to furtively introduce it among neighbors and members of the same political association. It is, in a word, an act of brutal selfishness that tolerates and punishes a moral and enlightened society.

No. IV. — DIFFERENCE THAT ONE NOTES BETWEEN THE MORTALITY OF BLACK PERSONS AND THAT OF WHITE PERSONS, OF FREE PERSONS AND SLAVES, IN THE UNITED STATES

When examining the tables of mortality in America, one is struck by a result that shows the privileges of the dominant race of white persons over the black race, even in respect to life.

At Philadelphia, from 1820 to 1831, only 1 white person died out of 42 individuals belonging to the white race; while 1 black man died out of 21 individuals belonging to the black race.

If we compare mortality among black slaves to mortality among free black persons, we arrive at a still more surprising result: at Baltimore for the last three years, 1 free black man died out of 28 free black persons,[4] and 1 slave out of 45 male black slaves.

Thus, slaves die less often than free men.

This is easily explained: the slave has no agitation of mind because he has no future; he never fights against poverty because one is obliged to provide for all his needs; finally, if his actions lack morality, not being free, they are at least regular and well ordered.

The emancipated are found without capital and without industry, exposed to every horror of destitution. To these difficulties of his position come to be added his small knowledge in the art of ruling himself; he does not know the use of reason that must now replace the whip of the master for him; his passions, like needs, shorten his life. What happens to him on a small scale happens to all peoples of the world who are suddenly rescued from arbitrary power. Liberty is certainly a beautiful and great thing, but those who first acquire enjoyment in it rarely receive its benefits.

Emerson's medical statistic p. 28, reports of the health office of Baltimore.

No. V. — TOTAL NUMBER OF INDIVIDUALS SENTENCED TO THE PUNISHMENT OF IMPRISONMENT IN THE STATE OF PENNSYLVANIA IN 1830

To discover, in an approximate manner, the total number of individuals sentenced to imprisonment during the year 1830 in the State of Pennsylvania, we have operated in the following way:

In Philadelphia, there are 51 counties that all have a prison, where individuals sentenced to short punishments must be confined. There are, moreover, two state prisons in Pennsylvania where criminals from all counties who are sentenced to a year of imprisonment are sent.

We know the exact number of individuals that the county of Philadelphia, the most considerable of all, sent in 1830 into the county prison. We also know the number of criminals who, this same year, had been sent to the central houses by every county of Pennsylvania. We lacked, therefore, only knowledge of the number of individuals sent, this same year, into the prisons of different counties, to know how Pennsylvania as a whole had furnished convicts to the prison in 1830.

Here is the method that we have followed to discover this latter point.

We thought that the number of individuals sent by the county of Philadelphia to the central prisons in 1830, which is 229, must be the number of individuals sent the same year by the same county of Philadelphia to the prison of the county, which is 1,431,[5] since the number of individuals sent by other counties of Pennsylvania into central prisons, which is 98, is to the number of individuals sent in 1830 by these same counties in their respective prisons the number that we do not know; in other words, we established the following proportion: 229:1431 :: 98: x, which gave for the fourth term 612. If the operation was rigorously precise, there would then be 612 individuals who would have been sent in 1830 to the various county jails, independently of those of Philadelphia.

But we have not thought it possible to give the figure of 612 as the expression of truth. There are, in fact, a host of small disorders that take place only in cities, and especially the largest cities, and there are a host of others that follow only where justice has all its activity. Proportionally speaking, therefore, fewer small offences and more large crimes are committed in the countryside than in cities.

On the other hand, Pennsylvania has many villages and even rather great cities, such as Pittsburg, Harrisburg, Lancaster, where the number of small offenses must be rather high.

We think, then, that by reducing the figure 612 in half, we must approach the truth. This gives us 306, which furnishes only an average of 6 convicts for each of the 50 counties that we are concerned with.

These calculations leave us more below than above the truth. But supposing that they were rigorously precise, it would result from it that in 1830 there were in the State of Pennsylvania 2,064 individuals sentenced to imprisonment.

The population being, this same year, 1,347,672, one would have counted 1 sentenced to prison out of 658 inhabitants.

No. VI. — Number of executions that have taken place in Maryland from 1785 to 1832

From 1785 to 1832, 78 persons have been sentenced to death and executed, which gives approximately (1.73) executions per year.

There were 19 of them in the last 12 years.

During this same period, the average population of Maryland has been 380,072 inhabitants: there has therefore been, each year, 1 execution out of 219,600 inhabitants.

(*Handwritten document furnished at Baltimore.*)

No. VII. — Table of individuals who, from 1821 to 1827, have been inmates in the prisons of the City of New York, tried, acquitted, and sentenced

In 1822, 2,361 persons have been jailed under prevention of crime or for offence.

Out of these 2,361 individuals, more than[6] 1,820 were not judged, either those who had been pardoned before trial or dismissed by the grand jury. Thus, out of 100 arrested individuals, more than 77 left the prison without trial.

Out of 541 who were tried, 361, or almost three-quarters (67 out of 100), were sentenced and 180 absolved.

Out of 2,361 individuals arrested in 1822, there were 2,000 of them that left the prison without having finished the sentence, or 85 out of 100.

In 1823, 1,920 persons were jailed under arrest.

Out of this number, 1,321 left the prison without trial (approximately 69 out of 100).

Out of the 599 who were tried, 422 were convicted (70 convicted out of 100 tried), 177 were absolved.

Out of the 1,920 individuals, 1,498 left the prison without having undergone conviction (78 out of 100).

In 1824, 1,961 persons were jailed under arrest.

Out of this number, 1,375 were released without trial (70 out of 100).

Out of the 586 who were tried, 417 were convicted (71 out of 100), 160 were absolved.

Thus, out of the 1,961 individuals, 1,544 left the prison without having incurred conviction (almost 79 out of 100).

In 1825, 2,168 persons were jailed under arrest.

Out of this number, 1,621 were released without trial (almost 75 out of 100).

Out of the 547 who were tried, 386 were convicted (almost 71 out of 100), 161 were absolved.

Thus, out of 2,168 individuals, 1,782 left the prison without having incurred conviction (82 out of 100).

In 1826, 2,273 individuals were jailed under arrest.

Out of this number, 1,611 were released without trial (71 out of 100).

Out of the 662 who were judged, 462 were convicted (almost 70 out of 100), 200 were absolved.

Thus, out of 2,273 individuals, 1,811 left the prison without having incurred conviction (almost 80 out of 100).

In England, the number of convictions is much smaller in respect to the accusations.

See: *Livingston's Introductory report to the Code of prison discipline*, pag. 32.

No. VIII. — Influence of the City of New York on the Criminality of the State of the Same Name

The city of New York, which during the year 1830 was peopled with only 207,021 inhabitants, furnished to it alone 400 convicts out of the 982 individuals who, during this year, were affected by arrests of ordinary justice in the State of New York.

Thus, in 1830, the inhabitants of the city of New-York were to the inhabitants of the entire State as 1 is to 9.24.

While the convicts of the city of New York were to the convicts of the entire state as 1 is to 2.45.

No. IX. — Total number of sentences handed down in 1830 in the whole State of New York by ordinary courts

The total number of individuals who, during the year 1830, were sentenced by ordinary courts either to death, or to imprisonment in the State jail, or to imprisonment in the houses of arrest, or finally to fines, rose to 982.

Out of these 982, one counted 903 men and 79 women.
The convictions are divided thus into the following:

To death.	3
To the state prison.	461
To the house of refuge.	12
To the houses of arrest.	295
To fines only.	211
	982

The statistical table from which these details are found is an official document that, at our request, was furnished to us by the authorities of New York.

It would be wrong to think, however, that the number 982 exactly represents the total number of individuals convicted in the State of New York during the year 1830.

The official table of which we speak contains only the number of individuals sentenced by ordinary courts, which is to say by the courts called: *mayor's court, court of oyer and terminer, court of quarterly sessions.* In addition to these tribunals, there exists a semi-administrative and semi-judicial authority, that of police officers. These functionaries have the right to carry to prison a very great number of petty delinquents, vagrants, disturbers of the order... who in France would be tried by the correctional courts and who would figure on the tables of criminal justice. The number of individuals convicted in this way must be very considerable in America, if one judges it by the genuine documents that we collected at Philadelphia. The only house of arrest of this city contained on average, from 1825 to 1831, 1,263 convicts each year. Most of them were sent there by police officers.

Notes

1. *Tocqueville and Beaumont excerpt a letter from Franklin Bache to Roberts Vaux, published broadly to the public at that time. Rather than inserting the original English text, I have translated the author's French. See Bache 1829 for comparison.
2. Mr. Bache is simultaneously doctor of the Walnut Street prison and of the new penitentiary [Eastern State Penitentiary].
3. We must warn that we neglect the fractions of months and days.
4. Bizarre thing! Free black persons die less in Baltimore, where the government is hard and oppressive for them, than at Philadelphia, where they are the object of philanthropy and public attention.
5. This figure appears no doubt very high; it hardly forms, however, that average of four years which preceded 1830.
6. *More*. This figure and the stubborn *corresponding figures* of the following years are below the truth. In fact, there were in 1822 five hundred forty-one individuals accused of *crimes* or *misdemeanors* having been judged; but [while] nothing indicates that those who had been tried had never been jailed under mandates (committed), it is still certain that many from among them had been bailed and had never been in prison. It is, then, not five hundred forty-one which is necessary to subtract from two thousand three hundred sixty-one, but a number smaller than five hundred forty-one, and whose exact figure we do not know.

References

Bache, Franklin. 1829. *Observations and Reflections On the Penitentiary System: A Letter from Franklin Bache, M.D. to Roberts Vaux*. Philadelphia: Jesper Harding.

Livingston, Edward. 1827. *Introductory Report to the Code of Prison Discipline: Explanatory of the Principles on which the Code is Founded, Being Part of the System of Penal Law Prepared for the State of Louisiana*. London: John Miller.

Philadelphia Society for Alleviating the Miseries of Public Prisons. 1831. *First and Second Annual Reports of the Inspectors of the Eastern State Penitentiary of Pennsylvania, Made to the Legislature at the Seasons of 1829–30, and 1830–31*. Philadelphia: Thomas Kite.

Appendix No. 17: Statistical Observations and Comparisons

No. I. Comparative table of individuals admitted into the different penitentiaries, classified by nature of the misdemeanor. — II. Average number of deaths in the penitentiaries. — III. Comparative table of recidivism. — IV. Proportion of men and women in the different penitentiaries. — V. Proportion of black persons among the inmates and in society. — VI. Proportion of Americans foreign to the State where they have committed their crime. — VII. Proportion of individuals foreign to America among the prisoners. — VIII. Proportion of Irish and English, properly speaking, among the prisoners. — IX. Proportion of individuals originating from the State where they have committed their crime. — X. Proportion of prisoners originating from the State where they have committed their crime, in relation to the population of that same State. — XI. State of pardons. — XII. Age of the convicts. — XIII. Report of the individuals sentenced to the State prison, with the population from various States.

---

*Tocqueville and Beaumont do not originally title Appendix No. 17; I have added "Statistical Observations and Comparisons" to lend clarity and consistency with the authors' footnotes citing this appendix throughout the main text.

No. I. — Table of individuals admitted into the penitentiaries of Pennsylvania, New York, Connecticut and Massachusetts, classified by nature of the misdemeanor

Connecticut (1789–1830)
Convicted for crimes against properties: 87.93 out of 100 c.[1]
Convicted for crimes against persons: 12.06 out of 100 c.

Pennsylvania (1789–1830)
Convicted for crimes against properties: 90.03 out of 100 c.
Convicted for crimes against persons: 9.97 out of 100 c.

Massachusetts (1820–1824–1830)[2]
Convicted for crimes against properties: 93.64 out of 100 c.
Convicted for crimes against persons: 6.36 out of 100 c.

New-York (1800–1830)
Convicted for crimes against properties: 93.56 out of 100 c.
Convicted for crimes against persons: 6.26 out of 100 c.

Convicted for crimes against mores
New York. (Same period.) 2.78 out of 100 c.
Massachusetts (Ibid.) 2.79 out of 100 c.
Pennsylvania (Ibid.) 2.72 out of 100 c.
Connecticut (Ibid.) 7.93 out of 100 c.

Convicted for forgery
Pennsylvania. (Same period.) 3.91 out of 100 c.
Massachusetts. (Ibid.) 9.60 out of 100 c.
New York (Ibid.) 13.28 out of 100 c.
Connecticut. (Ibid.) 14.26 out of 100 c.

APPENDIX NO. 17: STATISTICAL OBSERVATIONS AND COMPARISONS   289

If we take the average of these four States, whose inhabitants formed, in 1830, one-third of the population of the Union (4,168,905 inhabitants), we arrive at the following result:

Convicted for crimes against properties: 91.29 out of 100 c.
Convicted for crimes against persons: 8.66 out of 100 c.
Convicted for crimes against mores: 4.05 out of 100 c.
Convicted for forgery: 10.26 out of 100 c.

Comparison between the different periods

While comparing the different periods that we have indicated above with each other, we arrive at the following result:

Connecticut (1789–1800)

Convicted for crimes against properties: 95.40 out of 100 c.
Convicted for crimes against persons: 4.60 out of 100 c.
Convicted for crimes against mores: 3.44 out of 100 c.
Convicted for forgery: 10.34 out of 100 c.

1819–1830

Convicted for crimes against properties: 83.10 out of 100 c.
Convicted for crimes against persons: 16.90 out of 100 c.
Convicted for crimes against mores: 11.34 out of 100 c.
Convicted for forgery: 13.65 out of 100 c.

Pennsylvania (1789–1800)

Convicted for crimes against properties: 94.35 out of 100 c.
Convicted for crimes against persons: 5.65 out of 100 c.
Convicted for crimes against mores: 2.74 out of 100 c.
Convicted for forgery: 4.97 out of 100 c.

1819–1830

Convicted for crimes against properties: 94.61 out of 100 c.
Convicted for crimes against persons: 5.34 out of 100 c.

Convicted for crimes against mores: 1.72 out of 100 c.
Convicted for forgery: 4.84 out of 100 c.

State of New York (1800–1810)

Convicted for crimes against properties: 96.45 out of 100 c.
Convicted for crimes against persons: 3.54 out of 100 c.
Convicted for crimes against mores: 0.87 out of 100 c.
Convicted for forgery: 8.88 out of 100 c.

1820–1830

Convicted for crimes against properties: 90.12 out of 100 c.
Convicted for crimes against persons: 9.37 out of 100 c.
Convicted for crimes against mores: 5.06 out of 100 c.
Convicted for forgery: 16.76 out of 100 c.

We have not done the same work for Massachusetts, because this State furnished us with only one time period.

In Europe, it is generally acknowledged that, in proportion to society's progress in civilization, the number of crimes against persons cannot fail to decrease.

The figures that we have just presented prove that in America, at least, it is not the case. We see, on the contrary, that in the State of Pennsylvania the number of crimes against persons does not diminish with time, and that, in the States of Connecticut and New York, as civilization increases, it seems to increase with it. This augmentation takes place in an equal and uniform manner; it is difficult to attribute it to chance. It cannot be said, moreover, that it is due to causes foreign to America, such as the immigration of foreigners, the presence of the Irish... never, as we will soon see, have foreigners been less numerous than at the present time in the prisons of the United States, compared to the American population, and the number of Irish has not varied for thirty years.

Some other observations come to give new weight to this remark.

For example, not only do two States out of three exhibit a greater proportion of convictions for crimes against persons in 1830 than in 1790; but, in 1830, the State where one encounters the most convictions is that of Connecticut, which in respect to instruction and enlightenment occupies the first rank in the whole Union; and the State where one encounters the least convictions is the State of Pennsylvania, where the population is comparatively ignorant.

We see that from the crimes against properties, there is one whose number increases ceaselessly and very rapidly, in proportion to the spread of enlightenment. That is forgery.

In the State of New York, a very enlightened State, and one that stands at the head of the commercial movement in America, forgers come together to form one-sixth of all convicts. In Connecticut, which has only a little commerce, but where the entire population knows how to read and write, the forgers form approximately one-seventh of the number of convicts; while in Pennsylvania, a State peopled in great part by Germans, among whom instruction and especially eagerness to get rich is not nearly so developed, not one forger is counted out of twenty convicts.

No. II — Sanitary State

Mortality in the different prisons of America, on which we have recovered some documents, follows this progression.

At Walnut Street (Pennsylvania), 1 deceased person out of 16.66 prisoners.
At Newgate (New York), 1 deceased person out of 18.80.
At Singsing (Ibid.), 1 deceased person out of 36.58.
At Wethersfield (Connecticut), 1 deceased person out of 44.40.
At the Maryland penitentiary, 1 deceased person out of 48.57.
At Auburn (New York), 1 deceased person out of 55.96.
At Charlestown (Massachusetts), 1 deceased person out of 58.40.

It must not be forgotten that for three of these prisons, Singsing, Wethersfield, and the Maryland penitentiary, we have only been able to obtain an average of three years.

In the city and the outskirts of Philadelphia, from 1820 to 1831, mortality has been, each year, 1 inhabitant out of 38.85.

At Baltimore, in 1828, 1 individual died out of 47 inhabitants.

Thus, in two prisons, Newgate and Walnut-Street, mortality has been much greater than in the city of Philadelphia and that of Baltimore (these are former prisons). In one (at Singing), mortality has been approximately equal; in four (Wethersfield, Auburn, the penitentiary of Maryland and that of Boston), mortality has been less.

In the population of the prisons, one encounters fewer old men than in society; at first glance, it should not therefore seem surprising that mortality is less among the inmates than among free men; the result that precedes will not appear less remarkable if we think of the sedentary life that every convict leads; and if we especially consider that every class of society has furnished their quota to the figure of Philadelphia and Baltimore, while in the penitentiaries, the poorest classes, the most vicious and the most disordered, have alone contributed.

Nature of the diseases that led to death

In the Wethersfield penitentiary, the prevailing diseases have been those of the stomach and intestines. They even took an epidemic character in 1819. 9/10 of the inmates were affected; the doctor of the prison, in his annual reports, asked whether this state of things should be attributed to the discipline of the prison. He could not explain how it would be thus; the inmates are, he said, better fed than most farmers.

In the prisons of Auburn and Philadelphia, the prevailing diseases were those of the lungs. Out of 64 persons who, from 1825 to 1832, died at Auburn, 39 succumbed to chest diseases. Out of 60 persons who died in the Walnut Street prison in 1829 and 1830, 36 died because of the same kind of sicknesses.

During these same years, we counted in the city of Philadelphia only one death caused by chest diseases, out of 4 1/2 deceased persons.

Recorded Number of Maladies

At Auburn, from 1828 to 1832, each day there was 1 sick person out of 102 prisoners.

No. III. — COMPARATIVE TABLE OF RE-COMMITTALS IN THE DIFFERENT PRISONS OF AMERICA

It is very difficult to compare with each other the results obtained in the various prisons of America relating to recidivism. In facts, the documents that are reported for this object from our research indicate three bases that differ between them.

Thus, in certain prisons, the number of individuals in recidivism when they *re-enter* the prison is compared with the totality of individuals who *entered* with them into the same prison.

In others, the inmates in recidivism who are *found* in the prison are compared with the totality of criminals who *are prisoners* there.

In others, finally, the number of individuals who *return* to prison is compared with the totality of those who were put *in liberty*.

The numbers obtained by these different processes cannot be usefully compared to each other.

We cannot, for example, compare the relationship between recommitted convicts and other convicts with the relationship between recommitted inmates and other inmates. It is true, indeed, inmates entering each year end up composing the whole population of the prison; but these inmates do not remain there all at the same time; and if the recommitted inmates leave it sooner than others, fewer of them will be found in the prison after a certain time, proportionately, than there were of them among the convicts who entered successively into the prison. If, on the contrary, which almost always happens, the recommitted inmates remain longer in prison than the others, the prison, after a certain time, will contain more of them, proportionately, than are found among the convicts each year.

It is even more difficult to compare the proportions produced by the two procedures indicated above with the proportion produced by the comparison of recommitted convicts to the totality of free prisoners.

In one case, you compare the recommitted individuals with convicts having been sentenced for the first time arriving in prison, or prisoners of the same prison; in the other case, you compare these same individuals with those who were in the prison and are not there anymore. The terms of comparison are completely different.

Since we cannot reconcile these three bases, we have chosen to compare only the states where the same bases had been used.

First method of comparison

Thus, at Walnut Street (Pennsylvania), there entered [the prison] over 10 years (1810–1819) 1 recommitted convict out of 5.98 convicts.

At the Maryland penitentiary, over 12 years (1820–1832) there entered 1 recommitted convict out of 6.96 convicts.

At Newgate (New-York), over 16 years (1803–1820), 1 out of 9.45.

At Auburn (Ibid.), over 6 years (1824–1831), 1 out of 19.10.

Second method of comparison

At Walnut-Street (Pennsylvania), in 1830 there was 1 recommitted inmate out of 2.57 inmates.

At Newgate, former Connecticut prison, in 1825 there was found 1 recommitted inmate out of 4.50 inmates.

In Auburn (1824-1831), 1 out of 12.

Third method of comparison

Out of 6.15 prisoners released for 25 years in the Massachusetts prison, 1 has returned as recommitted.

Out of 19.80 inmates who were released since the opening of the Wethersfield penitentiary (1826) until the present, 1 has returned as recommitted.

It will be seen that, whatever the mode of calculating, the new penitentiaries have a decided advantage over the former.

But here an objection is presented: we compare a new prison to a former prison. It is obvious that those who return to the first are less numerous than those who return to the second. The first has handed over to society only a small number of convicts, while the other has delivered a great number. The criminals who left the first have had a much longer parole, and consequently many more chances to fail a second time.

If we consider the history of most recidivists, and when we reflect on what happens especially in America, this observation is less striking than at first glance. It is certain that, in general, recidivism occurs soon after leaving prison. If the freed convict triumphs over the first temptations that present themselves to him, and happily escapes the exercise of passions which constraint itself made more energetic, it can be believed that he will not succumb.

Let us add that as one gets further from the time of the first crime, it becomes more difficult to prove the state of recidivism. This difficulty is felt particularly in America, where men change without ceasing, and where one can take note of nothing.

We must, then, establish as an approximately certain fact, that when a former inmate has not fallen into recidivism for the first three or four years of his liberty, he has escaped the chance of committing a second crime, or at least the danger of seeing the state of recidivism noted.

The example of the Newgate prison comes to prove this observation: Newgate was founded in 1797. Four years later, in 1802, the proportion of individuals in recidivism there was already as strong as ten years later. It was at least double what existed at Auburn four years after the establishment of that penitentiary system.

No. IV. — Comparative table of men and women in the prisons of the United States

We lack this figure for the penitentiary of Charlestown (Massachusetts). The women in Massachusetts are not contained in the same prison as the men, and we have not been able to know what their number was.

(State of New-York) At Singsing, from 1828 to 1831, one finds

One woman out of 19.24 inmates of both sexes.
One white woman out of 33.73 white inmates of both sexes.
One black woman out of 9.87 inmates of both sexes belonging to the black race.

At Auburn, from 1826 to 1831, one finds

One woman out of 19 inmates of both sexes.

Connecticut, from 1827 to 1831, one finds

One woman out of 14.60 inmates of both sexes.
One white woman out of 16.14 white inmates of both sexes.
One black woman out of 11 inmates of both sexes belonging to the black race.

Pennsylvania in 1830, one finds

One woman out of 7.30 inmates of both sexes.
One white woman out of 15.64 white inmates of both sexes.
One black woman out of 3.40 inmates of both sexes belonging to the black race.

Maryland, in 1831, one finds

One woman out of 6.27 inmates of both sexes.
One white woman out of 86 white inmates of both sexes.
One black woman out of 3.56 inmates of both sexes belonging to the black race.

If we take an average of all these numbers, we find that, in the four penitentiaries of which we have spoken, one woman is found out of 11.85 inmates of both sexes;
One white woman out of 37.88 white inmates of both sexes;
One black woman out of 6.96 inmates of both sexes belonging to the black race.

The proportion of women in the prisons of the Union must become more considerable as we descend into the States where black persons are more numerous, because black women commit infinitely more crimes than white women. This is confirmed by the series of figures that we have just presented.

No. V. — Proportion of black persons in prisons and in society

In Massachusetts, there has been each year from 1822 to 1831, 1 black man out of 6.53 inmates.

In Connecticut, from 1828 to 1832, 1 black man out of 4.42 inmates.

In the State of New York, from 1825 to 1830, 1 black man out of 4.67 inmates.

In Pennsylvania, in 1830, 1 black man[3] out of 2.27 inmates.

In Maryland, in 1831, 1 black man[4] out of 1.82 inmates.

We see that the number of black men in the prisons increases as one advances towards the middle; it is the same in free society.

Here is, meanwhile, the proportion in which black men are found, in 1830, in the States of which we have spoken:

In Massachusetts, 1 black man out of 87 inhabitants.
In Connecticut, 1 black man out of 37 inhabitants.
In the State of New York, 1 black man out of 42 inhabitants.
In Pennsylvania, 1 black man out of 36 inhabitants.
In Maryland, 1 free black man[5] out of 6 inhabitants.

While calculating an average, we see that in the prisons of five States, of which we come to speak, there is found 1 black man out of 4 inmates.

In 1830, in these same States, we count one free black man out of 30 inhabitants.

No. VI. — Comparative table of prisoners who, born in the United States, are however foreigners to the particular State where they have committed the crime

We counted:

In Maryland, from 1827 to 1831, 1 inmate of this kind out of 5.14.
In the State of New York, from 1824 to 1832, 1 out of 3.48.
In Connecticut, from 1827 to 1831, 1 out of 2.86.
In Massachusetts, from 1826 to 1831, 1 out of 2.82.
In Pennsylvania, in 1829 and 1830, 1 out of 2.16.

We will note that Maryland is the one out of the five states where the smallest number of foreign Americans is found, compared to the totality of the prisoners; and Pennsylvania, the one where the most are encountered.

Maryland still only feebly attracts American industry. In Maryland, the stationary population annually commits more crimes than others;[6] when the total number of convicts is compared to the number of foreigners, it is natural that the relationship is weak.

It is equally understood that in Pennsylvania, which offers great charms to the industry of its neighbors, and where the sedentary population commits few crimes each year,[7] the convicted foreigners form a considerable portion of the total number of inmates.

No. VII. — Proportion in which foreigners are found among the prisoners

As we approach the present period, the proportion of foreigners becomes smaller in prisons, as in society.

Such a natural result is established in the following way:

From 1800 to 1805, there are in the state prison of New York 1 foreigner out of 2.43 inmates.
From 1825 to 1830, there are no more than 1 out of 4.77 inmates.
From 1786 to 1796, in Pennsylvania, we found 1 foreigner out of 2.08 inmates in prison.
In 1829 and 1830, there are no more than 1 out of 5.79.

Here is, in those surrounding the year 1830, the proportion in which foreigners are found among the prisoners of different penitentiaries:

From 1827 to 1831, we count, in Connecticut, 1 foreigner out of 13.27 inmates.
From 1827 to 1831, in Maryland, 1 out of 12.65.
In 1829 and 1830, in Massachusetts, 1 out of 6.
Ibid. — in Pennsylvania — 1 out of 5.79.
From 1825 to 1830, in the State of New York, 1 out of 4.77.

It is, as one has no doubt noticed, in the States that have the greatest cities and present the most resources for industry that foreigners are found in greatest number. This result explains itself.

No. VIII. — Proportion of Irish and English,
properly speaking, among the foreign prisoners

The proportion of Irish among foreigners is established thus by the following:

We counted

Connecticut, from 1827 to 1831, 1 Irish out of 3.66 entering inmates.
Massachusetts, from 1822 to 1831, 1 Irish out of 3.06 Ibid.
New-York, from 1825 to 1830, 1 Irish out of 2.11 Ibid.
Maryland, from 1827 to 1831, 1 Irish out of 1.85 Ibid.
Pennsylvania, from 1829 to 1830, 1 Irish out of 1.75 Ibid.

It appears that the proportion of Irish among foreign prisoners has always been tiny for the last thirty years. Hence, from 1800 to 1805, we counted in the prisons of New York 1 Irish out of 2.05 foreigners: it is almost the figure of 1830.

It is easy to indicate the reasons that bring such a great number of Irish into American prisons.

Of all the foreigners who land on the soil of the United States, the Irish are, without any percentage, the most numerous; they arrive poor and burdened with children. In the beginning of their emigration, they suffer all the horrors of poverty; afterwards they find, on the contrary, an ease to which they have never been habituated, and which their long privations, as well as their violent habits, cause them to often abuse.

The excess of evil, like prosperity, pushes them more than others into crime.

The two States where the percentage of Irish is the weakest are, as we have been able to note, those of New England. The Irish go infrequently to that part of the Union, mostly in Connecticut, where there are no large cities. On the contrary, the English, properly speaking, arrive there in greater number than all others. There they find mores, habits, and ideas more like theirs; the country more easily furnishes some employment for their kind of industry.

This fact, whose existence we have learned on the same sites, is found established by the following figures: in the greater part of the Union, the proportion of British among foreign prisoners is reduced to a little thing. In the Massachusetts penitentiary, on the contrary, we find 1 Englishman out of 3.74 foreigners; in Connecticut, 1 out of 2.50.

We have been able to see that the Irish became more numerous, as one descends towards the middle; this is owing principally to a general cause that is easy to make known: in the North, the white population begins already to find itself agglomerated, the black race is reduced, and slavery abolished; in the North, we find a greater number of white persons who necessity forces to engage in the hardest professions. In the North, moreover, labor is honorable.

In the middle, on the contrary, and especially in the States where slavery still exists, there are fewer men belonging to the white race who consent to subject themselves to the duties of domesticity or to the harder labors of agriculture and industry. To the black race is reserved pain as well as poverty. In the South, one mistakes labor as a servile work.

Now, these humiliating duties, these rude and unproductive labors, are those to which education and misery condemn the Irish emigrant, and he goes to the place where the competition of *white workers* is less formidable.

The Irish disperse in the cities, and not in the countryside: they arrive at the United States poor and ignorant; they have no money to buy land, nor industry to exploit it. The singular inconstancy of their national character renders them, for that matter, unfit to care for agriculture and the stationary life of the farmer. Only the activity and needs of cities suit them.

No. IX. — Comparative table of prisoners originally from the State where they have committed their crime

In Pennsylvania, in the years 1829 and 1830, there was 1 individual originally from the State out of 2.76 inmates.

In Massachusetts, from 1826 to 1831, there was 1 individual originally from the State out of 2.14 inmates.

In the State of New York, from 1827 to 1832, there was 1 individual originally from the State out of 2.12 inmates.

In Connecticut, from 1827 to 1831, there was 1 individual originally from the State out of 1.77 inmates in prison.

In Maryland, from 1827 to 1831, there was 1 individual originally from the State out of 1.43 inmates in prison.

We must point out that the calculations which precede are incomplete. Our principal goal, in making them, was to know the proportion in which the inhabitants of the same State are found among convicts. Now, the tables from which we have operated are based on the place of birth, not the place of residence. It is mostly, however, the residence which concerns us. It is certain that a great part of the convicts represented by the tables as foreigners were established and domiciled in the States where they have committed their crime.

No. X. — Proportion in which the Convicts originally from the State where they committed their crime are found in relation to the population of the same State

In Massachusetts, from 1826 to 1832, they have convicted, each year, 1 individual originally from the State out of 14,524 surrounding inhabitants.

In Pennsylvania, from 1827 to 1831, they have convicted, each year, 1 individual originally from the State out of 11,821 inhabitants.

In the State of New York, from 1827 to 1832, they have convicted, each year, 1 individual originally from the State out of 8,600 inhabitants.

In Connecticut, from 1827 to 1832, they have convicted, each year, 1 individual originally from the State out of 8,269 inhabitants.

In Maryland, from 1827 to 1831, they have convicted, each year, 1 individual originally from the State out of 3,954 inhabitants.

No. XI. — Comparative Table of Pardons

From 1799 to 1820, in the Newgate prison (New York), 1 prisoner out of 4.07 has been pardoned annually.

At Auburn from 1823 to 1832, 1 out of 10.17.
At Singsing, from 1828 to 1832, 1 out of 23.97.
At the Walnut Street prison (Pennsylvania), in 1829 and 1830, 1 out of 9.59.
In Maryland, from 1827 to 1831, 1 out of 21.25.
In Massachusetts, from 1827 to 1831, 1 out of 21.
In Connecticut, from 1827 to 1831, 1 out of 57.

Thus, for the last three or four years, they have pardoned 1 prisoner out of 25.56 in the five States.

The abuse of the right to pardon appears to have been widespread in America for 25 years; but today we note in public opinion an evident tendency to restrain the effects.

In several States, meanwhile, the executive still uses power without measure of his prerogative.

Out of 638 individuals who, from 1815 to 1832, have left the central prison of Ohio, 493, more than two-thirds have obtained their pardon; 145 alone had left after the expiration of their punishment.

In 1831, out of 163 convicts that the prison contained, 59 had been pardoned.

See, on the exercise of the right to pardon, the details and observations contained in the statistical notes, no. 16 §2.

No. XII. — AGE OF THE PRISONERS AT THE TIME OF THEIR CONVICTIONS

There is no table of this kind for Maryland.

Prisoners less than 20 years old

At Massachusetts, 1826-1831. 1 out of 12 inmates.
At New-York, 1826-1832. 1 out of 11 inmates.
Pennsylvania, 1830. 1 out of 10 inmates.
Connecticut, 1827-1832. 1 out of 8 inmates.
Average: 1 out of 10.

From 20 to 30 years

New-York. 1 out of 2 inmates.
Pennsylvania. 1 out of 2 inmates.
Massachusetts. 1 out of 2 inmates.
Connecticut. 1 out of 2 inmates
Average: 1 out of 2

From 30 to 40 years

New-York. 1 out of 4 inmates.
Pennsylvania. 1 out of 4 inmates.
Massachusetts. 1 out of 4 inmates.
Connecticut. 1 out of 7 inmates
Average: 1 out of 5

From 40 to 50 years

New-York. 1 out of 11 inmates.
Pennsylvania. 1 out of 9 inmates.
Massachusetts. 1 out of 9 inmates.
Connecticut. 1 out of 9 inmates
Average: 1 out of 9

From 50 to 60 years

Connecticut. 1 out of 29 inmates.
New-York. 1 out of 24 inmates.
Pennsylvania. 1 out of 24 inmates.
Massachusetts. 1 out of 24 inmates.
Average: 1 out of 25.

There are still some prisoners above sixty years of age, but they are too small in number for it to be useful to note them.

No. XIII. — Relationship of the convicts at the central prison (State prisoners) to the population in the States of Massachusetts, Connecticut, New York, Pennsylvania, and Maryland

It appears rather difficult, at first glance, to compare the five States of the Union that our tables refer to on this point.

First, there exist some notable differences between their penal laws. Thus, there are crimes for which, in some states, the guilty person is sent to the central prison (State prison), in others, to the county prison.

Second, the minimum punishment necessary to be sent to a central prison varies much. Now, it is natural to believe that, proportionately, the prison that contains some sentenced to a year will be more peopled than the one where they send those sentenced to three.

The differences originating from these variations in the laws are not, however, as great in result as could be believed. We are ourselves assured that the crimes that send one into the State prisons are almost completely the same. These crimes are punished with an imprisonment of varying length, according to the legislation of the various States; but all those who are rendered guilty are not less sentenced to the central prison; whether the minimum be fixed to one year or two. Thus, the adulterous husband will be punished by a year of prison in Connecticut, by two years in the State of New York; but in the one and the other he will be sent to the State prison.

Nevertheless, we must not lose sight of these preliminary observations in comparing the following results:

From 1820 to 1830, there have been annually

At Connecticut. 1 convict[8] out of 6,662 inhabitants.
At Massachusetts. 1 convict out of 5,555.
In Pennsylvania. 1 convict out of 3,968.
At Maryland. 1 convict[9] out of 3,102.
State of New York. 1 convict out of 5,532.

The relationship of criminals to the population increases in proportion to the number of foreigners and black persons in each State. Thus, Connecticut, where one can count only a few black persons and foreigners, has fewer convicts than the State of Massachusetts, which, without possessing more black persons, attracts much more foreign industry.

Massachusetts, on its side, counts fewer criminals than the State of New York,[10] which, with more black persons, also has much more foreigners. The State of New York has fewer crimes than Pennsylvania, and what demonstrates it more, without comparison, is Maryland, where the black race forms one sixth of the population.

Let us examine, however, whether, in the five States where it is the highest question, the number of crimes increases or diminishes with time.

Pennsylvania

1795–1800.[11] 1 convict out of 4,181 inhabitants.
1800–1810. 1 convict out of 4,387
1810–1820. 1 convict out of 3,028
1820–1830. 1 convict out of 3,968

Connecticut

1789–1800. 1 convict out of 27,164
1800–1810. 1 convict out of 17,098
1810–1820. 1 convict out of 13,413
1820–1830. 1 convict out of 6,662

Massachusetts

From 1820 to 1830, the only period that we know, the number of crimes has not stopped decreasing in Massachusetts. Consequently, it resulted from prison reports that, for these ten years, the annual number of convicts remained constantly the same. But, during this period, the population constantly increased; it was at 523,287 inhabitants in 1820 and 610,014 in 1830.

Thus, while the population increased one-seventh, crime remained stationary.

Maryland

The same observation applies to Maryland; for ten years, the annual number of convicts has remained the same, while, during this period, the population grew by one-eleventh.

New-York

1800–1810. 1 convict out of 4,465 inhabitants.
1810–1820. 1 convict out of 4,858 inhabitants.
1820–1830. 1 convict out of 5,532 inhabitants.

We see by this table that the number of convicts at the state prison diminishes, compared to the population, in the State of New-York. It tends to diminish in Massachusetts and Maryland.

After having increased in Pennsylvania, during the time of the War of 1812,[12] it approximately resumes its level and appears to want to almost diminish rather than increase.

In Connecticut, it is an inexplicable march: we see it double approximately all ten years. The reasons that we have been given in the country itself do not suffice to completely explain this phenomenon. The excessive increase for the cost of convicts in Connecticut is probably due to some local circumstances that we do not know. Connecticut, moreover, is of all the compared States the one whose merits least attract our attention. Its population does not exceed that of our smallest departments.

In general, we can say that, following the natural way of things, the number of criminals must ceaselessly tend to diminish in the greatest part of the States of the Union, without proof of an increase in morality resulting directly from it.

The population of the United States is composed of three very distinct elements:

1. White persons born in the country; 2. Black persons; 3. Foreigners.[13]

The morality of these three classes is very different. The white person, surrounded by his parents and friends and possessing some land, must be certainly less inclined to commit a crime than the stranger who arrives, unknown and surrendered to a thousand pressing needs, or the black person, whom public opinion as well as the laws join to degrade.

Nevertheless, the more time passes, the more the class of white persons born in the country tends to increase its preponderance over the two others. Consequently, the natural movement of the population will not be equal for the black race and the white race. In the entire North and center of the Union, ease reigns among the white race, poverty among the black race. Moreover, white persons are hired incessantly; black persons can only lose. If we compare the white persons born in the country to the white foreigners, we arrive at the same result. There are, however, undoubtedly, more foreigners each year in America than there were thirty years [ago]; but the natural increase of the American population still greatly exceeds the growth of immigration. For that matter, the immigrant can count only himself in the class of foreigners; his sons will come to increase that of the Americans.

Each year, comparatively speaking, there must therefore be found among the convicts more white Americans and fewer black persons and foreigners, and this is what in fact happens. (See the tables.) The sum total of convicts, in proportion to the population, must be annually less; for the class that is more and more called to furnish convicts is at the same time that where criminals, relative to the population, are and must be fewer in number. Does it follow that the morality of the country increases? No; because the white person born in America, the foreigner, and the black person can each keep their respective morality without it resulting in being less productive. The decrease of crimes proves, not that the elements which compose the population become more moral, but only that their relative proportion comes to change.

What can be affirmed with more certainty is that, as long as the increase of crimes in America follows only the progress of the population, far from resulting in the consequence that the morality of the people remains the same, we must on the contrary conclude that it diminishes. For if the sedentary class, the true American population, were not committing more crimes each year, the total number of convicts must decrease constantly, instead of remaining stationary.

The middle of the Union alone makes an exception to this principle.

In the country with slaves, there is one special cause that tends to continually increase the number of individuals sentenced to prison;[14] that is emancipation. Slaves, as we have seen previously, are not subject to the penal code of white persons; they are hardly ever sent to prison. To manumit a black person is then really to import him into society, and to introduce with him a new element of crime.

From all this it results that, in the actual state of the statistics in America, it is almost impossible to either determine with exactness what is, in respect to morality, the preeminence of different States of the Union between themselves or in relation to Europe; or to establish that there is an increase or decrease in crime.

To obtain a clear and truly significant result on this point, it would be necessary to know the number of crimes committed by the sedentary population, the only one that ought to be called American. If this figure was known for several different periods, then, and only then, could it be said with certainty that morality increases or decreases in America. But it has been impossible for us to obtain such a document, except for the three years which have preceded 1831. As incomplete as it is, we nevertheless reproduce it here; it will throw a new light on our thought:

From 1827 to 1831, there have been sentenced

1 individual originally from Massachusetts out of 14,524 inhabitants.
1 individual originally from Pennsylvania, out of 11,821 inhabitants.
1 individual originally from the State of New York, out of 8,610 inhabitants.
1 individual originally from Connecticut, out of 8,269 inhabitants.
1 individual originally from Maryland, out of 3,954 inhabitants.

Thus Pennsylvania, one of the States that retained the most convicts from 1820 to 1830,[15] is found to be really one of the most moral of the Union; while Connecticut, placed at the head of those with legal morality, in the tables to which we allude, is in reality one of the States that, from 1827 to 1831, has furnished the most criminals.

Notes

1. *Although not specified by Tocqueville and Beaumont, here "c" might be shorthand for *condamnés,* or, *convicts.* I have left the shorthand as it was recorded in the original.
2. We have not been able to obtain the table of convictions in the State of Massachusetts; but we found at the prison, alongside some names of the individual inmates in 1820, 1824 and 1830, the mention of crime that they had committed; which is more or less the same.
3. It is probable that in Pennsylvania the proportion of black men in the prisons in a little less considerable than it seems to be here. The number that we give above is that of one year only, and chance could have contributed to form it. We believe this even more, as in taking the number of all convicts, white and black, arriving at the penitentiary from 1817 to 1824 (number which is raised to 1,510), one finds the average of 1 black man out of 2.61 convicts. Now, the number of black men must rather tend to diminish than to grow in the prisons of Pennsylvania, since it ceaselessly diminishes in society.
4. It has been seen previously ([Appendix No. 16] statistical notes, no. 3) that when we say some black inmates in the Maryland prisons, it is a matter only of freed black men; slaves can never appear.
5. Since only free black persons enter the prisons, it falls to us in society to equally count only the free black persons. Without this, the argument from the comparison of two reports rested on a corrupted base. All black persons who inhabit Massachusetts, Connecticut, the State of New York, and Pennsylvania, are free, except for a very small number. Slavery is entirely abolished in these States.
6. 1 convict originally from Maryland out of 3,954 inhabitants.
7. 1 convict originally from Pennsylvania out of 11,821 inhabitants.
8. The minimum punishment necessary to be carried into these three penitentiaries is 1 year.
9. Minimum 2 years.
10. Mostly if one considers the difference in the minimum punishment.
11. We have not been able to place our point of departure until 1795, although the Walnut Street prison had been created several years before. But earlier,

only the convicts of the city and the county of Philadelphia were contained therein. Only on 11 March 1794 was a law introduced permitting the judges to send all criminals sentenced to more than one year in prison to Walnut Street. It can be remarked that the law of 12 March 1794 authorizes judges to send the convicts to the Walnut Street prison, but it did not oblige them. It is then possible that some sentenced for more than one year were retained in the county prisons. However, the thing is not probable.

12. This war has exercised a great influence on the number of crimes in America. It will be the same of all those undertaken by the United States. The Americans, strange as it is, have conserved in their arms the old usages of Europe. The soldier is a mercenary paid in pounds of gold, who fights without chances of advancement. Honors and glory belong to the privileged class of officers. When a war is ended, the greatest part of the American army is disbanded. The soldiers, who generally have neither homes nor industry, disperse in the country, and soon the number of crimes increases with rapidity. In 1814, more than two hundred thousand French had, one said, quitted the military career without having seen the costs of criminals in France grow. These names belong to the honest population of the kingdom; they have almost all an industry or some means of existence.

13. *The discussion of race throughout *On the Penitentiary System* seems to outline the preliminary principles behind Tocqueville's chapter on race relations in *Democracy in America*.

14. It is not necessary to clarify that these are those sentenced to prison who serve as the basis to increase the number of crimes in America.

15. See the Table at the beginning of this chapter.

Appendix No. 18: Some Points of Comparison Between France and America

No. I. Classification of convicts following their offences in France and in America. II. Comparative table of mortality in the main prisons of France and the American penitentiaries. — III. Comparative table of recidivism in the two countries. — IV. Proportion of men and women among the inmates in the French and American prisons. — V. Tables: 1. Of the number of foreigners among the individual convicts in France and in America; 2. Of the number of French born outside the department where they were prosecuted, compared to the number of Americans born outside the State where they were prosecuted. — VI. Age of convicts in France and America. — VII. Relationship of convicts to the population in France and America.

No. I — Classification of the Convicts in France and in America

In the year 1830, 10,046 individuals were sentenced in France, either criminally or correctional,[1] to a year of prison or more. Out of these 10,046 individuals:[2]

1,208 had committed crimes against persons, or 12.02 out of 100;
8,838 had committed crimes against property, or 87.98 out of 100;
195 had committed forgery, or 1.94 out of 100;
208 had committed crimes against mores, or 2.07 out of 100.

In the same year 1830, the average convictions pronounced in the States of Massachusetts, Connecticut, New York and Pennsylvania, provide the following result:

Convicted for crimes against persons 8.66 out of 100.
Convicted for crimes against property 91.29 out of 100.
Convicted for forgery 10.26 out of 100.
Convicted for crimes against mores 4.05 out of 100.

The proportion of crimes against persons has been, as is seen, a little more considerable in France than in America.[3]

The convictions for crimes against mores have, on the contrary, been a little more numerous in America than in France.

A great difference is recognized only in forgery.

The state of education in America, the great number of banks, and the immense commercial movement that is evident there, easily explains this difference.

In France, it has been observed that crimes against persons have had a slight tendency to become less frequent. Thus, in 1825 they counted 22 crimes against persons out of 100 crimes; in 1826, 22; in 1827, 22; in 1828, 19; in 1829, 18; and in 1830, 17.

For thirty years, on the contrary, crimes against persons seemed to become more frequent in America.

Statistical notes, no. 17, paragraph 1.

Tables according to Criminal Justice in France, 1830, p. 2, 114; 1829, p. 2; 1828, p. 2; 1827, p. 2; 1826, p. 2; 1825, p. 2.

No. II. — Comparative table of mortality in French central prisons and American penitentiaries

In 1828, the population of the main prisons of France was 17,560 individuals; out of this number, 1,372 died in the year: 1 death out of 12.79.

In 1829, the number of inmates was 17,586; the number of deaths, 1,386: 1 death out of 12.68.

In 1830, the number of inmates was 16,842; the number of deaths, 1,111; 1 death out of 15.16.

Thus, during the last three years the average mortality in the main prisons of France has been around 1 death for every 14 inmates.

In America, during the same years, on average, in the five penitentiaries of Singsing, Auburn, Wethersfield, Baltimore and Charlestown (Massachusetts), only 1 prisoner died out of 49 approximately.

This result will appear even more extraordinary if one considers that in America, in the five penitentiaries that we just spoke of, there is found little or no women. But, if we deduct the number of women in the French prisons, mortality would be even more considerable. Thus, we have said that in 1830 the average mortality has been 1 death out of 15.16 prisoners; it would have been 1 out of 14.03 if we were concerned with only male prisoners.

Documents furnished by the Minister of Public Works and Commerce. Comparative tables relating to the State of New York, p. 2.

No. III. — Comparative table of recidivism in France and in America

In France, for the last three years, 1828, 1829, and 1830, 95,876 individuals have been sentenced to imprisonment, of which 13,622 were in a state of recidivism.

Ratio: 1 convict in recidivism out of 7 convicts.[4]

In Pennsylvania, from 1810 to 1819, there was 1 convict in recidivism out of 6 convicts.

In Maryland, from 1820 to 1832, 1 convict in recidivism out of 7 convicts.

In the State of New York, from 1803 to 1820, 1 convict in recidivism out of 9 convicts.

At Auburn, from 1824 to 1831, 1 convict in recidivism out of 19 convicts.

Thus, France has had, each year, less convicts in recidivism than Pennsylvania, more than Maryland, and almost three times more than the State of New York since the establishment of Auburn.

It is necessary to note, moreover, that the comparison of these figures can never furnish anything other than approximations. The number of convicts in recidivism in America cannot be exactly compared to the number of convicts in recidivism in France. In America, criminal administration properly speaking does not exist. It is, in general, only the return of the guilty into the same prison that establishes his state of recidivism. In

France, one has a thousand means of knowing the previous conviction of a criminal.

As a result, in admitting that the figure of convicts in recidivism in America is the same as the figure of convicts in recidivism in France, we can still count that in reality America furnishes more of them than France. It cannot be doubted, for example, that in France there are less recidivists than in the State of Maryland, although the figures of two countries are identical to themselves.

Comparative Table of Recidivism, no. 17, par. 3.

Account given of criminal justice in France, 1828, p. 192 and 112; 1829, p. 193 and 114; 1830, *report to the King*, p. xi, xvil, and xviii; p. 165 and 94.

No. IV. — Comparative table of the number of women in the prisons of France and America

Out of 22,304 individuals who have been convicted for crimes in France from 1825 to 1831, there were 3,911 women.

Ratio: 17.53 out of 100 convicts of both sexes.

Out of 31,655 individuals, who in the same period were correctionally convicted to one year of prison and more, were found 8,687 women.

Ratio: 25.55 women out of 100 convicts of both sexes.

If we add these numbers, to make the comparison with America easier, we find that out of 53,959 individuals who, from 1825 to 1831, had been sentenced criminally or correctionally to a year or more of prison, there were 11,998 women.

Ratio: 22.23 women out of 100 convicts of both sexes.

Out of 104,709 individuals who, in the same period, had been correctionally convicted to less than one year of prison, we found 20,649 women.

Ratio: 19.72 women out of 100 convicts of both sexes.

In America, in the central prisons (State prisons) of New York, Connecticut, Pennsylvania, and Maryland, women were to men in the proportion of 9.34 to 100 inmates of both sexes.

If we compare to this figure that of those individuals criminally and correctionally convicted in France to one year of prison and more, figure composed of approximately the same elements, we see that the number of female inmates is more than double in France than in America.

Still, it is necessary to note that the figure of 9 out of 100 is applied to the totality of Americans, white or black men; but if we take only the figure of white women, the difference between France and America would be far greater; for in American penitentiaries, white women are to the entirety of white inmates of both sexes as 3.87 to 100.[5]

We cannot compare the figure of women sentenced to less than one year of prison with any corresponding figure in America. We know only that in America, as the punishment becomes weaker, the number of convicted women greatly increases; it is at least what we have observed in the States of New York and Pennsylvania. It is not the same in France. The proportion of women sentenced to less than one year in prison is not as considerable as that of women sentenced to more than one year.

Proportion of men and women in the different penitentiaries, no. 17, paragr. 3.

Table of criminal justice in France: 1826. p. 9 and 121; 1827 p. 9 and 132; 1828 p. 14 and 140; 1829 p. 14 and 151; 1830 p. 14 and 125.

No. V. Comparative Table: 1. In France,
of the number of foreigners among the accused,
and of the number of French born
outside the department where they were prosecuted;
2. In America, of foreigners among the convicts
as well as Americans born outside the State where
they were prosecuted

In France, out of 21,731 individuals who have been accused from 1827 to 1831, 697 were not French; 15,691 were born in the department where they were prosecuted; 5,303 were born outside that department.

Thus, foreigners were to the entirety of the accused as 3 to 100.

The accused born in the department were to the entirety of the accused prosecuted in the same department as 72 to 100.

The accused born outside the department were to the entirety of the accused prosecuted in the same department as 23 to 100.

In America, (in the States of Massachusetts, Connecticut, New York, Pennsylvania, and Maryland), the individuals sentenced to the state prison were divided thus as follows:

14 foreigners to America out of 100 inmates;

51 individuals born in the State where they had been prosecuted out of 100 inmates;

33 individuals born outside the State where they had been prosecuted out of 100 inmates.

The comparison of these numbers establishes a fact that we have already understood, namely: that the population is infinitely less sedentary in America than in France.

We will become even more convinced of it if we consider that our departments are, in general, much smaller than the States of the Union, and that no political links can attach those who were born there. It must therefore be more common among us than in America to change one's domicile; it is, however, the opposite that happens.

Statistical Notes, no. 17, paragr. 7, 8, 9.

Table of criminal justice in France: 1828, p. 26; 1829, p. 26; 1830, p. 27.

No. VI. — Comparative Table of the ages of convicts in France and America

Out of 21,703 individuals[6] who, from 1825 to 1831, were convicted in France for crimes, 4,251 were less than 21 years old, or approximately 1 out of 5 convicts.

7,504 were ages 21 to 30 years, or approximately 1 out of 3 convicts.

5,195 were ages 30 to 40 years, or approximately 1 out of 4 convicts.

2,800 were ages 40 to 50 years, or approximately 1 out of 8 convicts.

1,211 were ages 50 to 60 years, or approximately 1 out of 18 convicts.

483 were ages 60 to 70 years, or approximately 1 out of 46 convicts.

There are also several prisoners who are older than 70 years, but they are too few in number for it to be useful to deal with it.

If we compare these figures with the corresponding figures obtained in America, we note little difference between them.

The convicts less than 20 years old are in the proportion of 1 out of 10 in America.

Those aged 20 to 30 years, in the proportion of 1 out of 2.

Those aged 30 to 40 years, in that of 1 out of 5.

Those aged 40 to 50 years, in that of 1 out of 9.

Those aged 50 to 60 years, in that of 1 out of 25.

These are, as we have been able to observe, the two initial proportions that differ the most in the two countries.

But it is necessary to remember that in France the first proportion is composed of individuals less than 21 years old; in America, those less than 20 years old. It is this displacement of one year that causes the difference noted, a difference only apparent.

Statistical notes, no. 17, paragr. 12.

Table of criminal justice in France, 1826, p. 14; 1828, p. 22; 1830, p. 22; 1827, p. 14; 1829, p. 22.

No. VII. — Relationship of convicts to the population in France and America

In France in 1830, 10,261 individuals were sentenced to imprisonment of one year and under.

Ratio: 1 convict out of 3,118 inhabitants.[7]

This ratio is not the result of an accident; for it occurs again approximately in 1829, 1828, and 1827.

In the United States, from 1820 to 1830, if we make an average of all the results obtained in the penitentiaries of Massachusetts, Connecticut, New York, Pennsylvania, and Maryland, we find 1 out of 4,964 inhabitants sentenced to the State prison.

In France, as can be seen, there are more individuals convicted for serious crimes than in America. But it is necessary to say that for France we have adopted as the basis of our calculations the minimum convictions to one year in prison, while in two of the greatest States compared the minimum is 2 years.[8]

We have reason to believe that if it were possible to compare the total number of individuals sentenced to any kind of imprisonment in the two countries, the advantage would rest in France.

Here is what this opinion is founded on:

In 1830, in Pennsylvania, there were 327 persons sentenced to the main prison; there has been, therefore, 1 convict of this kind out of 4,121 inhabitants, proportion that is much closer to the average than we have indicated above.

In Pennsylvania during this same year, there were 1,431 individuals sentenced to less than one year of prison, only in the county of Philadelphia.

This number is not the product of an accidental year. It forms approximately the average of four years which preceded 1830.

By adding 1,431 and 327, we obtained the number 1,758.

It is evident that this number 1,758 is less representative of the entirety of individuals sentenced to prison in 1830 in the State of Pennsylvania, because one of the elements of which it is composed is furnished by a single county, and we do not know the results obtained in the 50 others.

We will, however, compare this figure, as incomplete as it is, with that of the inhabitants of Pennsylvania in 1830, and we will obtain for ratio: 1 sentenced to prison out of 767 inhabitants.

But in France in 1830, there was only one sentenced to prison out of 1,043 inhabitants, and this ratio is approximately the same in the years 1829, 1828, and 1827.

Thus, the individuals sentenced to the State prison in Pennsylvania, added to the individuals sentenced to less than one year of prison in the only county of Philadelphia, are already much more numerous, proportionately with the population of Pennsylvania, than the individuals sentenced to any imprisonment in all of France, in proportion to the population of the kingdom.

The comparison would be still more favorable to us if we could obtain the results of criminal justice in the 50 counties of Pennsylvania, whose reports we lack.

We estimate that if this calculation had been made, we would have found at least 1 convict out of 600 inhabitants;[9] while in France one finds of them only one out of 1,000.

This great number of imprisonments can be attributed principally to two causes:

1. First, to the severity of principles that the mores of the first inhabitants imported into the laws. There is a crowd of small disorders that our codes leave unpunished, and which the penal legislations of America repress, such as gambling of all kinds, oaths, noise, drunkenness, idleness in many cases.
2. These laws are severe; their enforcement is even more so. A great arbitrariness reigns.

In general, the liberty of the poor person is badly guaranteed in the United States. One of the principles of the British constitution is to leave to the superior classes the right to freely constitute the police of society.

In America, the English aristocracy does not exist, but a part of its regulatory attributions remained in municipal administrations that, composed of plebeian magistrates, have nevertheless until the present adopted the same doctrines.
Statistical Documents on Pennsylvania, p. 15.
Table of Criminal Justice in France, 1830, p. 12, p. 125.

Notes

1. *The *Trésor de la Langue Française informatisé* defines "correctionnellement" as: "What has relation to infractions called offences, as opposed to crimes and citations."
2. In the divisions of crimes against persons and properties, we have not completely adopted the order of the tables of criminal justice, to be able to establish a more exact comparison between France and America.
3. But it is necessary to remember that in America it is almost always the injured party who prosecutes, and often has interest in not pleading it. In France, in most cases, the public ministry takes care to avenge the offence and the State pays the costs of the procedure.
4. This figure represents only the proportion of re-committals judicially recognized in 1828, 1829, and 1830. But however great the activity of the judicial police, there is, even among us, a crowd of individuals whose past life remains unknown to the courts, and whose re-committal is recognized only in the prison. In 1830, out of 16,000 prisoners who submitted to their punishment in the main prisons, [there were] 4,000 re-committals, which gives 1 re-committal out of 4 prisoners.
5. It would be wrong, however, to compare the number of white women in the American penitentiaries with that of women in French prisons. White women in America, even those who belong to the lowest classes of society, occupy an elevated social position in comparison to black women. To be mixed with the latter seems to them the height of ignominy. The fear of a similar shame greatly prevents them from committing crimes. Often, also, the jury itself shies away from applying a punishment to which the idea of infamy is attached.
6. There have been, in reality, 21,740 convicts over these five years; but there are 37 who do not know their age.
7. Taking 32,000,000 inhabitants for the population of France.
8. Nor must it be forgotten that criminal justice in France is infinitely more active than in the United States.
9. See details on this point in the statistical notes, no. 16, §5.

Reference

"Trésor de la Langue Française informatisé." *Center National de Ressources Textuelles et Lexicales.* http://atilf.atilf.fr/lexicographie/. Accessed September 9, 2017.

Appendix No. 19: Financial Part

FIRST SECTION (OLD SYSTEM): STATISTICAL TABLE PRESENTING THE MAINTENANCE EXPENSE OF THE FORMER PRISONS, PRIOR TO THE PENITENTIARY SYSTEM

Daily expense, minus products of labor

Newgate (Connecticut)

Maintenance of the former Newgate prison (Connecticut) has cost during the last ten years as follows:

Year 1817 — 12,679 dollars 51 cents.
1818 — 12,494 dollars 27 cents.
1819 — 11,403 dollars 73 cents.
1820 — 9,704 dollars 11 cents
1821 — 6,000 dollars 00 cents
1822 — 5,263 dollars 65 cents
1823 — 5,500 dollars 00 cents
1824 — 8,002 dollars 80 cents
1825 — 7,284 dollars 90 cents
1826 — 6,301 dollars 08 cents
Total 88,634 dollars 05 cents.

In 1828, there were 93 prisoners in the new prison; supposing that a similar number were found in the former over the last ten years, each of these ten years having cost, on average, 8,863 dollars 40 cents (46,976 fr. 02 c.), minus the product of labor; consequently, the day of a prisoner cost the State, on average, 26 cents 10/10,000 (1 fr. 38 c. 38/10, 000). Notice that in taking the number 93 for the average number of prisoners in the former prison, from 1817 to 1826, we take a number certainly too high, unless it is demonstrated that the number of crimes is increasing in the State of Connecticut: it is therefore probable that the maintenance of the inmates costs less; but it is certain that it could not be higher than the number that we present.

Moreover, from 1791 until 1826 the Newgate prison has, for its maintenance alone, incurred for the State of Connecticut an expense of 204,711 dollars 38 cents. (1,084, 968 fr. 30 c.).

See *report of 1826 on the Connecticut prison.*

Lamberton (New Jersey)

The maintenance of the New Jersey prison has cost, during the ten years from 1820 to 1829, as follows:

Year 1820 — 1,872 dollars 50 cents.
1821 — 10,169 dollars 84 cents.
1822 — 5,805 dollars 00 cents.
1823 — 3,725 dollars 00 cents
1824 — 6,331 dollars 00 cents
1825 — 3,350 dollars 00 cents
1826 — 2,025 dollars 00 cents
1827 — 2,987 dollars 50 cents
1828 — 3,029 dollars 37 cents
1829 — 3,125 dollars 48 cents

In 1829 (the last year), there were 90 inmates in the prison: supposing that a similar number were found during all the other years, each of these ten years has cost, on average, 4,242 dollars 06 cents (22,482 fr. 91 c), minus the product of labor; consequently, one day of a prisoner cost the State, on average, 12 cents 90/10,000 (68 c. 44/10,000). It is to be remarked that, in taking the number 90 for the average term of the number of inmates in prison, from 1820 to 1829, we take a number probably too high, unless in every State of the Union the number of prisoners increased either by the growth of crimes in some or by the decrease of pardons in others; moreover, we can doubt whether the expense per day was not higher, but it appears very certain that it was not less.

From 1797 until 1829, the State of New Jersey paid for the maintenance of its prison 164,963 doll. 81 cents (874,298 fr. 19 c.)—See 5th Report of the Boston Society, p. 423.

It is fair to say that, in recent times, the Lamberton prison has markedly improved under the financial report. In 1831, its expenses have exceeded its income only by 1,038 dollars 65 cents (5,504 fr. 84 c.). — See *Report on the New Jersey prison, including a letter from Judge Coxe of Philadelphia.*

Walnut-Street (Pennsylvania)

During the eleven years that have passed from 1819 until 1829 inclusively, the State of Pennsylvania has paid the following sums to sustain the prison of Walnut-Street:

Year 1819 — 8,234 dollars 46 cents.
1820 — 7,110 dollars 75 cents.
1821 — 4,330 dollars 00 cents.
1822 — 3,050 dollars 40 cents.
1823 — 4,118 dollars 13 cents.
1824 — 4,065 dollars 83 cents.
1825 — 6,046 dollars 80 cents.
1826 — 4,046 dollars 80 cents.
1827 — 5,095 dollars 17 cents.
1828 — 56 dollars 80 cents.
1829 — 256 dollars 22 cents.
Total: 46,111 dollars 36 cents.
Or 244,390 fr. 20 c.

In 1827, there were in the Walnut Street prison 576 prisoners; supposing that a similar number was found there during the eight preceding and the ten posterior years, each of the eleven years having cost, on average, 4,191 dollars 94 cents (22,017 fr. 28 c.), minus the product of labor, consequently the day of an inmate in this prison cost the State, on average, 1 cent 99/10,000 (10 c. 47/10,000).

See *5th Report of the Boston Society of Prisons*, p. 354.

The causes that influence the high cost or economy of the administration of a prison are very well developed in the case of Walnut-Street, in the *5th Report of the Boston Society of Prisons (loco citato).*

Newgate (New-York)

In twenty-three years that have passed from 1797 until 1819 inclusively, the former New York prison has cost, for its construction as well as for its annual maintenance, 646,912 dollars (3,428,633 fr. 60 c). It appears that around 1,060,000 fr. (200,000 doll.) have been spent for the construction, leaving therefore 446,912 dollars (2,368,633 fr. 60 c.) for maintenance alone, minus the product of labor. Each of these twenty-three years has therefore cost, on average, 19,432 dollars (102,989 fr. 60 c). But, there have been in this prison, on average, 440 prisoners each year during the years we are talking about; consequently, the day of an inmate in this prison cost the State 12 cents 32/10,000 (65 c. 29/10,000).

Second Section (New System)

§1. — *Construction*

System of Philadelphia — System of Auburn. — Expense of construction (Philadelphia system).

Expense of Construction (Philadelphia System)

Penitentiary of Cherry Hill near Philadelphia. — 262 cells.

432,000 dollars (2,289,600 fr), bringing the price of each cell to 1,648 dollars 85 cents (8,738 fr. 93 c).

(Document received by us on the same site). See also *Report of the Commissioner Drafters of Pennsylvania and that of Judge Powers.* 1828.

Pittsburg Penitentiary. — 190 cells.

186,000 dollars (985,800 fr.), bringing the price of each cell to 978 dollars 95 cents (5,188 fr. 42 c.).

(See *Carey.*)

We arrange the Pittsburg penitentiary under the title of the Philadelphia system because it has been created for solitary imprisonment day and night, which forms the distinctive trait of this system; we must, however, note that the inmates of Pittsburg do not work; their cells have more resemblance with those of Auburn than with those of the Cherry Hill penitentiary.

Expense of Construction (Auburn System)

Washington Penitentiary. — 160 cells.

180,000 dollars (954,000 fr.), bringing the price of each cell to 1,125 doll. (5,962 fr. 50 c.).[1]

Charlestown Penitentiary near Boston. — 300 cells.

86,000 dollars (455,800 fr.), bringing the price of each cell to 286 dollars 66 cents (1,519 fr. 23 c.).[2]

Singsing Penitentiary. — 1,000 cells.

200,000 dollars (1,060,000 fr.), bringing the price of each cell to 200 dollars (1,060 fr.).[3]

Wethersfield Penitentiary. — 232 cells.

35,000 dollars (185,500 fr.), bringing the price of each cell to 150 dollars 86 cents (799 fr. 56 c.).[4]

Baltimore Penitentiary. — 320 cells.

46,823 dollars 44 cents (248,164 fr. 23 c.), bringing the price of each cell to 146 dollars 32 cents (775 fr. 51 c.).[5]

Blackwell-Island Penitentiary. — 240 cells.

32,000 dollars (169,600 fr.), bringing the price of each cell to 133 dollars 33 cents (706 fr. 86 c.).[6]

We do not exactly know the price of the Singsing penitentiary, which we indicate as having cost 200,000 doll. (1,060,000 fr.).

Accordingly, from some documents we find, whether in the reports to the legislature or in a note from Mr. Cartwright, engineer at Singsing, that the construction of the penitentiary has cost the State around 150,000 doll. (795,000 fr.). But it is necessary to add to this price the value of work made by the prisoners employed to build it instead of free workers. It is for this reason that we add 50,000 dollars (265,000 fr.) to the first sum. Clearly, this sum of 50,000 dollars greatly exceeds the value of the work performed by the prisoners. We are thus sure that in estimating the construction of Singsing at 200,000 dollars, we estimate higher than it actually cost, everything considered.

We see from the above table that the cell costs on average 257 dollars 47 cents (1,364 fr. 59 c.); still, it must be noted that the high price, and disproportionate with the others, of the Washington penitentiary, singularly expands the average; and it would perhaps be more accurate to determine an average taken on all the penitentiaries, with the exception of that of Washington, which has been built without any purpose of saving; in acting thus, we would get for [an] average price of the cell 191 dollars 11 cents (1,012 fr. 88 c). We must not forget that we are concerned here with the price of the cell and all its accessories in the prison.

§II. — *Maintenance*

Expenses — Products.

The statistical tables that follow are only the very succinct summary of an immense work that we have done on the financial situation of American prisons, such that its extent prevents us from publishing its entirety. We can, moreover, affirm that not one of our figures is not founded on an official document. We have filed all supporting documents at the Department of Commerce and Public Works.

Financial Situation of Auburn

Year 1825. — 386 inmates, on average.

Expenses of the prison. 24,275 dollars 92 cents (128,662 fr. 37 c.).
Revenue produced by labor. 13,976 dollars 10 cents (74,073 fr. 33 c.).
Total: 10,299 dollars 82 cents (54,589 fr. 04 c.).
Difference at the expense of the prison. 10,299 dollars 82 cents (54,589 fr. 04 c.).

Year 1826. — 433 inmates, on average.

Expenses of the prison. 30,736 dollars 05 cents (162,901 fr. 06 c.)
Revenue produced by labor. 20,522 dollars 17 cents (108,767 fr. 50 c.).
Total: 10,213 dollars 88 cents (54,133 fr. 56 c.).
Difference at the expense of the prison. 10,213 dollars 88 cents (54, 133 fr. 56 c.).

APPENDIX NO. 19: FINANCIAL PART 327

Year 1827. — 476 inmates, on average.

Expenses of the prison. 36,543 dollars 91 cents (193,682 fr. 72 c.).
Revenue produced by labor. 25,191 dollars 17 cents (133,513 fr. 20 c.).
Total: 11,352 dollars 74 cents (60,169 fr. 52 c.).
Difference at the expense of the prison. 11,352 dollars 74 cents (60,169 fr. 52 c.).

Year 1828. — 547 inmates, on average.

Expenses of the prison. 33,571 dollars 84 cents (177,930 fr. 75 c.).
Revenue produced by labor. 33,460 dollars 56 cents (177,340 fr. 96 c.).
Total: 111 dollars 28 cents (589 fr. 79 c.).
Difference at the expense of the prison. 111 dollars 28 cents (589 fr. 79 c.).

Year 1829. — 604 inmates, on average.

Expenses of the prison. 38,200 dollars 80 cents (202,464 fr. 24 c.).
Revenue produced by labor. 34,056 dollars 17 cents (180,497 fr. 70 c.).
Total: 4,144 dollars 63 cents (21,966 fr. 54 c.).
Difference at the expense of the prison. 4,144 dollars 63 cents (21,966 fr. 54 c.).

Year 1830. — 629 inmates, on average.

Revenue produced by labor. 36,251 dollars 79 cents (192,134 fr. 48 c.).
Expenses of the prison. 36,226 dollars 42 cents (192,000 fr. 02 c.).
Total: 25 dollars 37 cents (134 fr. 46 c.).
Difference at the expense of the prison. 25 dollars 37 cents (134 fr. 46 c.).

Year 1831. — 643 inmates, on average.

Revenue produced by labor. 36,209 dollars 44 cents (191,910 fr. 03 c.).
Expenses of the prison. 34,405 dollars 60 cents (182,349 fr. 70 c.).
Total: 1,803 dollars 84 cents (9,560 fr. 33 c.).
Difference at the expense of the prison. 1,803 dollars 84 cents (9,560 fr. 33 c.).
(*See Reports from the Inspectors of the Auburn prison for the years 1825, 1826, 1827, 1828, 1829, 1830 and 1831*).

Financial Situation of Wethersfield

Year 1828 (half a year). — 93 inmates, on average.

Expenses of the prison. 2,598 dollars 31 cents (13,771 fr. 04 c.).
Revenue produced by labor. 3,615 dollars 47 cents (19,161 fr. 99 c.).
Difference to the profit of the prison. 1,017 dollars 16 cents (5,390 fr. 95 c.).

Year 1829. — 115 inmates, on average.

Expenses of the prison. 5,876 dollars 13 cents (31,143 fr. 48 c.).
Revenue produced by labor. 9,105 dollars 54 cents (48,259 fr. 36 c.).
Difference to the profit of the prison. 3,229 dollars 41 cents (17,115 fr. 88 c.).

Year 1830. — 150 inmates, on average.

Expenses of the prison. 7,295 dollars 00 cents (38,663 fr. 50 c.).
Revenue produced by labor. 12,363 dollars 94 cents (65,529 fr. 08 c.).
Difference to the profit of the prison. 5,068 dollars 94 cents (26,865 fr. 40 c.).

Year 1831. — 174 inmates, on average.

Expenses of the prison. 7,342 dollars 16 cents (38,913 fr. 44 c.).
Revenue produced by labor. 15,166 dollars 18 cents (80,380 fr. 75 c.).
Difference to the profit of the prison. 7,824 dollars 02 cents (41,467 fr. 30 c.).

The new Wethersfield penitentiary has then, in the space of three and a half years, brought to the State, minus all expenses, 17,139 dollars 53 cents (90,839 fr. 50 c).

The former Connecticut prison (Newgate) has cost the State, from 1790 until 1826, 204,711 dollars, that is to say 1,000,084 fr. 30 c., for maintenance of inmates, minus the product of their labors.

(See *Reports from the Inspectors of the Connecticut penitentiary for the years 1828, 1829, 1830 and 1831.*)

APPENDIX NO. 19: FINANCIAL PART 329

Financial Situation of the Baltimore Penitentiary

Year 1828. — 317 inmates, on average.

Expenses of the prison. 15,883 dollars 79 cents (84,184 fr. 08 c.).
Revenue produced by labor. 27,464 dollars 31 cents. (145,560 fr. 84 c.).
Difference to the profit of the prison. 11,580 dollars 52 cents (61,376 fr. 76 c.).

Year 1829. — 342 inmates, on average.

Expenses of the prison. 16,265 dollars 00 cents (86,204 fr. 50 c.).
Revenue produced by labor. 36,216 dollars 25 cents. (191.946 fr. 12 c.).
Difference to the profit of the prison. 19,951 dollars 23 cents (105,741 fr. 62 c.).

Year 1830 (for 9 months). — 363 inmates, on average.

Expenses of the prison. 13,292 dollars 61 cents (70,450 fr. 83 c.).
Revenue produced by labor. 26,105 dollars 29 cents (138,358 fr. 03 c.).
Difference to the profit of the prison. 12,812 dollars 68 cents (67,907 fr. 20 c.).

Thus, in three years the Baltimore penitentiary, minus all expenses, brought to the State of Maryland the sum of 44,344 dollars 45 cents, that is 235,025 fr. 58 cent.

(See *Reports from the Inspectors of the Maryland Penitentiary for the years* 1828, 1829, 1830.)

Financial Situation of SingSing

Years 1828 and 1829. — 541 inmates, on average.

Expenses of the prison. 33,654 dollars 00 cents (178,366 fr. 20 c.).
Revenue produced by labor. 4,648 dollars 19 cents (24,635 fr. 40 c.).
Difference to the profit of the prison. 29,005 dollars 88 cents (153,730 f. 79 c.).

See *Report from 6 January 1830.*

Years 1829 and 1830. — 669 inmates, on average.

Expenses of the prison. 36,606 dollars 00 cents (194,011 fr. 80 c.).
Revenue produced by labor. 13,253 dollars 01 cents (70,240 fr. 95 c.).
Difference to the profit of the prison. 23,352 dollars 99 cents (123,770 fr. 85 c.).

See Report from the Inspectors of 5 January 1831.

Year 1831. — 875 inmates, on average.

Expenses of the prison. 51,703 dollars 31 cents (274,027 fr. 54 c.).
Revenue produced by labor. 40,205 dollars 33 cents (213,088 fr. 24 c.).
Difference to the profit of the prison. 11,497 dollars 98 cents (60,939 fr. 30 c.).

See Reports from the Inspectors of 12 January 1832.

In each of the reports from which these calculations are extracted, the figure of the annual expense is much higher than what we give here, because it includes the expenses incurred by the construction of the prison, while we count only maintenance expenses.

The figure of expenses thus reduced is precise; that of the revenue is not. Here is why: until 1831, most prisoners were employed at building the prison; consequently, their work, which was fruitful in the sense that it dispensed with an expense, did not, however, produce any revenue and did not bring in income. In 1831, 526 prisoners out of 875 have been occupied with productive labor: thus, the figure of the income has been singularly augmented; we can, in establishing a proportion, calculate what must be produced by 875 prisoners, by putting for the base what is produced by 526. But, in this regard, we would risk making an inexact calculation. Consequently, the product of labor does not always double with the number of workers: it often happens that the fabrication of manufactured objects exceeds consumption and goes beyond the needs of commerce; and one cannot know whether 1,000 inmates cutting stone in the quarries of Singsing will yield as much to the State proportionally as 526.

All that can be said is that, according to every probability, the prison will sustain itself and will cost absolutely nothing to the State, when the labor of every inmate is applied to productive industries.

Philadelphia System

We do not present any statistical table on the financial situation of Philadelphia, because it has been impossible for us to procure the documents that we desired on this point.

However, it follows from the 2nd report made to the legislature in 1831 that during the first fiscal year the product of their labor covered the maintenance of the inmates; and there remained to the responsibility of the State only the payment of the employee's salary. The report of the following year seems to report a similar result. However, it gives no number. It is necessary to note that the number of inmates in the new penitentiary of Philadelphia is very small; and Mr. Samuel Wood, the director of this prison, thinks that the labor of the prisoners will become proportionally more productive as the latter become more numerous.

See 27th Report on the Philadelphia penitentiary.

Expenses and Products Compared

Maintenance and Labor

Auburn. (Average of 7 years.)

The total expense for each inmate costs per day 17 cents 61 (93 c. 33).
The labor of each inmate produced per day 14 cents 59 (77 c. 34).

Singsing. (Average of last 3 years.)

The total expense for each prisoner cost per day 16 cents 33 (86 c. 68).
The labor of each inmate produced per day 10 cents 26 (54 c. 39).

Wethersfield. (Average of 4 years.)

The total expense for each inmate per day is raised to 13 cents 55 (0 fr. 71 c. 81).
The labor of each inmate produced 23 cents 35 (1 fr. 18 c. 46).

Baltimore. (Average of last 3 years.)

The total expense for each prisoner per day is raised to 13 cents 36 (0 fr. 70 c. 78).
The labor of each prisoner produced 26 cents 31 (1 fr. 39 c. 42).

Food Alone

Food alone for an inmate cost per day, on average:

Auburn. (Average of 6 years.) 4 cents 36 (23 c. 34).
Singsing (Average of 2 years.) 6 cents 00 (31 c. 80).
Wethersfield. (Average of 4 years.) 4 cents 72 (25 c. 01).

Cost of Surveillance Alone

The surveillance of an inmate (that is, the cost of the guards, salary of employees, et cetera) cost per day, on average:

Auburn. (Average of 6 years.) 6 cents 17 (32 c. 72).
Singsing. (Average of 3 years.) 6 cents 83 (36 c. 19).
Wethersfield (Average of 4 years.) 6 cents 87 (36 c. 37).

Cost of Food, Clothing, and Sleeping Combined

Food, clothing, and sleep of an inmate cost per day, on average:

Auburn. (Average of 3 years.) 5 cents 76 (30 p. 52).
Singsing. (Average of 5 years.) 8 cents 07 (43 c. 58).

If we approximate the above table of the statistical state relative to the former system, we will see that in the State of Connecticut the day of each convict has for the last four years brought to the State, minus expenses, 46 cents 65 (8 cents 80); while during the ten years that preceded the establishment of the new system, the day of each inmate cost the State on average 26 cents 10 (1 fr. 38 c. 38); which makes a difference of 1 fr. 84 c. 65 (34 cents 90) for the day of each prisoner.

Expense of Annual Maintenance (Auburn)

Over the 7 years that passed from 1825 to 1831, each prisoner cost, on average, each year, 63 dollars 76 cents 06 (337 fr. 95 c. 03).

The most that a prisoner has cost per year is 76 dollars 77 cents (406 fr. 88 c). The least that he has cost is 53 dollars 50 cents 8/1,000 (283 fr. 59 c.)

Salary of the Employees

	Auburn. 1831 643 prisoners	Singsing 1831 875 prisoners	Boston (old prison) 1829 276 prisoners	Wethersfield 1831 174 prisoners.
Superintendent	1,250 d.	1,750 d.	1,500 d.	1,200 d.
Other employees	13,700	18,370	11,671 d. 55 c.	2,513 d. 33 c.
Total	14,900 d. (78,970 f. 73 c.)	20,120 d. (106,686 f. 20 c.)	13,171 d. 55 c. (69, 809 f. 21 c.)	3,713 d. 33 c. (19,680 f. 64 c.)

Note. The superintendent of the Virginia prison receives $2,000.

END.

NOTES

1. The figure for construction expenses has been given to us by the present superintendent. The portion implemented by this penitentiary has therefore cost only 120,000 dollars (636,000 f.); but the expense that remains to be made is estimated at 60,000 dollars. It is probable that costs will exceed estimation.
2. See the brochure that contains the regulation of the new Charlestown prison (Massachusetts).
3. See handwritten note from Mr. Cartwright, engineer at Singsing.
4. See the handwritten notes of Judge Welles of Wethersfield and Reports to the legislature on the Connecticut prison.
5. See page 10 of the report of the inspectors of the Maryland penitentiary, from 23 December 1828.
6. See Carey, pag. 38.

Index[1]

A

Accountant, 32, 91
Administration, 113, 114, 208–210, 217, 313
  federal, 85
  local, 4, 32, 90, 91, 108–111, 115, 124, 130, 318
  of the penitentiary, 17n1, 40, 89–91, 97n7, 108, 173, 187, 189
Agricultural colonies, xl, xliin14, 114, 197–200, 211, 211n4
Alabama, 218
America, xxxi, 77, 158, 180, 207, 217, 275, 294, 301
  character of, 11, 13
Architecture, 83, 101, 102, 116
  architect, 85, 102, 239
Association, xxiii, 123, 217
Australia, 154–161, 164, 167n7, 168n16, 193
  See also Botany Bay

B

Bache, Franklin, xxxv, 55n57, 273, 274, 285n1, 285n2
Bagnes, xl, xliin13, 26, 53n41, 97, 108, 112, 167n12, 191, 192
Barbarism, *see* Inhumanity
Barrett, Gerrish, xxxii, 62, 64, 78n9, 78n13, 180, 265–267
Beaumont, Gustave de, xv, xvi, xxi, xxiii–xxviii, xxxvii
  Marie, or Slavery in the United States, xv
Belgium, xl, 114
Bentham, Jeremy, xix, 100
Blacks (Negroes), 69, 74, 78n11, 188, 221–226, 266, 280, 285n4, 295–297, 299, 304, 306, 307, 308n3, 308n5, 315, 319n5
  See also Emancipation; Slave, Slavery
Blosseville, Ernest, xliin17, 167n4
Bonaparte, Louis-Napoléon, xvii, 110

---

[1] Note: Page numbers followed by 'n' refer to notes.

Boston Prison Society, xxxv, 11, 18n9, 20n27, 54n54, 91n1, 171, 174
Botany Bay, 153, 154, 164

C
Capital punishment, 4, 12, 15, 18n4, 23n53, 23n55, 27, 151, 177, 189
Catholicism, 59, 162
Centralization, xxi, 13, 108–111
Chamber of Deputies, xvi, 109
Chaplain, 59, 62, 65, 105, 112, 221, 257, 258
Christianity, see Religion
Cincinnati, 13
Civilization, xix, 11, 15, 166, 306
Civil society, xxii–xxiii, 11, 15, 27–29, 36, 37, 61, 71, 72
 and agricultural colonies, 197
 in America, 48, 67, 74, 105, 160, 176, 206
 in Australia, 160
 and education, 203–206
 in France, xix–xx, xxii, xl, 106, 109, 116
 and houses of refuge, 124–127, 132–134, 138n9
 influences on, 58, 74, 79n25, 146, 190, 208
 interest of, 37, 103, 113, 117, 118, 144, 149–152, 182
 obedience to, 101, 179
 and penitentiaries, 68, 154, 180, 184, 187, 188, 220, 226, 274
 power of, 64, 84, 255
Classification system, 4–6, 26, 27, 86, 108, 128, 133, 172, 177, 178, 260–263
Clinton, George (Governor of New York), 8, 123
Colonists
 relations with natives, 154
 See also Agricultural colonies; Colonization; Penal Colonies

Colonization
 conditions for success of, 153–155
 cost of, 155
 difficulties for France, 161–166
Commerce, 70, 75, 79n25, 113, 159, 164, 193, 217, 291
 between penitentiaries and communities, 38, 52n34, 90
Congress, 21n35
 See also Legislature
Connecticut
 code of laws, xxxii, 22n48, 184, 226
 penal institutions, xxxii, 32, 247–255, 321, 328
 state of, xxxvi, 12, 15, 34, 41, 44, 69, 73, 84, 88, 189, 218, 239–241, 265, 288–291, 295, 296, 301–305, 307, 312, 315–317, 332
 See also Penitentiary: Newgate (CT); Wethersfield
Constitution, 126
Contract, Contractor, 38–40, 90, 130, 183, 191, 236
 See also Commerce
Corporal Punishment, xxii, 4, 11, 12, 22n48, 22n51, 23n52, 43–47, 104, 131, 132, 185, 234, 253
 See also Whip
Corruption, xxxix–xl, xlin4, 5, 10, 14, 27, 28, 58, 67, 71, 79n25, 80n30, 95–97, 101, 115, 142, 189, 193
 See also Vice; Virtue
Crime, xix–xx, xxxvi, 22n46, 175, 176
 causes of, xvii, 67–71, 149
 debt, 21n37, 75, 213
 forgery, 22n51, 75, 288–290, 312
 laziness, xix, 4, 10, 13, 28, 29, 101
 against mores, 288–290, 312
 murder, 12, 163
 against persons, 288–291, 312
 against property, 288–291, 312
 rape, 15
 theft, xix, 15, 215

INDEX   337

D
Decentralization, 9
  See also Centralization
Delaware, 16, 22n49, 22n51, 218
Democracy, xvi, 133, 204, 216
Departments, 13, 20n33, 109–112, 166n1, 170n20, 306, 315
Despotism, 48
  See also Tyranny
Discipline, 4, 5, 13, 17, 17n1, 19n20, 35–37, 40, 48, 71, 96, 100, 118n6, 189, 258
Doctor, 35, 48, 173, 229, 252, 253, 272–275, 292
Dwight, Louis, 11, 174, 177

E
Education, xviii, xx, 62, 70, 79n25, 201–206
  of children, 10, 127, 128, 136, 142, 144, 160, 270
  primary school, xxxvi, 106, 189
  of prisoners, 59–61, 77n5, 78n11, 219, 221–223, 230, 236, 265, 266
Emancipation
  of prisoners, xxxix, 18n10, 69, 73, 96, 107, 116, 149
  of slaves, 69, 187, 188, 280, 307
England, *see* Great Britain
Enlightenment, xviii, 11, 15, 62, 64, 66, 70, 79n25, 113, 114, 118n8, 124, 146, 159, 162, 174, 176, 194, 216, 279, 290, 291
Equality, 36, 96, 131, 177
Europe, 5, 20n28, 40, 48n2, 69, 74, 77, 79n25, 91n2, 101, 151–153, 159–162, 182, 206, 209, 215, 277, 307
Expense
  constructing penitentiaries, 83–87, 102, 103, 109, 111, 112, 239–243, 324–326
  houses of refuge, 130, 270
  maintaining penitentiaries, 88–91, 193, 240, 243, 321–324, 326–331
  public treasury, 6, 10, 28, 95, 102, 211
Experience, xx, 11, 12, 37, 58, 61, 69, 132, 145, 240, 274
Experiment, 4, 7, 10, 102, 172

F
Family, 125–127, 142, 146, 154, 201, 204, 206, 219–221, 225, 228, 230, 231n4, 241
Florida, 218
Foreign affairs, 79n25, 108
Foreigners, *see* German; Immigrants; Irish
France, xvi–xviii, xl
  comparison with America, 4, 15, 19n25, 26, 37, 39, 40, 74–77, 86, 87, 96, 99, 113, 138n6, 141–146, 188, 192, 193, 311–319
  courts in, 77
  government of, xv, xl, 95, 103, 117
  national character of, 104, 163, 234

G
Geneva, 101, 178
Georgia, 21n40, 218
German, xviii, xxxviiin6, 221, 291
God, 16, 64, 132, 259
Governor, 35, 65, 277
  See also Local government
Great Britain, xxxviiin6, 21n34, 70, 213, 283, 319
  as a colonial power, 116, 151–157, 161–166, 193
  laws of, 15, 208, 209
  penal reform, xxxix, 178
  people of, 230, 299
  use of treadmills, 38, 181, 182

Greatness, 164
Guards
  character of, 31, 32, 267
  duties of, 31, 45, 250, 251

H
Habits, 59, 66, 67, 73, 96, 105, 111, 130, 135, 136, 138n6, 142, 144, 160, 161, 179, 187, 188, 198, 199, 208, 209, 216, 216n3, 218, 223, 234, 235, 267, 269, 272, 273, 299
History, 3, 155, 164, 240, 294
Holland, xl, 114, 211n4
Honesty, xxii, 13, 28, 29, 33, 46, 63, 64, 66, 67, 72, 76, 113, 137, 151, 180, 185, 209, 258
Honor, 8, 9, 33, 34, 57, 59, 63, 65, 107, 109, 131, 159
House of Refuge, xxxviiin5, 12, 19n25, 25, 26, 123–138, 141–146
  Baltimore, 12
  Boston, xxxvii, 12, 123, 128, 131–134, 257–263
  discipline of, 125, 129, 142
  New York, xxxvi–xxxvii, 3, 9, 123, 130, 131, 134, 136, 137, 143
  Philadelphia, xxxvii, 12, 123, 130, 131, 134, 136, 143, 269, 270
  theory of, 9, 10, 134

I
Illinois, 218
Imagination, xviii, xx, xliii, 29, 58, 65, 103, 106, 153, 157, 162, 177, 209, 278
Immigrants, 68, 69, 74, 157, 290, 306
  See also German; Great Britain; Irish

Indiana, 190, 218
Indian, American, 177
Individualism, 85, 217
Industry, xxviinn11, 39, 74, 79n25, 86, 87, 90, 91, 135, 151, 181, 297
Infamy, *see* Shame
Inhumanity, 3, 15, 16, 18n3, 46
Innovation, *see* Experiment
Inspectors, 32, 35, 45, 50n15, 50n18, 60, 91
Institutions
  human, 64, 117
  penal, 58, 71, 103, 106, 110, 118n10, 124–127, 146, 200, 225
  political, 3, 65, 70, 133, 160, 204, 207
Intellect, intelligence, xxxix, 38, 60, 103, 127, 129, 134, 159, 217, 230
Interest
  public, xviii, 85, 143, 146, 163
  self, 40, 135, 150, 154, 181
Irish, 159, 209, 215, 290, 299, 300
  See also Immigrants
Isolation, punishment of, 3–5, 7, 11, 27, 28, 35, 42, 47, 58, 60, 61, 66, 85, 97, 101, 108

J
Judicial system, xxxvi, 3, 71, 125, 126, 132, 142, 144, 170n20, 188, 259, 284, 319n3
  jury, 44, 125, 160, 176, 185, 195n2, 282, 319n5
Justice, xxii, 37, 57, 76, 132, 165, 185, 210, 234
Juvenile delinquent, 12, 123, 125, 136, 142, 146, 269

INDEX 339

K
Kentucky, xxvin1, 12, 48n3, 175, 190, 213, 218

L
Labor, 3, 5, 11, 12, 28, 29, 36–38, 42, 53n45, 66, 89, 95, 107, 127, 129, 299
  in common workrooms, 7, 8, 29, 36, 39
  in solitary confinement, 20n27, 28, 219–221, 224–226, 230
Lafayette, Gilbert (General), 49n5
Lausanne, *see* Switzerland
Laws, 3, 7, 16, 30, 46, 48, 66, 67, 71, 101, 124, 161, 174, 175, 303, 306
  American, 75
  criminal, 3, 15, 150, 213
  French, xviii, 75, 102, 104, 109, 142
  and judicial power, 71
  poverty, 208–209
  reform of, 5, 12, 15, 107, 171
Legislature, xxxiii, xxxv, 4, 6–10, 12, 19n23, 20n28, 21n39, 32, 35, 44, 65, 109, 142, 172, 175, 185, 202, 203, 205, 233
  legislation, xviii, 16, 76, 107, 143, 169, 176, 192, 216, 304, 318
  See also Politician
Le Peletier de Saint-Fargeau, Louis-Michel, xviii
Liberty, 48, 59, 69, 73, 85, 159–163, 201, 280, 318
  of children, 125, 126, 130, 133, 135, 144
  of communication, 101, 116
  of poor, 208, 213
  of prisoners, 27, 31, 35, 61, 96, 107, 118n3, 150, 153, 157, 177, 178, 182, 187, 188, 191, 225, 229, 266, 272, 274, 293, 294

Lieber, Francis, xviii, xxi, xxiv–xxv, xxviiin12, xxviiin17, xxxviiin1, xxxviiin6, xlin3, xliin6, xliin7, xliin12, 17n1, 18n8, 19n15, 19n17, 20n29, 20n31, 51n29, 92n9, 119n12, 138n3, 244n2
Livingston, Edward, xxviin8, xxxv, 11, 19n21, 20n31, 23n55, 27, 46, 47, 50n11, 54n53, 72, 78n8, 79n24, 80n29, 80n31, 100, 176, 177, 191, 236
Local government, 15, 35, 149, 166n1, 201
  See also Administration: local, Township
Louisiana, xxvin1, 11, 21n39, 218
  See also New Orleans
Lucas, Charles, xix, xxviin8, xxviin9, 20n34, 72, 80n31, 100, 117n3, 163
Lynds, Elam, xxxiii, xxxvi, 3, 8, 19n18, 19n21, 19n24, 33, 39, 44, 53n47, 54n53, 64, 78n14, 104, 118n5, 172, 179, 233–237

M
Maine, xxvin1, 5, 12, 15, 20n27, 48n3, 175, 218
Manufacturing, 38–40, 70, 86, 87, 90, 91, 95, 180–182
Maryland, xxxiv, 5, 12, 20n27, 44, 48, 68, 69, 73, 79n21, 175, 184, 208, 218, 279, 282, 296–298, 301–304, 307, 313
  See also Penitentiary: Baltimore
Massachusetts, xxxi, 5, 12, 15, 22n48, 32, 33, 44, 68, 69, 71, 79n27, 175, 218, 288–291, 294, 296–298, 301–304, 307, 308n2, 312, 313, 315, 317
  See also Penitentiary: Boston, Charlestown

Material, xxxix, 28, 30, 64, 75, 78n11, 85, 87, 91, 100, 104, 106, 116, 117n1, 127, 146, 160, 175, 209, 240
Michigan, 218
Middle Ages, 84, 91n2, 159
Military, 70
  See also War
Minimum sentencing, 303, 304, 308n8, 308n10, 317
Mirabeau, Honoré-Gabriel de Riqueti, xviii
Mississippi, 218
Missouri, 218
Morality, xlin2, 30, 46, 59, 60, 65, 66, 71, 72, 74, 91, 96, 112, 116, 128, 132, 190, 218, 229, 259, 306, 307
  See also Corruption; Vice; Virtue
Mores, xxviiin15, xlin2, 11, 27, 49n4, 75, 102, 105, 109, 111, 127, 136, 142, 160, 201, 312, 318
Mortality rates, 47, 96, 274, 291, 292, 313

N
New England, 15, 159, 203, 206n3, 299
New Hampshire, 21n36, 218
New Jersey, 5, 13, 16, 20n27, 23n51, 172, 218, 322
  See also Penitentiary: Lamberton
New Orleans, 13, 21n39
  See also Louisiana
New York
  city of, xxxvi, 9, 283
  state, xxviin1, xxxii, 6–8, 10, 12, 13, 44, 45, 52n40, 68–71, 88, 112, 124, 172, 184, 187, 201, 202, 205, 209, 210, 213, 218, 275, 283, 288–291, 296–298, 301–304, 307, 312–315, 317

  See also Penitentiary: Auburn, Blackwell Island, Newgate (NY), SingSing
North America, 159
North Carolina, 218
North, the, 17, 21n40, 69, 299, 306

O
Ohio, xxviin1, xxxvi, 13, 15, 21n36, 190, 213, 218, 228, 302
Overseer, 249–250

P
Pardon, 7, 63–65, 78n15, 226, 229, 275–279, 301
Pécule, 40, 50n13, 53n41, 95, 96, 113, 191–193
Penal colonies, xvii, xxiv, xl, xliin17, 20n34, 117n3, 149–161, 193, 194
Penal reform, xx, 11, 17, 25, 100, 115
  debates on, xvi–xviii
  modern, xxii
Penitentiary
  Auburn, xv, xxviin1, xxxiii, 6, 7, 9, 18n11, 19n23, 20n27, 28–32, 35, 39, 43, 44, 47, 51n27, 54n55, 88–90, 180, 182, 187, 191, 275, 276, 291, 293, 295, 301, 313, 326, 327, 331, 332; compared with Philadelphia system, 59, 62–64, 67, 73, 78n8, 83–87, 102, 103, 272, 273; system of, xv, xxxiv, 7, 8, 10–12, 26, 30, 31, 42, 47, 175, 233, 325, 326
  Baltimore, xxviin1, xxxiv, 38, 41, 43, 47, 63, 85, 86, 88, 171, 178, 180, 182, 191, 280, 291, 292, 313, 325, 329, 332, 333; city of, xxviin1, xxxvi, 28, 215, 228

Blackwell Island, 21n42, 84, 86, 325
Boston, xxvin1, xxxi, 14, 23n52, 27, 28, 31–34, 39, 43, 47, 52n40, 54n50, 59, 62, 63, 73, 74, 171, 333; city of, xxi, 187
Charlestown, 291, 295, 313, 325, 333n2
Cherry Hill, xxvin1, xxxv, 3, 6, 10, 12, 18n13, 83, 324
Lamberton, 47, 175, 322, 323
Newgate (CT), xxxii, 12, 88, 265, 293, 294, 321, 322, 328
Newgate (NY), 47, 73, 88, 184, 279, 291, 293, 301, 324
Philadelphia, xxvin1, 5, 14, 28, 29, 32, 35, 38, 48, 51n26, 52n40, 54n55, 58, 91n1, 174, 219–231, 291, 292; city of, 3, 6, 12, 73, 280, 281, 291; system of, xv, xxxv, 3–6, 26, 30, 31, 42, 59–61, 67, 331; *See also* House of Refuge: Philadelphia
Pittsburg, 173
Pittsburgh, xxvin1, xxxv, 6, 10, 85, 175, 324
principles of construction, 6, 10
Singsing, xxvin1, xxxiii, 3, 9, 19n24, 27, 28, 31–33, 36, 39, 43, 44, 46, 47, 59, 62, 63, 73, 78n11, 84, 88, 112, 179, 182, 187, 237n4, 275, 291, 295, 301, 313, 325, 329–333
theory of, xl, 5, 21n36, 25, 71
Walnut Street, xxvin1, xxxv, 3–5, 10, 47, 54n55, 72, 73, 175, 189, 219, 222–228, 274, 291, 293, 301, 308n11, 323
Washington, DC, 84, 85, 218, 325
Wethersfield, xxvin1, xxxii, 3, 12, 27, 28, 31–35, 39, 43–45, 47, 53n40, 59, 62, 64, 74, 84, 88–90, 112, 115, 191, 240, 243, 244, 291, 294, 313, 325, 328, 331, 332
Pennsylvania, xxxv, 3, 6, 10–12, 15, 16, 18n4, 18n6, 21n41, 32, 46, 48, 68, 74, 79n21, 126, 190, 203, 214, 218, 280, 281, 288–291, 295, 296, 301–305, 307, 308n3, 308n7, 312–315, 317, 318, 323
See also Penitentiary: Cherry Hill, Philadelphia, Pittsburgh, Walnut Street
Philanthropy, xxxix, 11, 57, 100, 106, 117n1, 146, 150, 152, 186, 233, 285n4
Philosophy, xviii, xx, xxii, xxviin6, 11, 16, 23n55, 57, 61, 62, 100, 224
Poissy, xvi
Police, xxxvi, 71, 76, 113, 118n6, 137n2, 142, 157, 169n16, 176, 193, 284, 318, 319n4
Politician, xx, xxii, xl, 114, 152, 158
Poverty, xx, 37, 101, 114, 189, 203, 204, 207–211, 215, 306, 318
working classes, xxxix, xl, 86, 292
Powers, Gershom, xxxiv, 8, 9, 19n18, 33, 37, 51n30, 51n31, 52n33, 52n38, 52n39, 54n52, 54n53, 78n8, 79n24, 171, 180, 190
Press, 20n32, 163
Prison, types of, xviii–xix, 25
Prisoners, types of, 21n43
Progress, xix–xx, 8, 16
Protestantism, 59
See also Religion
Psychological, 29–31, 37, 85, 104, 106, 117n1, 133, 152, 185, 223, 225, 229
cause, xxxix, xlin2
suffering, 7, 18n2, 20n27, 28, 178
Publicist, xviii, xx, 20n28, 27, 100

Public opinion, xviii–xx, 20n29, 35, 46
  in America, 4, 7–9, 11, 19n21, 21n40, 65, 124, 173, 176, 218, 233, 306
  in France, xl, xliin17, 103–106, 109, 115, 116, 149
  power of, 16, 160, 240

Q
Quakers, 3, 46, 176

R
Race, *see* Blacks; Irish
Recidivism, xviii, xx, xxii, 72, 73, 76, 96, 162, 190, 222, 225, 279, 292–295, 313
Reformation, 5, 6, 16, 59, 71, 101, 105, 113, 117n3, 151, 248
  in children, 132, 136
  moral (radical), 7, 16, 27, 59, 64, 96, 105, 106, 115, 187, 188
  the possibility of, 63, 77n1, 78n16, 248, 266
  rational, 66
Religion, 163
  education, 59, 62, 66, 174, 189
  in houses of refuge, 128, 134, 257
  influence on individuals, 33, 60, 61, 63, 66
  in penitentiaries, 64, 77n7, 219–221, 224, 226, 228, 230
  social and political role of, 64, 66, 75, 105, 106, 115, 159
  See also Chaplain; Quakers
Restiveness, xxxix
Rhode-Island, 15, 22n48, 218
Rights
  of children, 125–127, 129, 133, 135
  of guards, 5
  political, 65, 100, 108, 111, 142–144, 178, 185, 186, 201, 202, 207, 216, 277
  of prisoners, 192, 199, 200, 248, 253
  of society, 23n53, 23n55, 40, 41, 45, 66, 100, 163, 178, 192, 193, 208
Rochefoucauld-Liancourt, François, xix, xxviin8, 3, 5, 18n7, 72
Romans, 159

S
St. Domingo, 159
Salary, 34, 50n20, 78n9, 87, 191, 192, 251, 333
Schools, *see* Education
Shame, 16, 107, 125, 319n5
Silence, 3, 29–31, 36, 42, 44, 66, 96, 101, 104, 108, 115, 127, 240, 254, 270
Slave, Slavery, 15, 16, 21n39, 22n45, 23n51, 69, 107, 153, 187, 188, 279, 280, 299, 307, 308n4, 308n5
  See also Emancipation
Solitary confinement, 4–7, 10, 20n27, 42, 43, 118n8, 131, 171, 177, 187
Solitude, 18n2, 27–29, 35, 59, 60, 219–230
Soul, 16, 23n56, 27, 29, 33, 42, 60, 63, 64, 107, 124, 131, 146, 152, 219, 220, 223, 230, 237
South Carolina, 218
South, the, 15, 21n40, 69, 299
Statistics, xxxi, xxxv–xxxvi, 67, 68, 70, 74, 79n26, 136, 209, 321–332
  limits of, 64, 75
Superintendent, 34, 90, 91, 112, 124, 131, 134–136, 185, 333
  responsibilities of, 32, 33, 60, 128

Supreme Court, xxxvi
Surveillance, 33, 35, 85, 88, 110, 111, 113, 114, 124, 126, 129, 131, 158, 183, 207, 235, 251
Switzerland, 101

T

Temperance society, xxxvi, 79n28, 217, 218
Tennessee, xxviii1, 12, 48n3, 175, 218
Theory, xx, xxxix, 4–6, 10, 16, 20n30, 45, 58, 73, 99, 100, 102, 208
  See also Experience; Experiment
Tocqueville, Alexis de, xv
  Democracy in America, xv, xxi, xxv, xxviii2, 49n4, 117n2
  Old Regime and the Revolution, xxi
Township, 199, 203, 204, 207
  See also Administration: local; Local government
Trade, see Commerce
Trial, xvii, 14, 132, 135, 176, 184, 223, 229, 257, 263, 282, 283
  See also Judicial System
Tyranny, 127, 217, 233
  See also Despotism

U

United States, xl, 15, 27, 33, 34, 39, 40, 48n2, 58, 86, 111, 159, 174, 176, 182, 201, 215, 309n12
  See also America

V

Vagrancy, xvii, 114, 136, 138n3, 143, 157, 207, 227, 284
Van Diemen, island of, 154
Vaux, Roberts, xxxv, 11, 18n6, 49n5, 50n11, 54n53, 72, 78n17, 79n24, 80n29, 80n31
Vermont, xxviii1, 12, 48n3, 175, 218
Vice, xl, 21n38, 22n44, 28, 29, 58, 63, 79n28, 96, 152, 158, 160, 269
  defects of prisons, 13, 41, 95–97
Virginia, 5, 20n27, 34, 190, 218
Virtue, 57, 63, 65, 106, 107, 160, 176, 186, 187

W

Wages, see Pécule
War, 70, 163, 164, 166, 309n12
Warden, 33, 247, 248
Welles, Judge, xxxvi, 86, 87, 91n4, 128, 129, 134, 138n4, 239, 333n4
Whip, 4, 22n48, 43, 44, 46, 53n43, 53n46, 114, 171, 184, 234, 280
Witnesses, xvii, 21n37, 215
Women, xvii, 41, 53n43, 74, 130, 160, 226, 265, 295, 296, 313–315, 319n5
Wood, Samuel, xxxv, 18n6, 33, 51n20, 178, 179, 331

The manufacturer's authorised representative in the EU is Springer Nature Customer Service Centre GmbH, Europaplatz 3, 69115 Heidelberg, Germany. If you have any concerns regarding our products, please contact ProductSafety@springernature.com

Printed and bound by CPI Group (UK) Ltd, Croydon, CR0 4YY

23/03/2026

02076735-0016